Knowing Differently

Knowing Differently

The Challenge of the Indigenous

EDITORS

G. N. Devy
Geoffrey V. Davis
K. K. Chakravarty

Routledge
Taylor & Francis Group
LONDON NEW YORK NEW DELHI

First published 2014 in India
by Routledge
912 Tolstoy House, 15–17 Tolstoy Marg, Connaught Place,
New Delhi 110 001

Simultaneously published in the UK
by Routledge
2 Park Square, Milton Park, Abingdon, Oxon OX14 4RN

Routledge is an imprint of the Taylor & Francis Group, an informa business

© 2014 G. N. Devy, Geoffrey V. Davis and K. K. Chakravarty

Typeset by
Solution Graphics
A–14, Indira Puri, Loni Road
Ghaziabad, Uttar Pradesh 201 102

All rights reserved. No part of this book may be reproduced or utilized in any form or by any electronic, mechanical or other means, now known or hereafter invented, including photocopying and recording, or in any information storage and retrieval system without permission in writing from the publishers.

British Library Cataloguing-in-Publication Data
A catalogue record of this book is available from the British Library

ISBN 978-0-415-71056-5

Dedicated to

The indigenous peoples in all continents who know that they belong to the earth, not that the earth belongs to them

Contents

List of Plates	ix
List of Tables, Figures and Maps	xi
List of Abbreviations	xiii
Glossary	xv

	Introduction K. K. Chakravarty	1
1.	Being 'Primitive' in a Modern World: The Andaman Islanders Vishvajit Pandya	13
2.	Co-Existence of Multiple Timeframes: Narratives of Myths and Cosmogony in India Vibha S. Chauhan	34
3.	*Pimatisiwin* Indigenous Knowledge Systems, North and South Priscilla Settee	51
4.	Metaphors of Fertility, Phallic Anxieties and Expiation of Grief in the Babukusu Funeral Oratory Chris J. C. Wasike	71
5.	The (Re-)imag(in)ing of the Oba of Benin in Nigerian Dramatic Literature and its Implications in Indigenous Studies Israel Meriomame Wekpe and Alero Uwawah	88
6.	'Kasapa': Mobile Telephony and Changing Healthcare Communication in Ghana Perpetual Crentsil	106
7.	Discourse of Resistance and Protest in Meitei Folklore Leisangthem Gitarani Devi	125
8.	Sovereign Ontologies in Australia and Aotearoa–New Zealand: Indigenous Responses to Asylum Seekers, Refugees and Overstayers Emma Cox	139

9. Indigenous Worldviews and Environmental Footprints:
   The Case of Prometheus *vs* Hermes   158
   A. O. Balcomb

10. Folk Heritage and Classical Lore: The Grand Narratives
    from the Aegean Archipelago and Derek Walcott's
    Caribbean Creole Readings   168
    Eckhard Breitinger

11. Conceptualizing Space and Indigenous Knowledge:
    Articulations and Considerations for Natural Resource
    Management in the Himalayas   198
    Seema M. Parihar, P. K. Parihar, Soma Sarkar
    and Shilpy Sharma

12. Breaking the Power of Patriarchy: Unity Dow's Novel
    The Screaming of the Innocent   225
    Geoffrey V. Davis

13. The National, the Indian, and Empowering Performance:
    Festive Practices in the Highlands (Bolivia)   241
    Ximena Córdova

14. Contemporary Maori Painting: Pictorial Representation
    of Land and Landscape   270
    Dieter Riemenschneider

15. Art, Landscape, and Identity in *She Plays with the Darkness*,
    The Madonna of Excelsior and *Cion*   289
    Gail Fincham

16. Indigenous Languages in the Post-Colonial Era   309
    Zahid Akter

17. The Struggle for Survival: Globalization and its
    Impact on Tribal Women in Kerala   317
    Lata Marina Varghese

18. Eco-Fraternity of Kurum(b)a Tribes in Wayanad, Kerala   327
    Nelson P. Abraham

About the Editors   338
Notes on Contributors   340
Index   346

List of Plates

1.1	Jarawas as they appeared on the West Coast of Middle Andamans in 1994	16
1.2	Enmey (centre) and His Mates at G. B. Pant Hospital in Port Blair, Displaying Ornaments and Clothes, Acquired in Port Blair, 1999	21
1.3	Jarawas at the Roadside in 2000	22
1.4	Jarawas at the Roadside in 2004	23
1.5	Jarawas Standing at the Roadside Wearing Clothes Given by the Non-Tribals	23
1.6	Road Sign Put up by the Administration along the ATR	25
1.7	Display of Jarawa Image in the Frontyard of the Andaman Bhavan, New Delhi, 2010	31
13.1	The GTADO Perform the Devil Dance at the Oruro Carnival Parade, 2008	247
13.2	Playing the *Tarka* at the Anata Parade, 2008	250
13.3	The Caporal Dance is Popular among the Youth and the Middle and Upper Classes in Oruro	251
13.4	At the End of the Parade Dancers Enter the Church and Meet the Image of the Virgin at the End	258
13.5	An Aymara Priest Performing Reciprocity Rites at the Sacred Sites (*Wak'as*) in Advance of the Anata Parade	261
13.6	Huge Poster of Evo Morales outside the Presidential Palace on the Main Square in La Paz	265
14.1	*Sketches of a Maori muru at Parawera*	272
14.2	'Mt Ventoux as seen from Mormoiron'	275

Between pages 50 and 51

   I. 'Ajay', 2009
  II. 'Buffy', 2009
 III. 'Crystal', 2009
  IV. 'Patricia', 2009

x List of Plates

Between pages 288 and 289

   V. *Papatuanuku, 1984*
  VI. *Catcher of the Sun*
 VII. *Giant Bearing Star*
VIII. *Claerhout Church and Parishioners*
  IX. *Musicians*

List of Tables, Figures and Maps

Tables

11.1	Evolved Relationship of Indigenous Knowledge with Space	217
11.2	The Meaning of Space as Perceived by an External Person and an Indigenous Person	218

Figures

10A.	Linear Plot Development in Eugene O'Neill's *The Emperor Jones*	196
10B.	Circular Plot Development in Derek Walcott's *Dream on Monkey Mountain*	197
11.1	Space of Indigenous Knowledge	220
11.2	Intrusion of Modern Scientific Knowledge System into the Sphere of Indigenous Knowledge System	221
11.3	Indigenous Knowledge Web and Space	222

Maps

11.1	The Study Area	201
11.2	Drainage Network of Tehri Garhwal and Almora	207

List of Abbreviations

AAJVS	Andaman Adim Janjati Vikas Samiti
ACFO	Asociación de Conjuntos Folkóricos de Oruro
AIDS	acquired immune deficiency syndrome
ATR	Andaman Trunk Road
BECE	Basic Education Certificate Examination
CBD	Convention on Biological Diversity
COSATU	Congress of South African Trade Unions
DOM-TOM	*départements et territoires d'outre-mer*
ELT	English Language Teaching
FSUTCO	Federación Sindical Única de Trabajadores Campesinos de Oruro
FYM	Farm Yard Manure
GCBII	Geospatial Capacity Building Initiative Index
GI	Geographical Indication
GPS	Global Positioning System
GSM	Global System for Mobile Communications
GT	Ghana Telecom
ICT	information and communication technology
IELTS	International English Language Testing System
IK	Indigenous Knowledge
IPR	Intellectual Property Right
ISD	Information Services Department
MC	master of ceremonies
NCA	National Communication Authority
NGO	non-governmental organization
NTFP	Non-timber Forest Products
NWU	North-West University
PDA	Personal Digital Assistant
PIC	Prior Informed Consent
PTC	Posts and Telecommunications Corporation
PTG	Primitive Tribal Group
SCOT	social construction of technology
SIM	Subscriber Identity Module
SMS	Short Message Service
SMS-MO	Short Messaging Service-Mobile Originating

SMS-MT	Short Messaging Services-Mobile Terminating
ST	Scheduled Tribe
TOEFL	Test of English as a Foreign Language
TRIPS	Trade-Related Intellectual Property Rights
UK	United Kingdom
UN	United Nations
UNAIDS	Joint United Nations Programme on HIV/AIDS
UNESCO	United Nations Educational, Scientific and Cultural Organization
US	United States
USAID	United States Agency for International Development
USSR	Union of Soviet Socialist Republics
VIP	Very Important Person
WHO	World Health Organization
WIPO	World Intellectual Property Organization
WTO	World Trade Organization

Glossary

abuelos (Aymara) — ancestors
adim-janjati (Hindi and several other Indian languages) — official Indian term for 'primitive' tribes
adivasi (Hindi and several other Indian languages) — the indigenous people
afwile sibuno safwile kumurwe tawe (Luhya) — the disembodied intellect
Agrakhal (Hindi) — man-made water pounding structure
akullikus (Aymara) — (Bolivian) coca-chewing ceremonies
ayllu (Aymara) — autonomous space for the continuation of pre-Hispanic Aymara knowledge
ayni (Aymara) — to 'live in harmony with nature and others'
Bali Jagar (Hindi) — a ritual involving recitation of a mythological narrative
bans keora (Hindi) — a kind of plant, a fragrant Champak tree
cargamento (Spanish) — decorated vehicle used in processions
chal (Hindi) — man-made water recharge zone
chhemi (Irula) — a variety of green beans (*Phaseolus vulgaris*)
Chisi chibona likonjo nio chaungakho (Luhya) — 'like flies that love buzzing around a wound'
Criollos (Aymara) — Creoles, people of European descent (Bolivia)
daivam kaanal (Irula and Kurumba) — an indigenous shamanic ritual among the Uralis of Kerala, India
Daivapura — place of worship of the Uralis of Kerala, India
danzarine (Spanish) — dancers
dhaan (Hindi) — pond used for bathing animals and irrigation
dhara (Hindi) — a stream, a source of clear and perennial drinking water
dipheko (Setswana) — ritual murder

ekhendie (Luhya)	a walking stick
ekutusi (Luhya)	a flowing robe
emakombe (Luhya)	the land of the ancestors
Falhari (Hindi)	one who survives by eating fruit alone
ganja (Hindi)	hashish, cannabis
garmo (Hindi)	fertile cattle
garu (Hindi)	sterile cattle
Gomalan (Malayalam)	chief of the hamlet
gools (Hindi)	network of channels to divert irrigation water from small rivers
ha (Maori)	expression of life breath among the Maori of Aotearoa–New Zealanders
haoringjen, nairingjen (Meitei)	will-power and death-defying nature of hill people
hapu whangai (Maori)	adopted members
hapu (Maori)	a sub-tribal grouping
jallupacha (Ayamara)	rainy season (in Bolivia)
jha (Hindi)	a forest patch of Deodar trees
jhupu (Hindi)	sterile pack animals
jolya (Hindi)	a variety of paddy in India
jumo (Hindi)	fertile cattlekalon kala (Hindi) a variety of paddy in India
kalon safed (Hindi)	an indigenous variety of rice
Kalpavriksha (Hindi)	the mythical tree that makes wishes come true; a variety of banyan
khagola (Hindi)	a variety of paddy in India
khakutusi (Luhya)	a colobus monkey
khal (Hindi)	man-made water pounding structure
khullu kala (Hindi)	a variety of paddy in India
khullu safed (Hindi)	a variety of paddy in India
khururwe yabebe (Luhya)	a ferocious python
khuswala kumuse (Lubukusu)	an after-burial performance among the Babukusu indigenous people in Kenya; the term literally means 'stepping in the area'
kumuse (Luhya)	a death ritual among the Babukusu in Kenya
Lachmi Jagar (Hindi)	invocation to Goddess Lakshmi
manuhiri (Maori)	guest among the Maori people of Aotearoa–New Zealand

masoor (Hindi)	a variety of lentil variety (*Pisum arvense*)
matar (Hindi)	green peas (*Pisum sativum*)
mayang (Meitei)	Hindu Brahmin in Manipur, India
Mayang Taath (Meitei)	the haughtiness of the *mayang*s
Mestizos (Spanish)	people of mixed descent in Bolivia
mole (Hindi)	practice of using fully decomposed organic matter for producing manure
muti (isi-Zulu)	a substance or object which has or is believed to have curative, preventive, protective, or harmful powers of a medicinal or supernatural kind, in some parts of Africa it is sometimes obtained through ritual murder.
Nag (Hindi)	cobra; also a serpentine God
Namunyu kabiila eyikila (Labukusu)	hyenas that love taking advantage of wounded prey
nanni dhal (Hindi)	a kind of lentil (*Vigna angularies*)
nala (Hindi)	tank used for collecting water from subterranean springs
ntu (Bantu languages)	being or life
Nosa (Yoruba)	God
Oba (Yoruba)	king
omusani (Yoruba)	a circumcised adult
omusecha owekiminie (Yoruba)	a prosperous person
omuswali (Yoruba)	performer of the *kumuse* ritual
Pachamama (Aymara)	Mother Earth
Panca-janah (Sanskrit)	five main clans among the ancient Aryans
Papatuanuku (Maori)	the Mother Earth
Parima (Hindi)	fairy mother
pataka	traditional Maori storehouse
pimatisiwin (Plains Cree)	life of happiness
poncho (Aymara)	traditional ceremonial costume of the indigenous
powhiri	(Maori) a welcome ceremony involving a warrior challenge
Puyas (Meitei)	traditional Meitei language manuscripts on varied subjects
rou (Hindi)	water pounding structure
ruru (Maori)	owl

srishtitatvas (Sanskrit)	the life forces or principles in nature
talbuni (Hindi)	cross-breed cattle
tal (Hindi)	large natural water body
taonga (Maori)	treasures or heritage
tarka (Anata)	traditional pre-Hispanic wind instruments of the highlands in Bolivia
Te Whenua	the land
Tija Jagar (Hindi)	a ritual performed during the monsoon season
tino rangitanga (Maori)	one among us
Tirelo Sechaba (Setswana)	national service
tor (Hindi)	a variety of lentil (*Cajanus cajan*)
ubuntu (Bantu languages)	an African concept of well-being and community empowerment; African humanism
Uch-alkali (Irula)	an indigenous festival involving singing and dancing in Kerala, India
upobhasha (Bangla and Assamiya)	a regional language variety or a sociolect
urd (Hindi)	same as kali dhal; a kind of lentil (*Vigna mungo*)
usos y costumbres (Aymara)	traditional knowledge of customs (among the indigenous in Bolivia)
wakotawin (Plains Cree)	the Cree concept of well-being and empowerment
whare whakairo	traditional Maori 'meeting house'

Introduction

K. K. Chakravarty

The present volume is one of three in a series, planned on the platform of Chotro,[1] for a 'polyphonic ... articulation and expression' of the 'existential disasters', faced by marginalized communities the world over (Devy et al. 2012: 6–7). If the disinherited, dispossessed, migrant communities narrate their struggles to visit, perform and preserve their identities in the other two volumes, this volume describes the way they know the world around them, relate with it and protect it instead of exploiting it. They retain the pristine mode of knowing nature homologically, as subject and object at the same time, in consonance with its rhythmic cycles, its visible and intelligible precepts, and live according to them, instead of trying to alter them.

A section of humanity has, on the other hand, tried to know the earth, its living and non-living environment, by trying to master its operational principles, by breaking these down into their constituent elements, in order to reconstruct them according to its own design. It suffers from the hubris of seeing itself as the weaver rather than as part of the web of nature. It has interfered, in the name of human welfare, with natural processes, through mega developmental projects for their extraction and exploitation. In consequence, the entire humanity has been overtaken by the nemesis of climatic change, natural disasters, extinction of species, and erosion of bio-cultural diversity. Development planners have treated the home and hearth of the community as a dome, a catchment, a range, a timber mine, a bio reserve, a carbon sink, an empty land for development. Armed with the historical entelechy to understand the community better than it understands itself, they have treated its knowledge as an imperfect first sketch of ecological thought, which is ambiguous and

---

[1] 'Chotro' is a word used by Rathwa Bhil tribals of the border areas of Gujarat, Rajasthan and Madhya Pradesh to describe a platform where villagers can assemble, discuss and resolve issues that concern them. The word has been used for international gatherings of indigenous writers, creative artists and activists, hosted by the Bhasha Research and Publication Centre, Baroda, Gujarat, India, since 2008, to discuss and resolve issues of indigeneity the world over.

barren in its native soil, and bears flower and fruit only when it is transplanted to the soil, fertilized by the technological and scientific thought of the West. Community knowledge, in their formulation, has to be appropriated and domesticated, by an act of reconstitutive chresis,[2] into their developmental text, after being stripped of what they consider to be the dross of its holistic, contextual elements. They have co-opted nature-based communities into this hegemonic mode of knowing as native informants. They have sequestered their knowledge from public domains, and commoditized it for profit and exploitation in the borderless ubiquity of global capitalism.

One of the instruments used for the subversion of this pristine mode of knowing has been the use of a foreign language as the language of commodity, knowledge, technology, and communication. In India, Bangladesh and Malaysia, a predatory appropriation of natural resources has proceeded apace, powered by a foreign language of development. Big dams and plantations have proliferated. Agriculture has been hybridized and corporatized. Traditional knowledge in medicine, horticulture and vegetable cultivation has been permitted to languish and die. Human habitats in hills and forests have shrunk. Tourist resorts have mushroomed. Life and well-being of women has diminished due to drinking, violence and death among men, caused by the toddy mafia. Local languages have been marginalized in print and electronic media (Chapters 17 and 18). As against such destruction of human and natural resources, the communities have evolved cognitive categories and strategies for the sustainable management of these resources. In the process, they have transformed their physical habitats into mental landscapes. In Tehri Garhwal and Almora, they have tapped subterranean and perennial springs, ponds, gullies and water-recharge zones for harvesting rain water. They have developed biofencing, organic farming, mixed cropping, sacred groves, and household animal care for dwelling in harmony with nature. They have validated their ecology, wisdom, traditions against state programmes that privilege the so-called scientific knowledge and technology. They have

---

[2] Derived from the Greek word *chraesthai*, 'chresis' is a theory of the Christian church, which speaks of discarding the gross and utilizing the best in other non-Christian traditions. This is done through transplanting the *logos* seed from the non-Christian soil (where it is barren) to one fertilized by the Judaeo-Christian stream of thought, in which it can bear flower and fruit. It deconstructs the other tradition into its constituent elements, and reconstructs it into a scheme supposedly superior to the original.

mapped nature naturally, symbolically, cognitively, and socially, in heterotopic layers (Chapter 11).

Local communities have also used various strategies to stop the invasion of their natural habitats and erosion of their identity markers. In Kerala, India, tribals have agitated at Plachimeda against Pepsi, or for land at Chengaru in Attapaddi (Chapter 17). Creation stories in *Tija*, *Lachmi* and *Bali Jagar* rituals mix Oriya, Desiya and Dravidian Pengo dialects. These describe the return of rice and millet to their genesis, with an allusion to the emergence of land from primeval waters. In Bengal, *kahar* Baan-*gosain* fights to substitute worship of Baba Ruddar for Narayan Hari. The snake goddess Vish-hari leads Santhali snake-charmers in wresting worship from Chand Saudagar. Tarashankar Bandopadhyaya assumes the mantle of Kakbhushundi, the eternal seer, and uses vernacular dialect and mythology to tell his stories (Chapter 2). The Ongee and Jarawa hunter-gatherers in the Andaman islands of India dress or undress for a consideration as they emerge from or return to their forests. Thereby, they try to retain agency for dealing with intrusive poachers, tourists and state welfare agents (Chapter 1). A revivalist movement has been mounted by the Meitei community in Manipur, north-east India, to reverse the Hinduization initiated by King Meetingu Pamheiba or Garibniwaz (1709–48) by using a collective memory of repression — of Meiteis being subjected to mercantile exploitation, religious persecution and cultural marginalization by Hindu immigrants. The Meitei script has been revived in place of the Bengali script. The god Sanamahi has been introduced in place of Hindu deities. Meitei place names, festivals, *salais* (clans) have replaced Hindu counterparts. *Maibas* and *Maibis* (emissaries of God) have been substituted for migrant Brahmin *mayangs* (Brahmin migrants from the west of Manipur) as healers, priests and divine emissaries. Hindu religious scriptures have been burnt to protest against the burning of Meitei religious texts — *Puyas* — in the 18th century. Elements of culture, shared by Meiteis of the valley with Kabuis of the hills, have been celebrated, to counter the description of Kabuis as rude and hostile in the pro-Hindu folktale, 'Kabui Keioiba'. Brahmin immigrants have been denigrated as wily and weak in martial arts game-rhymes. The Nupi Lan revolt has been staged by women against exploitation by Marwari traders (Chapter 7).

Apart from reasserting their identity, communities have raised the bar of human accountability to human society by building bastions against exploitation of nature on the bedrock of their ideas of concord with nature and concepts for education and knowledge production.

Cree Canadians have created the concept of *pimatisiwin*, good life, and *wakotawin*, to work for all, as all humanity is inter-connected. Seven healing fires of singing, dancing, laughing, talking, listening, playing, and crying have been used in pipe ceremonies, sundance ceremonies, sweat lodge camps, conducted by the late 19th-century Cree chief Big Bear in Saskatchewan, Canada. The Amerindian Lakota extended family has provided a platform for caring and sharing, to transcend pain, integrate emotional, spiritual, physical and mental well-being, and create a sense of belonging. In South Africa, the Khoi-San concept of *ubuntu* (concept of indigenous know-ledge, healing and community empowerment) has provided the foundation for Archbishop Desmond Tutu's efforts for spiritual healing and renewal. He has tried to cure both perpetrator and victim of the violence of apartheid, of their compulsion to inflict pain or remain enslaved to pain, through confession and dialogue in the Truth and Reconciliation Commission. North-West University has introduced a cross-disciplinary course on African socio-political thought in global perspective, on healing, water management, peace and conflict resolution, cultural and bio-diversity conservation, in response to local developmental needs. Communities have thus developed a benefit-sharing, reciprocal, affective protocol for generating, interrogating, communicating, valorizing, legitimizing, accrediting, and disseminating knowledge. They have countered Euro-American patterns of funding, research and scholarship which extract knowledge from communities for profit without returning benefits to them. In doing so, communities like the Xhosa have created epigrams like, 'I am because you are, not because I think', and '[A] bird builds its nest with another bird's feather ... [H]ands wash each other' (Vil-Nkomo and Myburgh 1999: 114) (see Chapter 3).

Ritual funeral oratory and carnival parades have also been pressed into service by communities to fortify their ancestral community identity against intrusive interference. In western Kenya, ritual has been used to link the living and the dead, past and present. The Bantu-speaking Luhya ethnic group, Babukusu, establish this link through *omuswali/baswali*, the Man of Memory, their official remembrancer. He performs the after-burial funeral oratory, through *khuswala kumuse*, by stepping into the arena. He extols the exploits of the deceased and his community, in the Lubukusu language, to provide security and peace for him in the ancestral land, and for his kith and kin on earth. He celebrates life and death as similar to phallic denudation and parturience, and grasslands burning to yield new sprouts. He performs the ceremony only for naturally deceased men of means and attainments, who have graduated into the circumcised state, and are, therefore, ready for life, marriage, war, conquest, and property (Chapter 4).

Aymaras in Bolivian highlands have used festive carnival parades to counter the official carnival — introduced by national authorities after the 1952 revolution in the Spanish colony Oruro — to create an integrated, imagined, national community. The Oruro association of folkloric troupes, sponsored by the authorities, has confected the carnival parade troupes out of urban kin and trade networks, to convey an evangelic, mercantilist, Christian Catholic message, excluding non-Catholic, indigenous elements. As against this nation-making exercise, comprising first nation Indians, European-descent Creoles and mixed-descent Mestizos, the Anata Andina carnival parade has been put together by the Oruro Peasants' Federation from indigenous kin networks of rural *ayllus*.[3] This parade celebrates ancestral customs, production needs and knowledge. It invokes the power of *pachamama*, Mother Earth, to nurture reciprocity between human and non-human communities. The official parade has created an original, based on mass-produced synthetic costumes, electronic musical instruments, documented texts, and a polyphonic selection of multiple cultural expressions. The unofficial parade uses traditional costumes, manual instruments, *ayni*[4] fertility rituals and animal sacrifices. Unlike the official parade, the rural parade has not been included in the list of World Intangible Heritage for United Nations Educational, Scientific and Cultural Organization (UNESCO) nomination. It is not received, as the official parade is, at its conclusion in the Church of the Mineshaft, in front of the painting of the Virgin, by the priest with a mass. It is organized as a symbolic protest against conversion of the indigenous tradition into an alter ego of the white in the official parade; exclusion of indigenous people from the right to vote, access to education, financial market, and natural resources; and against the 'pedagogical plenitude'

---

[3] *Ayllu* is a cultural space network of the indigenous Aymara community of highland Bolivia, linked by territory, production needs, kinship affinities, traditional knowledge, and political principles, received trans-generationally, and celebrated through ritual dance performances dedicated to Pachamama, or mother earth.

[4] *Ayni* is a concept of the Anata Andina carnival parade and dance rituals, performed by the indigenous Aymara people of highland Bolivia in rural *ayllus*. The concept is derived from the pre-Hispanic, ancestral principles of living well, in reciprocity with deities in nature, Pachamama and others. The rituals are designed to nurture fertility of the land, growth of crops, animals, and all forms of life.

of unilinear historicism' (Bhabha 1990, quoted in Radhakrishnan 2003: 314) and 'racialised biopolitics of white supremacy and brown subalternity' (Cadena and Starn 2007: 12) which consign indigenous Aymaras to the dung heap of history, as 'myths of the past, ruins in the jungle, or zoos' (Menchú 1992, in Porras and Riis-Hansen n.d.) (see Chapter 13).

Knowledge of a better and finer world dawns for the community also through confrontation with the pervasive complicity in amorality, within its own tradition. In the novel *Screaming of the Innocent* (2001), the Botswana novelist Unity Dow describes the abortive fight of a young woman health worker, Amantle Bokaa, to rouse villagers against the cruelty of the entrenched patriarchy, acquiescence of the corrupt police, administrative apathy, and silence of the superstitious and fearful eyewitnesses. They thwart her attempt to uncover the ritual mutilation and murder of a 14-year-old virgin by local elders for ensuring their success and prosperity by invoking supernatural or devilish powers. The horrible practice of harvesting not only plant, but also animal and virgin body parts, is known by the Zulu word *muti* or the Setswana word *dipheko*. The horror of the inhuman practice is brought home through the dying screams of the virgin Neo Kakang. The screams haunt Rra-Naso, an impoverished old man, who collaborated in the ghastly act, and drive him to suicide (Chapter 12).

Sovereignty is another plank on which aboriginal communities of Australia, New Zealand, Nigeria, and Kerala (India), have pitted their affective right to prior possession (as First Nation people) against the effective sovereignty claimed by Anglo-Celtic immigrants. These communities have taken their stand on their pristine entitlement to the land, embodied in their ancient king or possession, continuing through the transient interruption of colonial rule. In Australia, they have asserted this right by offering hospitality and Original Nation Passports to Sri Lankan, Tamil and Afghan asylum seekers from their tent embassy at Canberra, or by extending adoption and gifts to Iranian artists. Maoris of Aotearoa–New Zealand have sold Pakeha-style Maori visas to Polynesian Samoans after the expiry of their work permits; adopted them; given them Maori names; and welcomed them ceremonially through pressing of noses, exchange of life breath and language immersion programmes (Chapter 8). In Benin, Nigeria, *Oba Nosa*, the all-seeing God-king of unfading beauty, has been reinstalled as a cultural symbol, spiritual icon and political sovereign. The Ague-Osa ceremony has projected the sovereign through theatre. It shows that the British in the 19th century acted as prosecution, defence, judge, and jury in an illegal trial to condemn the king in a Kangaroo Court; that the king resigned himself to his fate with courage and dignity as a sacrifice intended for the gods; and that the person imposed by the British as king refused to take his place, since a wall gecko could never bear a lizard. The period of the ceremony is explained as a time of abstinence from social rites and music. The colonial British rule is treated as an interlude, the sovereignty of the king continuing to be respected as legitimate and valid (Chapter 5). In Kerala, the Tēn and Urali Kurumars see themselves as superior in education, food habits and hygiene to other tribal groups. They see the engravings and inscriptions in Edakkal caves as the work of their ancestral Vishnuvarman rulers. In recent past, they relate to the king who led Kurichiya tribals in guerrilla warfare against the British and killed himself on his failure (Chapter 18).

The communities have also peopled their physical habitats with the signs and symbols of their mental landscape, as a measure of cultural survival. The eco-fraternity of Kurumba tribes in Wayanad, Kerala recognizes tracks, honeybee hives, roots, tubers, yams and colocassia by sight and smell. They equate stages in the development of banana leaves with the pregnancy stages of their maidens, to anticipate *Aintinaii*, the fivefold ecological categorization of their biosphere. Their primordial man, Adimukhan, leaves the woman born of his pangs, for the other end of the universe. The bereaved woman dreams him out in a forest rivulet. Their *Mooppans* (hamlet chiefs) act as chiefs, priests and medicine men, and lead their offering to forest deities like Mariyamma, Bettu Chikkamma and ancestral spirits. They define taboos and prescriptions for harvesting their forests sustainably (Chapter 18).

Maori artists of Aotearoa–New Zealand, represent their landscape in art as Earth Mother, severed from the Sky Father, whose blood flows into sunset colours, and not, like European artists, as a picture framed by a horizon from a chosen viewpoint. Despite use of painterly means — substitution of chemical for natural colours — they relate to their gods, ancestors, land, sea, rivers, and mountains. They show their storehouse, meeting house and a diversity of coloured signs, shapes, letters, guardian figures, and words, in sculptures, installations, mixed media objects, and landscape art. Thereby, they suggest symbolic recovery of their *taonga*, or treasures of Mother Earth, in the face of legal euphemisms and subtleties. Air New Zealand has translated the layered use of texts and images in Maori art into its logo as a symbol of life (Chapter 14). The South African novelist Zakes Mda builds his story-worlds on Bushman paintings of healing San trance dances, Frans Claerhout's paintings of heliotropic sunflowers and mnemonic flight codes, embedded in crazy quilt designs and mourning traditions. He celebrates acquisition of self-knowledge by indigenous communities from cultural symbols embedded in the landscape, in the manner of freedom songs in apartheid South Africa and Negro spirituals in slave-owning America. He discovers the patterns of rock art in patterns in water, lichen, leaves, cracks in mud, *kokerboom* (aloe tree) branches, tortoise carapace, that are strewn over the grasslands in which the trance dancers painted, lived, died, and were buried. He pits the sunflower, intrinsic to a non-extractive, non-toxic, indigenous subsistence economy against the misogynous Afrikaans gaze, which feminizes the landscape for exploitation. He contrasts the exploding colours of a native church, a black Jesus and Mary, in purple and red, with the black slate, sandstone whites-only church. He speaks of South African bees that share the same pheromones as their keepers, send calming messages to them through airborne hormones, and are arranged in irregular rows in beehives according to colours which they know. He compares them with American bees that count, are looked after by their keepers instead of looking after the keepers, and are arranged in straight, regular rows. He describes 'crazy' patchwork quilt designs that embody topographical clues for the flight of American plantation slaves, and are adapted for joyful, ludic, asymmetric drawings in the context of chants of itinerant mourners (Chapter 15).

Communities have to acknowledge their primal epistemology in its own terms as a cognitive model for leaving a lighter footprint on nature. It is a viable alternative to the instrumentalization of reason, contractualization of transactions, domination, objectification, and exploitation of a seemingly inanimate nature. It personifies, anthropomorphizes and spiritualizes nature and treats it as alive. It accepts a sacramental relation of this life with the afterlife, universal kinship of every being with each other, genealogical filiation of everything with everything and with an original source. It unites the Bushman hunter with the hunted eland and anticipates the symbolic school of post-colonial anthropology. To acknowledge this epistemology is not to deny capacity of the 'primitive human' for reciprocity or self representation, suggest his vulnerability, or express nostalgia for a lost paradise or innocence (Chapter 9).

Indigenous and tribal communities across the world have provided lessons towards the reinvention of cognitive categories for conserving human habitats, mindscapes, natural resources, memories, identities, and symbols. It is essential to act on these lessons to bridge the gulf yawning between natural and social sciences, inductive and deductive, local and global, textual and contextual, tangible and intangible knowledge, ideas and expressions. The gap has originated from the particularistic, positivist, intellectual roots of the universal *telos* assumed for production and dissemination of knowledge by westernizing technifying elites. It has caused a shift from the complexity and variety of strategies in the management of natural and human resources to their radical simplification and homogenization. It is necessary to reverse this process and restore the diversity of narratives and scripts nurtured by local communities against the essentializing, proto-colonial master narratives bred by them for the production, classification, characterization, and utilization of such resources. Such a reversal of approach will facilitate a movement from heavy, capital-intensive technologies to labour-intensive and intermediate technologies, major to minor denizens of forest, single- to multi-tier forestry, mono-culture to poly-culture of crops, fiscal to non-fiscal assessments, consumptive to non-consumptive values.

The recollection and regeneration of the symbols of mental and cultural landscapes of communities has to accompany this course correction. The South African concept of *ubuntu*, the Cree Canadian concept of *pimatisiwin* or *wakotawin*, the Anata Andina concept of *aÿni*, the Maori concept of *taonga* or *whenua* (land), the concept of *Aintinaii* in Kerala and Tamil Nadu, described in this volume, all bind nature and culture, oppressor and oppressed, hunter and hunted in a relation of reciprocity and mutuality. These concepts are rooted in a perception of unity of subject and object, knower and known, the perceived distinction being created by nescience. They are opposed to a particularistic trend in the Western concept of knowing, which does not permit non-Western cultures to exist in their inappropriable otherness; the Christian eschatological concept of believing, which poses an unbelieving, objectifiable other; the European enlightenment idea of ineluctable human progress to a secular utopia; Georg Wilhelm Friedrich Hegel's identification of the secular history of the West as a sacred history of the progressive self-realization of God, spirit or reason; the Marxist notion of historical materialism; the Freudian venture of enlarging self-knowledge; and the perception of the human subject as *ego cogito* or monad — put forward by Immanuel Kant and Gottfried Wilhelm von Leibniz respectively — which carries an absolute idea, of living only by reason (Mehta 1985a: 218, 1985b: 1–2, 1985c: 69–82).

The community concepts of knowing perceive a universe not indifferent but sympathetic to humanity. Humanity has to work with rather than against the elements of the phenomenal world. If there is a defect in understanding in community concepts like *muti*, or murder by ritual mutilation, it has to be corrected by the effort of the community itself.

These concepts epitomize and articulate a protest against forcible enculturation and assimilation in the guise of development. They suggest that the coexistential space inhabited by nature-based communities is to be repossessed, repeopled and rehabilitated with meaning by them as their own, and not as a space assigned by the state and multinational corporations, or left unoccupied by them. They embody the transgenerational community title to prescriptive possession and cultural self-determination, against principles that supersede such a title in the name of national or universal interest. Lacking recorded titles, indigenous, contextually-oriented communities are being integrated into a textually-rooted developmental culture in which all factors are mobile, and monetary and legal transactions are prized above barter and oral agreements. They have suffered from traumatization of memories, fracturing of histories, psychological ennui and resorted to chiliasm,[5] infra-nationalistic movements for the restoration of their right to live according to their own values and norms. The history of discontent narrated in this volume suggests the urgent necessity of harnessing community festivals, arts, worldviews, cartographic codes, rites of passage and knowledge systems concerning sustenance of human and natural resources for building bridges between culture and development, and for social impact assessment of a project in a particular eco-cultural regime.

Amnesia and aphasia, loss of memory and speech is responsible for the erosion of the co-evolutionary interdependence of human communities with their non-human neighbours in nature. Loss of the language of sustainable development among communities is a phenomenon to be understood beyond the statistical terms of endangerment as defined in the UNESCO vitality index on language loss. It is to be understood instead in terms of the end of niche diversification keyed to a sustainable materials economy, which doesn't use most materials but makes the most of existing materials. There has been an unequal exchange of knowledge and resources between the bio- and capital-rich regions, and commodity diversity has been substituted for a genetic one. There has been a tendency to confuse technological efficiency with bio-cultural superiority, in a racially-rooted, individual-oriented, intellectual property right regime. The growing inequality and reductionism are consequences of a panoptic prison-tower view of colonial subjects, as analyzed by George Orwell. 'The people have brown faces. Besides, there are so many of them. Are they really the same flesh as yourself? Do they even have names? Or, are they

---

[5] Chiliasm is a futuristic, predictive theory, derived from the theological doctrine that Christ will reign upon the earth a thousand years.

merely a kind of undifferentiated brown stuff, about as individual as bees or coral insects?' (Orwell 1954: 187). The realization has to dawn that while every individual is made of a mosaic of genes, biologically human beings are essentially one, and that Mendelian genetics and experimental biology have eroded racist theories of cultural superiority being a biological phenomenon. It is necessary to rebuild a *sui generis* community-based collective Intellectual Property Right (IPR) regime, which will treat communities holding custody of eco-specific, bio-systemic knowledge as innovators and breeders of intellectual seeds, and not as mere consumers of proprietary seeds. Their micro-spatial knowledge of biotopes is mostly superior in extent and depth to lexically-grounded, cosmopolitan knowledge.

It is necessary, for human survival, to protect community knowledge and identity-markers against the normlessness of a permissive society and *lex mercatoria* (law of the market). Such protection is required to avoid the trivialization and misrepresentation of the look and feel, colour and texture of their folkways symbols. In the Mataatua Declaration of Cultural and Intellectual Property Rights of Indigenous People, 1993, New Zealand; the Inter-Apache Summit on Repatriation of Cultural Properties in the US; the Karioca Declaration of Indigenous People's Earth Charter, 1992, in Brazil; and the Bulun Bulun case on the commercial use of rock art motifs in Australian courts, communities have asserted their right to cultural self-determination. They have demanded reversal of culturally-based harm, restitution of grave goods, return of their space and resources in land and air, custodial rights for the protection of their dreaming, burial and ceremony places. In the Karioca declaration, they have said, 'we feel the earth as if we are with our mother. When the earth is sick and polluted, human health is impossible. To heal ourselves, we must heal the planet, and to heal the planet, we must heal ourselves' (Dialogue between Nations 1992). To know differently, like indigenous, nature based communities, is to know that all western knowledge is not scientific, nor all scientific knowledge western, and that modernization is not to be equated with westernization. However, in this era of planetary culture, west is not fully west, nor east fully east. To speak with Heidegger, '[i]f Europe is to fulfil or heal itself, it has to open itself up to other great beginnings. It should become a land of sunset, to prepare for a new dawn' (Mehta 1976: 479).

References

Bhabha, Homi K. 1990. 'DissemiNation: Time, Narrative, and the Margins of the Modern Nation', in Homi K. Bhabha (ed.), *Nation and Narration*, pp. 291–322. London: Routledge.

Cadena, Marisol de la and Orin Starn. 2007. 'Introduction', in Marisol de la Cadena and Orin Starn (eds), *Indigenous Experience Today*, pp. 1–30. Oxford: Berg.

Devy, G. N., Geoffrey V. Davis and K. K. Chakravarty (eds). 2012. *Narrating Nomadism: Tales of Recovery and Resistance*. New Delhi: Routledge.

Dialogue between Nations. 1992. 'Culture, Science and Intellectual Property'. Indigenous Peoples Earth Charter, Kario-ca Conference, 25–30 May, Kario-ca. http://www.dialoguebetweennations.com/ir/english/kariocakimberley/KOCharter.html (accessed 5 June 2013).

Dow, Unity. 2001. *The Screaming of the Innocent*. North Melbourne: Spinifex Press.

Mehta, J. L. 1976. *Martin Heidegger: The Way and the Vision*. Honolulu: University Press of Hawaii.

———. 1985a. 'Beyond Believing or Knowing', in M. David Eckel (ed.), *India and the West: The Problem of Understanding — Selected Essays of J. L. Mehta*, p. 218. Chico, California: Scholars' Press.

——— 1985b. 'Philosophical Issues in Representation', in M. David Eckel (ed.), *India and the West: The Problem of Understanding — Selected Essays of J. L. Mehta*, pp. 1–2. Chico, California: Scholars' Press.

———. 1985c. 'The Concept of Progress', in M. David Eckel (ed.), *India and the West: The Problem of Understanding — Selected Essays of J. L. Mehta*, pp. 69–82. Chico, California: Scholars' Press.

Orwell, George. 1954 [1939]. 'Marrakesh', in *A Collection of Essays*, p. 187. New York: Doubleday Anchor Books.

Porras, Silvia and Anders Riis-Hansen. n.d. 'Interview with Rigoberta Menchu Tum: Five Hundred Years of Sacrifice Before the Alien Gods'. Race & Ethnicity. http://race.eserver.org/rigoberta-menchu-tum.html (1 September 2010).

Radhakrishnan, R. 2003. 'Postcoloniality and the Boundaries of Identity', in Linda Martín Alcoff and Eduardo Mendieta (eds), *Identities: Race, Class, Gender and Nationalities*, pp. 312–30. Oxford: Blackwell Publishing.

Vil-Nkomo, Sibusiso and Johan Myburgh. 1999. 'The Political Economy of an African Renaissance: Understanding the Structural Conditions and Forms', in Malegapuru William Makgoba (ed.), *African Renaissance: The New Struggle*, pp. 270–73. Cape Town: Mafube Publishing; Sandton: Tafelberg.

1 Being 'Primitive' in a Modern World

The Andaman Islanders

Vishvajit Pandya

It is now widely accepted that the tribal communities on the islands of South Andamans have lost their culture and languages or are rapidly losing them with a steady decline in their population since colonial times. These communities identified by the Indian state as Primitive Tribal Groups refer (among others) to the Ongee and Jarawa communities of hunter-gatherers. Both academic and popular comment on the Islands has over the years remained focused on the impact of their incorporation within the structures of the modern state. Much of such writing, however, has served to reinforce a narrative of victimhood that sees these communities as passive subjects of exploitation or neglect. Although there is undeniable evidence of the culturally destructive aspects of state policies of welfare, there is also evidence that points to a series of community responses that constitute a narrative not of victimhood, but of resistance and engagement. This chapter focuses on some of the specific ways in which the Ongee and Jarawa have mobilized language and strategies of self-presentation that is not reflective of mere acculturation or incorporation but of self-assertion, of resentment and, above all, an active engagement with the changing world around them. Such acts of self-expression it is argued must be understood in the context of the larger cultural logic that informs their lives in the forest and their capacity to act as historically conscious agents in the world outside it. The central thrust of this chapter is to present and analyze ethnographic data that tell us how the Ongee and Jarawa use their bodies as much as their language to interpret, engage and resist the intrusive presence of the state and the 'Outsider' in their lives in the forest.

A 'Bizarre Incident'

Early in the morning of August 2006, a group of 12 young men entered the Reserve Forest from the coast of Shoal Bay with a supply of hunting equipment and water.[1] As they trudged along the mangrove into the thicker forest interiors, they were suddenly surrounded by a group of eight Jarawa men. A local newspaper from Port Blair reported the sequence of events that followed, describing it as a 'downright bizarre incident, strange, unbelievable and yet true!' (*Light of Andamans* 2006).

According to the report, as the Jarawas surrounded the intruders, the first question they asked in Hindi was whether they had brought any food with them. The poachers, already in shock and terrified by the intensely menacing presence, replied in the negative. The Jarawas, on not finding any food, started mercilessly slapping and kicking the men and hurling the choicest Hindi abuses all the while. The scuffle and resistance put up by the poachers was of no use. The Jarawas compelled them to remove all their clothes as a prelude to the next offensive. According to the report, the poachers, on removing their clothes, were asked to perform physical acts that were 'extreme and sexually perverse'. Finished with the assault, which allegedly included acts of sodomy, the Jarawas climbed on the shoulders of the naked poachers and asked them to proceed towards the Andaman Trunk Road (ATR), a major road running through the reserve forest.

A road gang was working on the roadside along with a police constable on duty, who was horrified at the sight. The Jarawas laughed and enjoyed the scene while the poachers could barely stand the mortification. The constable pleaded with the Jarawas to return the clothes. But the Jarawas refused to comply. Instead, they embarked on a different game. On hearing a vehicle arriving they would herd the naked poachers inside the jungle and bring them back once the convoy had passed. The game went on till dusk. Only after sunset were the torn clothes returned. The poachers returned home completely shattered, humiliated and exhausted. According to the weekly newspaper, *Light of Andamans* (2006: 3): 'This is a rare phenomenon in the behavior of Jarawas towards the civil society. Never before in the entire history of Jarawa interaction was such an incident of such extreme sexual perversity reported'.

---

[1] Jarawa reserve territory, a protected area for aboriginal tribes, was created on 30 June 1956 by the government notification no. 76/56. It primarily restricted the entry of non-tribals to areas designated as tribal reserves. In September 1991 certain coastal areas along the area associated with the aboriginal tribes were also brought under protective regulation. In September 2004 (No. 159/2004/F.No 1-752/2002-TW PF) the Jarawa reserve territory was expanded to accommodate the growing needs of the Jarawas and control the presence of non-tribals in Jarawa areas.

It is interesting to consider the response of the media as well as the state to the incident. The administration neither denied the incident nor confirmed it. While some expressed bewilderment at the shockingly bizarre nature of the incident, others took recourse to silence. Clearly the incident had upset the basic premises of the pacification narrative, the end of hostilities and the Jarawas' own gestures of friendship and reconciliation to the Outsider ever since their coming out in 1997. Why did the Jarawas take recourse to such a bizarre act of hostility on the body of the Outsider? Was it an act of spontaneous 'primitive' aggression? Or was it expressive of a deep-seated memory of conflict?

Why did the Jarawas seek to undress their captors and parade them naked across the ATR? Why was it not enough to just physically harm them? Was the idea of removing the clothes of the Outsider a deliberate effort to return the gaze of the Outsider or an attempt to unsettle the state narrative of pacification? These are some of the questions that this chapter seeks to explore in order to understand the larger implications of this incident in the cultural and political meanings that the Jarawas bring to bear upon their condition of marginality.

But was this incident of 2006 really a first in the history? It must be noted that what happened in post-independent India is perhaps not a unique phenomenon as far as the earlier colonial accounts are concerned. In the *Report on the Administration of the Andaman Nicobar Islands and the Penal Settlement 1874–75*,[2] it is reported that in the forests of the Luckrabama (Middle Andaman) in March 1875, Andaman islanders shot dead an escaped convict who refused to strip out of his clothes and told two naked escapees accompanying him to get out of the forest back to the settlement.

A close analysis of the range of contacts between the Andamanese and the Outsiders over a period spanning colonial and post–colonial regimes (Pandya 2002a, 2009) reveals a practised structure of resistance and subversion around dressing and undressing and the consequent processes of photographing and representations (see Plate 1.1). This aspect of the Andamanese relations with the Outsider is silenced in the State's narratives of pacification and welfare. In these narratives, there is little recognition of the fact that the Andamanese can and do utilize past experiences of contact to structure contemporary relations with Outsiders. In the Jarawa offensive of 2006 on the settlers, it becomes clear that

---

[2] Indian Office Library Records (IOLR), File no. V-10-591, 44, British Library, London.

Plate 1.1: Jarawas as they appeared on the West Coast of Middle Andamans in 1994

Source: Photographed by the author.

every act of violation of the settlers' body, every language of abuse and every gesture of hostility is embedded in a genealogy of the Andamanese experience of the Outsider and being a 'primitive' in the modern world.

Methodologically, this chapter draws upon history and ethnography in ways that call for a critical reading of both the 'modernizing' process that subsumes the representation and the very visibility of the 'primitive'. Interpretations of the Jarawa behaviour of August 2006, for instance, are read together with historical narratives and ethnographic studies of encounters between the Andaman islanders and the Outsider. This paper tries to understand how some of the constitutive features of colonial and post-colonial narratives of pacification in general, and of the Jarawas in particular, have been repeatedly unsettled by the Jarawas' attempts to convey the contingency and conditionality of their pacified selves. This chapter seeks to develop this argument by focusing on the Jarawas' engagement with their clothed bodies. The uncritical acceptance of clothing, particularly in the case of the 'Primitive Tribal Groups' (PTGs) of the Andaman Islands has often been regarded as one of the signs of the success of contact and pacification projects by the state.[3] In the case

---

[3] Out of the 698 Scheduled Tribes listed in the Constitution of India, 75 are identified as Primitive Tribal Groups (PTGs) and are considered more backward

of the Jarawas, this claim looks vulnerable not because the Jarawas have rejected clothing per se, but because they have used it suggestively and strategically to define the terms of their relations with the Outsider.

Jarawas can be ethnographically viewed by positioning them so as to comprehend the structure and practice that constitutes the history of relations between 'primitive' Andaman islanders and Outsiders. Constitutionally recognizing the Jarawas as a marginalized PTG is the State's acknowledgement of the fact that certain groups of tribals remain changeless and vulnerable, thereby requiring forms of special assistance and social welfare and protection in order to ensure their survival while they can be modernized and moved away from their marginalized position (see Pandya 2002b, 2005). Jarawas are a group consisting of about 350 hunter-gatherers, who are confined to a 570 sq. km demarcated territory known as the Jarawa Reserve Territory on the South and Middle Andaman Islands in the Bay of Bengal. In the Indian government's mentality, Jarawa as *adimjanjati* (primitive tribals) must be protected and fortified against continuous threats, as they continue to be living in a 'pre-agricultural natural state, with food insecurity and a host of diseases with no shelter and clothes' (Ministry of Tribal Affairs 2004). The 2004 National Policy formulated by the Ministry of Tribal Affairs was keen to display a degree of sensitivity in its policy measures by inserting a key proposal that to 'boost the PTG's self-image their being stigmatized as

---

than Scheduled Tribes. In 1979, they were defined by their inclination to live in a pre-agricultural stage of economy, very low literacy rates and stagnant or even declining populations. At 2,500,000, the PTG populations constitute nearly 3.6 per cent of the tribal population and 0.3 per cent of the country's population. To observers outside the bureaucracy, the PTGs have benefited little from the developmental initiatives planned for them. They face continuous threats of eviction from their homes and lands. They live in a pre-agricultural state, with food insecurity and a host of diseases like sickle cell anaemia and malaria. In recognition of these lacunae in state developmental efforts of the past, the National Policy of 2004 suggested a series of corrective measures. The document formulated by the Ministry of Tribal Affairs was keen to display a degree of sensitivity and correctness not only in its policy measures but also in the social implications of its use of particular classificatory terminologies for the PTGs. It had, for instance, inserted a key proposal which said, 'To boost PTGs' social image, their being stigmatized as "primitive" shall be halted. Efforts shall be made to bring them on par with other Scheduled Tribes in a definite time frame. Developmental efforts should be tribe-specific and suit the local environment' (Ministry of Tribal Affairs 2004).

primitive shall be removed' (Ministry of Tribal Affairs 2004). Here the contradiction was that the framers of the national policy had just followed the 1979 definition of a PTG, refusing to acknowledge the fact that the sources of the PTG's stigmatization were inherent in the very categories used to classify them as such. Both colonial and Indian administrators simply perpetuated a stigmatized construct of 'primitiveness'. Fundamental to both, the construction was the most visible marker of nakedness of hunters and gatherers moving in the forest. Being surrounded by ever increasing non-tribal settler populations has made the Jarawas extremely marginal. It is against this historical backdrop that the Jarawas as a 'PTG' perceive and articulate their 'nakedness', which calls into question the uncritical associations of 'nakedness' with 'primitiveness' that inform and sustain the disciplinary projects of the modern Indian state.

This chapter seeks to enter this zone of silence and retrieve the responses of those people whose nakedness has been the target of a whole range of disciplinary projects of both the British colonial state and the Indian ruling elites. The visual representation and culturally communicated notion of nakedness among the Jarawas historically maps out the utilization of the attributed primitiveness by the Jarawas to assert 'I am primitive as you have imaged!' or 'I was once a primitive not anymore!'

The constituted identity of the Jarawas is an outcome of a historical process that has always entailed events of contact between the non-tribal Outsiders and the marginalized Andaman islanders 'in the forest'. Non-tribals provided the tribals with materials with the intent of making them presentable in accordance to their own visualized images. When what is provided by the Outsiders is accepted by the tribals it actually articulates the Jarawas' power and capacity to communicate their own construct of history and identity through events of contact. In the contact events between the tribals and the non-tribals, a cultural and ideological calculation is made by interacting groups.

In post-independence India the statement made was that the tribals are the 'Other' along with the whole nation that is modernizing, but the distinct identity of the tribal will be maintained.

The analytical template for Jarawa primitive tribal identity will consider 'clothing' as a form of representation to reconstitute the Andamanese as new 'colonized subjectivities', that have altered from what is primitive and what is not primitive or what settlers refer to as 'ex-primitives' (*sudhrey huwey junglee* [reformed primitives] or *kabhee junglee thei* [once were primitive]). However, in some contexts the reverse process of discarding the clothes is also seen as a way to assert primitivism through nakedness and conveying the conserved identity of the primitive tribal in the state and society.[4] Let us consider the incident of August 2006 to draw attention to the fact that the Jarawas' engagement with clothing and by extension their bodies in contexts of 'visual' encounters with the Outsider reveals a structure of practice that needs to be understood as part of their larger efforts to negotiate the conditions of their marginality.

Clothing the Jarawas — The Friendly Way

The Andaman administration has for long held the view that, all the welfare activities of the state have had such an impact on the Jarawas that in September of 1998, after a lapse of 200 years, they decided to end all hostility and come out of the forest, with the intent of maintaining amicable relationships with the outside world. It celebrated the fact that the treatment of a young Jarawa boy named Enmey in Port Blair hospital had convinced the Jarawas to befriend the Outsider. Enmey was held up as the mascot of the friendly Jarawa and his story was constitutive of the Indian state's pacification of the Jarawa. Pictures of Enmey in colourful tee shirts and Bermudas lounging around the corridors of Port Blair's G. B. Pant Hospital appeared in newspapers and other media signifying the dramatic entry of the naked primitive into the civilized space of the modern state.[5]

---

[4] In 1979, tribal Ongee women from Little Andaman were trained to put on clothes, over a body that only used to have a palm-fibre apron. They were to be brought to Port Blair by the administration to meet Prime Minister Indira Gandhi visiting Port Blair. On seeing Ongee women all dressed up the prime minister insisted that they should be asked to remove the imposed-upon dress and let them remain natural and authentic for the official photograph. Ongee women were subject to the authorities telling them to get in and out of a dress in accordance to the image the 'outsider' has of the tribal 'Other'. For the state and its citizen's image Andamanese are unique as 'primitive' since tribals have 'costumes' and non-tribals have clothes, but 'primitives' are those devoid of both. Sociologically, all that a non-tribal presents is what the 'primitive' lacks and 'primitive' is indexical of what the 'modern' is not. Perception of nakedness has been a primary constitutive factor in the tribal and non-tribal encounters in the region, within the Indian state and civil society's representational systems.

[5] Capture and return of the Andaman Islanders has a long history in the formation of the colonial power and attempts at civilizing the savage (see Hellard 1861; Mukhopadhyay et al. 2002; Naidu 1999; Sarkar 1989). Some of the earliest

Yet there was a curious twist in Enmey's story which was carefully ignored in this narrative. Enmey, it may be noted at this point, was admitted to the hospital after he was found nursing a fractured knee on the edges of the Jarawa Reserve forest in the Middle Andamans. Villagers who heard him groan in pain informed welfare officials who later brought him to Port Blair for treatment. Enmey's presence in Port Blair was said to have encouraged other ailing Jarawas in the forest to come out of the forest to receive medical attention. The part of the story that is instructive relates to the time following Enmey's release from the hospital. On 28 December 2000, Enmey and 19 other Jarawa men were discharged from the G. B. Pant Hospital. They were taken back to the roadside camp at R. K. Nallah under the supervision of welfare officials. They received a whole range of presents and bade tearful good-byes before they made their way back into the forest. At the drop-off point they were received by 20 other Jarawa men and women in their traditional attire. After a brief exchange of gifts and food items from those who returned from Port Blair, the whole group was said to have walked back together. What was interesting was that the group returning from Port Blair took off all the items of clothing they had acquired in Port Blair and hung them around in the shrubs and undergrowth. What had been received with much enthusiasm in Port Blair was summarily discarded the moment they reached the forest.

Although several explanations are offered for the Jarawas' motivations to come out of the forest, there is little understanding of Enmey's own reflections on his perceived role as a 'messenger of peace' in the forest. Enmey's keenness to present himself as the reformed Jarawa amenable to the civilizing influences of the Port Blair medical facility where he was admitted for treatment of a fractured knee was taken to be a sign of a change among the Jarawas as a whole. Yet, on being asked why he was happy to wear the coloured vests and track pants given to him in Port Blair, and why he had brought many other Jarawa boys with him many of whom were hitherto hostile to outsiders in general, he replied:

> By coming to Port Blair, we get things at the hospital. Just as by climbing a tree we find irritating bees but also find honeycombs. So coming to Port Blair is good and to get good things we come to the hospital. In Port Blair, on seeing you all, we want to be like you; you all who gather around to see us. We want

---

records of it date back to 1792. See the letter from Captain Kyd to Lord Cornwallis (IOLR, Eur.F 21/1). See also Mouat (1863); Temple (1903).

to be seen in clothes, shoes, caps, and coloured handkerchiefs. Just as you all are seen by us! By doing so soon we will be left to see your place freely — when we try to be like you we find more and more new things. So, it is good to come to Port Blair where we get all that you want us to have. It is not hard work! So, others want to come with me. But in the forest, I cannot really climb trees or hunt if I wear shoes! Can I? Just as I cannot wear clay paints in your hospital. In the forest, I discard all that we get in Port Blair and get more of it at the roadside (interview with Enmey, Port Blair, 2001).

Enmey's reflections offer a completely different way of reading of what one may call compliance or collaboration. If clothing offered the possibility of moving unhindered within the hospital and brought with it more 'things' then of course, they were welcome. The adoption of clothing, in other words, was in no way any indicator of the acceptance of civilized ways. It was a strategic engagement with the structures of surveillance and protection offered by the hospital. Wearing clothes in the hospitals offered the possibilities of both relative freedom and easy subsistence. From my conversations with Enmey and his friends I was led to understand that the Jarawa had formulated a new self-image of the 'primitive'. Enmey was once 'primitive' but now he was also an ex-primitive, as the modern state wanted him to be — he was both exotic and accessible (Plate 1.2).

Plate 1.2: Enmey (centre) and His Mates at G. B. Pant Hospital in Port Blair, Displaying Ornaments and Clothes Acquired in Port Blair, 1999

Source: Photographed by the author.

Theatre on the Andaman Trunk Road

The notion of dressing and undressing as routes to relative freedom and easy subsistence has found further elaboration on the segment of the ATR which runs through the Jarawa reserve territory in the Middle Andamans. Jarawas acquire clothes when they are out of the forest and this facilitates their limited movement and interaction in Port Blair where they are seen as changing from being primitive and naked. However, on returning to the forest, items provided to them are discarded and they revert to presenting themselves as relatively 'under or un-dressed', drawing the attention of those who provide them food items for consumption and clothes to cover themselves. Since the year 2000, Jarawas on this stretch of the road have been seen to draw the attention of tourists and commuters by switching back and forth between conditions of 'naked primitiveness' and 'clothed civility' (Plates 1.3 and 1.4). Their keenness and ability to switch appearances comes from the understanding that posing naked in front of tourist cameras offers yet another opportunity for easy foraging. Commuters, tourists, and passers-by in fact have encouraged this understanding by offering the Jarawas food, money and the odd trinket. The promise of a good collection encourages the younger ones amongst them to dodge the surveillance of welfare workers and run after the buses that ply along the ATR. While tourists and commuters look on with wonder, settlers in the nearby villages see the roadside exchange of goods and gazes with cautious optimism. The Jarawas' acceptance of the Outsider's food and their willingness to present the more 'benign' attributes of their 'primitiveness' brings with it the hope that they are consciously moving away from their earlier stance of hostility (Plate 1.5). Yet, observations

Plate 1.3: Jarawas at the Roadside in 2000

Source: Photographed by the author.

Being 'Primitive' in a Modern World 23

Plate 1.4: Jarawas at the Roadside in 2004

Source: Photographed by the author.
Note: It is interesting to note the sunglasses acquired from the tourists and bananas made into a headband.

Plate 1.5: Jarawas Standing at the Roadside Wearing Clothes Given by the Non-Tribals

Source: Photographed by the author.

on the ground over a period of time prove how misplaced such optimism can be. With the increasing consciousness and experience of perceptions of their nakedness, the Jarawas are seen to have developed the capacity to use their bodies to destabilize the meanings of 'primitive' and the narrative of 'pacification' built around it.

As a consequence of the strategy of moving back and forth within the stereotypical frames of the 'savage' and the 'civilized', the Jarawas have been able to negotiate a parallel mode of subsistence on the margins of the forest. While there is much truth in the argument that livelihood within the reserve is under threat, Jarawa behaviour on the roadside cannot be explained away by deprivation alone. Although the administration accepted the deprivation argument and increased the supply of food and resources in the forest, attempts to keep them away from the visible range of the road have in most instances remained limited in impact. Since 2005, the administration has made considerable attempts to strengthen policing on the ATR, restraining both the Jarawa and the tourists who plied along its length in the fervent hope of catching a glimpse of one of the few remaining 'savages' in contemporary India. The government's increased efforts in this direction was also in response to range of concerns expressed by human rights groups and the Indian judiciary which indicted the government for allowing the Jarawas to 'beg' by the roadside. Jarawa visitations on the ATR as well as in the neighbouring villages were also seen as a potentially disruptive influence on the precarious structures of the settler economy. Welfare agents had to constantly pacify irate villagers complaining of incidents of destruction of their gardens and homesteads.

In order to restrain the Jarawas' keenness to roam around the ATR and allow themselves to be photographed, the Andaman Adim Janjati Vikas Samiti (AAJVS) workers tried to warn them that if they exposed themselves to the flashbulbs they would burn their skins which would cause sores.[6] Such warnings clearly went unheeded as the Jarawas

---

[6] The constitutionally-endorsed notion of 'tribal reserve' (Article 243, Clause 2, June 1956) guaranteed protection of a tribal culture by judiciary and administrative powers in a 'non-interference' and 'non-imposition' manner. However, in 1975, for the further protection of the Jarawas, the Central Government of India allocated a budget and formed the *Andaman Adim Janjati Vikas Samiti* or the AAJVS, which translates as Andaman Primitive Tribal Welfare Association, within the administration of the union territory of the Andaman Islands. The AAJVS started looking exclusively after the future of the 'primitive' tribes on the islands (AAJVS 1977; Krishnatry 1976; Sharma 1981). The small size of

continued their practised habits of stopping before buses and cars and holding out their palms for bits of betel nut or tobacco leaves or a few rupee notes and then posing before the cameras (Plate 1.6).

Plate 1.6: Road Sign Put up by the Administration along the ATR

Source: Photographed by the author.

By 2005 the administration had put up a series of signboards and spread the idea that road users are not to photograph or give anything to the Jarawas.[7] Welfare staff and police were posted along the road to

---

the Jarawa population and their pursuit of hunting and foraging made them unique as compared to other tribal cultures of the Indian subcontinent; hence the term *adim* (primitive) was a prominent component. The then prime minister, Mrs Indira Gandhi, saw this programme for the 'primitive' as a special priority in relation to the process of modernization of the islands. The role of the AAJVS was to oversee a number of measures and processes with the stated objectives of protecting and promoting development essential for survival and growth (Krishnatry 1976: 25). Particularly for the Jarawas, being a 'primitive tribe' was seen as an important way of dealing with the problems generated by the 1956 Regulation of Aboriginal Protection Act (AAJVS 1977) as the project of building the ATR through the Jarawa reserve forest was finally approved.

[7] On 1 June 2006, the administration reissued strict orders to the users of the ATR that legal action would be taken against tourists and tour operators who

ensure that Jarawas without clothes or partly dressed were not at the roadside to draw attention; the Jarawas were constantly pushed away from the roadside. The new restrictions however have not restrained them — they now stand at the roadside partly clothed and attracting renewed interest in their predicament. They have learned Hindustani, and are capable of silencing welfare staff attempting to restrain them with the argument that they are merely 'sitting at the roadside and not disrupting the traffic'. Why should they be compelled to go back into the forest?!

There is a clear understanding that their studied road act will not be without effect. My recent travels along the ATR revealed the maturing of an act I had already witnessed some years ago. The encounter with the Outsider is scripted around what could be described as astute verbal and body-play. Once the Jarawas succeed in slowing down the traffic and luring the eager tourist or commuter to fish out his/her camera, the Jarawas at the roadside quickly assume a stance of reproach and convey the stern message, 'Do not photograph me! If you do, you'll have to give me something!' My own understanding of this new assertiveness (informed by several years of studying the Jarawas in various contexts) is that the verbal and body language comes close to that of the braying displays of command and authority by the local police posted on the fringes of the Reserve. The situation becomes even more dramatic and intense as the Jarawa youth acquire a stance of belligerence by flailing sticks and banging the bodies of vehicles, swearing and cursing all the while. When the startled outsiders comply and start offering gifts or try engaging in some form of dialogue, a dramatic scene begins to unfold. Like performers waiting in the wings for the final act on the stage, younger Jarawas, particularly women, glide out of the shrubbery in traditional body attire with clay paints, bows and arrows to perform a swift and studied parade in front of the anxious photographers, who are then compelled to comply with the demand for more generous gifts. If the officials patrolling the road arrive while this scripted drama conducted by the Jarawas is on,

---

tried taking any kind of photographs of the Jarawas anywhere. The 'Dos and Don'ts for travellers on the ATR in the Jarawa area' reiterated that the Jarawas were one of the primitive tribes of the islands and were not to be promoted as a tourist attraction. In the final declaration, the administration mentioned that these steps and regulations were essential for all in order to protect their own lives and property, making it clear that these regulations were not just for the protection of the life and property of the Jarawas but for that of all those who tried to engage with them (Plate 1.6).

they swagger into action hurling abuses at both the photographers and the photographed, brandishing their sticks and commanding the Jarawas to retreat into the Reserve. At times the offenders, whether they are tourists or commuters, are threatened with legal action or let off after paying a small fee or bribe. Before the next convoy of traffic comes by the Jarawa groups along the ATR get dressed up and are ready for yet another round of body-play wherein the assertion of a fluid 'primitiveness' is heightened by the carefully scripted entry and exit of clothed and unclothed performers along the roadside.

This incident reflects an escalation of the awareness among the Jarawas that their image is itself a commodity that can be transacted to advantage. It also shows their increasing capacity to dodge the structures of state surveillance. Police outposts and AAJVS workers along the ATR struggled to sustain the structures of the optical regime that sought to restrain both the inadvertent visibility and the deliberate display of the Jarawa body. The pressure of commerce and tourism on the one hand and the Jarawas' purported collusion with their agents on the other has made the ATR a zone of deep conflict. Although Jarawa visits on the ATR seem to have registered a relative decline in recent years, there are also increases in the number of poachers entering the Jarawa reserve forest where incidents like that of August 2006 take place and where the semiotic charge of the naked body and the clothed body are utilized to re-negotiate the terms of marginality in more dramatic ways.

The Jarawa relation with clothing in particular and to the disciplines of the body in general indicates the reflexive processes that have characterized the Andamanese relation with the Outsider over time. The Jarawas have learnt as perhaps have other Andamanese groups, to use the structures of discipline as vehicles of resistance. Whether in Port Blair or near the roadside the Jarawas follow the principle of aligning themselves with the historical relations unfolding in a particular space–time. By appropriating material from a range of contexts and contacts, the Jarawas create a symbolic surplus that sustains an imposed discourse of historical change. This however is not a history that moves through clearly demarcated stages — from 'naked, primitive and uncivilized' to 'dressed, modern and civilized'. It rather reflects a historical consciousness marked by the collisions and inter-reflexivities of two different worldviews and identities. It is a consciousness that plays out in sequences of friendship and hostility, each time reflecting the experience of a past contact and the specific positioning of the present particularly through dressing and undressing. The process of clothing and its utilization to assert and contest identities in fact goes all the way back to the colonial period. A couple of early examples would help explicate the point.

Subversion to sartorial disciplining among the Andaman islanders has a long history. Talbot Clifton was an orchid collector who visited the islands in 1907. In the course of her early encounters with the Andamanese in the homes set up for them, she commented that the Andamanese were expected to be dressed in the presence of settlers. She also described them as being 'shy' about getting photographed without clothes (Clifton 1911). In other words, there seems to have been a strange ambivalence towards clothing or covering the body. While there were times when they complied with the commands of the sartorial discipline imposed on them, there were on other occasions sudden displays of rebellion against clothing. This is borne out in the accounts of a range of visitors to the islands intent on photographing the islanders. Stanley William Coxon (1915) — posted to the islands in 1876 — was, for instance, fascinated with the possibilities of photographing the 'natural Andamanese' and his recollections of native women at a sports event organized by the colonial administrators in 1876 on Ross Island show how the 'discipline' of clothing imposed on the tribals was got around. The episode marks not just the ability of the tribals to rid themselves of what they saw as an artificial encumbrance, but the delight of the settlers in the spectacle of what they strove assiduously to cover up:

> Andamanese live on the outside island in a state of absolute nature. Whenever permitted to cross over to Ross Island, it was the duty of one of the officials to see that their nakedness was covered ... On this particular occasion, the precaution had been taken of wrapping the entrants for the ladies' race in pieces of sacking, tied round the waist with string. The parade being over, some sixteen dusky damsels formed up abreast of the starter. The course was cleared and all eyes were on the straight-point. 'Are you ready?' said the starter. 'Off!' and off went every wrap they had on them! No stupid piece of English sackcloth was to be allowed to interfere with the chance of any of our black beauties winning the much-coveted money prizes. We were all simply in convulsions, and the laughter of the Tommies could be heard reverberating in the hills ... We heard afterwards that on their way to the starting-post the ladies had contrived to cut through their waist strings with their fingernails, so that they clearly engaged in the fray ... with no false modesty. What a priceless snapshot this race would have made! But alas! We had no Kodaks in those days (ibid.: 50–51).

This practice of subverting the sartorial discipline imposed by the British colonizers on the Andamanese is repeated by the Jarawas under the regime of the Indian state too.

The Jarawa 'performance' on the ATR, as much as in the confines of the G. B. Pant Hospital in Port Blair, resonate with similar strategies and modes of negotiation with regimes of sartorial discipline and more significantly the act of photography. For the Indian state and the agencies of welfare however, such incidents fail to cohere into meaningful practice. Hence, the sense of outrage and utter disbelief was expressed at the event of August 2006.

Concluding Issues

Coming back to the events of 2006, one can perhaps argue that the incident reveals that acts of friendliness and hostility and the interpretation of these by the Outsider have reinforced the boundaries defining the world of the tribal and the non-tribal. Far from bringing the tribal communities, the settlers and the state into a shared discourse, projects of pacification, welfare and contact or befriending have multiplied misunderstandings in more than one context. The status of the Jarawas as a PTG 'pacified, but not quite' defines the terms of their marginality in slightly different ways than that of the Great Andamanese or the Ongee. What makes their position ambivalent and potentially disruptive for the state is that the Jarawas have called into question some of the basic premises of the state's project of welfare — particularly the terms in which it seeks to understand and facilitate the inclusion of the primitive in the structures of the modern state.

My ethnographic intervention in the history of contact as it plays out between the asymmetries of the state and a marginalized people 'without history' has led me to re-engage with history as unfolding in a complex semiotic system — one in which signs like the clothed body or the naked body keep acquiring new material and visual values and meanings. Because the objective world to which signs are applied has its own refractory characteristics and dynamics, the signs, and by derivation the people who live by them, particularly those understood as 'primitive', are open to being interpreted as 'once primitive', 'no more primitive' and 'primitive but not hostile' in different locations or even sometimes at the same time. Repeated contacts but lack of shared discourse between the Jarawas and the Outsider has further perpetuated the problem of them being perceived not as agents of their historical course but as a generic category of PTGs, constructed by the representational practices of the state and the discourses of welfare.

If we deconstruct the narratives of the colonial and post-colonial narratives of pacification (Awaradi 1990; Portman 1899) what we see is that our triumphant narratives have sought only to reinforce the state's ability to confront and eventually neutralize the tribal's hostile nature. However, the basic premise of the given narrative is questionable, particularly in light of the Jarawas' engagement with the Outsider that reflects a historical subjectivity and agency that is seldom acknowledged or addressed. In doing so, what comes to the surface is a sense of marginal identities that have been shaped and are expressive of the historically constituted relation of distrust between the Andamanese tribal communities and the Outsider, whether in the guise of the colonizer, the welfare agent, the tourist, the poacher, or of non-tribal settlers on the island.

Negotiating marginality challenges the terms of welfare and unsettles the narrative of pacification. The Jarawa's gestures of friendship with the Outsider are evidently conditional, their gestures of compliance often contingent. To acknowledge this fact prompts us to question the certitudes of the state's narratives of pacification and point to the prevailing relations of distrust. Much of this mutual suspicion is rooted in a fundamentally flawed understanding of welfare. The humanitarian discourses of state welfare and the ideology and practice of *Adim Janajati Vikas* is premised upon an understanding of the subject of welfare as a subject without agency. For all its claims to promote *vikas* or progress, all that the state welfare agency or the AAJVS seek to do is to attempt to discipline the primitive into a modern subject of welfare, duly disempowered and devoid of agency. The policing of the ATR as a way of protecting the Jarawas as a prized 'Primitive Tribal Group' symbolizes the dilemmas of a modernizing state keen to showcase the trajectory of its evolutionary graph while following the path of 'development'. It is little wonder then that at the Andaman Nicobar Bhavan, the island's official guesthouse and office in New Delhi, a huge 20-foot tall statue of a naked savage aiming an arrow is installed in the frontyard (see Plate 1.7). There is also an installation of an Andamanese tribal sculpted without clothes but with bows and arrows in front of the Lieutenant-Governor's residence at Port Blair. The state in all senses continues to grapple with the issues of the image, imagination and the 'visibility' of the 'primitive' groups under its jurisdiction. The self-image of the state requires the visual display of the virile savage protected and preserved by humane governance.

This chapter examined how Jarawas themselves emerge as producers of images of their 'identity', using possible combinations of materiality and visuality to conform to the expectations of 'primitives' and 'ex-primitives', both being marginal, to their advantage. In Port Blair, the act of wearing clothes works to project an image of having left behind the state

Plate 1.7: Display of Jarawa Image in the Frontyard of the Andaman Bhavan, New Delhi, 2010

Source: Photographed by the author.

of 'primitivity'. Yet this composed identity is dismantled once they are in the forest where they manage to recover their identity by undressing. At the roadside, the staged performance for the tourists comprising of dressing and undressing demonstrates their skill in manipulating identity through materials to align to the image imagined for them by curious outsiders. Historically, Jarawas have learnt about identity as being performed and communicated through the contexts of contact and they perhaps express the marginal identity in their worldview of the poachers who entered their world by commanding them to undress. Though the combined power of the optical regime of the state, the social imagination of the 'primitive' and the standardized representational practices in the global image flows, what is created ironically is zones of blindness that prevent us from seeing how history works its way in making Jarawa more 'modern' without making it any less 'primitive'.

References

Andaman Adim Janjati Vikas Samiti (AAJVS). 1977. *Retrieval from the Precipice: A Unique Experiment to Prevent Extinction of the Remaining Negrito Primitive Tribes in Andaman & Nicobar Islands*. Port Blair: Andaman Adim Janjati Vikas Samiti.

Awaradi, S. A. 1990. *Master Plan 1991–2021 for Welfare of Primitive Tribes of Andaman and Nicobar Islands*. Port Blair: Andaman Nicobar Administration.

Clifton, Talbot. 1911. *Pilgrim to the Isles of Penance: Orchid Gathering in the East*. London: John Long.

Coxon, Stanley William. 1915. *And That Reminds Me: Being Incidents of a Life Spent at Sea and in the Andaman Islands, Burma, Australia, and India*. London: John Lane, The Bodley Head.

Elwin, Verrier. 1959. 'Do We Really Want to Keep them in a Zoo?', *Sunday Statesman*, 3 October, p. 32.

Hellard, S. 1861. 'Notes on the Andamanese Captured at Port Blair', *Journal of the Asiatic Society of Bengal*, 30: 259–63.

Krishnatry, S. (ed.). 1976. *The Prime Minister and the Andaman Nicobar Archipelago*. Port Blair: Government Press.

Light of Andamans. 2006. 'Bizarre Incident at ATR', issue 37, 2 September.

Ministry of Tribal Affairs. 2004. 'National Tribal Policy (Draft)'. Ministry of Tribal Affairs, Government of India, New Delhi.

Mouat, Frederic J. 1863. *Adventures and Researches among the Andaman Islanders*. London: Hurst and Blackett.

Mukhopadhyay, K., Ranjit Kumar Bhattacharya and B. N. Sarkar (eds). 2002. *Jarawa Contact: Ours with Them and Theirs with Us*. Kolkata: Anthropological Survey of India.

Naidu, Thalapaneni Subramanyam. 1999. *Action Plan to Save the Jarawa: An Anthropological Perspective to Conserve the Endangered Stone Age Aborigines*. Pondicherry: Centre for Future Studies, Pondicherry University.

Pandya, Vishvajit. 2002a. 'Contact, Images and Imagination: The Impact of Roads in Jarawa Reserve Forest of Andaman Islands', *Bijdragen tot de Taal-, Land- en Volkenkunde* (Leiden), 158(4): 799–820.

———. 2002b. 'Jarwas of Andaman Islands: "Their Social and Historical Reconstruction"', *Economic and Political Weekly*, 37(37): 3830–34.

———. 2005. '"Do not Resist, Show Me Your Body!": Encounters between the Jarawas of the Andamans and Medicine (1858–2004)', *Anthropology and Medicine*, 12(3): 211–23.

———. 2009. *In the Forest: Visual and Material Worlds of Andamanese History (1858–2003)*. Lanham, MD: University Press of America.

Portman, Maurice Vidal. 1899. *A History of our Relations with Andamanese*. Calcutta: Superintendent of Government Printing Press.

Sarkar, Jayanta. 1989. *Jarawa*. Calcutta: Seagull Books and Anthropological Survey of India.

Sharma, S. 1981. *Brief Résumé of the Activities of the AAJVS*. Port Blair: Government Press.

Temple, Richard. 1903. 'Official Record of Dealings with the Jarawas', in *Census of India 1901*, vol. 3. Calcutta: Superintendent Government Printing Press.

2 Co-Existence of Multiple Timeframes

Narratives of Myths and Cosmogony in India

Vibha S. Chauhan

I

In the beginning there was no earth, no sky, no underworld, nothing. There was only water — an ocean of water. A lotus flower arose from the ocean; Lord Bisnau was born from that lotus. A flood swept Lord Bisnau away as he was being born. Basut Nang, the snake was there... Then from Lord Bisnau's navel, a lotus flower arose. Baram, his brother was born from that lotus flower. Mahesar was born from Lord Bisnau's pubic area.

... Kalikmata did battle with the demon and killed him. After the death of the demon, Lord Bisnau created the world. At first he created it the size of a sesame seed, then the size of a coin and then the size of a palm. After that it was big enough to place his foot upon; then he made it the size of a plate and the three brothers placed their feet on it... After that he made the three worlds: the upper world, the middle world, the underworld (Gregory and Vaishnav 2003: 1–5).

The above lines are excerpts from the creation myth sung by the Halbi speakers of north Bastar in the state of Chhattisgarh as a prelude to the annual ritual of *Lachmi Jagar* (invocation of goddess Lakshmi). *Lachmi Jagar* is ritually performed as a part of the harvest festival falling between October and February and generally lasting for around 11 days.

This creation myth incorporates several features and themes — like primeval chaos, endless waters, the gradual emergence of land, the creation of siblings/parents by a conscious and planned act of deities, and the division of land and duties — that exist in creation myths of many other traditional communities.

What is significant is that the creation myth quoted here forms just a prelude to the much longer *Lachmi Jagar* song of 30,939 lines. When transcribed, the text would cover around 1,000 pages. This narration consists of two parallel stories: that of King and Queen Mengin who descend from the upper to the middle world (earth); and that of Mahadev and his wife Parbati. It is at Parbati's insistence that the first rice field is planted:

> One day Queen Parbati thought, "We have made the earth. We have created the three worlds but we have no fame. We have done nothing for the people of the middle world. How will they survive?" She then sat on a couch next to her husband, King Mahadev, and said ... "Mark out two farm plots, O beloved, ... cultivate them.... Go to the blacksmith's workshop, O beloved, and get an axe, a hoe, an adze, a chisel, a ploughshare and a reaping hook forged."
>
> Mahadev and Bhikhander then picked up the tools and a gourd of gruel and went to clear the land ... The two of them worked together and cleared a site. They fired the land and cleared the stumps and shrubs. They divided the land into plots. ...
>
> "I have neither oxen nor seed, O beloved", Mahadev [said], "How will I sow?" "Please go to Barandpur, O beloved", Parbati said, "Sona and Rupa the oxen are there. Please ask for them and bring them. Then go to the store of Kuber, O beloved, ask for seed and bring it" (ibid.: 34–37).

And so the story goes on. After an initial failed attempt, the field finally yields rice.

It is significant that another ritual called *Tija Jagar*,[1] similar to *Lachmi Jagar*, is performed in the wet season. A kindred ritual called *Bali Jagar*[2] is performed in the neighbouring state of Orissa in the hot season. Similar performances also take place in nearby places like Jagadalpur, Kondagaon, Narayanpur, Dantewada, Bijapur, Koraput, and Nowrangpur. While some variations do exist amongst these narratives, the major theme of production of rice — and millet as a subsidiary crop — remains the same. Interestingly, the spread of the various *jagars* overlaps with the rice- and millet-producing regions of the Dandakaranya plateau that is drained by River Indravati. The expanse is situated on the border of Dravidian-speaking south India and Indo-European speaking north India. However, the proximity of different tongues acts as no deterrent

---

[1] The ritual finishes on the third (*tij*) day of the rising moon of *Bhadon* (August–September) from whence comes the name *Tija*.

[2] It literally means 'sand-bringing' ritual.

to such performances. In fact, we discover that a narrative like *Bali Jagar* is sung in the Indo-European language (Desiya Oriya) as well as the Dravidian language (Pengo) (Gregory and Vaishnav 2003: viii–ix). That is probably because despite the presence of deities as *dramatis personae*, the basic emphasis of the myth happens to be the rather pragmatic and essential requirement of the human world — the production of food — with various parallel narratives becoming an extended allegory for the production of rice.

A close analysis of the above narratives reveals them as being fairly representative of some of the major approaches in the study of myth in traditional communities. Besides telling us the story of creation and cultivation of rice, the *jagars* also establish and explicate features essential for collective existence. These include norms of familial relationships, equality amongst occupational groups, the desire to do something beneficial for humankind, and to earn everlasting social prestige and praise. They may be read as samples of Émile Durkheim's notion of social facts and features like religion, family values and socio-legal systems that exert immense influence on personal and social actions, generating shared beliefs and opinions that unify and consolidate social cohesion — in short, the creation of what he calls, 'collective or common consciousness' (Durkheim 1933: 79).

The narrative of *Lachmi Jagar* indicates the coexistence of two rather contradictory features. Despite the events being implausible and completely arbitrary, these myths share several common aspects across cultures, reminding us of the paradox that Claude Lévi-Strauss sees in the study of myths and mythical structures when he wonders: 'If the content of myth is contingent [i.e., arbitrary], how are we to explain the fact that myths around the world are so similar?' (Lévi-Strauss 1963: 208).

While some scholars believe that myths are narratives about gods and demi-gods, others like Geoffrey Stephen Kirk confidently assert that '[t]he dogma that all myths are about gods can be easily disposed of' (1973: 9). Mircea Eliade regards myth as a 'sacred story', and hence a 'true history' (1963: 6). Ranajit Guha (1985) sees myths — especially those of deprived communities — as an expression of the subversion of the ascendant myths, symbolically protesting against the dominant social order.

The above opinions however, fall short of becoming representative. In fact, myth is an extremely complex cultural reality and needs to be approached from multiple perspectives. The situation becomes even more intricate when it comes to the representation of myth in literature, especially during the process of transformation of oral narratives into written scripts and forms like the novel. The task becomes highly contentious, interconnecting politics with poetics and culture with economics. However, an investigation of creation of mythical patterns in novels and potential conflicts/collusions between myths and characters in the narrative pattern can be an extremely rewarding exercise. Imbued with the writer's ideology, the matrix of individual and community existence, articulation of protest as well as reproduction of the existing social order, the analysis holds the potential of reflecting and investigating the palimpsest of multiple relations between myths, communities and characters that people the fictional universe of the novel. It is this that the discussion that follows hopes to achieve, through an analysis of two Bangla novels — *Hansuli Banker Upokatha* (Bandopadhyay 1951) and *Nagini Kanyar Kahini* (Bandopadhyay 1992) by the renowned Bangla novelist Tarashankar Bandopadhyay (1898–1971).

II

Hansuli Banker Upokatha and *Nagini Kanyar Kahini* are often described as *britimoolak upanyas* [novels about occupational communities] since they create and interrogate the lives and psyche of characters of the *kahars*[3] (palanquin bearers) and the Santhali[4] snake-charmer communities. Novels such as these also narrate the *srishtitatva* (cosmogony) of these communities through a careful recreation of the *upobhasha* (dialect) of these communities. The need for novels based on authentic and close association with 'small' and depressed sections of society was expressed by several writers like Manik Bandopadhyay (1908–1956), who rejected the contemporary novel's obsession with the middle classes. Manik Bandopadhyay says that: 'The life of the middle class people is mechanical, perverted and full of contradictions. It is mainly governed by meanness, selfishness and the desire to reproduce their conventions' (1981: 18).[5] His novels like *Putul Nacher Itikatha* (1936) and *Padmanadir Manjhi* (1939) exemplify his artistic credo of 'leaving the middle classes and integrating with the isolated and deprived communities' (ibid.).

---

[3] 'Risley (1891) describes the *kahar* as a large cultivating and palanquin-bearing caste ... many of whose members were employed as domestic servants by natives and Europeans. *Kahar* is derived from the words "kand" and "bhar", i.e. one who bears a burden on his shoulder' (quoted in Singh 1993: 645–46).

[4] Santhal are the largest indigenous community in India, who live mainly in the states of Jharkhand, West Bengal, Bihar, Orissa, and Assam.

[5] All translations from Bangla into English have been done by the author.

Forming sub-narratives within the novels, the *srishtitatvas* in *Hansuli* and *Nagini* are articulated in the *upobhasha* of the communities. Embedded within the context of the main narrative — dealing with wider external forces — these *srishtitatvas* symbolize the dialectics of isolation and proximity of these communities with the external societies. The narrators too are persons who combine within themselves the contrasting features of someone who is rooted in the community, even while belonging to a distant place or/and time. Very similar to Walter Benjamin's storyteller, these narrators simultaneously co-exist in their own, as well as in remote mythical time and space. This co-existence at more than one plane facilitates the narrators of myths to usher in dualities like past and present; traditional and contemporary; sacred and secular; collective and individualistic; coercive and collaborative. Myths often symbolize the root cause of such contradictions as well as their resolutions. Though, as Roland Barthes suggests, 'myth makes itself look neutral and innocent' (1972: 124), narrations of myths assimilate a great measure of this paradox and thus need to be read as complex narratives.

There is a fairly strong consensus amongst scholars that myths become knowable only if they are experienced in their extant forms within the contexts that engender them.[6] However, it is this 'lived experience' that the writers attempt to duplicate through the creation of a fictional but credible universe with complex characters and relational ties. The narrators actually delineate the complex content and impact of myths in traditional communities like those of the *kahars* and the Santhali snake charmers. Rooted simultaneously in various timeframes, these narratives may be seen as representing concepts of the ideal, the real and the desirable. The narrators recreate that 'sacred' space and time through the narration of *srishtitatvas* when their world and its various attributes, cultural practices and social norms had been codified and put in place. Thus, far from being only fanciful, myths may be perceived as congealed history of social codes.

Suchand — the narrator in *Hansuli* — combines these various characteristics of narrators of myths within herself, becoming the eye that sees through the haze of time to recreate the primordial time through narration of the community myth. Suchand was there when 'the intense darkness of the primordial era' (Bandopadhyay 1951: 62) covered the *bansvan* (the bamboo forest) at the spot where the *kahar* community finally struck root.

---

[6] For instance, scholars like Wilhelm Wundt and Bronislaw Kaspar Malinowski.

'I am Kakbhushundi, There is nothing more left for me to see' (ibid.: 44), says Suchand, the narrator of the myths of the *kahar* community in *Hansuli*. Kakbhushundi — the character she compares herself with — is the mythical narrator in Tulsidas' *Ramcharitmanas* (1979). Kakbhushundi is known to have been granted the gift of living through a thousand lives along with the freedom of taking any physical form. Lord Ram in *Ramcharitmanas* had blessed him with everlasting life and infinite vision. After moving through innumerable incarnations, Kakbhushundi chooses to live on in the physical form of the crow, for it was in that form that he had received the blessings of Ram. He becomes an ideal narrator of the events of the life of Ram since he possesses the ability of penetrating through time and space to view, as well recreate the story of Ram.

The novel *Hansuli* traces the process of change from the isolated state of existence of the *kahars* to the point in time when its inhabitants 'went out and mingled with the stream of people on the major pathway' (Bandopadhyay 1951: 349). The story of the origin and history of the *kahar* community is narrated by the 'primordial old woman' Suchand (ibid.: 315). We hear the story of the creation of their community deity Baan-*gosain* in the battle between humans and deities, along with the 'cargo myth' generating wealth and prosperity for the Choudhury and Ghosh families, who are located at the apex of the hierarchical caste structure. Suchand traces the changes that creep into the community through generations. The novel describes the conflicts and dilemmas accompanying this process of change that continues well into the era of World War II. Naturally, this goes hand in hand with the dissolution of the *srishtitatva* within the *upokatha* (sub-narrative) of the *kahar* community till the 'riverlet of *upokatha* of the kahar narrative gets lost in the colossal river of history' (ibid.: 351).

Suchand articulates the mythical story of the *kahar* community — its gods, religion and rituals — thus:

> Oh Shiva! The oldest amongst the old . . . the old God Shiva, Baba Kalaruddar! Baba under the wood apple creeper, the gods of the kahars! Even his God is Kalaruddar. . . . The chief worshipper of Baba Kalaruddar is always someone who belongs to the low caste. It has been like this since primordial times . . . since the time of Baan-gosain . . . (who) was a low-caste king and a worshipper of Bhola Maheshwar Kalaruddar. He drank alcohol, ate meat but always worshipped Baba with flowers. He became an ascetic during *gajan* [a major Shiva festival]. He sat on burning embers and called out for Baba. He slept on the bed of iron nails . . . Day and night he played *bum bum* (a call for Shiva) on his cheeks. . . .

Gosain has one hundred wives. He had only one child – a girl named *Rusha*, that is, Usha. Narayan's grandson became restless when he saw Usha. He once entered her room on the sly and Baan-gosain found out about this. He threatened, "I am going to cut Narayan's grandson to pieces." Narayan's throne became unsteady. His crown shook....

There was confrontation between the two. The earth started quaking. The earth's bosom cracked; and boiling water poured forth. The stars fell off the skies; the world echoed with the cries, "Gone! Gone!"

Narayan sliced off Baan-gosain's legs and arms with his *chakra*.[7] Even then Baan-gosain did not die — did not accept defeat. Even when he seemed dead, he repeatedly sprang back to life. It was then that Baba Ruddar entered the scene. Kalaruddar and Narayan — *Hari* and *Har*. The twain met! Baba Ruddar intervened and got Narayan's grandson married to Rushavati.

Narayan said to Baan-gosain, "Make any desire of yours known to me and that will be fulfilled. Your arms and legs will become whole again. I can make you the king of the world." Baan-gosain replied, "No, I don't want my limbs back. I will not even become the king. If you want my desire to be fulfilled, then grant me the wish of being worshipped along with Baba Ruddar. Only the people from my caste, *gotra*,[8] and family should be allowed to worship at the *gajan*." Hari and Har both said, "So be it." Since then Gosain has no limbs — only the trunk and the forehead ... First Ban-gosain must be worshipped. It is only after that Baba Kalaruddar accepts any worship or offering (Bandopadhyay 1951: 142).

A similar violence exists in the narrative that traces the origin of the *nagini kanya* (snake girl) in *Nagini Kanyar Kahini* as it narrates the long battle for power between Manasa, the goddess of snakes and Chand Saudagar,[9] the worshipper of Shiva (Bandopadhyay 1992). Mahadev, the headman of the community of Santhali snake-charmers, narrates the story thus:

The snake charmers consider Dhanvantari [he is believed to have come out of the churning of the oceans holding a pot of ambrosia and is therefore

---

[7] The divine wheel used as a weapon.

[8] John Henry Hutton explains what *gotra* is by saying, 'Like the clan, the *gotra* or *got*, by derivation a "cowshed" (the family cattle usually shared the family dwelling), is an exogamous unit of individuals theoretically descended from a common ancestor ... the *gotra* is a normal exogamous sub-division of the endogamous whole, but as in the case of composition of a caste by sub-castes, *gotra* is extremely variable and often anomalous' (1961: 55).

[9] 'Saudagar' literally means 'trader'.

accepted as the first guru of the Santhali snake charmers] to be the first man to possess the knowledge of poisons. He had protected the Santhali Mountain [the original home of the snake charmers] with his *mantra*. Ghosts, demons, witches, snakes could not enter it. Their death was certain if they entered. Peacocks and mongoose severed them into pieces.... Poison sucking stones were scattered amongst the rocks. They sucked poison like water. The snakes that entered this territory fell like chopped creepers. They lost consciousness. Such was the power of breeze that was loaded with the aroma of plants that killed all poison.

Dhanvantari had given the responsibility of the Santhali Mountain to his disciples. Dhanvantari was a friend of Chand Saudagar [Chand, the trader and the owner of seven ships was a worshipper of Shiva and a reviler of Vish-hari, the daughter of Shiva and the goddess of snakes]. He took no tax from the disciples of Dhanvantari and allowed them to settle on the Santhali Mountain. The disciples of Dhanvantari, the curers of snakebite enjoyed status and respect in society. They were not untouchables. They had the right to wear the creeper of the poison killing plant round their shoulder like a *janeu*,[10] the sacred thread. They were like the ascetic bauls.[11] Since the knowledge and cure of poison is priceless, they took no money to cure snakebite. Just a small gift of charity.

The enmity between Vish-hari and Chand Saudagar continued. There was confrontation. The battle started ... The immense knowledge vanished. Dhanvantari went! All the curers of snakebite were desperate. Their *guru* was gone, the *mantra* was forgotten. The six sons of Chand Saudagar died. The only child of the headman of the poison curers — a daughter — died.

... Lakhinder, a beautiful boy, was born to Chand Saudagar. The astrologers prophesized that he would die of snakebite on his wedding night. Chand Saudagar turned a deaf ear to all this. He broke the pot of Manasa with his staff. Lakhinder was married to Behula. An iron fort was constructed on the Santhali Mountain. It had an iron vault as the wedding chamber of Lakhinder (ibid.: 19–22).

The friends of Chand Saudagar, the Santhali snake-charmers and their followers, the peacock and the mongoose, surrounded the whole area, making it impossible for snakes to enter the area. It was then that Manasa deceived the headman. She made the black poisonous *nagini*

---

[10] A symbol of high caste.
[11] A syncretic sect of religious, mystic minstrels from eastern part of India, mainly Bengal.

take the form of the headman's dead daughter and sent it to him. The headman was deceived:

> The girl called, "Father".
>
> The headman wept. He spread out his arms and said, "Oh! My lost treasure! Oh! My daughter, come and embrace me" ... The girl opened her eyes and said, "You are my father."
>
> The headman said, "Yes, my daughter, yes." Then he said, "But you must give me word never to leave me and go."
>
> ... The girl danced in a way in which only the headman's daughter and the snake girl could dance ... She breathed into the nostrils of the headman ... The headman fell asleep with that breath in his nostrils. So did whole nature (Bandopadhyay 1992: 22–27).

The girl once again took the form of the *nagini* and entered the iron vault through a small hole deceitfully left open for her. It bit Lakhinder to death. Behula tried to cut it to pieces but could only manage to chop off its tail with a nut chopper.

It was then that Chand Saudagar cursed the headman:

> You have not kept your word. I trusted you and you stabbed me in the back. You and your fellows are ungrateful and untrustworthy ... you must be exiled if you deceive the man who bestows his faith on you. I had given you the gift of staying on the Santhali Mountain without paying tax. I cancel that deed. I take away your right of staying on this mountain, this area and this community. Your settlement, caste, respect, wealth — all has left you. This is Shiva's command and my curse. Nobody will touch you. Nobody will allow you to settle with them (ibid.: 27).

Life, however, must go on. The Santhali snake-charmers had no option but to leave the Santhali Mountain. Before leaving, the headman caught the black *nagini* and imprisoned it in the basket hanging from his shoulder. He soon heard her speak:

> Dear father, it's me. I am with you ... The dictates of Chand have made you homeless. Mother Vish-hari will provide you with a new place to settle down. Float down the lap of Ganges ... Settle down on the fertile ground anywhere on the banks. Chand's dictates will not be followed there. Chand has taken away your lineage and caste. Mother Vish-hari gives you a new lineage ... Mother Vish-hari will receive water and flowers through your worship. You will not lose your caste. Your complexion has become black due to Chand.

It will now have a new glow. Mother has provided you with a new knowledge different from Dhanvantari's. This *mantra* will control all living creatures in the world. The most poisonous bite of snakes, unless it is the bite of death, will be cured, the poison evaporating like camphor ... You can extract my poison and give it to the curers of snake bite. It will become life-giving when treated. A tiny amount of this on the needle can bring a man back from the mouth of death ... And father, I will always remain your black daughter ... I will be born as a daughter in your group of people ... and will carry the responsibility of worshipping Mother Vish-hari for you. She will bring about the welfare of all people. She will obey you, read the mind of Mother Vish-hari and communicate it to you (ibid.: 29).

The *nagini* gave directions to the Santhali snake charmers till they reached Hijal Bil.[12] She then said to them, 'This is the seat of Mother Vish-hari. The seven ships of Chand Saudagar have been hidden here under the water by mother' (ibid.: 30). The novel goes on to tell us how several ships of the Santhali snake charmers abandoned the group on this long journey during the migration from Santhali Mountain to Hijal Bil. 'In the end three boats reached the banks of Hijal Bil ... Three homes laid the foundation of the new Santhali village. In Santhali now there are thirty homes of the *vish vaidya* (poison curers) that have grown from these three' (ibid.).

III

The myths in *Hansuli Banker Upokatha* and *Nagini Kanyar Kahini* impact both the communities materially as well as spiritually. They play a significant role in making the *kahars* and the snake-charmers what they finally become. The myths govern tenets regarding their skills, profession, religion and methods of procuring food, besides attempting to rationalize their physical, emotional and spiritual state of existence. Actually, the *kahars* and the snake-charmers perceive themselves as having been fashioned through a set of mythical events that occurred in the remote past. Their lives and their living are constituted to a large extent by the notion that despite being flesh and blood creatures, they existentially belong to a scheme of things that has been designed by deities and immortals. Their conviction in the supernatural origin of their world is coupled with the assurance of its unbroken continuation in their physical world, existing

---

[12] Wetlands of eastern Birbhum and western Murshidabad districts in West Bengal.

along with the possibility of recovering it. Time for them, therefore, is not sequential but something that is recoverable essentially through myth and the mythical re-creation of the drama of cosmogony. 'By "living" or "recreating" myths one emerges from the profane, chronological time and enters a sacred time at once primordial and indefinitely recoverable' (Eliade 1963: 18). Myths of this 'strong time' (ibid.: 31) and their renewal through re-enactment, reiterate the inter-connectedness and not opposition between the realms of present and past, here and there.

Narration of cosmogony — that serves as a model for all kinds of creation — becomes a mythico-ritual means of rediscovering and reliving the original moment of creation of the living social structure. This overlapping of the biological, psychological, material and transcendental states of existence enfolds within itself the potential of uncovering the prevailing conditions of life, rationalizing these, as well as providing hope. The unity between various timeframes and distant spaces finds expression through repeated narrations of the moment when the community got created. Since the original structuring had been initiated and organized by gods/demigods, that moment is naturally touched with divinity. Any narration or recreation of that moment too — it follows — would partake at least of a portion of that divinity. It would be profanity to even attempt to approach that moment without taking special care to glorify and preserve it. Rituals need to be performed to mark the distinction of these moments and specially ordained people and specially prepared spaces would be prerequisites of such narration. The moment of the past along with its energy is believed to overtake the present during these narrations. In *Hansuli Banker Upokatha* it is Suchand the Kakbhushundi who is the narrator of various mythical moments and events leading to the crystallization of the *kahar* community (Bandopadhyay 1992). We find that in *Nagini Kanyar Kahini* only the headman of the Santhali snake charmers community has the distinctive privilege of narrating the myth of their exile from their 'original' home and the subsequent resettling (Bandopadhyay 1951). This moment of narration is generally in consonance with the surrounding natural phenomenon that duplicates the wonder of the original ethos too.

In *Nagini*, the moment of narration of the creation myth is marked not just by the awe and dread of both the narrator and the listeners but also by a mysterious disturbance in nature all around. Each time the myth is retold, it symbolizes the recreation and regeneration of what Mircea Eliade calls the spirit of primeval time, along with all the awesome spiritual power that is associated with it. The atmosphere, the narrator and the listeners undergo a transformation each time the myth of their original home and lost status is narrated. The novel tells the story thus:

> In the grasslands on the banks of Bhagirathi is Hijal Bil. In the thick forest of grass — the headman of the Santhali snake charmers — resettles himself as he tells the story of those times. The thick bones of his shoulder blades begin to tremble due to the stormy passion in his breast. They [the Santhali snake-charmers] have small eyes, as if slit by sharp blades. Even these eyes have become large with wonder... A stormy thunder rages around the region of the Santhalis. Trees are shrouded with the fluttering of wings; the flopping of wings of the peacock sound like an approaching storm. The echoing sound of *keieyoon, keieyoon* continues to startle everyone. A long line of mongooses stand erect with bristles on their bodies straightening and the sound of *fiss-s-s, fiss-s-s, fiss-s-*singing out of the mouths and noses. The peacocks on the branches spread their claws, stretch out their necks and beaks, encircle around and restlessly come down sometimes on one branch and sometimes on another. The teeth of the mongoose gleaming in a straight line are sharp like the razor's edge. These flicker in the dark (Bandopadhyay 1992: 21).

An annual narration like *Lachmi Jagar* of Chhattisgarh quoted in the beginning also tells the story of the emergence of rice for the first time. This in fact, becomes a part and parcel of the esoteric community knowledge. The ritual of *Lachmi Jagar* recounts the exemplary creation of rice and by doing so persuades the rice to go back to its genesis. The act is actually a replication of the divine act of creation of rice and the person enacting it is believed to be imbued with some of that divinity. Thus the moment of this recreation of the original moment becomes a moment of remembrance and evidence of the presence of the supernatural in the mundane, routine existence of the community.

It is thus that even ordinary acts like cooking or/and consuming food become acts determined by the divine. All elements and forms of life have their own stories of origin with an aura of the supernatural wrapped around them. This is evident not just in *adivasi* societies structured around the bonds of blood and clan but even in caste societies like the one in *Hansuli Banker Upokatha* (Bandopadhyay 1951). The existence of caste formally recognizes and legitimizes the principle of inequality as a part of the divinely given order of things. This concept of stratification is so comprehensive that it divides society into a vertical as well as a horizontal hierarchy of *varna*,[13] castes and sub-castes. 'There are Brahmin parts of the human anatomy, deities, cosmological worlds, cardinal directions, times of the day and year, animals, foods, plants, trees' (Smith 1994: 13). These impose a structured order on both the human and non-human universe. Discussing different species of snakes in *Hansuli* the writer comments: 'The real (Chandrabora) snake is probably a Brahmin. That is why these people cremate it if it gets killed' (ibid.: 30).

The norm of sharing in a community with meagre resources is essential for the existence of its members (Firth 1961: 135). This however, is not left to individual whim but ordained as an inescapable obligation on the part of all members of the *kahar* community through a mythical account that Suchand narrates thus:

> (Everything around us) exists because of Baba's grace ... That was the time of the devastating flood ... It happened very long back. We had still not been born. I heard the story from my father. The flood raged through the night; it raged violently through the whole night. Intense darkness shrouded everything. And *jham jham* rained the water from the skies ... A boat came to the banks of (the river) ... Suddenly ... Baba emerged ... a clean shaven head; glowing complexion; a long *janeu* of *rudraksh*[14] around his shoulder; a red garment wrapped around him; *khadau*[15] on his feet; he walked on the water and came close ... he pointed the boat to Choudhury and said, "Have you seen that boat? That is yours. Worship me; bow your head to gods; offer water to guests; give alms to the beggar; show sympathy to the poor; speak sweetly to a sad person ... This wealth has been given by me. It will stay as long as you obey me. It will vanish if you ever disobey me and break the rules I just announced" (Bandopadhyay 1951: 14).

Thus, we find that the wealth that the Choudhury family acquired came coupled with Baba's command to share it with others. The mythical story quoted above rationalizes the presence of unequal wealth in the community. By tracing the source of the wealth to Baba's grace, the myth provides unquestionable ground for the deprived to accept their poverty as well as the Choudhury's wealth without any grudge. Moreover, by making it mandatory for the Choudhury to share his wealth, the myth

---

[13] The *varna* system in Hinduism stratifies society into four major caste groups: Brahmins, Kshatriyas, Vaishyas and Shudras. These are further divided into innumerable sub-castes.

[14] Seeds of a tree that are considered to be holy and used in rosaries.

[15] Wooden sandals.

further ensures the sustenance of the poor along with continuation and reproduction of inequity without risk of conflict.

Such interpretation, however, can at best be only partial and incomplete. While it is true that myths function as 'a charter of customs, beliefs, rights and institutions' (Von Hendy 2002: 22), they are at the same time, dynamic and paradoxical, holding within themselves the potential for subversion. Myths do function as instruments for sustaining relations of dominance and power, as constructs working themselves out in ways very similar to the ones articulated by Terry Eagleton in his discussion of ideology:

> A dominant power may legitimate itself by promoting beliefs and values congenial to it; naturalizing and universalizing such beliefs so as to render them self-evident and apparently inevitable; denigrating ideas which might challenge it; excluding rival forms of thought, perhaps by some unspoken but systematic logic; and obscuring social reality in ways convenient to itself. Such 'mystification', as it is commonly known, frequently takes the form of masking or suppressing social conflicts, from which arises the conception of ideology as an imaginary resolution of real contradictions (2007: 5–6).

Nonetheless, while it is possible to perceive myths like ideology, they cannot be contained fully in the framework because of being susceptible to several contradictory meanings. While apparently sustaining and propagating the existing relations of power, myths actually enfold the concept of protest and insubordination within themselves. The 'small' communities like those of Santhali snake-charmers and the *kahars* exist only in relative isolation from the external caste society that remains a constant threat to their very existence. The socio-economic domination often gets expressed in the cultural arena through an interpenetration and subversion of existing myths, rituals, values, as well as personages that achieve godhead. In *Hansuli*, Baan-*gosain* is a defiant king who challenges Narayan and despite belonging to a low caste is successful in getting his daughter married to Narayan's son (Bandopadhyay 1951).

In a story in *Srimad Bhagwat* of the *Mahabharata*, the Vaishnav myth tells the story of how Lord Krishna as a young lad jumps into the river Yamuna to retrieve his ball from its deep waters. He has a battle with Kaali Nag (snake) there and emerges victorious, standing on the Nag's hood, playing his flute. Krishna, the incarnation of Vishnu becomes the undisputed master of Kaali Nag. The snake-charmers in *Nagini* however believe that things happened very differently:

They say, the Nag did not accept defeat in the battle. After a long battle the Nag said to Krishna, "I will die but not accept defeat. I will do that only on one condition, which is that you must become my son-in-law. You must marry my daughter. I will accept defeat if you agree to this." The cunning Kanhaiya [another name for Krishna] agreed. The marriage music started playing in Naglok [land of snakes]. The Nag bent his head in defeat. Kanhaiya took the Nag's most deadly and poisonous weapon, the jewel on his forehead and promised to come back. "I will soon be back," he said and went away. But he did not return. He went to Mathura and then to Dwaraka (Bandopadhyay 1992: 140).

D. D. Kosambi discusses how 'the basis of the Krishna legend is that he was the hero and later demi-god of the Yadu tribe, one of the five main Aryan people (*Panca-janah*) in the oldest Veda; but these Yadus were alternately blessed or cursed ... in constant fighting between ... tribes' (1972: 115). Krishna is also a saviour of cattle and thus symbolizes the pastoral society that needed to burn down forests to steadily increase grazing land for cattle. Conflicts between 'forest' and 'pastoral' communities were naturally both frequent and inevitable. Culturally, the hostility would have resulted in an appropriation and subversion of myths and legends of each other, and it is this that probably gets reflected in multiple versions of the Krishna myth.

IV

Repeated narration of myths not only reaffirms the role of divinity and superhuman personages but also periodically renews and regenerates the community. This is what ensures the establishment of the sacred order that furnishes the pattern for profane time and events. However, we discover that though myths do set rules for social structuring and order they are far from static, frozen constructs and continuously respond to transformations that creep into the inter-personal as well as collective existence of people over time. Becoming a reminder of the continued presence of the past in contemporary existence, myths connect contemporary life with codes established since the origin of communities and thus become a symbol of the interconnectedness between apparently contradictory aspects like the divine and profane, the remote and contemporary, collusion and conflict.

Located at the intersection between fantasy and history, mythic tradition may also be seen as representing an internal logic and order through which communities make sense of their suffering. This is achieved through appropriation and mutation of myths across diverse socio-cultural cultures. Myths may be both the agents of cohesion and continuity as well as instruments of articulating protest. The myth of Baan-*gosain* in *Hansuli Banker Upokatha* for instance, illustrates the social degradation of the *kahar* community, the low status of their women, as well as the desire to overcome these (Bandopadhyay 1951).

Myth can also facilitate the writer in negotiating with class, clan and caste in novels dealing with collective forms of social existence. They become relevant for fictional constructs in various ways because of their potential of representing the continuity of the past along with the fissures and tensions that accompany transformations within the community and the wider, external social order. A potent tool in the hands of the writer, myths may be used to articulate one of the most fundamental conditions of human condition — the fall from the order of being and a desire to return to it.

References

Bandopadhyay, Manik. 1981 [1957]. *Lekhaker Katha*. Calcutta: New Age Publishers.

Bandopadhyay, Tarashankar. 1951. *Hansuli Banker Upokatha*. Translated by Hanskumar Tiwari as *Hansulibak ki Upkatha* (New Delhi: Bharatiya Gyanpeeth, 1991 [1984]).

———. 1992 [1952]. *Nagini Kanyar Kahini*, trans. Gauri Banerjee. New Delhi: Bharatiya Bhasha Prakashan.

Barthes, Roland. 1972. *Mythologies*, trans. Annette Lavers. New York: Noonday Press.

Durkheim, Émile. 1933. *The Division of Labour in Society*. New York: The Free Press.

———. 1995. *The Elementary Forms of Religious Life*. New York: The Free Press.

Eagleton, Terry. 2007 [1991]. *Ideology: An Introduction*. New York: Verso.

Eliade, Mircea. 1963. *Myth and Reality*. New York: Harper and Row.

Firth, Raymond. 1961 [1951]. *Elements of Social Organisation*. London: Watt.

Gregory, Chris A. and Harihar Vaishnav (trans. and eds). 2003. *Lachmi Jagar: Gurumai Sukdai's Story of the Bastar Rice Goddess*. Kondagaon: Kaksad Publications.

Guha, Ranajit. 1985. 'Career of an Anti-God in Heaven and on Earth', in Ashok Mitra (ed.), *The Truth Unites: Essays in Tribute to Samar Sen*, pp. 1–25. Calcutta: Subarnarekha.

Hutton, John Henry. 1961 [1946]. *Caste in India: Its Nature, Function and Origin*. London: Oxford University Press.

Kirk, Geoffrey Stephen. 1973. *Myth: Its Meaning and Functions in Ancient and Other Cultures*. Berkeley: University of California Press.

Kosambi, D. D. 1972 [1970]. *The Culture and Civilization of Ancient India in Historical Outline*. New Delhi: Vikas Publishing House.

Lévi-Strauss, Claude. 1963. *Structural Anthropology*. New York: Basic Books.

Singh, K. S. 1993. *People of India: The Scheduled Castes*, vol. 2. New Delhi: Oxford University Press.

Smith, Brian K. 1994. *Classifying the Universe: The Ancient Indian Varna System and the Origin of Caste*. New York: Oxford University Press.

Tulsidas. 1979. *Shri Ramcharitmanas*. Gorakhpur: Geeta Press.

Von Hendy, Andrew. 2002. *The Modern Construction of Myth*. Bloomington: Indiana University Press.

Plate 1: 'Ajay', 2009

Source: Courtesy of Bindi Cole.

Plate II: 'Buffy', 2009

Source: Courtesy of Bindi Cole.

Plate III: 'Crystal', 2009

Source: Courtesy of Bindi Cole.

Plate IV: 'Patricia', 2009

Source: Courtesy of Bindi Cole.

Plate V: *Papatuanuku,* 1984

Source: Robyn Kahukiwa, Oil on hardboard, 1180 x 1180 mm. Reproduced in Robyn Kahukiwa and Patricia Grace, *Wahine Toa: Women of Maori Myth,* Auckland: Penguin Books, 2000 [1980], p. 23. Reprinted by permission of the author and the publisher.

Plate VI: *Catcher of the Sun*

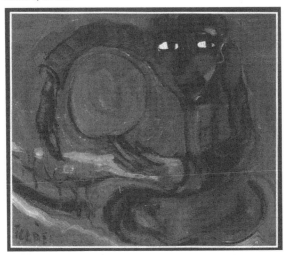

Source: Reproduced with permission from Dirk Schwager and Dominique Schwager, *Claerhout: Artist and Priest,* Maseru: Visual Publications, 1994, p. 72.

Plate VII: *Giant Bearing Star*

Source: Reproduced with permission from Dirk Schwager and Dominique Schwager, *Claerhout: Artist and Priest*, Maseru: Visual Publications, 1994, p. 18.

Plate VIII: *Claerhout Church and Parishioners*

Source: Reproduced with permission from Dirk Schwager and Dominique Schwager, *Claerhout: Artist and Priest*, Maseru: Visual Publications, 1994, p. 16.

Plate IX: *Musicians*

Source: Reproduced with permission from Dirk Schwager and Dominique Schwager, *Claerhout: Artist and Priest*, Maseru: Visual Publications, 1994, p. 44.

3 *Pimatisiwin* Indigenous Knowledge Systems, North and South

Priscilla Settee

This chapter begins with an examination of some of the critical issues relating to Indigenous Knowledge Systems. I have asked the questions, such as what is the nature of Indigenous Knowledge Systems? How can these systems improve the situation for indigenous peoples? How can this knowledge influence the development of curricula?

In Canada, I spoke with elders from Joe Duquette High School, now called Oskayak, a community-based initiated school for indigenous students. In South Africa I interviewed people working within two separate universities. I focused the inquiry on how the universities were developing Indigenous Knowledge Systems as resistance and also as a way to enable a better quality of life for communities. I also asked participants to describe the indigenous knowledge components and courses within each of their institutions. In most instances, personal storytelling became the medium for learning about developments at the different sites. Storytelling is a way of creating knowledge that is fundamental to indigenous peoples, who for the most part originated from oral cultures. Storytelling remains a method of teaching life lessons in present-day indigenous communities (Jolly et al. 1995).

For indigenous peoples and others whose realities have been marginalized by the academy, it is about having our voices recognized as essential pillars of intellectualism (Belenky et al. 1986; Mihesuah 1998; Justice 2004). Indigenous cadres need to take the initiative to start the process of curricular and pedagogical overhauls focusing on increasing the level of connectivity and complementarity between the formal education system and Indigenous Knowledge Systems in the communities (Barnhardt and Kawagley 2005). Of equal importance is the fact that they need to be models of academic inclusivity. I believe that as the critical mass of indigenous academics continues to grow, there will be tremendous opportunities for an emerging field of scholarship that has, at present, started to make important contributions (Cook-Lynn 1998). Thus, think tanks serve as a tool for indigenous groups for 'reframing' (Smith 1999), which is to take 'greater control over the ways in which indigenous issues and social problems are discussed and handled' (ibid.: 154). Reframing occurs within the way indigenous peoples engage in conversation about what it means to be indigenous. The third Chotro conference provided such a think tank where community people, scholars, artists, and healers came together to contribute to the ongoing discussion of indigeneity within learning.

Speaking from a northern scholar's perspective, we cannot overlook the important parallel scholarship that has been developing with indigenous peoples in the global south as demonstrated by my research. As Paulo Freire postulated, '[d]ialogue with others ... not only has the ability to accomplish social goals; it also "humanizes" the individual through creating the "role of man as Subject in the world and with the world"' (1970: 46). Very little of the cutting-edge content of these community-based meetings ever makes it into scholarly publications or university curricula. However, social change at the community-level is evident. Grounding their work in a contemporary issue, community members making decisions based on their experiences, traditions, values, and motives. In this way they develop deeper understanding and even greater control over their circumstances.

> Also in this category are professors who are well aware of the concerns Native scholars have over their propensity to ignore Native voices yet require their graduate students to write according to the status quo (that is, to ignore Native versions of the past and present and not to focus on tribal concerns), and they tend to dwell excessively on Euroamerican theory and will not approve students' theses and dissertation unless they adhere to those standards. These professors are particularly difficult to combat because of the established power base that has been created from their politicking abilities and published works about Native peoples that make money for publishing houses (Mihesuah and Wilson 2004: 35).

As indigenous peoples, the impact of the colonial system has been one that manifests itself in relationships of control and domination by colonizing powers against the colonized. This relationship calls for intensive realignment of power relations and a healing of those relationships.

Indigenous Knowledge: A Pedagogy of Healing

It is acknowledged that indigenous communities have suffered from centuries of oppression caused by colonial societies. I believe that Indigenous Knowledge Systems have a capacity to help us heal from our collective oppression, which has deep and complex manifestations. Structural and complex pathologies have impacted our communities, which in turn have repercussions throughout the larger society. Indigenous peoples often face racist and discriminatory treatment from colonials. Historically in Canada, religious institutions imposed physical, sexual and emotional abuse on our people through the residential school experience resulting in intergenerational abuse. Added to this, our people are marginalized, economically and socially, by the ongoing colonial structures present in public policies, formal schooling and the employment practices of the dominant society. Our communities experience violence and are in desperate need of healing and rebirth. The prisons are filled with our people who have lost hope and turned to crime to alleviate poverty. Urban Indian gangs create communities where there are none, but base these on violence, exploitation and death. Drugs and alcohol numb the pain of daily living. Our research as indigenous scholars must drive the educational experience to help heal the abuse, pain and community breakdown because they are a fundamental impediment in our ability to develop our nations. Our educational practice must help our students and others develop a critical awareness of colonialism and its impact on daily living. I believe educational reconstruction should be a collective academic undertaking and part of the role of knowledge creation. Knowledge creation must take a central position in deconstructing the tragic situation of the oppressed; 'the understanding of the oppressed exposes the real relations among people as inhumane: thus there is a call to political action' (Hartsock 1998: 241). Finally, our actions — including research — must direct policies that will develop social and economic systems to support the marginalized. This is one way to ensure a shift of power to the community.

In the Canadian indigenous world, elders have played an essential role as carriers of traditional knowledge and its role in community healing. Saulteaux Elder Laura Wasacase attributes community dysfunction to unresolved residential school abuse and the breakdown of community and family structures created by the residential school process (personal communication, May 2003). Elder Wasacase talks about the need for community healing and the creation of balance in our lives. She states that there are many people in our community who are wounded from generations of abuse. Elder Wasacase uses the medicine-wheel concept and model to address how our communities need to create balance. She describes the need for balancing the four parts of the human psyche — the physical, mental, spiritual, and intellectual forces. In healing circles, Wasacase uses talking circles in which individuals are encouraged to talk about their abuse in a circle of confidentiality. Fundamental to youth healing is the need to be listened to and be acknowledged. Our communities have many youth who have never belonged or are seldom listened to. They join gangs in their quest to satisfy their need to belong. Wasacase maintains that healing from past abuses and trauma and returning to sacred ceremonies are fundamental to community well-being. A case in point is one in which three men sexually assaulted a 12-year-old Native girl in which two of the men were acquitted. This event occurred during the time when many Aboriginal men and women were found dead as a direct result of white police actions and several Indian girls were murdered by a serial killer (Goulding 2001). Both cases have irreversibly damaged both Aboriginal and non-Aboriginal communities and cases speak to the need for healing within the communities.

Indigenous scholars have lent their voices to the healing of community relations. I first heard Martin Brokenleg, a Lakota psychologist from South Dakota, give a keynote address at an Indian education conference (Brendtro et al. 2002). Brokenleg began his powerful presentation by displaying a slide of his parents. He proceeded to tell audiences that his strength as a balanced professional originated in the belonging he first experienced within his nuclear family and his large extended Lakota family, referred to as *tiyospaya* in the Lakota language. Brokenleg states firmly that the reason so many of our people are despairing is because of our need to belong and because of our collective need to recover our lost values of caring, sharing, community, and belonging, which have been the principles of Indigenous philosophies. I believe that these are values that all of humanity needs. Too often in education, we attempt to work with the intellect at the cost of the emotional, mental and spiritual. Brokenleg bases his work with troubled youth on the native model of the medicine wheel. The medicine wheel teachings tell us that human beings need balance to live productive lives. This *being in balance* is based on emotional, spiritual, physical, and mental well-being. Brokenleg states that communities suffer because individual needs are not being met, and this eventually means that whole communities are in discord.

In Canadian indigenous communities the historical and systemic abuse is now manifest in multi-generational symptoms and community conflict. Many communities suffer from inter-family and community discord. There is a great need for healing. In *Strong Women Stories, Native Vision and Community Survival* (Anderson and Lawrence 2003), the words of Shelley Bressette, whose cousin was shot and killed by police on her reserve community of Ipperwash, Ontario, during a land dispute in September 1995, reverberate:

> Healing is letting go of our pain, whether that be personal pain inflicted upon us or the kind of collective pain or trauma we experienced during the Ipperwash Crisis. Letting go means to resolve it or understand it and see it for what it is, and to move beyond it, so that it no longer takes a hold on our daily lives. Recently, at a gathering, I heard a teacher say: "We all experience great suffering in our lives, and we don't know why. But if we look at these times as teachings and ask ourselves what can we learn from these painful moments, then we can give them new meaning" (ibid.: 240).

Oskayak High School — A Model for Community Healing

The Oskayak High School, established by indigenous parents in Saskatoon, is an example of one in which learning focuses on the important role of culture and healing and establishes connections to the land through the restoration of traditional ceremonies and practices. The urban Aboriginal High School's annual *Big Bear Walk* takes place in northern Saskatchewan. I interviewed the late school Elder Simon Kaytwayhat about the walk. Elders, staff and students were the originators of the walk, which has been taking place annually since 1998. It was named after the honoured Cree leader, Chief Big Bear, who was wrongfully jailed in 1885 for defending the land sovereignty rights of his people (Dempsey 1984). In 100 years, human rights for indigenous peoples have not improved. Chief Big Bear's political struggle inspired the annual walk, whose goals include:

(a) remembering the four peoples of the world and that representatives of each walk with us;
(b) the recognition of our people as a Nation;
(c) the spiritual renewal that comes from sacrificing something of ourselves for our families, our community, our nation, ourselves and all of humankind because we are all related;

(d) to honour Big Bear's memory as a man of peace and a spiritual leader who was wrongfully imprisoned;
(e) to ask Big Bear's spirit for help in our healing from the diseases of drug and alcohol addiction, family violence, childhood sexual abuse and incest, and the dark legacy of residential school atrocities;
(f) to inspire and motivate spiritual leadership (with Big Bear as our role model);
(g) to hear from our Elders of the history of that time (1885), those places and those events so that we, in turn, will be able to share that knowledge with others;
(h) for the return of Big Bear's Sacred Bundle from New York's Manhattan Museum to our Indian Nation;
(i) to create a Healing Lodge to be built on the battle and massacre site;
(j) to express our gratitude for life, breath, prayer, consciousness, and choice to the Creator of us all because we are all related.

Every four years, the healing staff (a symbolic pole that represents healing) is carried by the group that organizes the walk. Oskayak carries the staff at the beginning and then passes it to the community of Loon Lake and then to the community of Onion Lake where it remains. As part of the walk, youth voluntarily choose to walk over 80 kilometres cross-country to learn about their own limits, test their patience and ability to live in close quarters with their fellow students and teachers, and to be connected as a whole. They spend one week on the walk and along the way they learn about the land and plants, and also listen to oral traditions and take part in spiritual ceremonies, such as the pipe ceremony, sundance ceremony and sweat lodge.[1] Students are expected to be active participants in the daily activities of setting up camp, cooking, cleaning-up, and breaking up camp. Elder Kaytwayhat states that the trek is an example of learning that involves all four aspects of humanity: the physical, spiritual, intellectual, and emotional. He describes it as a healing journey for the youth. He talks about the seven healing fires that are singing, dancing, laughing, talking, listening, playing, and crying. A person can heal when he/she participates in these seven activities. Oskayak just celebrated its 30th year of operation — it had been

---

[1] These are spiritual and cultural ceremonies largely specific to the Great Plains tribal peoples.

established in 1980 as a Native Survival School by a group of parents to help students who could not cope with the regular school system (personal communication, April 2006). Oskayak High School is an example of how healing must be central to the process of Aboriginal learning and also an example of how indigenous knowledge, Aboriginal culture and ways of knowing become central to student activities and learning. I have been a member of the Kitotiminak (Parent) Council since 1996, which helps administer the school, and for me it has been foundational to the work that has led me to the international sphere and Indigenous Knowledge Systems within educational institutes.

Learning from the Global South

This section examines how higher learning utilizes Indigenous Knowledge Systems in South Africa. International scholars and activists have referred to these regions as the Global South. My research involved spending several months at the University of Pretoria and North-West University in South Africa. The purpose of my visits was to understand, as a participant observer, the process of indigenization of formal educational institutes such as universities to learn about the curricula that have been developed at these centres. I also wanted to know how governments were supporting the process of indigenization through the development of public policy. I believe that many models, curriculum examples and methodologies can be replicated or adopted as we indigenous peoples share similar world views and ways of knowing, as well as face many of the same developmental issues.

South Africa is an amazing land of contrasts of plains, mountain ranges, vast farming areas, and vistas leading to rugged and tranquil coastal regions. The discovery of diamonds in 1867, and gold in 1886, encouraged economic growth and immigration, intensifying the subjugation of the indigenous populations. Despite the end of apartheid, millions of South Africans, mostly black, continue to live in poverty. My invitation from North-West University in the city of Mafeking provided me with a vibrant centre whose mandate is to develop indigenous knowledge courses from the undergraduate level, graduate level, to the doctoral level. North-West University is a black university. I met H. O. Kaya, who provided leadership in the development of the range of indigenous knowledge curriculum. Kaya is originally from Tanzania and was educated there during the exciting era of social and political transformation under the leadership of Julius Nyerere. Kaya's work is indeed impressive and has provided much inspiration for my own curriculum work at the University of Saskatchewan. Through this experience at North-West University I realized the important contributions that graduate and doctoral programmes could make in Indigenous Knowledge Systems. My research also took me to the University of the Western Cape, where I met some Khoi-San people, members of South Africa's oldest indigenous group. Finally, I visited the University of Pretoria with Catherine Odora Hoppers in Pretoria. It has been an enriching experience to learn from all of these individuals. I noticed the parallels in the African concept of indigenous knowledge, healing and community empowerment known as *ubuntu*. This concept runs analogous to the Cree concept of *wakotawin*; and it describes how humanity is inter-connected and must work for the good of all:

> In *ubuntu/botho* we can draw sustenance from our diversity, honoring our rich and varied traditions and culture, and act together for the development, protection and benefit of us all. This philosophy recognises the indivisibility of human nature and the commonness of purpose of human beings which make our interests, aspirations and objectives intertwined. It believes in the totality of human effort and a holistic involvement in the quest for love and peace in the family of man, in the universal order of things (Teffo 1999: 169).

Ubuntu had been deeply and negatively impacted by the South African brutal apartheid system. But in 1994, South Africa's history of apartheid came to a close with the free elections that year. A tripartite agreement, which included the Government of South Africa, the Congress of South African Trade Unions (COSATU), and the African National Congress, ended a racist and brutal regime in South Africa's history that has left many deep psychological scars among the people. One of the means of closure to apartheid was the Truth and Reconciliation Commission headed by the renowned cleric Archbishop Desmond Tutu. This commission heard the testimonies of the victims of apartheid as well as the perpetrators. A record of some of the horrors of the apartheid era is recorded in Antjie Krog's *Country of My Skull* (1998), her report of the Truth and Reconciliation process that started in December 1995. Following are the words of a woman who survived an attack by whites. She lost contact with her husband who, she later learned, had died in the attack:

> The undertaker took us to his mortuary. I saw him; I was with my elder daughter. When we got there, his eyes were hanging; we could see that there were

dots, black dots all over his body. And we could see now the big gash on his head, the gash cause by the ax. I am still sick ... my feet were rotten and my hands were all rotten, I have holes, I can't sleep well. Sometimes when I try to sleep, it feels like something is evaporating from my head until I take these pills, then I get better. All this is caused by these bullets that I have in my body. My son Bonisile, who was smeared with his father's blood on him, was never well again after that, he was psychologically disturbed (ibid.: 101).

Theoretically, after 1994, the black people of South Africa gained their political independence, but in many ways economic power still rests with the white population and much poverty remains:

> The socio-economic legacy is summed up by a single fact that the United Nations Development Programme published a few years ago. If white South Africa were a country on its own, its per capita income would be 24th in the world, next to Spain; but if black South Africa were a separate country, its per capita income would rank 123rd globally, just above the Democratic Republic of the Congo (Mamdani 1999: 127).

For South African blacks, land is the essential issue regarding development. Whites continue to own and occupy the most productive land; they own most of South Africa's businesses and natural resources. White universities still enjoy better funding and produce knowledge that promulgates white superiority and hegemony. While a significant number of blacks have been incorporated into various levels of government and public service, the majority continue to live in substandard conditions. A common feature of South Africa is crowded townships, such as Soweto and Alexandra, bordering on the wealthy community of Sandton, both of which I visited. There is a disparity between living conditions of the black and white populations. These townships have no resources, such as good housing or clean drinking water; and, often, these townships become the fertile grounds for crime, poverty and desperation. The cost of living in South Africa has escalated by 18 per cent in one year, and the average wages do not provide for a life of dignity. Violent crimes, a legacy of the apartheid era, are commonplace. Rather than blaming these conditions on the will of politicians only, they must be viewed within the complex process of cultural domination and globalization that plagues other parts of the world. Many black academics have made indigenization a priority in their effort to reclaim their country, politically, intellectually and practically. As in other regions of the world, several conferences have been organized on the topic of the indigenization of political, civic and educational processes. Eager to meet some of the people involved and learn of the process within universities and their link to public policies, I attended two meetings that introduced me to many new indigenous knowledge colleagues, who I subsequently interviewed in my research. Africans believe that the ingenuous and life-giving knowledge force of *ubuntu* needs to be re-established at the centre of the formal learning and community revitalization movement. According to African Renaissance scholars, there is a need to build on the ancient strengths of the many African cultures:

> Embodied in the African philosophy of *ubuntu*, a new universalism, which seeks to affirm a concept of development in which fear is replaced by joy, insecurity by confidence and materialism by spiritual values, promises to emerge. *Ubuntu* is humaneness, care, understanding, and empathy. It is the ethic and interaction that occurs in the African extended family. The *ubuntu* concept is found in proverbs from many African societies and communities such as "the stomach of the traveler is small," "a home is a real one if people visit it" (Zulu): "a bird builds its nest with another bird's feather" and "the hands wash each other" (Xhosa) (Vil-Nkomo and Myburgh 1999: 114).

Ubuntu values the contributions of other cultures and integrates similar values. It recognizes the inter-connectedness of human kind and celebrates all we hold in common.

Catherine Odora Hoppers, a world-renowned black scholar, states that this philosophy differentiates African society fundamentally from European and Western societies in that it emphasizes reciprocity, responsibility and the embracing of the stranger. 'I am because you are' is very different from 'I am because I think'. *Ubuntu* is a philosophy that emphasizes a 'turned toward-ness' just like the plant turns naturally towards the light, so as human beings we should see ourselves in each other's eyes. It is very different from a worldview in which no kind of psychic or spiritual communication or communion between humans and Earth or nature is possible, or where nature is seen as consisting of inert, random, machine-like processes and which have to be conquered, subdued, controlled, and dominated. It is this philosophy, as it underpins human relations and extends respect for nature, that distinguishes the African worldview from the Western one, in which the reified inclination has been to exploit until decimation, promote untrammelled competition, and establish relationships with 'others' through conquest. This Africanist philosophy spoke to my own Cree worldview of *pimatisiwin*.

I met Catherine Odora Hoppers for the second time at the University of Pretoria. I had met her at the University of Venda at the Indigenous Knowledge Systems conference a year prior, where she delivered the keynote address. Hoppers was originally born in Uganda and lived there until she was exiled under the brutal regime of General Idi Amin Dada, but not before many of her family members were viciously murdered. None of their bodies were ever recovered. Because her family organized politically against and criticized the dictator Amin, Hopper's life was also under threat. This forced her into exile, first in Zambia, and later on, with her children, to seek asylum in Europe. She managed to escape to Europe after being forced at gunpoint into the back of a truck with her three-month-old son. The upbringing she had received from her father, a respected chief and leader, and from a mother who was an outstanding women's leader and political mentor to several generations, would form the basis for her strong African indigenous identity. Sweden became her home for the next decades. In between, she took up posts overseas in Zimbabwe and, later, in South Africa where she has, since then, become central to the struggle for the implementation of indigenous knowledge within government policies, in the research community and in institutional practices. Researchers have long been aware that cultural understanding involves making sense of the means by which others make meaning. Listening to the story that she crafted to depict her life gave me an understanding of her personal autobiography alongside her institutional biography. She has worked as chief research specialist at the Human Science Research Council in Pretoria from where she led the national transdisciplinary initiative to take the question of indigenous knowledge and the integration of knowledge systems to the scientific community. Concurrent with this, she has served on the United Nations Interagency Steering Committee on Education for All, provided technical expertise on education policy to the Organization of African Unity, on community intellectual property rights to the World Intellectual Property Organization (WIPO), as well as to the World Economic Forum. She was a Professor at the Faculty of Education, University of Pretoria, South Africa, and is presently a visiting professor at Stockholm University in Sweden. Hoppers remains a leading and respected scholar of Indigenous Knowledge Systems throughout Africa. Not surprisingly, her perspective on honouring Indigenous Knowledge Systems takes on a critical perspective of the process of globalization and, specifically, the global market place mentality, which Africa and other regions are today thrust into.

What follows are highlights from an interview I did with Hoppers at her home in South Africa on her views of Indigenous Knowledge Systems and its development within the African context (Interview, September 2002, Pretoria). I asked her how the South African government was accommodating Indigenous Knowledge Systems. She started by describing her role as Technical Advisor in supporting the Parliamentary Portfolio Committee on Arts, Culture, Science and Technology as it grappled with this complex issue, and moved on to her work within the national steering committee and her contributions to the articulation and delineation of the issues during and after the first national workshop to a wide cross-section of the academic and policy audiences.

In 1997, in preparation for the National Year of Science and Technology, the then Chairman of the Parliamentary Portfolio Committee on Arts, Culture, Science and Technology, Mongane Wally Serote, and the national steering committee, made up of political leaders, community holders of knowledge and the top people in the science councils had undertaken an audit on indigenous technologies as a first step towards documenting the living technological knowledge of local communities. This was undertaken in order to initiate the process of identifying some of the knowledge for further value addition in order to improve the quality of life in the rural areas.

Hoppers had strong words for the classical research-led model of extracting knowledge from communities as it led, whether intentionally or not, to the theft of knowledge in national and regional systems. These systems had neither infrastructure nor organized authority to demand negotiations on ownership rights to such knowledge or to demand compensations in the event of acts that were already committed. She insists that the usual pre-packaged argument that the 'stolen' knowledge is not lost as their intellectual property rights are sucked out through the backdoor! It is, therefore, a case of stolen knowledge reaching humanity but by wrong methods, with wrong protocols and intentions, and definitely with pretentious consequences. Moreover, the assimilationist model places profit-making over the purposes of sharing. The issue of integration is, therefore, a challenging one and needs to be looked at with vigilance, sensitivity and empathy on a continual basis. Hoppers describes the need to include the lost generations of Africans who have a right to dialogue and to exist in multiple identities, including a global identity. They should not feel inferior but should be anchored with an ancestry and a culture within a system that helps form their backbone as the future citizenry of Africa. She sees real value in listening to voices of the extended community and sees their citizenship as essential.

The South African Ministry of Arts, Culture, Science and Technology played an instrumental role in laying the groundwork for the Indigenous Knowledge Systems policy. Study teams were organized to travel to India and China to examine the issues of integration of Indigenous Knowledge Systems into formal national systems. This built on the previous work of the National Steering Committee, which had organized a task team made up of sector ministries and members of the scientific community and arranged for public hearings in all the provinces of South Africa. Hoppers led the task team that prepared the policy background document from which the White Paper and legislation are evolving. From this a Directorate was created in the Department of Art, Culture, Science and Technology, which is leading an ongoing inter-ministerial task team and projects. In addition, the Ministry of Agriculture and the Ministry of Environmental Affairs and Tourism are involved in the work of the Convention on Biological Diversity (CBD). This involvement will ensure that the concerns of millions of African farmers, who use a subsistence model, mixed cropping and sustainable types of farming methods, are considered when negotiating the terms of the CBD. From a continental perspective, the Organization of African Unity has developed model legislation for the protection of Indigenous Knowledge Systems which highlights several groundbreaking issues such as Prior Informed Consent (PIC), provides guidelines for other national systems, and takes into account local situations. The continental strategy of Indigenous Knowledge Systems protection is developing with other African countries, whereas earlier, culture and knowledge were considered separately. The continental approach has made it possible to look at culture in a deeper, lateral and longer-term way. This has enabled more complex debates to be fostered, such as jurisprudence and legal systems, post-conflict healing and reconciliation systems, intellectual property rights, value addition and benefit-sharing protocols, and sustainable development and poverty reduction questions to be fostered. It has also situated these issues within the international arena.

In the area of the need for Indigenous Knowledge Systems to be centrally located within the context of higher learning, Hoppers states that higher education is the authority mandated by the state, and hopefully by the citizens, to generate, develop, legitimize, accredit, and disseminate knowledge. Higher education is responsible for defining what constitutes legitimate knowledge. Yet, in South Africa, as it is the case with so many parts of the world in which colonizing and colonized elites unilaterally established the conquering worldview as the unquestioned 'norm', entire education systems have found it almost impossible to develop methodologies and instruments with which to respond to the knowledge base existing within the original society.

'Knowledge' is defined in a way that cuts off that which the majority of its citizens actually have and own, and which they have perpetuated for centuries. Instead, within the African context, that knowledge is largely Western-based; it is not reflective of knowledge systems of African people, and appears to have no intention whatsoever of ever valorizing and validating either that local knowledge or the technologies that sustain as much as 80 per cent of African people. Yet, it is the people who emerge from these education systems that hold senior positions in state and international governance systems. The situation is thus maintained in which the definition of knowledge is so skewed and where the routine violation of cognitive rights of people is built deeply within the heart of the academy. Research — as a knowledge-generating instrument — therefore, has a lot to answer and to learn if it is to serve the basic needs of the majority of the people in Africa. Hoppers argues that as it stands, researchers never see the need to build transparency into their research ethics when doing research in local communities, leading to a double exploitation. The first level of exploitation is in terms of the extraction being one-sided, with research conclusions never finding their way back to the communities. The second relates to the situation in which the research, for instance, involves disclosures of knowledge of plants or herbal products with commercial value to researchers who then siphon off this information to a pharmaceutical company without any memory of who gave that information and what should accrue to such a source. She claims that the only way the higher education sector is going to have to deal with Indigenous Knowledge Systems is by approaching the issue from a human rights perspective and reconstructing the bridges that it burnt. Hoppers describes her relationship with research thus:

> I discovered the ambiguity of my presence in a research establishment because I said; I cannot go to the field because I am the field. I am she that you would all go to research. I am an African child. I am from a rural part of Africa; I am the classical object of research. How should I participate in research without us clarifying the ethical grounds for what we are going to do? (personal interview, February 2006).

She links her personal situation and that of her people within the framework of cognitive subjection and ascribed poverty. She locates her work on Indigenous Knowledge Systems within heuristic tools she has consolidated from gender and peace studies, from international relations, and from scrutinizing the problems of education and the academy.

She describes the healing aspects of Indigenous Knowledge Systems: the wounded person wishes to be healed but to also heal, to be the brother/sister-healing of the other. We want the world to recover its humanness. It is like a dance, the healing is both for the victims and also for the perpetrators. Any person who can perpetrate so much violence and inflict so much pain on others can never be free. The weaker persons may not have the opportunity to enter the places where they can speak with their oppressors about the need to heal and mend relations, but our connection with humanity is maintained only through the empathetic attention to the faint echoes of those cries of anguish. Hoppers is poetic when she describes the need for a healing process between the colonizer and the colonized, the oppressor and the oppressed:

> within the colonizing groups. Human spirit rebels wherever it is. And as for me, I have derived a lot of insights and a lot of wisdom in relating with people across the globe ... Across the globe in actually finding people who are similarly seeking to heal. People who I think have to carry on and bang on these doors and say come out and heal because there's something qualitatively amiss, with the way things are really going. So I think that when we now look at what this kind of trajectory means for global linkage, ... what we begin to see is the recovery of humanity occurring in different points. If you think of it like you're looking at the stars above, you see the twinkle, see how they twinkle and it's like it's occurring in different points. In terms of the bigger template of the world, it is really occurring; human spirit rejecting certain kinds of afflictions; certain kinds of inhumanity. Human spirit rebelling. And here it is not something to say it is only for the indigenous communities; it is also for the broader group we refer to as the colonized people, but also are similarly committed to reconstructing broken relations. Similarly committed to usurping faith in the future and really rebuilding the therapy (personal interview, February 2006).

She describes the struggle for re-establishing Indigenous Knowledge Systems as the struggle to recover and reclaim our humanity. Parallel to Hopper's thoughts, Antonio Gramsci (1995) in *Further Selections from the Prison Notebooks* describes how the chaos in schooling and the larger society should be met with humanistic goals. In his discussion of vocational versus classical schooling:

A rational solution to the crisis ought to adopt the following line. First a common basic education, imparting a general, humanistic, formative culture; this would strike the right balance between the development of the capacity for working manually (technically, industrially) and the development of the capacities required for intellectual work (Gramsci 1995: 27).

What I learned from Hopper's story and others is that if our stories of self are to help us reform institutions or recover communities, we need to be willing to reinvent them. We must replace time-worn renditions of 'who we are' that in Toni Morrison's words, are 'unreceptive to interrogation, cannot form or tolerate new ideas, shape other thoughts, tell another story, fill baffling silences' (1994: 14). Instead, our scholarship and activism must tell new stories in many voices. As an academic I have always chosen to serve my community rather than only work with the square boxes of tenure and promotion requirements. Some of this service includes developing courses that respond to local development needs to truly reflect the conditions in our communities and to provide liberation tools from all oppressive conditions. I believe our local conditions warrant and require this support from people within higher learning. As academics, I believe, we must always be guided and inspired by the local conditions of our people.

Indigenous Knowledge Studies at North-West University, North West Province

The land in this region is hot and dusty and borders on semi-arid desert-like conditions. South Africa has nine provinces and North West province is the home of the North-West University (NWU), which was established in 1980 by the then Bophuthatswana black homeland government. The NWU was established to provide university education to the black communities in the homeland of, primarily, the Batswana (Botswana) people. It falls under the jurisdiction of the National Department of Education, which, apart from student tuition, is its main source of funding. The university houses the faculties of Education, Human and Social Sciences, Law, Agriculture, Science and Technology, and Management and Commerce. It has about 6,000 students. A second campus was established in 2001 in Mankwe, about three hours from the main campus at Mafeking. Formally, the Indigenous Knowledge Systems programme was established in February 2001 to contribute to the human resource needs of its indigenous peoples, who are mostly rural. However, its roots were established in 1997–98 with sociology students who were registered in honours and master's degrees in indigenous technologies. According to Kaya, when the South African government took the initiative in Indigenous Knowledge Systems, the NWU already had a practical background. The collaboration took place in 1998, and a proposal for conferences and seminars on Indigenous Knowledge Systems was developed. In 2001, seven South African scholars travelled to the University of Saskatchewan to present at the Indigenous Peoples Program Indigenous Knowledge Conference, which was chaired by me. In 2000, the NWU was asked by the South African government to come up with new programmes and when they were accredited, finances would be secured.

The Indigenous Knowledge Studies programme at NWU offers courses at the undergraduate level, with space for 192 students; the honours level, with space for 13 students; the graduate level with space for eight students; and the PhD level, with space for one student. Courses that focus on indigenous knowledge that are largely taken by black students but intended for all, include:

(a) *Introduction to the Nature and Patterns of Indigenous Knowledge Systems*: enables the student to define and explain major concepts and practices, such as cultural and bio-diversity.
(b) *Introduction to African Social and Political Thought*: presents the development and characteristics of African social and political thought before and after Africa's colonial period.
(c) *Indigenous Land and Water Management Systems*: promotes indigenous water and land management systems for sustainable development.
(d) *Comparative African and Western Political and Social Theory*: prepares the student to compare and analyze the foundations of western and African political and social theory, including the patterns and ideologies of liberation movements. Gender reflections in liberation movements are also included.
(e) *Comparative Healing Systems*: examines the difference and complementarity between western and traditional healing systems.
(f) *Comparative Patterns of Indigenous Knowledge*: presents the nature and significance of indigenous knowledge in sustainable development.
(g) *Indigenous Approaches to Peace and Conflict Resolution*: equips learners to facilitate conflict resolutions using indigenous approaches.

(h) *Indigenous Knowledge, Cultural Diversity and Bio Diversity, and Conservation and Sustainable Development*: will qualify students to have a critical knowledge of the relationship between cultural biodiversity and sustainable development.

According to Kaya, the programme is growing tremendously and is integrated across disciplines. Students can take law, sociology, economics, and peace studies. There are future plans to teach Indigenous Knowledge Systems in schools and in the College of Education. There was resistance and many of the ideas did not become institutionalized. The NWU is primarily, but not exclusively, for black students; however, both Kaya and Hoppers state that universities that are primarily for black students have historically enjoyed less governmental funding.

Some challenges faced by the programme include the need for networking and collaboration with other institutions and the need to expose students to other indigenous parts of the world. More challenges include the teaching capacity of current instructors. There are not enough faculties equipped to teach Indigenous Knowledge Systems. Capacity-building for the current programme is limited. The existence of teaching materials is a critical problem; and while NWU is trying to be self-reliant, there is a great need to collaborate and share resources. The interest in the Indigenous Knowledge Systems programme at NWU is growing. This is evidenced by the fact that numbers have grown from 10 students to well over 200 since the late-1990s. The university administration remains very supportive, as does the National Research Foundation. Black universities, such as the NWU, which were state-controlled, have had major impacts on civil society and have resulted in a racialized democracy. The African scholar Mahmood Mamdani sums up those impacts:

> The white universities were islands of privilege, in which intellectuals functioned like potted plants in greenhouses. They had intellectual freedom but lacked social accountability. In contrast, black universities coming out of apartheid were the intellectual counterparts of Bantustans. They were designed to function more as detention centres for black intellectuals than as centres that would nourish intellectual thought. As such, they had little tradition of intellectual freedom or institutional autonomy. They were driven by the heavy hand of bureaucracy. And yet they were far more socially responsive than their white counterparts (1999: 131).

Despite the revolutionary social transformation of 1994, many power structures within South Africa are slow to change, and universities are no exceptions. Many of the predominantly-black and predominantly-white structures remain the same.

The clustering of indigenous knowledge courses has made an impact on the university community, in both a negative and positive sense. Students see indigenous knowledge as something to take pride in and can relay that back to their home communities. According to Kaya, the act of establishing systems of study in this area has also created some resentment among some of his colleagues. According to Kaya, this has been reflected in the limited resourcing of the programme of studies.

Conclusion

As indigenous peoples we are instructed that whatever decisions we make, we should consider the next seven generations of humanity, and not just indigenous humanity, but all humanity. The particular teaching is reflective of our Anishnabe cousins' teachings about the seventh fire. The Anishnabe teaching states that the fifth fire is the time of the arrival of the non-Anishnabe. The sixth fire is a time of difficulty and suffering for the Anishnabe. The seventh fire will be a time of healing for communities and individuals and a celebration of our survival and rebirth. The re-introduction of Indigenous Knowledge Systems, locally and globally, is about honouring life-giving systems, developing healing capacities from all forms of oppression, and celebrating *pimatisiwin*, 'the good life'. *Pimatisiwin* and *ubuntu* are similar concepts shared by separate indigenous peoples. These indigenous concepts are invaluable sources in transforming educational practices and must be at the centre of our learning.

References

Anderson, Kim and Bonita Lawrence (eds). 2003. *Strong Women Stories: Native Vision and Community Survival*. Toronto: Sumach Press.

Barnhardt, Ray and Angayuqaq Oscar Kawagley. 2005. 'Indigenous Knowledge Systems and Alaska Native Ways of Knowing', *Anthropology & Education Quarterly*, 36(1): 8–23.

Belenky, Mary Field, Blythe McVicker Clinchy, Nancy Rule Goldberger and Jill Mattuck Tarule. 1986. *Women's Ways of Knowing: The Development of Self, Voice, and Mind*. New York: Basic Books.

Brendtro, Larry K., Martin Brokenleg and Steve Van Bockern. 2002 [1990]. *Reclaiming Youth at Risk: Our Hope for the Future*. Bloomington: National Educational Service.

Cook-Lynn, Elizabeth. 1998. 'American Indian Intel-lectualism and the New Indian Story', in Devon Abbott Mihesuah (ed.), *Natives and Academics: Researching and Writing about American Indians*, pp. 111–39. Lincoln: University of Nebraska Press.

Dempsey, Hugh Aylmer. 1984. *Big Bear: The End of Freedom*. Vancouver: Greystone Books.

Freire, Paulo. 1970. *Pedagogy of the Oppressed*. New York: Herder and Herder.

Goulding, Warren. 2001. *Just Another Indian: A Serial Killer and Canada's Indifference*. Calgary: Fifth House.

Gramsci, Antonio. 1995. *Further Selections from the Prison Notebooks*, trans. Derek Boothman. London: Lawrence & Wishart.

Hartsock, Nancy C. M. 1998. *The Feminist Standpoint Revisited and Other Essays*. Boulder: Westview Press.

Jolly, Grace McKay, Alice Aby and Stan Cuthand. 1995. *Kisewatotatowin: Loving, Caring, Sharing, Respect*. Saskatoon: Kisewatotatowin Aboriginal Parent Program.

Justice, Daniel Heath. 2004. 'Seeing (and Reading) Red: Indian Outlaws in the Ivory Tower', in Devon Abbott Mihesuah and Angela Cavender Wilson (eds), *Indigenizing the Academy: Transforming Scholarship and Empowering Communities*, pp. 100–23. Lincoln: University of Nebraska Press.

Krog, Antjie. 1998. *Country of My Skull: Guilt, Sorrow, and the Limits of Forgiveness in the New South Africa*. Johannesburg: Random House.

Mamdani, Mahmood. 1999. 'There can be No African Renaissance without an Africa-Focused Intelligentsia', in Malegapuru William Makgoba (ed.), *African Renaissance: The New Struggle*, pp. 125–36. Cape Town: Mafube Publishing; Sandton Tafelberg.

Mihesuah, Devon Abbott. 1998. *Natives and Academics: Researching and Writing about American Indians*. Lincoln: University of Nebraska Press.

Mihesuah, Devon Abbott and Angela Cavender Wilson (eds). 2004. *Indigenizing the Academy: Transforming Scholarship and Empowering Communities*. Lincoln: University of Nebraska Press.

Morrison, Toni. 1994. *The Nobel Lecture in Literature, 1993*. New York: Knopf.

Smith, Linda Tuhiwai. 1999. *Decolonizing Methodologies: Research and Indigenous Peoples*. London and New York: Zed.

Teffo, Lesiba. 1999. 'Moral Renewal and African Experience(s)', in Malegapuru William Makgoba (ed.), *African Renaissance: The New Struggle*, pp. 149–69. Cape Town: Mafube Publishing; Sandton Tafelberg.

Vil-Nkomo, Sibusiso and Johan Myburgh. 1999. 'The Political Economy of an African Renaissance: Understanding the Structural Conditions and Forms', in Malegapuru William Makgoba (ed.), *African Renaissance: The New Struggle*, pp. 270–73. Cape Town: Mafube Publishing; Sandton: Tafelberg.

4 Metaphors of Fertility, Phallic Anxieties and Expiation of Grief in the Babukusu Funeral Oratory

Chris J. C. Wasike*

For many people, death and the dying process arouse thoughts of pain, discomfort, loss of control, separation from loved ones, and resoundingly the cessation of all form of physical experiencing. Indeed the emotions associated with death make it necessary that the individual and collective units of a social group will seriously reflect on their very personhood and identity. For the Babukusu, in many ways, every death seems to shatter and rattle the core of self-belief and self-definition of both personal and collective identities. More importantly, the corporeal reality of an actual corpse is always an unsettling and disarming reminder of the sheer destructibility of the human body. Part of the reason for such morbid restlessness and trepidation associated with death emanates from the traditional and religious beliefs that lay claim to the view that a dead person turns into a spirit that roams in the ethereal presence of the society until it is properly appeased through a proper burial and performance of the necessary rituals. This view is underlined by Robert Hertz's analysis of African thanatology in which he argues that:

> [t]he corpse is feared because until its reconstruction in the life beyond is complete, part of its spiritual essence remains behind, where it menaces the living with the threat of further death. Thus the death of any person causes anxiety and fear; but this reaction varies in scale depending on the social status of the deceased (1960: 70).

---

* A draft of this paper was first presented at the Chotro III 2010 Conference on 'Local Knowledge, Global Translation', 11–16 September 2010, University of Delhi and Shimla, India.

Benefitting from the preceding general remarks on death, this paper proposes to examine how a peculiar after-burial oratory performance (*khuswala kumuse* in the Lubukusu language) among the Babukusu community of western Kenya can be interpreted as a textual exposition of morbid and sexual anxieties. Our analysis also acknowledges *khuswala kumuse* as a concatenation of verbal imagery and well-choreographed narrations that can be read as cultural texts that simultaneously construct and dismantle certain forms of cultural masculinities and identities. In this ritual performance that is usually enacted to honour the passing away of a renowned male elder, a traditionally recognized and approved community sage elder strides up and down an open performance area as he narrates a medley of oral art forms and recounts the community's past events, heroes and monuments. My argument in this chapter is anchored on the idea that even in death the human body remains a locus of gender-sanctioned powers, meanings and anxieties. Essential to my analysis is to unravel the extent to which the Babukusu definition of masculinity is based, as in most patriarchal societies, on the biological and metaphorical phallus as a symbol of power and the concomitant castration fear that eternally haunts it. I hope to demonstrate how the orator's rendition of this gender-conscious genre, deliberately or otherwise, continuously re-creates and re-imagines various forms of hegemonic masculinity that seek to valorise circumcision as a marker of Bukusu male personhood. I will also argue that while the orator uses his performances to express genuine fears and anxieties on how death destabilizes the hierarchies of masculinity, the same fears and anxieties, in our view, seem to be premised on the unstable over-reliance on the 'circumcised phallus' as a symbol of defining masculine virility and male personhood. Basically, I seek to examine how the funeral orator not only uses his narrations to mourn and expiate grief because of the demise of the physical male body but in fact bemoans the 'death of the phallus', so to speak.

As a way of giving background information on the Babukusu funeral oratory, I will begin by first outlining the death and funeral practices among the Bukusu and how the after-burial oratory fits into the whole cultural milieu. I will then proceed to theoretically examine how Jacques Lacan's concepts of phallic symbolism and castration anxiety dovetail with the practice of male circumcision and consequently relate to death and the performance of masculinity. Finally, I will give examples from one recorded text of John Wanyonyi Manguliechi, a revered, respected and renowned Bukusu after-burial performer, in order to illustrate how he employs rhetorical strategies that elucidate anxieties about death, anxieties of the phallus, and a general depiction of masculine continuities and discontinuities.

'Confronting Death With Words': Bukusu Funerary Rites and the Structure of the After-Burial Performance (K*huswala Kumuse*)

The Babukusu are one of the 17 sub-tribes[1] of the larger Luhya ethnic group that presently inhabit the western part of Kenya. Among the other sub-tribes of this conglomeration of related ethnic identities that speak almost similar Bantu dialects are the Wanga, Maragoli, Idakho, Isukha, Samia, and Banyala to mention just a few (Makila 1976: 43). For the Babukusu, as in many African societies, it is extremely difficult for any kind of death to be considered as having happened because of 'natural causes'. Death and the sight of a corpse are subjects of great anxiety. In the event of an inexplicable sudden death, suspicion ranges from witchcraft, poisoning to an evil eye instigated by a 'bad neighbour' jealous of the deceased person's successes. In their worldview, death is certainly believed to be caused by 'external forces'. Even in instances where a visibly aged older man dies eyebrows are still raised and questions posed about the cause of his demise. All the same, the death of an elderly man/woman is often celebrated as the beginning of an after-life in the spirit world inhabited by ancestors who continue to live and communicate with their families through dreams and apparitions. In the community's cosmology everyone, especially the elderly, aspires and looks forward to be remembered after they have gone to *emakombe* or the 'land of the ancestors'. For this reason it is imperative that every person, but more so a high-ranking man, is accorded a proper burial complete with all the traditional trinkets, rituals and customary practices. If not, it is feared the dead might turn into 'a wandering ghost' that is uncomfortable with life in the after-world and therefore a danger to the living. A proper burial is 'a guarantee of peace to the living and a respectable and secure passage for the dead' (Makila 2004: 13).

But not everybody is assured of a good burial. According to Manguliechi, abominable deaths such as those associated with suicide,

---

[1] Written accounts indicate that the Luhya tribe might have more than 17 sub-tribes. For more on the history of the Luhya in general and the Babukusu in particular, see also Makila (1976).

lightning, drowning, a curse, and deaths due to strange and infectious diseases such as leprosy do not warrant a decent burial (interview with John Wanyonyi Manguliechi, Kibingeyi, Bungoma, 3 June 2008; hereafter Interview). It is also traditionally agreed that social miscreants like wizards, thieves, murderers, and sorcerers do not deserve decent interment. The burials of such social misfits are thus characterized by thin crowds consisting of only their family members and their graves are dug deep as a symbolic gesture of contempt and the urgency with which the society wishes to completely forget them. In extreme cases, the corpses are whipped, burnt, chopped to pieces, or fed to wild animals. The spirits of such persons are regarded as unwelcome even in the ancestral world and are expelled, thereby turning into 'wandering ghosts' that have to be exorcized from the community's sanctum of continuity and memory.

Because death is regarded as a transition from a lived material presence to an ethereal spiritual and super masculine existence in the afterworld, care is taken by the Bukusu to ensure that the correct passage rites are performed to ensure that the dead man's journey to the world of the ancestors is smooth. My fieldwork interviews with Manguliechi also confirmed that a typical funeral of a once powerful man culturally referred to as *omusecha owekiminie* — meaning 'a man of means' or note — is in fact a celebration of his achievements. His family stages for the community a funeral that is as elaborate as it is showy (ibid.). The elaborateness and glitz on such occasions is a measure of the success of the deceased and is commensurate with his circumcision age-grade (*sisingilo*). Bukusu funerals are punctuated by the slaughtering of an animal, preferably a fattened bull for sacrificial ritual although the meat serves as food for the mourning throngs. The size of the bull has to match the status of the dead man because the hide of the slaughtered animal (*lisielo*) is symbolically used to wrap the corpse before burial to underscore the fact that the deceased was indeed 'a man of means' in his lifetime and has been dispatched to the other world in similar fashion.

Ideally, the burial of a Bukusu man has to take place either early in the morning or late in the afternoon. Elderly men are laid to rest late in the afternoon as the sun goes down, to again signify that a man as the head of the family does not really die, but 'goes to rest' in order to watch over the homestead from the other world. On the third or fourth day after burial (referred to as *lufu* — meaning 'reincarnation') the deceased's relatives and friends normally bathe at a nearby river and shave their hair to signal rebirth and continuity of life after death. The bathing and hair-shaving are part of the process of cleansing and shedding of the streak of bad luck, tragedy and 'darkness' that occasioned the death of a loved one. On the same day, the deceased's belongings and liabilities are distributed among relatives.

When all the burial and mourning obligations have been fulfilled on the day of *lufu*, the family of the deceased may decide to give a final ritual of sending him off to the 'ancestral world' by inviting a special ritual 'man of memory' to perform *khuswala kumuse* (literally meaning 'stepping in the arena'). This ritual is a rare occasion that bestows on the dead man the highest honour of being incorporated into the community's annals of history and memory. During the performance of this genre, the narrator, who is specially trained but is believed to be spiritually-inspired by ancestral powers to perform such a ritual, moves within a randomly configured open space away from the grave as he recounts the community's history and genealogy from the very beginnings. The performer engages public-speaking skills in a style reminiscent of Greco-Roman funeral orations. He demonstrates verbal flamboyance at its best in this ceremonial re-enactment. In the process he also idolizes and valorises the great achievements of the deceased man alongside the feats of other communal heroes who lived before him. As he moves up and down the arena his peripatetic movements eventually create a path in the midst of his audience that is usually gender-segregated with women seated on one side (often the left) and men on the other (right). All through, the performer is always adorned in ritual regalia that consist of a special head gear called *ekhorere* (made from the skin of a colobus monkey and embellished with cowries and an ostrich feather), a walking stick called *ekhendie* and a flowing robe called *ekutusi* (usually made from the skin of a colobus monkey). The performance attire is symbolic of the orator's high status in the community's hierarchy.

As a rule, only circumcised Bukusu men who have sired sons as firstborns and have living grandchildren at the time of their death qualify to have *kumuse* performed for them. However there are exceptions to this rule, especially in instances where the community's elders using their discretion think that a deceased man's social achievements warrant a waiver of these cultural requirements. In such cases the ritual can be performed for a younger deceased male. However, this ritual is the preserve of males and can never be performed in honour of any deceased woman whatsoever. The performer of this genre — *omuswali* — is held in such high esteem and near religious awe because his talent is regarded as a calling and the preserve of mature wise men from special Bukusu clans that do it.[2] In the Bukusu hierarchy, these clans are considered the custodians of the Bukusu history and cultural archives. It is this archival knowledge and history that *baswali* — the 'official remembrancers' — retrieve and pass on to the audience on the occasion of a male death.

In my analysis I will focus on one collected and transcribed text of a live performance by an oral artist called John Wanyonyi Manguliechi. The late Manguliechi, who passed away in July 2012, was a polygamous man (now survived by one wife out of the original three) who lived in Maturu village near Kimilili town, a rural urban centre overlooking Mount Elgon on the south-eastern side. His village and home fall under what was formerly the larger Bungoma district of the Western Province in Kenya. As a communally acclaimed performer of the funeral genre, Manguliechi's fame bordered on religious reverence, although his rhetorical and idiomatic command of the Lubukusu language made him stand out amongst similar performers of this ritual. I was lucky to have watched him live several times in his lifetime including on the particular occasion when I had his performance video-taped for purposes of this research. The rationale for my choice of Manguliechi's performances was because of his fame and idiomatic prowess in funeral performance. His fame stemmed from the high-profile personalities at whose funerals he performed. Among the prominent personalities for whom he presided over *khuswala kumuse* was the late Kenyan Vice-President Michael Wamalwa Kijana who passed away in August 2003. Indeed, a transcribed video text of Manguliechi's performance at Wamalwa's funeral congregation is the main focus of our current analysis. In the next section we will look at Jacques Lacan's concept of phallic symbolism as influenced by Sigmund Freud's views on castration anxiety, and at how his views can be appropriated and reformulated in the context of Bukusu male circumcision, death and the after-burial ceremony.

'Anatomy of the Phallus' and Masculine Anxieties

After Sigmund Freud, perhaps no other scholar of psychoanalysis has influenced cultural studies more than Jacques Lacan. As one of the key

---

[2] Traditionally, not everybody can be *omuswali*. F. A. Makila (1976) claims that the Bukusu clans that do this are: Batukwika (Bakwangwa, Basakha, and Bakitang'a), Babulo, Bachemayi, Bayemba, Bakhwami, Babuya, Bakabo, Bayitu, Basang'alo, and Babangachi. However, oral accounts from my fieldwork pointed to the fact that there could be more clans that practise or perform this genre.

founders of French structuralism, Lacan sought to explain the human subject by attempting to understand his/her cosmology through the structuralist framework of language. While Freud's figuration of the human unconscious asserted that it is only through the appreciation of the presence or absence of the penis that children become aware of human sexual differentiation, for Lacan the penis is more symbolic than biological, hence his reference to the 'phallus' (Lacan 2002a). Within the same psychoanalytic thinking, Freud's concepts of 'penis envy' (the lack of the phallus in girls) and 'castration anxiety' (the boy's fear of losing the phallus) became, at least for Lacan, more like linguistic codes that are beneficial in interpreting human beings within different social contexts. For this reason, Lacan believed that the ultimate reduction of sexual difference to the presence/absence of the phallus is 'a symbolic law', which is a product of patriarchy; simply put as the 'Law of the Father' (ibid.: 271–81). In this symbolic configuration Lacan argues that everything is done and understood in the name of the father, who is a metaphorical representation of patriarchal hegemony. He further maintains that the idea of the phallus basically constitutes women in terms of their 'lack of' and men in terms of the 'threat to lack' (ibid.). Thus any human subject in Lacanian view can only be identified with reference to one sex (male/phallic) and its 'other'. The phallus is therefore a 'privileged signifier' and the penis as the anatomical object of differentiation becomes fetishized and invested with multiple signifying functions (Lacan 2002b). Ultimately Lacan's 'phallus' appears to create a sense of difference from an illusion of power that is fantasized by the mere possession of the biological gadget.

Lacan's symbolic theory has been recast and domesticated by many cultural scholars and literary theorists. In masculinity studies, for instance, it is acknowledged that the anatomical and symbolic significance of the phallus has been at the centre of many debates that seek to delineate the biological and social construction of gender. Yet the phallus on its own is meaningless unless it is associated with men's eternal search for dominance through sexuality. Catherine MacKinnon (1982) reminds us that 'sexuality in and of itself is at the heart of male dominance [and] male sexual dominance is at the heart of all other power relations in society' (quoted in Segal 1992: 208). However, this fight for sexual dominance is more pronounced in heterosexual sexuality. Feminist scholar Wendy Holloway amplifies this view when she observes that:

> [h]eterosexual sex is the site of politics because it is contradictory; because it is a primary site of women's power and of men's resistance ... [The] power of

the penis is a 'knowledge' produced by sexist discourses; a knowledge which is motivated and thus reproduced by men's vulnerability to women because of the desire for the other/mother (Holloway 1984: 34).

To a large extent, discourses and imagery of male sexual conquest and subjugation of women have not only continued to define many patriarchalized masculinities, but also dominate and seek to validate the ways in which men perform their authority over women. What rings true according to Holloway is that men repress their own sexual anxieties and insecurities by supporting myths and stereotypes that associate heterosexual acts with masculine dominance (ibid.). Probably *kumuse* is one such cultural instrument of heterosexual dominance, as I hope to ascertain shortly.

While it is true that many cultures recognize the significant force of the equation of the phallus with masculine power, the symbolism of phallic power is often trapped in contradictions. In the words of Lynne Segal, phallic power is 'embroiled in anxious vicissitudes of constantly striving to validate itself amid the changing social experiences' (1992: 210). Segal's point is valid but, perhaps the biggest threat to phallic power is the fact that men have to regularly confront and reckon with the lived experiences of frequently reinventing and reasserting themselves in heterosexual contests where the female 'other' is fast claiming more ground in the fight for sexual dominance. This is true especially in relation to the emergence of feminist studies and the agitation for more political, cultural and economic representation of women in the public sphere. But it is important to note here that the symbol of the phallus appears to condense multiple meanings and realities that make it practically unavailable for possession for many men especially in their individual capacities.

To fully appreciate how anxious and tenuous the phallus is as a benchmark of traditional Bukusu masculinity, it is important to juxtapose it with male circumcision and death. For one, the Babukusu are one of the several Kenyan communities that practice traditional circumcision. In fact their way of doing it is usually characterized by cultural emotions and elaborate practices that are attested by many Kenyans. For this reason, members of the community who have successfully undergone the traditional ritual openly express their braggadocio by claiming to be a community of *basani* — 'the circumcised men'. The details about the genealogy of this practice will be discussed later in this chapter. However, at this point, let us briefly outline how the ritual of circumcision constructs masculinities in general and the Bukusu identity in particular, and how this correlation is emphasized even in death. In his comparative analysis of male circumcision in European-Christian and sub-Saharan African communities, Eric Silverman observes that:

> [i]t is all about culture, a symbolic message concerning personhood, gender, cosmology, status and community inscribed in the body. Male circumcision in Africa is associated with symbolic themes such as enhancement of masculine virility and fecundity, arboreal fertility, complementary opposition between men and women, preparation for marriage and adult sexuality and the hardening of boys for warfare (1995: 45).

Silverman's description of the ritual is closer to how the ritual has long been practiced by the Babukusu. For this community, the ritual was traditionally (and ideally) carried out on teenage boys who have to openly declare that they want *khukhwingila* (literally meaning 'to enter') or *khukhebwa* (to be circumcised).[3] Once the father of the young man agrees to his wishes, the boy will go ahead and acquire *chinyimba* (cow bells with which he will knock on some metallic braces worn on the wrists) as he dances to circumcision songs sung for him by a retinue of young adults — mostly cousins, brother/sisters or neighbours. Before the actual day of circumcision, the boy who wishes to be circumcised runs around with the cow bells inviting his relatives and neighbours to come on the material day to witness him facing the knife. The circumcision operation itself usually takes place in the father's or another male relative's courtyard. A specific spot where the boy stands during the operation is chosen by his relatives on the morning of the ritual. Then the circumcision candidate is taken to a nearby river early that same morning to bathe in cold water before being smeared with mud in what is believed to be traditional anaesthesia. When the boy is coming from the river to the homestead a special song called *sioyaye* is sung by a throng of elderly men who psych the candidate to brace himself for the ultimate moment. In the song, he is also taunted to give up early enough if he is having second thoughts about facing the knife. The actual circumcision however takes a very short time and when successfully done it is usually followed by ululations from women and bellows of approval from the men.

---

[3] For a more detailed explanation of the processes involved in Bukusu male circumcision, see also Wanyama (2006); Wasike (2012, 2013). A similarly elaborate process of male circumcision among the Bagisu of Uganda (an ethnic group that is fondly referred to as 'cousins' of the Babukusu) is explained by Heald (1989).

The successful initiate is usually fêted with gifts from family and relatives and songs of praise are sung to congratulate him.

Overall though, the Bukusu believe the practice is never so much about the actual operation but a mental preparation for the boys to face life with a mixture of resilience and stoicism. Although the initiates are expected to endure the cut without so much of a flinch or blink of an eye, the rite is meant to inculcate in the youngsters the sense that any stumbling block can be overcome just like the pain of the circumciser's knife. After the ritual the initiate moves from being *omusinde* (uncircumcised/boy) and becomes *omusani* (circumcised adult). More importantly, the rite appears to promulgate the ideology that women, sex and nature can be conquered by men. Given the physical brutality, testing of resilience and patience, gruelling dances (that involve initiates knocking cow bells [*chinyimba*] and dancing to circumcision songs) the initiates really have to overcome energy-sapping challenges. By the time they are done with the whole ceremony, they actually feel they have survived the worst and are therefore prepared to face the future with pride and valour. For the same reason, many Bukusu initiates were traditionally believed to be ready to marry, have children and own property after circumcision.

Nonetheless, while the rite is meant to inspire young adults to think and feel elevated to a special hierarchy of masculinity and cultural identity, actual experience has shown that the contrary also happens. Indeed as Jacqueline Rose has argued, 'the assumption of identity in relation to the phallus is itself a loss and castration; an index of the precariousness of sexual identity' (1982: 41). She insists that 'the phallus stands at its own expense and any male privilege erected upon it is an imposture' (ibid.). Silverman underscores this view in relation to the circumcision when he notes that the 'rite plagues boys and adults men with unresolved anxieties surrounding the social significance of sexuality' (1995: 5). He goes on to emphasize that the rite is both phallic and feminizing because on the one hand it 'crafts a parturient phallus' yet there is always a looming fear that circumcision leads to a 'denuded phallus' in literal and metaphorical sense; an emasculated rather alternative masculinity (ibid.). Traditionally, the Bukusu viewed the rite as both a symbolic and a literal passage from 'uncircumcised' boyhood and dependence to circumcised adulthood and self-sufficiency. However, the intricacies and realities of modern capitalism make such a marked transition from 'uncircumcised' dependency to 'circumcised' economic self-sufficiency virtually hard to attain. This disconnect between the physical and cultural achievement of manhood and a corresponding attainment of economic power certainly creates anxieties for the newly circumcised Bukusu men because the moral, psychological and economic import of the ritual is often subverted by the social realities of unfulfilled expectations and idealized masculinities. These anxieties (which we are referring to as phallic anxieties), we argue, are heightened on the occasion of a high-ranking male death because such an occurrence often signals both the loss of the human body and the cessation of phallic desires. To a certain extent, therefore, death feels like the final castration of the circumcised phallus. Let us now move on to illustrate how the after-burial performer deploys his rhetorical skills to expiate not just grief but phallic anxieties through his narrations.

Mourning the Dead Man, Mourning the Dead Phallus: Examples of Phallic Images and Metaphors of Fertility from the After-Burial Oratory

Although *khuswala kumuse* is a narrative genre, its mode of rendition is not as formulaic as the usual folk narratives. In fact Manguliechi's formulas of narration are more personalized though widely acknowledged by many in the Bukusu community. At the beginning and end of his performances, he usually literally storms in and out of space as if engaging in a wrestling match with the unseen enemy of death. He often starts his performances by walking up and down the length of the space in total silence. During this period, he often appears to be in a trance as he summons sacred powers that will enable him to carry out his duties. In traditional parlance, the silence at the beginning and end of his narration delineates the performance arena as hallowed ground. Similarly, his pronouncements are also deemed sacrosanct. But on many occasions his opening remarks are more like spiritual incantations that seek to calm the audience's anxieties about death. For example in one of his narrations he says:

> *Ndarakikha khumwene nono. Ndeba papa Wele! Ndi Wele enche! Ne Wele mwana! Ne Wele murumwa, ne kuka Mukhobe, omwene wakaba! Waana lifwa! Mala wacha wabola oli, oli lifwa nilio ndikhembana. Oli kubili kukwa kundi kwelao kwosi kwakelaho kwakwa! Oli ebonga eya, oli engeleo ekindi yakelao yaya. Oli chiselukho chiunananga. Oli nemuselukho naramo likhuwa nandaliana, oli murianana nio mwamenya, murianana nio mwasabana.*

English translation:

Let me start with Himself (God). I ask God the Father! God of the Universe! God the Son! God the Messenger Angel, and the Grandfather God Mukhobe, the one who gave! The one who gave us death! Then you said, 'It is death that I give you. Even bodies fall to give way for the regeneration of others that also fall. Even tropical grasslands burn and cause others to also burn. Even those in the same age-cohort regularly fight. In an age-cohort disagreements make them not eat together, yet people have to disagree in order to live, they disagree so as to borrow from each other'.[4]

In this extract the after-burial narrator bemoans the disruptive nature of death. However, he reminds his audience that death is in fact God-given. He also alludes to the fact that although death is destabilizing it is also a starting point of life's regeneration and of new continuities. John Bowker echoes similar views when he argues that 'where you do have death, there immediately you have the possibility of life' and 'death is an opportunity as well as an end ... a case of life yielding for life; life giving way so that other, more complex life can come' (1991: 221). In the same example, Manguliechi acknowledges the mortality of the human body that has to 'fall to allow for others to also fall' and also compares human life to 'grasslands that have to burn to give way for the sprouting new ones'. Indeed like the Biblical grain of wheat, the funeral performer insists that the human body has to die to give forth more life; a kind of discontinuity that ensures continuity.

Although he is always aware of the grief that his audience goes through, the performer of this *khuswala kumuse* reiterates the fact that death has been around since time immemorial. He repeatedly seeks to placate the anxieties of his listeners by reminding them that *kamasika bubwasio* — meaning 'death is like a duty roster and everyone has his time' — and *engunyi ekhale* (grief is as old as human life). He even uses the analogy of a chicken running around with the entrails of another slaughtered chicken totally oblivious of the fact that one day its own intestines will face the same fate. In a sense, the narrator seems to be harping on the inevitability of death for all humans. But perhaps the most prevalent anxiety about death that is voiced by Manguliechi is the mortal vulnerability of the human body. Given its finality, it seems nothing exposes the corporeal destructibility of the human body better than

---

[4] All translations in the chapter unless otherwise mentioned are by the author.

death. Judith Butler reminds us that death exposes the human body as 'a site of desire and vulnerability, as a site of publicity at once assertive and exposed' (Butler 1990: 20). The sense of loss and vulnerability according to Butler is informed by the view that human bodies are 'socially constituted ... attached to others, at risk of losing those attachments and exposed to others' (ibid.).

In his attempts to gesture towards an innately destructible human body flesh Manguliechi says:

> Warera lifwa. Wareramo bindu binee. Oli lola omutayi nio khuumbile nakhuumba khwiloba lifwa nilio ndikho khuwelesia. Wamuelesia omwana wasalwa ne engobi. Nga ne wasalwa ne engobi, mala engobi yayukhilakho, oli wakwa mala engobi yayukhilakho. Engobi yakwa basikha engobi. Engobi likobi! Wabukula lifwa! Warema munyama cho omundu, walanga oli kamafuki, nga nokendanga ne kamafuki. Kamafuki kamafu niko! Wabukula siakhulia waelesia omundu walia. Kabele kamaindi namwe bubele bulo. Ngawasia, mala bwekhola bufu nga nolichanga bufu, mala ewe omufu Wabukula omundu wamuelesia lifwa likhola khane. Nga nokonanga lilo obechanga, obechanga mwiloo. Bibindu ebio bikhubolela bali olifwa; nga nolikonanga lilo aba oli mwiloo nilio! Mala bibindu bino bili bibiefwe nibio, khukendanga nenabio, sekhubilekhanga enyuma ta. Mala wabola, nosalile omwana, mala keche akhutiukhe, nga nakhutiukha aba wetiukhile lifwa! Notiukha omwana aba watiukhile lifwa sikila watiukhile omundu wafwa khale!

English Translation:

God you brought death! It is manifested in four ways. You created man out of dust and you said that it is death I have given to you, to dust you will return. A child is born with a placenta. When it is born with a placenta, the placenta is soon buried, the child is born and the placenta is soon buried, the placenta is pushed out of the mother's womb and buried. The placenta is a debt! You took death and put it in the flesh of a person. You called it blood. Man lives because of blood flowing in his veins, blood is death! You took food and gave it to man to eat; be it maize or be it millet, once grounded into flour and man consumes flour, flour is death! Man is a walking corpse! You also remind man of death through a fourth sign! When man lies down to sleep, when he is asleep, he is in a grave-like hole! These things remind us that man will die one day. When one sleeps he is normally in a hole. All these things remind us all, we live with them, and we can't afford to forget them. Then you said that when you have a child who sires his own child and names him after you, once he names his child after (dead father) you then he has put death upon the head of the named child. Once you name a child, you will have death upon him, since you named him after a dead person!

In the preceding extract, the narrator chooses innocuous examples from daily experiences to explain the inevitability of death. The analogy of the placenta as a debt that has to be repaid by the eventual death of the child born with it is contingent as it signifies the double-edged meaning of birth as the ushering in of a new life and the beginning of the journey towards death. As the funeral orator moves up and down the arena in a restless mode, he literally and metaphorically re-enacts the anxieties of the corpse and the eternal fear and inexplicable ubiquity of death. It is as if he is worried about his own and the audience's bodies which are like moving corpses.

On the other hand, the performer's anxieties can also be read as a collective and individual mourning of the dead phallus. As we mentioned earlier, the Babukusu as a community are quite emotional about the significance of male circumcision as a yardstick of masculinity. Popular Bukusu folklore has it that circumcision was founded by a legendary figure called Mango. Mango is said to have killed a fiery python (*khururwe yabebe*) that had been terrorizing and killing his kinsmen at a place called *Mwiala*. As a gesture of recognizing his magical and brave feat, the *Sebei* — a Kalenjin sub-tribe that lived next to them — offered to circumcise him and give him a beautiful maiden as a wife. To this day, many older members of the community believe that Mango was the bravest man that ever lived among the community. Since his times, the Babukusu have continued to practice male circumcision in honour of Mango. But within the context of *kumuse* performance, the narrator not only recounts the myth to his audience but emphasizes the symbolic and reproductive significance of circumcision. In many ways, the celebration of male circumcision as a symbol of masculine achievement is a recognition of its role in male virility, fertility and reproduction. For example, he urges his listeners thus: *Okhacha wabola oli oyuno omutesio. Tawe. Lusimo lulio lubola luli musalane, musalane mala musomie babana* (Don't discriminate and say this one is Teso. No. There is a proverb that urges us to procreate, let us procreate and educate our children). By urging his Bukusu audience to intermarry, procreate and educate children, Manguliechi underscores the reproductive and unifying purchase of the 'circumcised phallus', so to speak. As we all know intermarriages foster unity amongst different ethnic groups. But the narrator goes further to underline the importance of educating young people and in the process appears to deconstruct the meaning of circumcision as the only phallic symbol of success. In a way he points to the fact that education is a better signifier of masculine power than a scarred penis; a better marker of masculine continuity.

In addition, the prominence of formal education as a marker of masculine success is emphasized by the funeral orator in one of his direct references to the late Vice-President of Kenya Michael Wamalwa Kijana. Performing at the late politician's funeral, Manguliechi bluntly praised him for giving birth to healthy and bright children. He particularly singled out his ability to have children with different women — including a white woman — as a mark of virile masculinity. And true to the orator's assertion, at the time of his death in August 2003, Wamalwa had hardly lasted a year in his last marriage with a young woman many years his junior with whom he had one daughter popularly known as Chichi. In an apparent allusion to these events, the narrator congratulates him as 'a bull that died with grass in its mouth' — an image that points to his virility and metaphor of his fertility. He also bemoans the communal and national loss of the late politician's gift of English oratory skills for which he was renowned throughout the country. He even urges the audience to always remember that Wamalwa has died from the 'waist downwards but his head remains' (*afwile sibuno safwile kumurwe tawe*). This is obviously a strong reference to the binary of intellectual and bodily capabilities as markers of masculinity. In a sense the orator appears to insinuate that although the politician's anatomical phallus has died, his 'intellectual phallus' and legacy still lives on.

But grimly aware of the debilitating effects of the HIV/AIDS pandemic, the *kumuse* performer does not sanction sexual licentiousness. If anything he warns and chides both the young and old to desist from sexual promiscuity. In one instance he admonishes young men who are fond of looking for sexual favours with older women. Using scathing proverbial analogies he refers to such youngsters as uncouth lads who behave 'like flies that love buzzing around a wound' (*Chisi chibona likonjo nio chaungakho*) or 'hyenas that love taking advantage of wounded prey' (*Namunyu kabiila eyikila*). In a way the orator forewarns the youths to be careful if they wish to live long and leave a legacy. And for adults, he admonishes them to be wary of the dreaded HIV/AIDS pandemic. Metaphorically referring to it as the traditionally prohibited *kumunandere* tree — a well-known tree in Bukusu folklore that is believed to give forth attractive and sweet but poisonous fruits — he advises them to avoid the temptation of being promiscuous because the 'poisonous fruit tree' beckons such people.

Conclusion

From our analysis it is quite clear that male circumcision as practiced by the Bukusu is a rite that constructs and deconstructs its own intended symbolism. To a certain extent the rite also flirts with castration and hence the anxiety that haunts the perceived power it is supposed to symbolize. Nowhere is this anxiety more evident than on the occasion of the death of a famous male Bukusu elder. Indeed we hope to have shown how the occasion of a male death for the Babukusu is not only a forum of performing masculine power memories, but it is also an opportune moment that helps reformulate traditional definitions of masculinities, social expectations for men and new meanings of trying and living as a man. The funeral performer's imagery clearly demonstrates that death subverts the power of the standing phallus and renders any related signification a subject of contestation and conjecture. Like Lacan's 'phallus' the narrator seems to argue that the Bukusu masculine figuration based on the circumcised phallus cannot stand forever. In fact it can never survive death. But even when alive it is always anxious and therefore not worthy as a signifier of maleness.

References

Bowker, John. 1991. *The Meanings of Death*. Cambridge: Cambridge University Press.
Butler, Judith. 1990. *Gender Trouble: Feminism and the Subversion of Identity*. New York: Routledge.
Heald, Suzette. 1989. *Controlling Anger: The Sociology of Gisu Violence*. Manchester: Manchester University Press.
Hertz, Robert. 1960. *Death and the Right Hand*, trans. Rodney Needham and Claudia Needham. New York: The Free Press.
Holloway, Wendy. 1984. 'Women's Power in Heterosexual Sex', *Women Studies International Forum*, 7(1): 63–68.
Lacan, Jacques. 2002a. 'Position of the Unconscious', in *Ecrits: A Selection*, trans. Bruce Fink, Héloïse Fink and Russell Grigg, pp. 702–21. New York and London: W. W. Norton & Company.
———. 2002b. *Ecrits: A Selection*, trans. Bruce Fink, Héloïse Fink and Russell Grigg. New York and London: W. W. Norton & Company.
MacKinnon, Catherine A. 1982. 'Feminism, Marxism, Method and the State: An Agenda for Theory', *Signs*, 7(3): 515–44.

Makila, F. A. 1976. *An Outline History of Babukusu*. Nairobi: Kenya Literature Bureau.
———. 2004. *Bukusu Cultural Traditions*. Nairobi: Kenya Literature Bureau.
Rose, Jacqueline. 1982. 'Introduction II', in Juliet Mitchell and Jacqueline Rose (eds), *Feminine Sexuality; Jacques Lacan and the École Freudienne*, pp. 27–57. London: Macmillan.
Segal, Lynne. 1992. *Slow Motion: Changing Masculinities, Changing Men*. London: Virago.
Silverman, Eric. K. 1995. 'Anthropology and Circumcision', *Annual Review of Anthropology*, 33: 419–27.
Wanyama, Melitus. 2006. 'Current Trends in the Form and Content of African Music: A Case Study of Bukusu Circumcision Music'. Unpublished PhD Thesis, University of Pretoria.
Wasike, Chris J. C. 2012. '(Re-)configuring the Soloist as a 'Nomadic' Modernity Trickster: The Case of 'Composer' in *Bukusu* Circumcision Folklore', in G. N. Devy, Geoffrey V. Davis and K. K. Chakravarty (eds), *Narrating Nomadism: Tales of Recovery and Resistance*, pp. 55–80. New Delhi: Routledge.
———. 2013. 'Textualizing Masculinity: Discourses of Power and Gender Relations in the Babukusu After-Burial Oratory Performance (Khuswala Kumuse)'. PhD Thesis, University of the Witwatersrand.

5 The (Re-)imag(in)ing of the Oba of Benin in Nigerian Dramatic Literature and its Implications in Indigenous Studies

Israel Meriomame Wekpe and *Alero Uwawah*

The Benin people of Nigeria enjoy a primogeniture tradition. The *Oba* (King) of Benin is a cultural symbol, a spiritual icon and a political figure. The Oba is a demi-god personified. In him, the Benins substantiate their unique identity. However, these images of the Oba are finding a slippery terrain in contemporary times, especially in certain Nigerian dramatic literature. The 1997 centenary celebration of the British Punitive Expedition reflected this reality when the Benin people commissioned a notable playwright to (re-)enact a 'work' reflective of the perceived superhuman image of the Oba; in this case, Oba Ovonramwen. This obviously caused an eruption in the Nigerian theatre firmament.

This chapter seeks to critically study how the Oba of Benin is (re-)imag(in)ed in contemporary Nigerian dramatic literature, and how within indigenous discourse this (re)presentation has had a profound implication for the person(a) of the Oba of Benin. Thus, this chapter takes a historical detour on the origin of the institution of the Obaship juxtaposing it with contemporary realities within the purview of a playwright's artistic mandate and impetus. In this regard, it appreciates plays indicative of the various perceptions of the person(a) of the Oba. The paper concludes that the Oba, though a representation of Benins and their identity, is at times now (re-)imag(in)ed within a 'global' perspective.

I

Linda Tuhiwai Smith succinctly remarks, 'Imperialism frames the indigenous experience. It is part of our story, our version of modernity.

Writing about our experience under imperialism and its small specific expression of colonialism has become an indigenous project of the world' (2005: 94). Importantly, within the context of this chapter, this may have fertilized and propelled the drive of certain African writers. We appreciate the efforts of Ngũgĩ wa Thiong'o and Micere Githae Mugo in *The Trial of Dedan Kimathi* (1976); Ebrahim Hussein in *Kinjeketile* (1970), and of course, Ola Rotimi in *Ovonramwen Nogbaisi* (1974) and Ahmed Yerima in *The Trials of Oba Ovonramwen* (1997) especially, as these playwrights vigorously respond to perceived historical biases by colonizers in their attempt to undermine the heroism of some Africans.

These playwrights, in a sense, attempt to interpret or rewrite history via the theatre space while presenting these characters as heroes and justifying their character's actions as not only heroic but exemplary as against the colonialists' perception of the villainy of these characters. These African writers see these actions of the colonialists and portrayal of these African heroes as rather derogatory. This would be why, wa Thiong'o and Githae Mugo elevate Dedan Kimathi to a folk hero and surround him with a mythic presence, thus disconnecting the British portrayal of Kimathi as a criminal and cannibal. For Hussein, Kinjeketile becomes an artistic creation to justify the historical Kinjeketile as a heroic fighter against German colonial impunity and this is quite antithetical to the misconception of him as a religio-magical trouble-maker. In the case of Oba Ovonramwen, the British are wont to present him as a king ever-thirsty for blood whose preoccupation is to send innocents to the slaughter chambers as excuse for rituals and sacrifices to the ancestors and gods.

However, the portrayal of Oba Ovonramwen in Rotimi's *Ovonramwen Nogbaisi* (1974) and Yerima's *The Trials of Oba Ovonramwen* (1997) finds itself on a slippery terrain since both plays have contrasting representations of Oba Ovonramwen. This is so because the Benin people have in a manner rejected Rotimi's Ovonramwen and so commissioned Yerima to redress and address certain historical inadequacies, misconceptions and misrepresentations contained in Rotimi's *Ovonramwem Nogbaisi* on the same Benin expedition saga (Anon 1996: 28).

Actually, Osayande Ugiagbe, secretary of the Benin Centenary Celebration Committee, elaborated that Oba Erediauwa (who is the present king) was discontented with the manner in which Oba Ovonramwen — especially being the exalted Benin monarch — was presented in Rotimi's play as a weakling who had to desert his throne when the colonial army led by Captain Philips invaded his palace (Rotimi 1974: 28). He goes on to elaborate further: 'That is unbecoming of a Benin Monarch and a gross misrepresentation of the institution regarded as the strongest of its type in the whole world' (Rotimi 1974: 28). Ugiagbe also criticized Rotimi's play as 'having been written from the perspective of British historians, who would rather underplay facts to absolve the colonial masters of any blame in the crime they committed against Bini people and by extension all Africans' (ibid.).

Indeed, at the celebration of the centenary in February 1997, this historical contestation played out. Thorold Masefield, the British High Commissioner, spoke about the misconceptions surrounding the punitive expedition. He justified the fact that the British had to be despotic on the world's behalf: the kingdom was uncivilized and needed outside contact, and human sacrifice was abominable. He rationalized that the brass objects removed from the palace had not been so much looted as dug up — a kind of archaeological dig. The Oba's address, however, focused on British imperialism in southern Nigeria and the illegality of the Ovonramwen trial in which British officers served as prosecution, defence, judge, and jury. His explicit objective was to rewrite the history of invasion and the punitive expedition from the eye of the conquered. Obviously, these two Cambridge University graduates offered a notable contrast in white and black (Nevadomsky 1997: 4–5).

These two views by the present Oba of Benin and the former British High Commissioner subtly provide an impetus for the discussion of both plays and any other(s) within the context of how the Oba is imagined or imaged in the Edo worldview and, in the context of this chapter, in Nigerian dramatic literature.

It is, however, instructive at this juncture for us to make an excursion on the origin of Benin as well as tangentially appreciate the Edo worldview while underlining the Benin people's perception of their king.

II

According to oral tradition, there are two dynasties of the Benin Kingdom. The first was the Ogiso dynasty, and the second, the Oba dynasty, which was short-circuited in 1897 by the British exile of Ovonramwen to Calabar but would resume in 1914 with the crowning of Eweka II. To date, there have been 39 Obas. One tradition states that during the reign of the last Ogiso, Ogiso Owodo, his son and heir apparent, Ekaladeran, was banished from Benin as a result of one of the queens changing a message from the oracle to the Ogiso. Prince Ekaladeran was a powerful warrior and well-loved. On leaving Benin, he travelled in a westerly direction to the land of the Yoruba. He arrived at the Yoruba city of Ife and finally rose to the position of the Oba. Ekaladeran would change his name to 'Izoduwa' which means, in Edo, 'I have chosen the path of prosperity'. The name 'Izoduwa' has been corrupted to 'Oduduwa'.

On the death of his father, Owodo, a group of Benin chiefs led by Chief Oliha came to Ife, pleading with Oduduwa to return to Benin to ascend the throne. His reply was that a ruler cannot leave his domain, but he would ask one of his sons to go back to Benin to become king.

One account indicates that the ancient Benin kingdom began around 900 CE. From its base located in what is now Nigeria, it became a large empire. Benin was and is still famous for its oral history traditions and for its highly-skilled craftsmanship and arts. Around the 16th century, the captain of the Portuguese ship, Lourenço Pinto, had observed that:

> Great Benin, where the king resides, is larger than Lisbon, all the streets run straight and as far as the eyes can see. The houses are large, especially that of the king which is richly decorated and has fine columns. The city is wealthy and industrious. It is so well governed that theft is unknown and the people live in such security that they have no door to their houses (cited by Chuhan 2010).

Benin social order is organized around divine kingship and is suffused with a male ethos. The Oba is the quintessence of male perfection, the peak of accomplishment. He presides over a vigorous palace arrangement composed of not more than 300 chiefs who in earlier times would have helped direct the kingdom's warfare, governance and economy. The Oba's overwhelming influence is extremely manifested in the salutations of the Benin. The greetings in Edo are:

> Obowie [Oba-owie] (King of Morning: Good morning);
> Obavan [Oba avan] (King of Noon: Good afternoon); and
> Obota [Oba ota] (King of Evening: Good evening).

This is also extended to references to man and woman. Thus, a matured man is called *Okpi Oba* (Oba's man), while a woman is *Okhu Oba* (Oba's woman).

It becomes relevant to say here that the story of the Edo people is incomplete without reference to the Oba. It is not far-fetched that everything revolves around the Oba. He is a cultural symbol, a spiritual icon and a political figure. The Oba is a demi-god personified; hence one of his appellations is *Oba Nosa* (God-king).

Edo oral tradition acknowledges these various appellations as a sign of deep respect and awe for the Oba:

> *Umogun* (mighty one),
> *Uku Akpolo kpo lo* (the mighty that rules, the one greater than all the kings),
> *Ekpen'owa* (home leopard),
> *Ovbi abi'hia* (the son of the creator, the one who has all the knowledge),
> *Ovbi'Ekenekene ma deyo* (the son of beauty that never fades),
> *Ovbio 'Ekuabo N'olo* (the son of the rocky arm, the brave and powerful),
> *Nohien utete no gh'ughe s'omwan* (the king on a hill, who sees more than everybody).

The entrance of the Oba at any occasion may be preceded by songs reflecting his awe and mythic presence. Hence, the renditions at such gatherings of: *Gh'oba gh'oba, gh'oba no gboriri* (see our Oba, our Oba whose presence causes goose pimples).

The metaphorical nature of these appellations and songs plus the salutations more than ever visualizes the Oba as superhuman. To say he is idolized/worshipped may be to state the obvious. This may be a reason why a new Ovonramwen has to be created or recreated (or reinvented) to reflect an idealized Oba who cannot be removed from his throne forcefully.

III

A forum for writers whose works have been nominated for the 2010 Nigeria Prize for Literature once again set the tone for the divide between drama and history. Irene Isoken Salami-Agunloye emphasized that her work — *Idia, The Warrior Queen of Benin* (2008) — cannot be categorized as an historical play even though it appropriates historical resources. She reflected that it is a play from a feminist perspective to demonstrate how women are perceived in the Benin kingdom. However, another nominee, Emmy Idegwu, noted: 'You have to be careful the way you interpret history' (Abodunrin 2010). While citing Rotimi's *Ovonramwen Nogbaisi* (1974) and Yerima's *The Trials of Oba Ovonramwen* (1997) as plays that interpreted history differently, Idegwu substantiated that the Binis rejected Rotimi's work, which was more historically correct, by saying the Oba bowed before the portrait of the Queen, while gladly welcoming that of Yerima which downplayed the point to celebrate their centenary.

Idegwu reiterated that as a writer it is imperative that one appreciates and understands the border between falsification and interpretation. Akinwumi Isola, whose play *Madam Tinubu: The Terror in Lagos* (1998) portrays that great matriarch and trader, disclosed that the Efunsetan family of Ibadan did not like the way their matriarch was portrayed. But Isola argued that drama is not history; it is a way of interpreting history. He elaborated that using history in drama is not very comfortable. If the family is still alive, they can challenge you for trying to blackmail their parents (Abodunrin 2010).

History and historical characters/figures have always been common denominators in Nigerian literature. In other words, the treatment of historical characters has enjoyed a substantial proportion of the Nigerian literary landscape. Indeed, it can further be extended that these historical materials are excerpted or culled from oral sources. Need we mention here that Nigerian literature could be categorized into modern and traditional, but it has to be emphasized at this point that this categorization is not sacrosanct; rather, it is an attempt to distinguish between written and oral literature: where written is modern, and oral is traditional. These two forms happen side by side. Necessarily, the corpus of major modern writers is derived and reinforced by traditional and cultural nuances that are indigenous to Nigeria.

The thrust of modern Nigerian literature or the thematic concern of playwrights of literary tradition radiates between two observable tendencies that have emerged with reference to the use of myth: the mythopoeic and the revolutionary imperative (Onwueme 1991: 59). Sometimes however, it may become visible to have a blend of the mythopoeic and revolutionary wherein one can deduce the overlapping of both tendencies. This is obviously reflective of the works of Rotimi and Yerima.

We may now transit to appreciating both plays in a critical manner, emphasizing how they have portrayed the historical Ovonramwen within the context of our discourse.

IV

Rotimi's *Ovonramwen Nogbaisi* (1974) begins in a rather sombre manner but he is quick to reflect in the 'Background' of the play to describe Ovonramwen as 'a man long portrayed by the biases of Colonial History in the mien of the most abominable sadist, but in actuality, "a man more sinned against that he ever sinned"' (ibid.: xi). The first time we encounter

Ovonramwen, which is just a few minutes into the play, Rotimi presents him in this manner:

> Silence.
>
> With slow dignity, Oba Ovonramwen now disengages himself from his supports, strides unrushed towards the prisoners, and stops, glowering down at them (Rotimi 1974: 4).

His entrance is actually an attempt, a fact-finding exercise, to hear from some of his rebellious chiefs why they killed one of their own — Uwangue Egiebo. His demeanour at this time is not one of someone who would shy away from intense opposition and scheming. His words do not convey any sense of fear or weakness. In fact, he bellows:

> Or who here was so blind to the obstacles which those scoundrels hurled upon my rise to the throne of Adolo, my father?
>
> [*To prisoners.*]
>
> Your brothers threw ashes in the face of a rising wind; in reply, the wind smothered them with the same ashes from their very hands. And you — you killed Uwangue Egiebo. Why? (ibid.: 4–5).

His stand at this moment is one of an uncompromising ruler, a no-nonsense leader and an earthly god, capable of sentencing one to death or taking a life — in this case, lives. Not even the pleading by other chiefs led by the Iyase and the song of placation by the women cult of Isikhien could lower the sentence by Oba Ovonramwen. Ovonramwen affirms, strongly:

> [L]et the land know this: Ovonramwen Nogbaisi is henceforth set to rule as king after the manner of his fathers before him. Some men there are who think that, by honour of years, or the power of position, or too much love for trouble, they can dull the fullness of my glow and bring darkness on the empire! But they forget ... They forget that no matter how long and stout the human neck, on top of it must always sit a head. Henceforth, a full moon's, my glow — dominant, and unopen to rivalry throughout the empire ... (ibid.: 6–7).

The language of Rotimi all this while and throughout the play gravitates between the sublime and the surreal. Rotimi skilfully articulates the story in mime, spectacle, music and we subsequently encounter another persona of Ovonramwen, a decisive king imbued with wisdom and exuding confidence in matters of state and diplomacy. See how he handles the *Ekpoma* elders and their insistence on their rejection of their *Enogie* or king:

> [*calmly*] And I say: In every land, big or small, there must be a Head. The Enogie of Ekpoma is no more, so you now bear hatred towards his son, and resist his becoming the next Enogie. What are you? Crabs? — that you seek contentment in just a belly and a back and no head? I will have no human crabs in my empire ... You will follow these Elders back to Ekpoma. When you come back here, I want it to be with the proof that the eldest son of the dead Enogie has been crowned Head of Ekpoma ... (ibid.: 11).

Before this encounter, he had cleverly warned the *Ijekiri* traders to be fair in their dealings of trade with him and the whiteman. He demands from them 20,000 zinc sheets as compensation for their 'dubious' dealings with the whiteman. A snippet of the following encounter reinforces the subtle acceptance that the Oba is not against change. In fact, the allusion to zinc and thatch (*emaha*) may be an agreement by him that change is a welcome and dynamic phenomenon.

> Ovonramwen: Look up. [The men obey.] What do you see?
> 1st Ijekiri Trader: The roof, Great One.
>
> Ovonramwen: Roof, yes, but what kind of roof?
> 2nd Ijekiri Trader: Zinc roof
> [*Traders stare at each other, baffled.*]
>
> Ovonramwen: You are both right. A small portion of my roof is the pride of the whiteman — Zinc sheets. But a wide area of it is humble, native 'emaha! A funny match is it not? (ibid.: 10).

What he cannot accept or reconcile is the dubiousness and doublespeak of the whiteman. Ovonramwen actually sees and senses:

> Gallwey.
> [*Gallwey is too perplexed to answer.*]
> Show me your hand.
> [*Gallwey extends a hand.*]
> Give me the hand.
> [*Gallwey reaches for Ovonramwen's hand.*]
>
> White One, your face shows love but does your heart? (ibid.: 19–20).

This last rhetorical question further justifies Ovonramwen's virtue, not only as a listener but as a man capable of relating to and accommodating others only if they manifest an amiable disposition.

Being an Oba requires Ovonramwen to perform spiritual duties and functions. Being an Oba also requires his participation in religious ceremonies which are for thanksgiving and propitiation of ancestors and gods. One of such ceremonies is the *Ague*, which is:

> a sober time. No burials or marriages took place, no guns were fired, and no drums or calabash rattles were played. While all Edo avoided eating new yams, only the Oba and certain chiefs, priests, and courtiers were full Ague participants. Their abstinence extended to other types of fresh produce and to sexual celibacy for up to four "Benin months". Ague-Osa's preparatory period concluded with seven days of isolation ... (Bradbury n.d., Nevins 1928; cited in Curnow 1997: 46).

The Ague ceremony was in progress when the British forcibly wanted to visit the Oba. Because the Ifa priest had instructed Ovonramwen to heed 'caution', he tactfully deals with the situation, but his over-zealous chiefs kill the white men. This precipitates a chain reaction. Kathy Curnow puts it in this manner:

> Against all advice, Acting British Consul-General James R. Philips insisted on visiting Benin City in early January 1897. The Oba had asked him to delay because of Ague, a ritual requiring his complete isolation from visitors. Although the subsequent British colonization was probably inevitable, Ague's timing and Philip's obstinacy catalyzed the chain of reactions which led to the conquest of the kingdom (1997: 46).

Subsequently, the Oba is arraigned before a Kangaroo Court convened by the British. Before the trial begins, Ovonramwen is made to pay obeisance to British imperialism which he subtly refuses. Only the placating of the chiefs who predict doom for his obstinacy makes him yield. The trial begins in earnest with the British as witness, judge and jury. From Rotimi's account, judgement was already served even before the trial began. Rotimi appropriates his creativity in this trial when he inserts Obayuwana's suicide as the main reason for Ovonramwen's reinforcement of his glowering personality:

> For me ... I know ... for me ... he died for me ... he killed himself for me ... he honoured me still ... me ... say all you can ... my people still accept me — me, as their ... their k-i-n-g! Me — me ... [*Rises proudly.*]

I am still Idugbowa, the son of Adolo ... Home-Leopard of the Benin Empire — O-v-o-n-r-a-m-w-e-n N-o-g-b-a-i-s-i!

[*Dons his crown and strides off with defiant dignity. Soldiers rush forward to intercept him, but Moor stops them.*] (Rotimi 1974: 62).

Eventually, Ovonramwen would seek the deep recesses of the forest from where he and his warriors wage a war of insurgence against the British imperialists. He is eventually captured, having been betrayed by Ezomo, his trusted war lord.

Roupell: Go on, Overami — run off.

Ovonramwen: [*surprised, but stoically calm, rises slowly from the debris*] Ovonramwen will not run!

Roupell: Why not? Are you too tired?

Ovonramwen: If the ground runs away, where will it go? Nowhere ... except ... except to pile up against as ground — which makes the previous running useless. I run no more!

Roupell: [*to soldiers*]. Tie him up!

Ovonramwen: Don't worry ... [*Stepping out*]. I shall follow you without a struggle! (ibid.: 76).

Some moments later, Ovonramwen asks Moor to deliver 'one small message' to his Queen:

Tell Queen Victoria that at last the big pot of corn has been toppled; now mother hen and her children may rejoice! (ibid.: 78).

Rotimi dramatically concludes in a deep-seated sense that the British may hold sway for the moment, but Benin remains Benin; that the Obaship may not reside in Benin but the Oba is still king; kingship as an institution never dies.

In a sense, Rotimi's portrayal of Ovonramwen, though laced with indecision on Ovonramwen's past, presents Ovonramwen as the king who was

troubled within by political unrest, and threatened from the outside by the commercial ventures of a white world, the powerful empire of Benin, like the great kingdoms of Ashanti, Opobo, and the Zulu Empire in the nineteenth century, suddenly found itself in an age of turbulence never before known to its peoples (Rotimi 1974: xi).

Ovonramwen's eventual death in 1914 restored the kingdom to its pristine past as primogeniture would once again be restored.

V

In studying Yerima's Ovonramwen, our first impression is that of a deeply subdued person:

> The Oba is in leg chains and he wears a velvet robe. He has no crown or beard on. He is seated and looks lost and agitated. There is a melancholic mood of subdued power on his brow. He has bushy hair and looks unkempt... (Yerima 1997: 19).

And when he allows Ovonramwen to speak, it is in this manner:

> *In a slow, hoarse voice he speaks*:
>
> Here I am. Seated in my glory. The once most feared, most respected. Oba Ovonramwen's son of Adolo. Here in subdued glory... Here I am posing for the white man's jeers. I ruled strong, powerful, supreme, independent and unquestioned. No one dared the leopard... but the white man. Here I am aboard the British yacht leg irons (*Raises his voice.*) Me, Oba Ovonramwen. The leopard whose eyes emit fire. The giver of life and death, Me... Pity? No, never! Regret? Never... The gods ordained this and like a sacrifice fit for the gods, I must look good and bear my new garb with dignity... (ibid.: 19).

The last sentence portrays the Oba in a clearly unfortunate no-win situation laced with a personality of extreme dejection. Inadvertently, Yerima has *ab initio* portrayed Ovonramwen as one incapable of doing or saying anything. At first sight, Ovonramwen seems to be helpless; his words are incapable of showing us anything more than a captured and pathetic king who has been forcibly dragged away by his colonizers. The humiliation presented is disturbing, since it shows a once powerful king's inability to speak in the face of his captors. One would have expected that an innocent man, like the Ovonramwen Nogbaisi even in leg chains, should speak as a Benin King.

This is so because the name 'Nogbaisi' emits fear. The historical Ovonramwen manifested awesomeness and sent shivers down the spines of his subjects but this does not remove him from the love of his people. Indeed, it would be as a result of his love for his people that he stands resolute but voluntarily retreats from continuing the six-month armed struggle against the British imperialists.

Yerima's *The Trials of Oba Ovonramwen* (ibid.) appropriates a storytelling approach but lacks the vigour to sustain the mythic presence of Oba Ovonramwen, and thus, when we get to see Ovonramwen again, it is much later when he is with Ologbose, one of his chiefs and his son-in-law. This encounter dovetails into a meta-theatrical episode, nostalgic in nature, recalling Ologbose's marriage to Ovonramwen's daughter, Evbakhavbokun. The import of this insertion, this play within a play, does not in any dramatic sense portray the Oba as a strong and serious person. Immediately after this we see Ovonramwen parleying with Obaseki, and the Ijekiri trader/bookkeeper, Omatshola, in a light-hearted manner which again suggests that he is indecisive when it comes to state matters.

All of this softly reinforces Yerima's Ovonramwen as deferring to other characters in the play, especially the prominent ones. He makes the Oba the 'other' character in the play, too flat even to take any decisive action. There is a sense of an Oba who at various times allows himself to be carried away by 'trivial' matters. We can infer from these actions that Yerima's portrayal is antithetical to the Benin worldview of how an Oba should be.

The idealized Oba in Benin cosmology and mythology is markedly distanced in Yerima's portrayal. The Ague ritual in which the Oba is partaking that necessitated later fatal chain reactions did not present the Benin's strong sense of tradition and their adherence to cultural values:

> Ovonramwen: My back scratches me, and all my friends offer to help me scratch it, they even tell me how to scratch it, but no one knows the spot. No one even ask me how the pain goes. No one! Ologbose no harm must come to the white men. I repeat no harm! Eyebokan shall take you there. Tell them that I will see them but only for some hours. No more. Bring them in the dark through *Urho' kpere* (ibid.: 38).

Ologbose and the other chiefs' acceptance of the near destruction of the age-long Ague tradition lack substantial reason. There is an attempt hereby by Yerima to excuse the Oba and justify his action. This justification finds itself on a slippery surface since some of his chiefs disregard Ovonramwen and kill the white men. The Oba's reaction to the killing further presents him as an Oba caught between two worlds unable to generate a firm personality:

> (*He rises and walks through the two lines formed by the chiefs who are standing as if in a trance*) From now on, we walk at the edge. From now on, we sleep no more. Let us now go home and await the white man's visit. The cobra ready to strike ... so we move closer for the strike. Go home all of you. Tonight, you tilt my crown for blood to flow (Yetima 1997: 47–48).

From this indication, it is obvious that Ovonramwen has resigned himself to fate. Now, let us quickly contrast this against Rotimi's Ovonramwen. When Rotimi's Ovonramwen heard about the whiteman's entrance into Benin, he reacts in this manner:

> Send trusted warriors out. If in truth it is the white men, alert our forces along the road to Ughoton. But they must not attack. Let them stand by and await further word from us. (Ologbosere leaves). Ohonsa of Akpakpava, pray bear with us. Iyase!
>
> Iyase: My Lord.
>
> Ovonramwen: Summon the council for war (Rotimi 1974: 28).

And when later he hears that the white men have been killed, Ovonramwen says:

> Children of our fathers, Benin, I fear, has this day swallowed a long pestle; now we shall have to sleep standing upright (ibid.: 37).

Even when Ovonramwen says this in a dizzily sober manner with physical support from his chiefs, his words do not convey a general sense of foreboding with resignation to Fate but that Benin should bravely prepare for whatever consequences.

So, when Yerima's Ovonramwen appears in the white man's court, we find a man, an Oba whose chiefs, faced with the death threat of a gun, submit to British imperial impunity.

> Alright, tell them to stop. Enough Bini blood has been shared already. Tell them to stop ... I will do it (Yerima 1997: 70).

What later transpires as a trial of the Oba is nothing more than a ridiculous judicial activity for which judgement has been decided by the

British beforehand. Ovonramwen's comportment in Yerima's play, and especially at this trial, reflects a Benin king who is sheepishly led to the proverbial stake — alone.

It must be reinforced within the thrust and context of this chapter that Yerima's Ovonramwen markedly draws Ovonramwen away from the imagined and imaged perceptions of the Benin people.

VI

A detour to at least three other plays within the Nigerian dramatic space should provide other (re)presentations or re-imaginations.

The first is Pedro Agbonifo-Obaseki's *Obaseki: A Historical Play* (1997) which saliently records in a theatrical manner the story of the historical Obaseki in the Ovonramwen saga. Rotimi sees Obaseki as a friend and ally to Ovonramwen but Yerima finds him a betrayer and sly conniver with the British. The inclusion of *Obaseki* in this chapter is apt since it is Obaseki who will surreptitiously fill the vacuum created by the British exile of Ovonramwen to Calabar. Agbonifo-Obaseki presents Obaseki as a man caught in the web of ambition woven by the British and the dubious connivance of some other chiefs who secretly hold a grudge against the high-handedness of Ovonramwen. Obaseki will rule Benin for 17 years from 1897–1914. However, Benin is restored to its primogeniture tradition when Ovonramwen's heir, Oko-o Aiguobasimwin, is installed as Oba Eweka II following the death of Ovonramwen.

The tale of *Obaseki* revolves around the intrigues surrounding Ovonramwen's forced exile to Calabar and his later death. At Ovonramwen's death, tradition demands that Aiguobasimwin ('You never tussle with the Oba') become Oba since he is the first son but the British wanted otherwise; they prefer Obaseki who they installed and who has been ruling for 17 years.

> Resident: Right. I definitely want Chief Obaseki crowned the Oba. More or less, you have been king over your people for about seventeen years. I find you agreeable and I am recommending you, if you so desire, and if your people support, to be king.
>
> Obaseki: Who are the people white one? Who? I cannot be king. A wall-gecko never bears a lizard. I do not find the prospect of being one attractive. It appeals to me, but I do not want it, Our Obaship is divine, and not even the white ones can change that. If you do, you will have a king with no subjects. Give the crown to he whom God has ordained (ibid.: 40).

The British insistence on changing the order is antithetical to the religious and cultural beliefs of the people. One of the most senior chiefs, Ero, reiterates:

> *Awua!* White one. Our Oba is divine, he rules all of Benin. The Gods have decreed (Agbonifo-Obaseki 1997: 4).

From these indications, we can pronounce that kingship in Benin is divine. The divine nature of the kingship corresponds to being god-king. Thus, we can maintain that the divine essence of the Benin Oba represents a deep religious and cultural symbol for the Benin people. The thinking here is that representing the Oba of Benin in literature or in any other media should reflect his superhuman personality. Any attempt otherwise would be to demean and reduce his stature in the eyes of his people and this may create serious implications or imbalance. It may also affect the perceptions of an indigenous people who value their Oba as totem.

We must add that we have also noticed other situations in history where certain chiefs or subjects have tried to counter the omnipotence of the Oba. Such actions and occurrences subtly reinforce the institution of the Oba as well as affirm his enormous glory. Take the case of Ossa Earliece's *Nekighidi* (2001) which appropriately transposes the historical Elekighiridi to the stage. Nekighidi is unhappy with Ozolua, who he feels is not the rightful heir to the throne. Nekighidi takes up arms against the Oba, Ozolua. The people of Benin see this as an affront and an insult to the exalted and sacred institution of the Obaship. Thus, at Nekighidi's fall we see the restoration and elevation of the sanctity of an indigenous people's tradition, any dent to which might create cataclysmic proportions. Earliece's attempt here indirectly questions violent agitations as negative but positively supports the pristine tradition of the Benin people and their Obaship (ibid.).

Significantly, Agbonifo-Obaseki and Earliece have employed the various performative nuances within the indigenous repertory of the Benins to substantiate their artistic mandate.

However, Evinma Ogieiriaixi's *Imaguero* (1972) largely follows the path of seeing the Oba as a Lord but who is more human even as the playwright reveals the cleverness of Oba Esigie and his domineering person(a). *Imaguero* presents, in another manner, the foxy nature of the Oba who is ultimately overwhelmed by Imaguero, wife of Oliha (a ranking chief of Esigie). Ogieiriaixi makes the Oba fundamentally crafty and cunning to a fault: Oliha boasts at council meetings that his wife, Imaguero, is ever faithful to him and Oba Esigie uses his crippled court jester to lure Imaguero to prove otherwise. Interestingly, Oliha is also married to the Oba's daughter, Amighen. This action by Oba Esigie forces Oliha to join forces with the people of Idah to wage war against Benin. Ogieiriaixi's thoughts about his mandate are apt here:

> One would like to believe that monarchs ... are by virtue of their stations in life well placed to escape being made play things by woman. *Imaguero* tells a story which makes this unlikely, and confirms the historical assertion that woman has been the cause of many wars.
>
> This is not a historical play in the sense that art is introduced into the narration of recorded story. By this I mean that I am not writing history (ibid.: 7).

From historical accounts, it would take another woman (Queen Idia, mother of Esigie) to end the war and give victory to the Benins.

VII

What we can observe from our study of these plays is the appropriation of songs and costumes in conveying in a deep sense the awesome stature of the Oba of the Benin and the rich cultural heritage of this indigenous people. To a large extent, the songs are derived from the royal court and gloriously reinforce the person(a) of the Oba. As the songs dramatically elevate the thought of the plays, they also strengthen the character of the Oba. Also, the costumes markedly show the superhuman stature of the Oba. However, what may be rather interesting in this regard would be the Oba of Benin, Oba Erediauwa's condemnation of the public presentation of Yerima's play. Adepeju Layiwola remarks:

> The records we have of Oba Ovonramwen leaving for Calabar, as captured by British photographers, is a king clad in a simple wrapper with a few neck beads on ... Even in that subdued state, the king, whom the Edo people regard as a god-king, must not be portrayed as completely defeated ... Thus, the opening scene where the Oba appears in chains might not go down well with such an audience (2005: 109).

If we properly articulate Oba Erediuwa's remark, could there have been any reason for the Benins to engage Yerima to counter Rotimi's play, especially since both of them were writing historical plays and not *history*?

We must realize that we are talking about historical plays. We understand that historical plays are not history. They are only plays that deal with history. The import here is that the characters treated in the plays are artistic and authorial representations by the playwrights to justify their social vision and thus may not necessarily be the actual persons in history. 'It may be an imaginative reconstruction of history or recreation and interpretation of the ... colonial torture and oppression by the British ... and their continued determination to resist exploitation, oppression and new forms of enslavement' (wa Thiong'o and Mugo 1976: viii). The thoughts of Thiong'o and Mugo may justify both Rotimi and Yerima's plays but fundamentally, the Benins' criticism of Rotimi's (re)imag(in)ing of Ovonramwen may subtly find a soft landing in the thoughts of the East African playwright, Ebrahim Hussein (1970: v):

> Kinjeketile — is not an historical evocation of the real man. Kinjeketile here is a creature of the imagination, and although the "two men" closely resemble one another in their actions, they are not identical. I have had to mould my character to suit artistic needs, borrowing freely from the imagination when historical facts did not suit my purpose. History should not be used as the measuring stick for this play therefore, rather, its failures or successes should be gauged against rules determining a work of art.

References

Abodunrin, Akintayo. 2010. 'Eight Writers and a Book Party'. *Next*, 7 August.
Agbonifo-Obaseki, Pedro. 1997. *Obaseki: A Historical Play*. Lagos: Design Concept and Systems.
Anon. 1996. 'Ola Rotimi rages over Ovonramwen'. *Guardian*, 3 February.
Bradbury, R. E. n.d. Unpublished Notes, University of Birmingham Library.
Chuhan, Kuljit 'Kooj'. 2010. 'The Empire of Benin and its Cultural Heritage'. Revealing Histories: Remembering Slavery. http://www.revealinghistories.org.uk/colonialism-and-the-expansion-of-empires/articles/the-empire-of-benin-and-its-cultural-heritage.html (accessed 30 August 2010).
Curnow, Kathy. 1997. 'The Art of Fasting: Benin's Ague Ceremony', *African Arts*, 30(4): 46–53, 93–94.
Earliece, Ossa. 2001. *Nekighidi*. Benin City: Bards Culture Company.
Hussein, Ebrahim N. 1970. *Kinjeketile*. Dar-es-Salaam: Oxford University Press.
Isola, Akinwumi. 1998. *Madam Tinubu: The Terror in Lagos*. Ibadan: Heinemann Educational Books.

Layiwola, Adepeju. 2005. 'Depicting Illusion as Reality: The Role of a Visual Designer in Sustaining Theatre Practice in Nigeria', *Nigerian Theatre Journal*, 8(1): 105–12.
Nevadomsky, Joseph. 1997. 'The Great Benin Centenary', *African Arts*, 30(3): 1, 4, 6, 8, 10.
Nevins, H. N. 1928. 'Intelligence Report'. Benin Division, Benin Province.
Ogieiriaixi, Evinma. 1972. *Imaguero*. Benin City: Emoton Publishing Company.
Onwueme, Tess Akaeke. 1991. 'Visions of Myth in Nigerian Drama: Femi Osofisan versus Wole Soyinka', *Canadian Journal of African Studies/Revue Canadienne des Études Africaines*, 25(1): 58–69.
Rotimi, Ola. 1974. *Ovonramwen Nogbaisi*. Benin City: Ethiope Publishing Corporation.
Salami-Agunloye, Irene Isoken. 2008. *Idia, The Warrior Queen of Benin*. Jos: Saniez Publications.
Smith, Linda Tuhiwai. 2005. 'Imperialism, History, Writing and Theory', in Gaurav Gajanan Desai and Supriya Nair (eds), *Postcolonialisms: An Anthology of Cultural Theory and Criticism*, pp. 94–115, Oxford: Berg.
wa Thiong'o, Ngũgĩ and Micere Githae Mugo. 1976. *The Trial of Dedan Kimathi*. Nairobi: East African Educational Publishers.
Yerima, Ahmed. 1997. *The Trials of Oba Ovonramwen*. Ibadan: Kraft Books.

6 'Kasapa'
Mobile Telephony and Changing Healthcare Communication in Ghana

*Perpetual Crentsil**

In the past, health messages in Ghana were mainly delivered in face-to-face interaction, for example, in doctor–patient communication or between the herbalist and a client. In villages, the traditional ruler's announcer went round shouting out health-related messages before radio, television, newspapers, posters, and billboard advertisements became more popular in cities and towns. The mobile phone has become the latest tool for delivering information on healthcare services. As communication by phone does not require literacy, mobile phones are now increasingly adopted in regions with no extensive form of communication prior to the new information technology (Tenhunen 2008: 515).

The pace of change brought about by the mobile phone as the new technology has had a significant effect on the way people live, work and share information, especially concerning health issues. The new communication systems are influencing and drawing from local social, cultural and political processes. The emerging phone technologies challenge the traditional processes of communication (Elegbeleye 2005: 193). Anthony Giddens (1990: 18–19) sees the ability to foster relationships with absent others as a central facet of modernity's globalizing dynamism. To him, in conditions of modernity locales are penetrated and shaped in terms of social influences quite distant from those locales. In this sense, as Sirpa Tenhunen (2008: 516) has pointed out, the mobile phone's ability to influence sociality's place-based conditions of existence and changing forms makes it anthropologically interesting.

---

* The research on which this paper is based is part of the research project 'Mobile Telephony, Gender and Development in Africa, India, and Bangladesh', funded by the Academy of Finland.

This chapter both draws from and contributes to the understanding of the role of cultural meanings in technology studies. In examining healthcare communication with mobile phones, it also explores anthropological understandings of agency and social practice. Technological determinism is the notion that technological development shapes society but is not influenced by it (Mackay and Gillespie 1992). The change of terminology from 'the use' or 'the adoption of technology' to 'domestication' or 'the appropriation of technology' exemplifies the theoretical shifts and cultural underpinnings in social studies of technology. 'Appropriation' generally refers to how artefacts are used, but also to how they are adapted in use and subsequently interpreted (ibid.). Rich Ling (2004), who has researched the appropriation of mobile phones in Norway, represents the mainstream in social studies of technology in moving beyond both technological and social determinism and employing the domestication approach. This approach centres on questions of how technology is adapted to everyday life and how everyday life, in turn, is adapted to technology.

Mobile phones provide numerous forms of social, political and economic empowerment to people. Studies have focused on economic and social aspects, on questions of poverty reduction, women's increased earnings, empowerment, and development. The Grameen Bank project in Bangladesh has been lending women money to obtain mobile phones since 1997 and providing 70 million people with access to phone networks (Tenhunen 2008). There is now a huge interest in the domestication of mobile phone technology in everyday life and cultural appropriation of such technology. For example, Heather Horst and Daniel Miller (2005) focus on social aspects of mobile phone communication in kinship and social relations in Jamaica.

In Africa, much of the studies of mobile phone use have been dominated by the appropriation of such a device in economic and social concerns (see, for instance, Elegbeleye 2005; Hahn and Kibora 2008; Overå 2006). Studies of mobile phone communication for health issues are mainly survey-based and project evaluations. The Cell-Life project, a non-governmental organization (NGO) in South Africa, concentrates on mobile phones for communicating information on HIV/AIDS and has attracted studies into how it uses mobile technologies as a mass information channel (see Tolly and Alexander 2009). There seems to be no rigorous study done on the use of mobile phones for disseminating healthcare information in Ghana.

My approach here in outlining the appropriation of mobile phones for dissemination of healthcare information in Ghana is similar to that of Horst and Miller (2005) and Hans Peter Hahn and Ludovic Kibora (2008), in that I prefer to frame my discussion using the domestication paradigm. The paradigm makes it possible to grasp how society shapes technology and how, conversely, technologies can have effects on the organization of society. As Tenhunen (2008: 517) has pointed out, this approach has, however, been developed to understand the acquiring of technology in Western societies, how users position technology while at the same time making it useful and meaningful. Consequently, the approach has its roots in Western epistemologies (such as the concept of domesticity itself). A similar approach that has gained considerable attention for the analysis of the social aspects of technology use is the social construction of technology (SCOT) theory, a dimension of the social shaping of technology that highlights the active role of the user in shaping and defining a technology's meaning (Klein and Kleinman 2002). An aspect of the SCOT theory suggests that technology design can produce different outcomes depending on social circumstances of development, and I find it appropriate for looking at the ways mobile phones are put to use and its social embeddedness in health information delivery. In this endeavour, I follow scholars such as Bryan Pfaffenberger (1988) who argue that technology and society cannot be separated. Such symbolic fields as gender, power, status, knowledge, and health constitute values and enduring meaning structures that cannot be ignored or overlooked.

I start off with the pattern of communication in Ghana and trace the changing forms (both indigenous and modern), an endeavour that heightens the need to historicize communication processes and devices from pre-colonial and colonial past to the post-colonial situation in order to take account of change and continuity. The ethnographic description relates mobile phones in health information delivery to other communication patterns, the social and cultural system that prevailed before the introduction of mobile phones, and ongoing processes of change. I have observed and interviewed several mobile phone owners, medical personnel, HIV/AIDS counsellors, patients, care givers, and mobile phone operators. Interviews were conducted in the form of informal conversations (in English and in local languages), lasting from a few minutes to one or two hours. In addition to these materials, I draw from my prior research in Ghana. As a Ghanaian and having conducted several periods of fieldwork in the country since 1999 (see Crentsil 2001; 2007), I already have an understanding of forms of healthcare (and social impacts of HIV/AIDS in Ghana), and the place of mobile phone technologies in the communicative ecology.

Indigenous Communication Systems and Health Messages in Ghana

Many forms of indigenous communication for disseminating health information prevailed in villages and towns in pre-colonial Ghana. Traditional communication devices and processes allowed health information or messages to be disseminated in oral, face-to-face (person-to-person) interaction. For example, the herbalist delivered messages of health to his or her client in face-to-face relations. The divine healer who became possessed and acquired information from the gods or spirits of the land through clairvoyance, was himself or herself a device for health information dissemination to individuals and/or to people of the community. Communication over long distances (from one village to another, for instance), necessitated sending an emissary.

Another form of communication was the traditional ruler's messenger who went round each ward of the village or town beating the *Dawuro* (gong-gong — a metallic device) and shouted out health messages from the traditional ruler on personal cleanliness, cleaning of surroundings, etc. The *Akyeame*, or 'meta-linguists', are important for performing 'multiple roles as councillors, counsellors, advisors, and information officers for kings/chiefs' (Adjaye 2008: 237). As the principal holder of power and authority in the society before the arrival of British colonizers, the traditional ruler (locally known as the chief or king) was the custodian of the society. It was the chief's duty to ensure a 'clean' and healthy society. Individual cleanliness was treated as personal and was left to people's own initiatives. People also listened to their lineage elders. Even so, the chief sometimes reminded people to be clean by instructing his messenger to beat the gong-gong and send the message around.

Social cleanliness was arguably the sole responsibility of the traditional ruler and it was seen to occur on two levels — in the spiritual and the physical worlds. Oral accounts about health and healing indicate that traditional healers such as diviners and fetish priests were important in disseminating health information to clients and adepts (Twumasi 1975). In the spiritual realm, it was the chief's duty to ensure that he and his ritual specialist(s) engaged in sacred performances to cleanse the society from witch activities. This was done fairly low-key without much to do with gong-gong beating. The fetish priest was a vessel for communication; he received information or solutions to problems from the gods and ancestral spirits through spirit possession and clairvoyance, and revealed these to the traditional ruler for onward transmission to the people of the community. Concerning physical cleanliness, however, things were done outwardly with gong-gong beating. For instance, according to an elderly woman I interviewed in 2003 (Crentsil 2007: 93) during outbreaks of epidemics (*oguekro* — literally, destroyer of towns) such as smallpox, the chief and his fetish priest led in preventive rites. A day was set aside and a gong-gong was beaten at the instructions of the chief to inform people of the community to dump their garbage on stalks of the plantain tree erected at the outskirts of the village and burned to cleanse the society of the epidemic.

The gong-gong is not the only device for communication. There is a wide range of multi-channelled, multi-media indigenous, non-verbal communication; people 'talk' with the cloth they wear, the way they dance and even with the way they play the drum (Yankah 2007). The talking drum, like the gong-gong, is an important indigenous communicative device used even today to communicate news, for calls or invitations to functions, produce music and dances of insinuations, and pleas, especially at funerals as an important social event. Storytelling, proverbs, drama, and traditional theatre form another range of indigenous communication systems or devices for sending health messages and other forms of information. The advantage of the indigenous communication systems is that they are small-group oriented, often geared to small rural audiences. They tend to be inclusive, dialogical, and interactive, eliciting audience participation (Adjaye 2008: 238).

Colonial Media and Social Change

One area that underwent modernization during British colonialism in Ghana was communication, and Kwesi Yankah (2007) claims there was an attempt to supplant or pluralize the legacy of indigenous languages and the face-to-face communication highly cherished in Ghana. The advent of colonialism in mid-1800s saw the springing up of electronic media. The telegraph was first established in Ghana (then Gold Coast) in 1881 (Allotey and Akorli, 1999, cited in Overå 2006). This made it possible for the landline (fixed telephone) to be established and thus it became an important communication device over long distances.

Even though 70 per cent of Ghanaians live in rural areas, over 80 per cent of all telephone lines were in urban areas, out of which 53.6 per cent were in Accra (Overå 2006: 1304). Postal services were also established as part of the communication process and telegrams were one of the important ways of communicating health messages. Such was the popularity of telegram messaging that a common joke exists about a funny telegram message — 'Seriously Kwesimintsim, hospital the wife' — which was sent to a man whose wife was seriously ill at a hospital at Kwesimintsim in a town in south-western Ghana.

Newspapers, radio, and later fixed telephones (landlines) and television were major sources of information on health. Various audio-visual aids such as the cinema became popular, and information vans with loudspeakers mounted by the Information Services Department (ISD) and the Red Cross (and later the Red Crescent) also came into existence after independence in 1957. Initially, the main function of newspapers, radio and television was to disseminate news and information about the political front to the public. K. A. B. Jones-Quartey (1975: xxi) points out that the press, mainly the newspapers, was undoubtedly the main instrument of agitation for social and political change at the disposal of the aroused leaders. The *Gold Coast Times*, one of the earliest newspapers in Ghana, paid close attention to burning social issues, and more importantly, the political scene (ibid.). Later, the mass media became a big tool for communicating health and development messages; but they supplemented and never supplanted the indigenous communication systems, especially the beating of gong-gong by the king's messenger. Colonialism caused many transformations about the chief's power; however, chieftaincy has survived and persisted in the face of post-colonial central state politics because the authority of the traditional ruler could never be obliterated. Today, people learn about health messages and are mobilized to participate in activities through radio broadcasts and information vans with loudspeakers, followed by gong-gong beating by the chief's messenger. This signifies the interface between tradition and modernity.

Although the mass media had and still have enormous potential for spreading health messages owing to their wide circulation, they still face peculiar problems. Rural audiences are 'non participatory' in terms of their use of mass media, and three factors may account for this. First, the newspapers and television exist mostly in the cities and towns and many rural dwellers have no access to them. Second, many people are not Western-educated and literate enough to read the newspapers or listen to television programmes that are mainly in English. Third, even the radio, which has a better penetration into rural areas, has its own problems; there are millions of listeners, but not everyone listens to most radio programmes. People still want to be told about particular information in face-to-face interaction. As Judith Sanders et al. (1991) have pointed out, even today with written communication and literacy, oral social interaction is highly prized in Ghana, just as it used to be before the introduction of Western education and mass media in the country.

Other types of media for disseminating health information that evolved after colonialism include seminars, symposiums, workshops, and face-to-face counselling sessions at hospitals. When hospitals were established during colonial rule, informal communication was mainly through doctor–patient interaction. State-owned or big private hospitals and those established by the missions (Christian churches and also by the Ahmadiyya variant of Islam) usually organize seminars, workshops or symposiums on health issues. The churches, including the recently fast-growing faith (spiritual church) healers, have become an important channel of health information dissemination through preaching to their adherents.

Drama and films are another channel for disseminating information and educating people on health issues through entertainment. 'Edutainment' is a word coined to indicate the use of entertainment to educate through drama, films, storytelling, etc. The Nollywood and Ghallywood film industries, which are Nigerian and Ghanaian versions respectively of America's Hollywood, are fast becoming 'edutainment' channels.

Latest Technologies in Ghana: The Internet and the Mobile Phone

The internet and the mobile telephone have become the two latest tools of communication in Ghana. As in many parts of Africa, the growth of the internet and mobile phones in Ghana has been exponential. In 1995, the Ghana Posts and Telecommunications Corporation (PTC) was privatized as Ghana Telecom (GT). In that same year, Ghana became the second African nation to have full internet connectivity (Overå 2006: 1304). From the mid-1980s, there was an enormous increase in the number of landline subscriptions within a very short time. Ragnhild Overå (2006: 1305), quoting GT figures of 2003, says the number of landlines reached 1.3 per 100 persons in 2003 — well above the average in sub-Saharan Africa. During 1997–99, 5,000 payphones were installed

Mobile Telephony and Changing Healthcare Communication in Ghana 113

throughout the country — quite a change from only 25 payphones which were all in Accra (Segbefia 2000: 83, cited in Overå 2006). A large number of small telephone businesses were set up, locally known as 'communication centres' (or Comm Centre), which provided public access telephone services in Ghana. Public access to telephones improved substantially; however, the physical environment and lack of infrastructure in rural areas still hamper a wider coverage.

The internet has emerged on the Ghanaian scene at a time when the unequal distribution of resources in Ghana's weak economy has engendered the rise of a commercial class which dominates its use. Although penetration is still considered to be low, in 2010 there were 1.2 million internet subscribers in a population of about 24 million. This was a huge leap from only 323 subscribers in March 1996 (Opoku-Dapaah 2009). Internet operates mostly in major cities and towns and has played an important role in the economic and social development of the country. It has enhanced instant communication among Ghanaians on one hand, and between Ghanaians and people around the globe on the other. The internet has indeed seen a rise in employment and infrastructural expansion (ibid.).

The phenomenal growth of mobile phones has been the most important change in communication devices. When multiple licences for mobile networks were awarded in 1992, Millicom, a subsidiary of Millicom International UK/Luxembourg, had started its operations in 1991 as the first mobile phone network operator and by 1998, it had over 22,000 subscribers. Mobitel (1992), Celltel (1993), Spacefon (1996), and Onetouch (the mobile phone arm of Ghana Telecom in year 2000) followed suit. By 2003, Mobitel, Celltel, Spacefon, and Onetouch together had 600,000 subscribers (Overå 2006). Today, there are more than 16 million mobile phone subscribers in a population of about 24 million.[1] Six mobile phone companies existed in Ghana in 2010: Kasapa, Vodafone, MTN, Tigo, Zain, and Glo (yet to start operations).

At a time when urban Ghana is fast shifting towards the use of mobile phones and surfing the internet, most parts of rural Ghana still have neither electricity nor landlines. The mobile phone is currently a near-universal phenomenon in its use and has the potential to be the most used device because, unlike landline telephone networks, mobile phones are not centralized and at a fixed spot. The fact that mobile phones can

---

[1] http://www.researchandmarkets.com/research/3c6117/ghana_telecommunic (accessed 30 November 2010).

be used even if an individual can neither write nor has an office, or is on the move most of the time, has made them the most appropriate communication technology (Overå 2006: 1302).

And since the majority of Ghanaians are not Western-educated or are semi-literates, verbal communication remains the most important mode of information exchange. The belief that the information and communication technologies (ICTs), especially the internet and the mobile phone, can engender socio-cultural, economic and political change has resulted in a shift in development discourse. In effect, the notion that new information technologies would change the poor quality of lives to improved ones with hope has been rife. This is the instrumentalist fashion in which these new technologies are being presented as a panacea for change and development. Yet, other social processes influence social change and this is true with mobile phone usage in Ghana.

Mobile Phones in Ghana: Ownership, Access and Affordability

By the first half of 2010, there were 16 million cellular phone subscribers in Ghana, one of the highest growths in Africa.[2] When the government deregulated its telecommunications in 1994 (one of the first in Africa), there were only eight mobile phone subscribers per 100 inhabitants (ibid.). There are many ways for users to get access to mobile phones. The devices can be purchased by the user, and those who can afford it sometimes acquire two or three phones in order to reach through on different networks (cf. ibid.: 1305). Mobile phones can also be received as gifts from relatives and friends; they are common gifts from abroad. Interestingly, while the phone received as a gift is valued because it saves the receiver purchasing it, it nevertheless creates the cost of keeping the connection active (cf. Slater 2005).

In Europe, the standard way of paying for a mobile phone service is on the basis of the potential customer signing a contract with a telephone company. In Ghana, mobile phone service providers mainly use a pre-payment system which involves buying cards that provide phone time, counted in units with the lowest rate at 1 Ghana cedi (US$ 0.10 in 2010) and allows a user to talk for some minutes. Customers can use the pre-paid card as they like over a period of weeks during which they keep

---

[2] http://www.researchandmarkests.com/research/3c6117/ghana_telecommunic (accessed 30 November 2010).

control over the usage. Pre-paid cards are widely available in local stores and from roadside sales agents of the various telephone companies in Ghana. Once the pre-paid 'outgoing call budget', as Warren A. Kaplan (2006) calls it, has been depleted, the phone can still be used but only for receiving incoming calls until its expiry date.

Mobile phones can also be shared. There are multiple dimensions to mobile phone sharing, which refers to allowing another person to use one's mobile phone for any communication purpose. Araba Sey (2009: 67) delineates two kinds of sharing — non-commercial (interpersonal) and commercial (payphone) sharing of handsets and airtime. Borrowing a subscriber's phone to receive calls on relatives' and friends' devices is fairly common (ibid.: 71). Those who do not have their own phones and cannot arrange sharing with relatives or friends can easily rent from roadside operators in kiosks, booths and even under trees and large umbrellas. In 2010, the basic charge was 20 Ghana pesewas (or US $0.10) per minute. Mobile phone call charges used to be very high in early 2000 — 3,800 cedis (US$ 0.44) per minute for a call to a mobile phone and 600 cedis (US$ 0.07) per minute to a fixed telephone (Ghana Telecom 2003, cited in Overå 2006). Such charges have reduced dramatically due to competition among the various phone companies, which has also prompted firms to be more concerned with the quality of their service delivery. In early 2010, the National Communication Authority (NCA) issued a directive for the free registration of all mobile phone Subscriber Identity Module (SIM) cards. On the whole, the average Ghanaians' low purchasing power still hampers access to and ownership of mobile phones.

Penetration of Mobile Phones in Ghana

Mobile phones in particular have relatively increased much more rapidly in number than fixed-line telephones and are much more widely used than the internet in many places in Ghana (ibid.: 1303). A few years after the deregulation of telecommunications, the demand for mobile phone subscription grew far beyond what the then four service provider companies were able to provide (ibid.: 1305). Between 2002 and 2005, networks were often congested, making it impossible to make phone calls. People had to climb trees or walk some 100 metres away from the vicinity to have a good reception. Even today, network problems can be frequent.

The NCA had been established by the Parliamentary Act, 1996 as a central regulatory body to regulate the telecommunications sector, to promote a stable operating environment for all, fair competition and efficiency (Addy-Nayo 2001). The main task of the NCA includes the licensing and regulation of telecommunications system operators and assigning or allocating systems frequency. Mobile telephony has indeed penetrated into different areas of Ghanaian society. All the operators cover most parts of Ghana — cities, towns, villages, and even hamlets.

Mobile phone coverage and fixed line networks largely reflect population density and they follow the main roads in Ghana — there is an urban bias in access to telecommunications, and only 69 of Ghana's 110 district capitals had fixed lines in 1999 (Segbefia 2000: 77, cited in Overå 2006). Although mobile phone coverage is constantly improving, many rural areas are still without any telecommunication facility (Overå 2006: 1305).

Patterns of Mobile Phone Usage

The mobile phone in Ghana is being put to a variety of uses; that is, they are being used for different ends. Like other ICTs, mobile technology facilitates the dispersion of transnational capital. People can now store and transfer their monies electronically such as in MTN's 'mobile money' and Zain's 'Zap', effectively turning a mobile phone into an ATM machine (Kutsoati 2010). Farmers and traders are able to check market prices on agricultural products and goods (Overå 2006), and others can check their bank account balance. A tool for social networking, the mobile phone is also being used for educating and giving key information on health and social issues. For example, through mPedigree the problem of fake medicines will be addressed because mobile phones can be used to check the authenticity of a drug by sending a free Short Message Service (SMS) message to a central number. Students of the Basic Education Certificate Examination (BECE) are given a code with which they can check their placements from their mobile phones (*Ghana Business News* 2010).

Connectivity, however, remains restricted mainly to economic responsibility and sociality. Users make requests for money from family members, boyfriends and ordinary friends. There are also countless stories of mobile phones being used as bait, especially by young women before they agree to an intimate relationship with a man, and for monitoring husbands and boyfriends. Connectivity to wireless technology has linked Ghanaian youth in particular to the information revolution and globalization. Mobile phones have made it possible for Ghanaians to increasingly participate in interactive radio programmes by calling to air their concerns or desires. By facilitating popular participation in the discussion of national or local issues, mobile phones have contributed to the institutionalization of democracy in Ghana (Opoku-Dapaah 2009).

Communication by mobile phones is mostly through voice calls, voice mails and SMS texts. In the voice calls, the caller makes a call to the receiver and talks straight away with him or her. However, the vast majority of mobile phone use in Ghana takes the form of 'flashing', in which the caller dials a contact and hangs up after one or two rings (Slater 2005: 770). The receiver of such a 'call' interprets it as a plea to call back. But the use of internet and SMS in Ghana has become a very popular means of communication in recent years. Spacefon (now MTN) was the first to introduce the use of SMS into the mobile phone industry. Although voice calls are arguably the easiest and frequently used mode of communication, SMS, which initially took time to catch on, has become one of the regularly used modes of mobile communication, fuelled by many factors that include the pricing policies, pre-paid and SMS roaming services (Addy-Nayo 2001). There are two types of SMS services — SMS-MO (Short Messaging Service-Mobile Originating) and SMS-MT (Short Messaging Services-Mobile Terminating). SMS-MO enables the customer to send short messages to other Global System for Mobile Communications (GSM) users. It can be used anywhere in the world where the service provider has a roaming agreement with a network that supports SMS. The SMS is charged per message sent. SMS-MT, on the other hand, enables the user to receive short messages of up to 160 characters in length and it is provided free of charge to all subscribers (ibid.).

Some mobile phone language has crept into certain aspects of Ghanaian life. The phrase 'out of coverage area' has now been appropriated in other domains; at a wedding, the master of ceremonies (MC) told friends of the bride that henceforth 'she is out of coverage area', meaning that she was not available for any other love relationship (see Yankah 2007). SMS texts are also being used as greeting cards with inspirational words: 'May all who seek your downfall get network problem, may the Devil be out of coverage area in your life, may problems that come your way be put on Call divert, may any call of death be your missed call, may your incoming calls be victory and prosperity. Stay Blessed! Happy New Year'.

But mobile phones are being put to negative uses too. As one writer in a newspaper column article wrote, armed robbers have used the mobile phone to exchange information for their evil operations many times (*Daily Graphic* 2010a). Also, people often receive recycled text messages or even anonymous phone calls with scary details, warnings or prompting. While some invariably turn out to be false, sometimes others jerk people into action with fear and despair (*Daily Graphic* 2010b). In the early hours of 18 January 2010, someone created a huge nationwide panic with what was claimed to be a text message that there was going to be an earthquake in Ghana. The source of that hoax message was never known. Three months later in March 2010 the government, through the NCA, issued the directive for all SIM cards to be registered from 1 July 2010 to 30 June 2011 or be blocked out of use.

Many possibilities from a variety of formal and informal arrangements have been offered through access to wireless telephony. Mobile phones in Ghana are mainly for communicating (and social networking) but are being used on a wide scale for educating, monitoring election results and ensuring democratic rule, commerce, and communicating health information.

Mobile Phones and Healthcare Communication

Mobile phones are facilitating the spread of healthcare services to many people who are looking for health information and intervention in order to eliminate or at least ameliorate their suffering and reduce their financial burden (Kaplan 2006). In Ghana, patients usually call directly to health counsellors and talk straight away or they 'flash' the personnel and wait to be called back or send SMS (text) messages. With respect to aspects of healthcare counselling for HIV and other chronic diseases, some patients may prefer text messaging but the potential to create problems is enormous. The ease of mobile phones could spell doom when a text message is opened accidentally and viewed inadvertently by the wrong person because of theft. This is likely to increase exposure instead of secrecy about a person's HIV status, for example, and may result in shame and stigmatization.

Nevertheless, one area in which mobile phone is making inroads in health communication is HIV/AIDS and related health issues. Through voice calls or text messages, patients were able to ask about the next counselling date, their treatment regimens, CD4 levels, etc. Trust is easily built, and stigma and shame may somewhat be reduced or avoided. Talking about personal health on a mobile phone may look easier than in face-to-face encounters. One HIV-positive woman is said to have readily given her mobile phone number instead of being visited at home for fear of her mother-in-law becoming aware of her HIV status and instigating divorce by the patient's husband. This is a key gender aspect of HIV/AIDS and the notion that women suffer worse repercussions than men.

Mobile phones enable appointment dates to be scheduled and rescheduled to ensure people keep attending counselling and treatment sessions. During a visit to a hospital in a town in the eastern region of Ghana, the HIV counsellor received a call on his mobile phone from one of the 'clients' [HIV patients]. I reproduce below only what the HIV Counsellor (H. C.) said since I could not hear what the caller was saying:

H. C.: Hello... Oh, hi. Yes, today [it was a Thursday] is counselling day.

Caller: --

H. C.: You are not coming... Oh, you want to know if you need to come today?

Caller: --

H. C.: Okay, what was your CD4 load count from the last session [two weeks ago]?

Caller: --

H. C.: Okay, it is quite good; if it is above 380 and you still have some of the medication from the last supplies, then you don't need to travel all the way to this place.

Caller: --

H. C.: Okay, thank you too and see you at the next session. Bye-bye.

Messaging and calls allow health workers to set up dates with patients, know their clinical health, psychological, moral, and financial conditions at any point in time. Patients' adherence to medication can be monitored. Clients who absent themselves can be tracked down and restored to reduce the level of absenteeism.

Another area is maternal health. Mobile applications are being used to assist community health workers feed patients' medical records on post-natal health into a computer database. Affordable handsets were provided for pregnant women in the Ashanti and upper east regions of Ghana to enable them to receive answers to common ante- and post-natal questions as well as reminders about check-ups and vaccinations.

This reduced maternal deaths — there were none in 2008 — which is important because according to United Nations (UN) figures, 560 out of 100,000 women in Ghana die each year during childbirth or from pregnancy complications (IRIN 2009).

The healthcare system and other social services are severely limited in Ghana. Researchers and health authorities acknowledge lapses in the provision of healthcare in the country; there is an uneven distribution with many rural areas completely lacking medical services (Bonsi 2000). This is obviously one of the major contributing factors to patients' failure to report again after an HIV-positive test; other factors include shame, secrecy and stigmatization by neighbours. Many patients who test positive do not attend follow-up treatment. In most cases, they cannot even be traced to their homes because they give false addresses (Crentsil 2007). Where health services are inaccessible, it is significant that mobile phones are available for people to get health information without transport cost and waste of time over long distances at great risk. Mobile phones may ensure privacy and protection from stigmatization.

Benefits and Constraints

It is now possible for an HIV patient to simply phone in and discuss his or her CD4 load (viral count). SMS texting is rapidly growing in Ghana. It costs less than voice messaging and it can reach people whose phones are switched off (because it can reach them as soon as they switch on the phone). As Kaplan (2006) has pointed out, SMS messaging is quite silent, which means that messages can be sent and received in places where it may not be practical to have a conversation. Another advantage of mobile phone in healthcare communication with respect to adherence to medicine in HIV/AIDS and other chronic illness is its ability to create a dyadic interaction between patient and health or care provider(s) in a short time. Trust is easily built.

Whereas access to internet services may be enjoyed mostly by the affluent and urban educated segments of Ghanaian society, mobile phone users need not be literate. Mobile phones address problems of cost of transport and risk of travelling by patients and health workers. Since they are widespread, quite cheap due to calling cards that make pay-as-you-go calls possible (Overä 2006) and because they reduce travelling time over long distances, mobile phones have become a general purpose technology and reach a wide spectrum of society. This makes important Bryan Pfaffenberger's (1988: 241) point that 'any technology should be seen as a system, not just of tools, but also of related social behaviours and techniques'. When one examines the 'impact' of a technology on society, therefore, one is obliged to examine the impact of the technology's embedded social behaviours and meanings (ibid.).

Since the World Health Organization (WHO) and Joint United Nations Programme on HIV/AIDS (UNAIDS 2005) have concluded that the mass media are one of the best channels for responding to the AIDS pandemic, there is an imperative to look at how devices such as the mobile phone can be harnessed to this end. Nevertheless, there are still daunting challenges such as poor access to some people, illiteracy and inability to read messages. A pertinent question is how language in SMS messaging will be addressed for those who cannot read and understand English.

Moreover, while there is the problem of poor network coverage, lack of electricity in remote areas to recharge batteries poses equally daunting challenges. Some people go hungry so that they can pay for mobile usage, and others must walk three to seven kilometres two or three times per week in order to recharge their mobile batteries. Despite all this, people still purchase mobile telephones, and so consensus on how we should measure 'benefits' is changing. A study of domestication and cultural appropriation of mobile phones in Burkina Faso (Hahn and Kibora 2008) found that they are regarded as devices to communicate with but also cause economic problems and may affect social relations through uneven disposition. All the same, the widespread usage of mobile phones (and over a wide area) is helping to promote health education and care.

Conclusions

Technological determinism defends the idea that technology leads to social change and that technological change is an independent factor that impacts on society from outside that society. The SCOT theory's consideration of social elements in looking at technological change is important and Kaplan's observation (2006) that living in resource-poor conditions is not a barrier to use of mobile phones for several cultural and economic reasons seems to apply to Ghana. Many people in rural areas have access to mobile phones and often use them. In this sense, the social value of a mobile phone is high even in resource-poor areas (Hahn and Kibora 2008). Mobile phones are easier for people with lower level of skills in technology or literacy than those needed for using a computer or the internet.

So, *Kasapa* (good talk) refers to one of the mobile phone operators in Ghana but demonstrates how mobile phones are being put to 'good use' (*pa*) in social, political, economic, and healthcare communication. Mobile phones are tools not merely for talking (*kasa*) but are being put to new uses, especially in the healthcare sector. The revolution in mobile phone communication is producing a massive surge in the development of electronic information, education, entertainment, political participation, and financial and healthcare services. This will even be further enhanced with the development path into the 3G (Third Generation) or smart phone and wireless technologies. 3G and other new mobile phone technologies have massive potential for communication and data transmission that will improve lives and enhance development. Mobile phone's new technology is providing many people with access to information that might improve the quality of their health and lives.

The course of mobile phone usage for healthcare communication is still unpredictable since artefacts are interpretatively flexible and may be put to different usages. It still cannot be imagined what new areas of health information dissemination can be evolved through mobile phones. One can only hope that areas such as graphics on HIV/AIDS and texts in local languages will soon evolve. Hence, a focus on the great promise for mobile phones to alleviate health-related problems becomes salient.

References

Addy-Nayo, Chris. 2001. '3G Mobile Policy: The Case of Ghana'. International Telecommunication Union. http://www.itu.int/3g (accessed 29 November 2010).

Adjaye, Joseph K. 2008. 'The Technology of the Human Voices: Oral Systems of Information Dissemination and Retrieval among the Akan of Ghana', *The International Information and Library Review*, 40(4): 236–42.

Allotey, Francis K. and Felix K. Akorli. 1999. 'Ghana', in Eli M. Naom (ed.), *Telecommunications in Africa*, pp. 178–92. Oxford: Oxford University Press.

Bonsi, S. Kofi. 2000. 'Health Care', in Kodzo Gavua (ed.), *A Handbook of Eweland: The Northern Ewes in Ghana*, vol. II, pp. 200–12. Accra: Woeli Publishing Services.

Crentsil, Perpetual. 2001. 'Informal Communication and Health-Seeking Behaviours in Ghana'. Master's Thesis, University of Helsinki.

Crentsil, Perpetual. 2007. 'Death, Ancestors and HIV/AIDS among the Akan of Ghana'. PhD Dissertation, Research Series in Anthropology 10, University of Helsinki.
Daily Graphic. 2010a. 'Mad Men, Ghosts And Spies', 22 January.
———. 2010b. 'The Catastrophe That Never Was', 27 January.
Elegbeleye, O. S. 2005. 'Prevalent Use of Global System of Mobile Phone (GSM) for Communication in Nigeria: A Breakthrough in Interactional Enhancement or a Drawback?', *Nordic Journal of African Studies*, 14(2): 193–207.
Giddens, Anthony. 1990. *The Consequences of Modernity*. Cambridge: Polity Press.
Ghana Business News. 2010. 'GES Introduces SMS Short Code for 2010 BECE Placement', 20 August. http://www.ghanabusinessnews.com (accessed 30 November 2010).
Hahn, Hans Peter and Ludovic Kibora. 2008. 'The Domestication of the Mobile Phone: Oral Society and New ICT in Burkina Faso', *Journal of Modern African Studies*, 46(1): 87–109.
Horst, Heather and Daniel Miller. 2005. 'From Kinship to Link-up: Cell Phones and Social Networking in Jamaica', *Current Anthropology*, 46(5): 755–78.
IRIN. 2009. 'Ghana: Cell Phones Cut Maternal Deaths', IRIN: Humanitarian News and Analysis Service of the UN Office for the Coordination of Humanitarian Affairs, 1 December. http://www.irinnews.org/PrintReport.aspx?ReportID=87261 (accessed 5 December 2010).
Joint United Nations Programme on HIV/AIDS (UNAIDS). 2005. 'Getting the Message Across: The Mass Media and the Response to AIDS'. UNAIDS Best Practice Collection. http://whqlibdoc.who.int/unaids/2005/9291734659_eng.pdf (accessed 15 November 2010).
Jones-Quartey, K. A. B. 1975. *History, Politics and Early Press in Ghana: The Fictions and the Facts*. Accra/Tema: Ghana Publishing Corporation.
Kaplan, Warren A. 2006. 'Can the Ubiquitous Power of Mobile Phones be used to Improve Health Outcomes in Developing Countries?', *Globalization and Health*, 2(9): 1–14.
Klein, Hans K. and Daniel Lee Kleinman. 2002. 'The Social Construction of Technology: Structural Considerations', *Science, Technology and Human Values*, 27(1): 28–52.
Kutsoati, Edward. 2010. "SIM Card Registration: A Chance to Formalize an Informal Economy, Digitally'. http://www.afrik-news.com/article18447.html (accessed 6 December 2010).
Ling, Rich. 2004. *The Mobile Connection: The Cell Phone's Impact on Society*. San Francisco: Morgan Kaufman.
Mackay, Hughie and Gareth Gillespie. 1992. 'Extending the Social Shaping of Technology Approach: Ideology and Appropriation', *Social Studies of Science*, 22(4): 685–716.

Opoku-Dapaah, Edward. 2009. 'Internet Cafes in Ghana: Economic Benefits and Social Costs'. Presentation prepared for the 7th International Conference on Open Access, University of Ghana, Legon, Royal Swedish Institute of Technology (KTH), Stockholm and Ghana Academic and Research Network (GARNET), 2–3 November, Accra. 'http://www.wideopenaccess.net/files/OA2009-Opoku-Dapaah.slides.ppt (accessed 10 November 2010).

Overå, Ragnhild. 2006. 'Networks, Distance, and Trust: Telecommunications Development and Changing Trading Practices in Ghana', *World Development*, 34(7): 1301–15.

Pfaffenberger, Bryan. 1988. 'Fetishised Objects and Human Nature: Towards an Anthropology of Technology', *Man*, 23(2): 236–52. http://www.jstor.org/stable/2802804 (accessed 23 January 2013).

Sanders, Judith A., Richard L. Wiseman and S. Irene Matz. 1991. 'Uncertainty Reduction in Acquaintance Relationships in Ghana and the United States', in Stella Ting-Toomey and Felipe Korzeny (eds), *International and Intercultural Communication Annual*, vol. XV, pp. 79–98. Newbury, California: Sage Publications.

Segbefia, Alexander Yao. 2000. 'The Potential of Telecommunications for Energy Savings in Transportation in Ghana: The Dynamics of Substituting Transport of Persons with Telecommunications in the Greater Accra Region'. MPhil Thesis, University of Ghana, Legon.

Sey, Araba. 2009. 'Exploring Mobile Phone-Sharing Practices in Ghana', *Info*, 11(2): 66–78.

Slater, Don. 2005. Comment on 'From Kinship to Link-up: Cell Phones and Social Networking in Jamaica', by Heather Horst and Daniel Miller, *Current Anthropology*, 46(5): 755–78.

Tenhunen, Sirpa. 2008. 'Mobile Technology in the Village: ICTs, Culture, and Social Logistics in India', *Journal of the Royal Anthropological Institute*, 14(3): 515–34.

Tolly, Katherine de and Helen Alexander. 2009. 'Innovative Use of Cellphone Technology for HIV/AIDS Behaviour Change Communications: 3 Pilot Projects'. http://www.w3.org/2008/10/MW4D_WS/papers/kdetolly.pdf (accessed 10 November 2010).

Twumasi, Patrick. 1975. *Medical Systems in Ghana: A Study in Medical Sociology*. Tema: Ghana Publishing Corporation.

Yankah, Kwesi. 2007. 'Mobile Phones and our Cultural Values', *Ghanaian Times*, 9 February, pp. 26–27.

7 Discourse of Resistance and Protest in Meitei Folklore

Leisangthem Gitarani Devi

Cultural history of any nation, region or community tells of politics of certain kinds. And the cultural history of Manipur tells of the politics of religion. Since the 17th century, the trajectory of religious developments in Manipur has not been without conflicts and contestations. To understand the politics of religion and the ensuing resistance against religious forces, a cultural reading of select Meitei folklores has been attempted in this paper.[1] Various forms of folklore have been selected as the premises of this study because folklore is considered the reservoir of culture. Moreover, when folklore is regarded as 'autobiographical ethnography, a people's own description of themselves'[2] by Alan Dundes (quoted in Bronner 2007: 53), what could provide a deeper insight into the cultural politics of the Meiteis than their own folklore!

Meitei folklore tells of creation and continuity, gods and goddesses, kings and nobles, human activity and relationships, battles and conquests, farming and fishing, trade and commerce, and more. As is the general characteristic of folklore, Meitei folktales and other forms of folklore are simple and unassuming. And yet beneath the guise of simple narratives lies the hint of resistance and protest. In this chapter, I wish to talk about bipolar resistance: resistance to the outside culture brought

---

[1] The Meitei are the predominant ethnic community of Manipur. They mostly inhabit the valley, while other ethnic communities mostly dwell in the surrounding hills. Other major ethnic communities are the Naga, Kuki, Kabui, etc.

[2] In the overwhelming work of elucidating and analyzing the conceptions and theories of folklore by Alan Dundes, Simon J. Bronner recalls Dundes's observation about folklore being 'autobiographical ethnography' — texts that provide a view from the inside and enable an expression of 'what people think in their own words and actions ... expresses what they might not be able to in everyday conversation' (Bronner 2007: 1).

upon by the Hinduization of Meitei society on the one hand, and resistance to pre-Hindu culture deemed profane by new Brahminical values on the other hand.

Despite the overwhelming Hindu culture prevalent since the 18th century, traditional Meitei culture has persisted even to this day because of its elasticity and accommodating nature.[3] Though much of its pristine nature is lost, yet it could adapt to the rapidly-changing cultural environment. Therefore, Meitei culture today is an amalgamation of both traditional Meitei values and Brahmanical Hindu ideology. But I state this, however, not at the risk of a happy assumption that the cultural history of the Meiteis has not seen any trace of antipathy and power struggle. There indeed has been a constant power struggle between Sanamahi followers[4] and Hindu believers since the time Hinduism was embraced. While on the one hand Sanamahi Meiteis are striving to revive the pre-Hindu socio-religious culture of the Meiteis and construct a pre-Hindu identity, Hindu Meiteis on the other remain rooted to a conservative Hindu lifestyle and values. This has ensued in an uncomfortable and hostile relationship between staunch followers of both the faiths.

During the pre-colonial days, the king himself was the champion of Hinduism and any form of opposition was met with stern hands. It was especially during the reign of Meetingu Pamheiba (re-named according to Hindu tradition as Maharaj Garibniwaz) that Hinduism was imposed on the common people *en masse*. They were not only made to convert to Hinduism but were also forced to adopt the Brahminical Hindu way of life. Saroj Nalini Arambam Parratt in *The Court Chronicle of the Kings of Manipur* recounts how beef eaters were penalized and publicly

---

[3] Khuraijam Bijoykumar Singh agrees with Clifford Geertz that a cultural group can adopt a new religion only if it has the capacity to do so. For, Geertz was of the belief that religion is but an 'orderly system of symbols' (quoted in Singh 2005: 91). Some prominent examples of switching symbols include: re-naming of Manipur as Kangleipak; tracing the origin of the Meiteis to Pandava Prince Arjuna and Manipuri Princess Chitrangada; alignment of the seven *salais* (clans) with Hindu gotras; re-naming of deities and shrines according to the Hindu pantheon, identification of Meitei festivals with Hindu festivals, etc (ibid.: 91–100).

[4] 'Sanamahism' is a term given to traditional Meitei religion and social beliefs. Sanamahism is derived from the term 'Sanamahi', an important Meitei deity. Adherents of Sanamahism are known as Sanamahi Meitei. Sanamahi is considered the creator of the world according to Meitei myth and religion (See Laisram 2009: 101).

humiliated upon the order of Maharaj Garibniwaz. Strict measures were implemented to ensure a Hindu lifestyle (Parratt 2005: 131). Undoubtedly, the process of Hinduization of Meitei society was not without its challenges. Sporadic incidents of protest were recorded here and there. However, as the king had the ultimate authority in those days, Hinduism was successfully introduced as the official religion of the state in the 18th century, even as people covertly resisted.

The socio-religious life of the Meiteis was greatly re-configured with Hindu protagonists taking over the reign of the Meitei society. New modes of eating and dressing were adopted to suit the Brahminical Hindu culture. Bengali script replaced the existing Meitei script; observance of traditional rites and rituals was either restricted or conducted by the migrant Brahmins; deities and places of worship were re-named to suit the Hindu pantheon and mythology; religion-based discrimination became the order of the day. In fact, the greatest single impact of Hinduization, which is deeply felt even to this day, is the divide among ethnic communities created by discriminating policies. Ardent supporters of Hinduism constructed narratives to separate the valley people from the hill people. The orthodox and discriminating custom introduced by Hindu agents denominated the hill dwellers as an unclean and uncultured section of society. Thus, a sense of socio-cultural divide was instilled between the hill people and the valley people despite the age-old belief in a brotherly relationship between them.

Various myths, legends and historical studies support the common origin of the hill people and the valley people. However, an equal number of counter myths and folk renderings that support and reiterate the notion that the valley dwellers and the hill tribes do not share a common ancestry also exist. While the pro-Hindu school of thought traces the origin of the Meiteis to Babrubahan, son of Princess Chitrangada of Manipur, and Arjuna, the Pandava Prince, many ethnographers and scholars believe in the theory that Meiteis are descendants of the hill tribes. Thomas Callan Hodson, former political agent in Manipur and ethnographer, in *The Meitheis* considered the narratives tracing the origin of Meiteis to Hindu mythology to be 'tainted by the influence of Hinduism' (1908: 6). Hodson supported the theory that the Meiteis are descendants of the surrounding hill tribes and the similarity of language and custom affords him enough reason to do so. As a counteractive measure, pro-Hindu myths, superstitions, customs, and beliefs embodied narratives of cultural superiority over that of the hill tribes. Hindu ideology introduced a new lifestyle and set of beliefs that pushed the non-Hindu followers to the periphery. The process by which Hindu culture was introduced was replete with challenges. The opinion is that Hinduism was rather forcibly adopted in the land.[5] Such a violent conversion of the Meiteis into Hinduism created feelings of dissent among people. Coercive measures by the monarch nevertheless suppressed any acts of defiance. This feeling of un-belongingness and strangeness towards the outside culture, however, found oblique expression in various forms of folklore.

Simon J. Bronner in *The Meaning of Folklore: The Analytical Essays of Alan Dundes* (2007) affirms Alan Dundes's belief that folklore is a form of sublimation. It is folklore that gives an outlet to things one cannot express overtly otherwise. Folkloric methods, through the garb of metaphors and symbols, give expression to rebellious ideologies. In fact, folklore is considered an escape-mechanism. Folklore is not a perishing relic, as it is often misunderstood to be, but rather continuity and it is created anew for the very reason that it offers a 'socially sanctioned outlet for the expression of taboo and anxiety provoking behaviour' (ibid.: 3).

In Meitei culture, the repressed desire of upsetting the equation of Hindu followers and believers of indigenous faith is allegorized through the use of conflict between animals or between animals and human beings. Very often animals like cats, jackals, monkeys, bats, crows, and rats are used to symbolize proselytizing Hindu Brahmins or the *mayangs*[6] in Manipur. They are often represented as predatory and destructive in nature. Conveniently, folklore has enabled the people of Manipur to rewrite their shared experience of frustration and anxieties. It offers them the opportunity to exact revenge for the injustices inflicted upon them by Hindu agents. An illustration of upsetting the power relations between non-Meiteis (the migrant Brahmins) and Meiteis can be seen in the game-rhyme given below:

Rat-a-tat,
Cut is your tail
Rollicking around the edge of barrel

---

[5] Parratt hypothesizes that Maharaja Garibniwaz fined his own brother for having protested against the introduction of Hindu idols and Hindu custom (2005: 143).

[6] In the present day context, the term *mayang* refers to non-Manipuris, especially people from mainland India. However, during pre-colonial and colonial times, *mayang* referred to Brahmin migrants from the west of Manipur (Sylhet and Cachar) (see Singh 2005: 19).

Here comes the sparrow!
Phadrang [*sound of fluttering wings*].[7]

This game-rhyme, in the guise of animal metaphors, could be read as the enactment of the imagined ousting of the migrant invaders. If read within the context of the power relations between non-Manipuris (migrant Brahmins and traders) and Meiteis, the animal metaphors used in the texts are employed to give vent to one's resentments towards non-Manipuris. In the text, the rat symbolizes the migrants from the west of Manipur, while the sparrow is the emissary of freedom. The underlying meaning of this game-rhyme could be construed as a protest against the hoarding of opportunities by migrant non-Manipuris.[8]

Even though their origins can neither be traced nor dated, folktales reflect various contextual, contemporary situations, be they social, political or economic. Franz Boas in *General Anthropology* claims that if indeed 'myths are built on the experiences of everyday life, we may expect that the dominant cultural interests are reflected in them. The incidents mirror the life of the people and their occupations, and social life may in part be reconstructed from these tales' (Boas and Benedict 1938: 622). The game-rhyme obliquely condemns the domination of administrative, economic and even religious activities by non-Manipuris during the pre-colonial and colonial times. It reflects the angst felt by the natives in the face of the threat assumed by migrants who had become important players in every aspect of Meitei society. Even though the game-rhyme may not necessarily reflect a particular historical instance, yet it bespeaks of the common problems faced by the people of Manipur.

An instance of the increase in domination by the migrants from the west is recounted in *The Court Chronicle of the Kings of Manipur* (Parratt 2005). There was a gradual usurping of the role of the native religious officers by the migrant astrologers, and tension ensued during the 18th century when *Konoks* or migrant astrologers were given predominance over *Maichous* or Meitei scholars in the socio-religious life of the Meiteis. The arrival of *Konoks* threatened the position of *Maichous*, who not only

---

[7] This is a game-rhyme popular among children. The translation is by the author and no recorded source or transcription of the same could be found. The current transcription of the rhyme is based upon oral rendition of the same.

[8] A similar interpretation of the game rhyme, given by Moirangthem Kirti Singh, goes: 'Oh Rat, thy tail is cut/One who plays on the edge of the jar/The cock is coming, Phadrang' (1993: 57).

functioned as astrologers but also as advisers to the king (Parratt 2005: 122). Even the role of officiating at religious ceremonies of local deities was handed over to migrant Brahmins, thus pushing the *Maibis* and *Maibas*[9] to the background. In fact, some Brahmins even had the privilege of being the royal adviser.

Apart from religious and political space, another area of migrant domination was the 'market'. Improvement of roads and transportation facilities highly facilitated cross-regional movement and many migrant traders started establishments in the Imphal valley. In the due course of time they started monopolizing trade and commerce in the valley and Manipuri traders felt deprived of their space. A particularly noted historical incident that corroborates the feeling of antipathy expressed in the game-rhyme quoted earlier is the Second Women's War in Manipur, also known as the Nupi Lan, in 1939 (Yambem 1976: 326–27). Among the events leading to the Second Women's War was predominantly the monopoly of trade by the migrant traders. In the late 1890s, the rice export trade was jointly in the hands of both native and migrant Marwari traders. The introduction of vehicular transportation, however, changed the character of the rice export trade and only the rich immigrant Marwari traders could afford to continue it. The dramatic increase in the export of rice coupled with the failure of the crop harvest in the early 18th century resulted in an artificially-induced famine in Manipur, and hence the outbreak of the Nupi Lan on 13 December 1939. The events leading to the Nupi Lan are an example of how the migrants not only pervaded the economic sector but also usurped the day-to-day livelihood of the Manipuris with their ingenious market skills. Such incidents and situations posed a threat to the natives, thus resulting in a xenophobic attitude. The 'rat' in the game-rhyme can thus be interpreted as a shape given to the dark insecurities and threats felt by the natives.

A close reading of the game-rhyme reveals the suppressed antipathy towards the rat, which is here portrayed as an invader and opportunist. Not only is the choice of animal significant but the comment on its body is political as well. The rat's tail is half cut, thus suggesting an attitude of strangeness towards the physical and racial features of the migrants. The colour of the rat is symbolic as it is an indirect comment upon the colour of the non-Manipuris. Hence, through the use of the 'rat', a cultural

---

[9] *Maiba* and *Maibi* were considered the emissaries of God. It is they who communicated the message of God to common people. They functioned not only as religious priests but also as healers in Meitei society.

difference is projected stressing the near impossible assimilation between the two parties and their cultures. We can also focus upon the movement of the rat in general. Rats are known for their scurrying nature. Therefore, the 'rat rollicking around the edge of the barrel'[10] might be scurrying in search of food. The barrel represents opportunity; and the rat gambolling around it suggests the monopolization of opportunities.

In continuation with this context, another folk text that corroborates the stereotype of the non-Manipuris is the saying *Mayang Taath*. This phrase would roughly translate as 'the wiliness of the *Mayangs*'. This folk saying is employed frequently in everyday context. It is used in a derogatory context when someone wants to point out the craftiness of another person. This folk text serves the purpose of heightening the sense of cultural and temperamental divide between the Manipuris and non-Manipuris. Such a feeling of a cultural divide has been well-contained in collective memory. Another similar example of covert challenge to the invading culture is as follows:

> Se Se Seboti
> Bhavani, son of Laishram,
> Let us have a duel
> To see who defeats who
> will pluck you like a reed
> will snap you like a lotus stem
> Let girls challenge each other with their dress
> Let boys challenge each other with their *khudei*[11]
> Swaa! (Devi 1974: 62–63)

This game-rhyme is popular among boys and girls and tests endurance and strength. It requires young boys and girls to sit in a squatting position. Then they have to stretch both the left leg and the right leg one after another and jump at the same time. The person who can jump

---

[10] This is an excerpt from a game-rhyme popular among children and the translation is by the author. No recorded source or transcription of the same could be found and the current transcription of the rhyme is based upon oral rendition of the same.

[11] *Khudei* is a short woven cloth worn by men around the waist and covers the knee. It is now basically a household dress. After the adoption of Hinduism in Manipur, the dhoti (a long white woven cloth worn by men around the waist and covering till the ankle) was the dress for men, worn on public and formal occasions.

in this position for a long time emerges as the winner. Manipuri men were known for their valour and physical prowess in olden times. Sports like wrestling, coconut races, horse polo, boat races, and martial arts are popular forms of sports demonstrating one's physical prowess. The prehistorical days of Manipur were characterized by constant wars and feuds that demanded that Manipuri men be physically energetic. Thus, Meitei folklore is also replete with glorification of the valour and strength of men.[12]

The game above is a challenge to test the might of the non-Manipuris. The underlying politics of this game is to instil a sense of being a misfit among the migrant settlers in Manipur. A common stereotype constructed about the non-Manipuris is that they are chicken-hearted and weak in nature. Through this game, the otherwise unexpressed grudges and antipathy towards the migrant settlers are given an outlet. Here again, the *mayangs* are challenged to a real and manly duel through which their strength could be tested. The politics of power relations between the non-Manipuris and the Manipuris are reconfigured in this game-rhyme. With a sense of hatred and disgust, the speaker in the game challenges his opponent to pluck the root of the migrant settler as that of a reed, and to snap his body as he would snap a lotus stem. Such strong imagery of hostility embodies the Meitei folks' unconscious desire to annihilate the spreading monopoly and cultural imperialism of the migrants.

The last two lines of the game-rhyme express the cultural difference in the mode of dressing. With the adoption of Hinduism in the 18th century and the immigration of non-Manipuris thereafter, food habits and dressing modes came to be largely influenced by Hindu culture. Meat eating was prohibited and the dhoti was introduced as the official dress. This game-rhyme embodies the resistance against new modes of life imposed upon them under the patronage of Hindu kings.

However, the collective effort of fighting against what seemed a cultural misfit is counteracted by narratives of Hindu supporters among the Meiteis. The royal family, and Brahmin society in Manipur particularly, left no stone unturned to de-familiarize the Meiteis with their indigenous culture. With the intensification of Brahmanical control over the Meitei society, the concepts of 'sacred' and 'profane' were introduced during

---

[12] Singh offers a similar interpretation of the game rhyme in his book, however the translation varies: 'Let us measure strength and/See who can win/Let us root out it as in the case of Kauna [reed]/Let us break it with a jerk/as in the case of Lotus fibre . . .' (1993: 56).

Discourse of Resistance and Protest in Meitei Folklore 133

colonial times. Khuraijam Bijoykumar Singh points out how such a concept has led to a divisive society which had otherwise been egalitarian:

> The Hinduisation of the Meiteis not only isolated the hill tribes as polluted group but is also a process of creating an 'ideological territorialization' of the geography into two binary opposite categories of 'sacred' (valley) and 'profane' (hills) (2005: 10).

With this 'ideological territorialization' was ushered in the politics of 'pure' and 'polluted', 'sacred' and 'profane'. The newly-formed Hindu society at that time was keen to segregate things and people as 'pure' and 'polluted'. This custom is deeply-rooted even today. The firm belief in the concept of 'pure' and 'polluted' is visible in the adage 'a grain of leftover rice pollutes when it touches a clean bowl of rice'. The existence of such folk sayings counteracts the narratives of pre-Hindu culture. It shows the control of Hindu values over the everyday life of the Meiteis. Hindu favourers among the Meiteis found a new status when they were instilled with the myth that they are the descendents of the Pandava Prince Arjuna. This theory of descent as a corollary affected the age-old ties with surrounding hill tribes. With the concept of 'pure' and 'polluted', the hill tribes were gradually segregated into the 'polluted' or 'profane' ones. This led to discrimination against the tribes, thus ensuing in an environment of hostility between the Meiteis and the hill people even to this day.

The feeling of cultural indifference and hostility among the ethnic communities was also heightened by prevalent stereotypes and notions constructed around the hill communities. Existing folktales like 'Kabui Keioiba' ('A Kabui Turned Tiger') deepened the sense of divide between the Meiteis and the hill people. It abuses the simplicity of the hill people and treats them as ignorant and dangerous people. Kabui is one of the largest ethnic communities in Manipur which has a very close affinity with the Meiteis. They share similar food habits, rituals and religious beliefs. Apart from their traditional deities, the Kabuis also worship Sanamahi — the prime, household deity of the Meiteis (Das 1989: 155). However, Hindu customs that emphasized a cultural superiority over traditional customs of the Meiteis as well as other ethnic groups upset the status quo. Therefore, Singh sees pro-Hindu narratives that denigrate people of other communities as a 'cultural project of Meiteis to discourage the age old practice of matrimonial alliance between the Meiteis and hill tribes that they had once upon a time before Hinduisation of the Meiteis' (2005: 25).

'Kabui Keioiba' is the story of a well-built, strong Kabui man who knows how to shape shift between tiger and man. One day, however, he failed to get back to human form. Thereafter, he was compelled to remain half-man, half-tiger. He becomes a predatory creature and terrorizes the neighbourhood. One day he abducts a young girl named Thabaton to make her his wife. The girl is the only sister of seven brothers. The brothers learnt of the abduction of their sister in their absence. Even though they were seven in number, they knew they were no match for the mighty Kabui tiger-man. So, they used their wits to free their sister from his clutch. Eventually the Kabui tiger-man met his end at the hands of his wife. He fell into the conspiracy led by his wife.

In this folktale, the seven brothers could be understood as the seven *salais* or clans — the grouping of families that serves as the backbone of the Meitei community. Earlier Manipur was inhabited by independent clans and there was constant wrestling for power among them. It was with the domination of the Meitei clan that a confederacy of seven clans was formed and thus came to be designated by the term 'Meetei' or 'Meitei' (Parratt 2005: 3–4). Since the time of the first historical king of Manipur, Meetingu Pakhangba, there is a record of matrimonial alliance between people of different groups. Throughout the royal chronicle of Manipur there are instances of inter-region or inter-community marriages. And therefore marriage between Meiteis and the hill tribes was common during the pre-Hindu period in Manipur. However, cultural changes brought upon by Hinduism discouraged matrimonial alliances between Hindu Meiteis and non-Hindu hill people. During the heyday of Hinduism, any matrimonial alliance between a hill person and a Meitei was not tolerated and such people were ostracized by the community. So deeply rooted is the sense of cultural superiority instilled by Hindu custom that even to this day an alliance between a Hindu Meitei and a hill person is not acceptable without certain reservations.

In this folktale, the Meitei woman would have been the connecting link between the Meiteis and the other ethnic community. Locating this text within the context of strife between Hindu Meiteis and non-Hindu ethnic communities, the act of abduction could be read as an act of coveting a transferrable name, object or property. Thus, the violent retrieval attempted by the brothers of the woman. In another rendition of the same story, the woman burns down the house of the Kabui tiger killing her child born of the Kabui and escapes from his clutches. What could be understood from this violent act of burning her child and the house is the aversion to mixing of blood and raising a lineage of 'impure' blood.

That is why the child, who would have become a symbol of polluted Hindu blood, is annihilated.

The portrayal of the Kabui man as mighty, ignorant and predatory is also significant. It is a common stereotype in Manipur to portray a tribal man as strong, adamant, hostile, and ignorant. A saying in Manipuri goes *haoringjen, nairingjen*, which refers to the will-power and death-defying adamant nature of the hill people. In the kingly days, *hao* was a term used to denominate commoners who are not of royal birth (ibid.: 35). In the present-day context, *hao* refers to the hill people; and the cultural baggage brought upon by Hinduism has now reduced the term to a more derogatory level. This folktale, according to Singh, has served as a 'social fencing' to bar sexual and marital relationships between Meiteis and the hill tribes (2005: 137–38).

Today, despite the presence of socially and culturally insidious narratives and the age-old Hindu tradition characterizing the Meitei society, there is a movement for the revival of pre-Hindu culture and identity of the Meiteis. Since the third decade of the 20th century, there has been a steadfast endeavour to bring to the fore traditional and indigenous cultural practices. It is an ongoing movement to free the Meitei culture of Hindu elements, if not to uproot them entirely. In fact any attempt to entirely annihilate Hindu custom from the Meitei society would indeed be a very violent one, for Hindu ways of life have become deeply ingrained in the lives of the Meiteis. Some of the Hindu customs such as prefixing the Sanskrit honorific title *Shri* or even cremating the dead body by fire has been in practice since 1713 and 1724 respectively during Maharaj Garibniwaz's reign (Parratt 2005: 123, 133). Such Hindu customs, among others, remain inseparably intertwined with the indigenous practices even to this day.

The seed for the revivalist movement, known as the Sanamahi Movement, was sown when Naoria Phullo, popularly known as Laininghal, established a religious and social organization known as Apokpa Marup in 1930. The aim of this organization was to revive indigenous Meitei religion and culture. The revivalists stood thick in their principles even through humiliations and ostracism (Sairem 1991: 118). What they preached to people was not hatred of Hinduism per se but renunciation of the adopted religion and with it the revival of pre-Hindu ideological beliefs. Apart from reviving the past religion and culture of the Meiteis, the revivalists also strove to regain the cordial relationship that was punctured by the discriminating attitude of Brahminical ideology.

Besides renunciation of certain Hindu rites and ceremonies, the revivalists reclaimed places of worship and deities that had been forcibly re-named and associated with Hinduism. In this collective endeavour of reviving Sanamahi tradition, folklore has played its part by being the reservoir of shared frustration, anxieties and antipathy; in a nutshell, a reservoir of collective, cultural memory. This collective memory which has been transmitted through narratives and activities has contained the natives' resistance against the overwhelming force of Hindu culture. It is this collective memory of resistance transmitted across time that has rekindled the revival of pre-Hindu values and practices. The covert resistance continuing since time immemorial through the conduit of folklore has today been translated into a major revival movement that seeks to re-establish not only the pre-Hindu Meitei identity but also restore the indigenous value system.

One historical event that has been imprinted on to the collective memory is the burning of the *Puyas*, traditional Meitei manuscripts on varied subjects. The *Puyas* are considered sacred by the Meiteis and more than 120 *Puyas* were burnt under the instruction of Santi Das Gosai, the religious guru of the then king Maharaj Garibniwaz (1709–48) (Sairem 1991: 122). This incident exterminated almost all written records of the Meitei language, myths and culture. Undoubtedly, the Meiteis have suffered heavy losses — from script to culture, to ideological values. Today, what comprises the Meitei society is the coexistence of both Hindu custom and Sanamahi tradition. But there are not many people who have renounced Hinduism and reverted to indigenous faith. It is this equation that is challenged by Sanamahi revivalists. The incident of *Puya* burning is today commemorated annually by Sanamahi revivalists to remind people of the atrocities done to them by the protagonists of Hinduism. This collective memory of blasphemy committed to indigenous faith and the losses incurred due to Hindu agents is re-kindled every year as a strategy to convince the Meiteis to renounce their adopted faith.

The revivalist movement today has taken a radical turn. The revivalists, in their endeavour to steer their movement to mass success, committed the same atrocious act of burning numerous Hindu books to avenge themselves for the *Puya* burning (ibid.: 122–23). Insurgent groups who are ardent supporters of Sanamahi revivalism have banned Hindi channels, films and songs in Manipur to uproot the influence of *mayang* culture in the everyday lives of the people. People are persuaded to give up their Hindu names and embrace Meitei names. In fact, Meitei films have started the trend of naming the characters using Meitei nomenclature.

Hindu festivals like Saraswati Puja, Rath Yatra, Durga Puja, Karthikeyan Puja, Deepawali, and others that used to be observed on a grand scale are celebrated in a low tone today. Those mentioned here are some of the measures adopted by the Sanamahi revivalists to resuscitate the traditional Meitei culture in its pristine form. Even as the Sanamahi revival movement continues through various courses — from ideological to activism, from students' participation to the role of civil societies — folk tradition remains a private affair in reinforcing the cultural difference between the Meiteis and the non-Manipuris at an individual level, and a public affair in maintaining a continuity of the collective memory of oppression and resistance at the community level. In this sense, folklore plays a pivotal role in the revivalist movement for it is through revival of folk traditions, rituals and the rendition of folk sayings that the people are reminded of their past glory and identity.

References

Boas, Franz and Ruth Benedict (eds). 1938. *General Anthropology*. New York: D. C. Heath and Company.

Bronner, Simon J (ed.). 2007. *The Meaning of Folklore: The Analytical Essays of Alan Dundes*. Logan: Utah State University Press.

Das, Shiva Tosh. 1989. *Life Style, Indian Tribes: Locational Practice*, vol. II. New Delhi: Gian Publishing House.

Devi, Rajkumari Tamphasana. 1974. *Manipuri Lok Sahitya*. Manipur: Rajkumari Tamphasana Devi.

Hodson, Thomas Callan. 1908. *The Meitheis*. Delhi: Low Price Publications.

Laisram, Rena. 2009. *Early Meitei History: Religion Society and the Manipuri Puyas*. New Delhi: Akansha Publishing House.

Parratt, Saroj Nalini Arambam. 2005. *The Court Chronicle of the Kings of Manipur: The Cheitharon Kumpapa*. London and New York: Routledge.

Premchand, Nongthombam (ed.). 2008. 'Manipuri Folklore: Towards a Performance Approach', *Indian Folklife*, 30: 1–23.

Rodriguez, Jeanette and Ted Fortier. 2007. *Cultural Memory: Resistance, Faith, and Identity*. Austin: University of Texas Press.

Sairem, Nilabir. 1991. 'The Revivalist Movement of Sanamahism', in Naorem Sanajaoba (ed.), *Manipur Past and Present: The Ordeals and Heritage of a Civilisation*, vol. II, pp. 109–26. New Delhi: Mittal Publications.

Singh, Khuraijam Bijoykumar. 2005. 'Sanamahi Movement among the Meiteis of Manipur: A Sociological Study of a Socio-Religious Movement'. PhD Dissertation, Jawaharlal Nehru University, New Delhi.

Singh, Moirangthem Kirti. 1993. *Folk Culture of Manipur*. New Delhi: Manas Publications.

Yambem, Sanamani. 1976. 'Nupi Lan: Manipur Women's Agitation, 1939', *Economic and Political Weekly*, 11(8): 325–31.

8 Sovereign Ontologies in Australia and Aotearoa–New Zealand

Indigenous Responses to Asylum Seekers, Refugees and Overstayers

Emma Cox

In October 2009, the then Australian Prime Minister Kevin Rudd telephoned the Indonesian President Susilo Bambang Yudhoyono to request that a boat carrying 255 Sri Lankan Tamils, heading for Australia's Christmas Island, be intercepted and escorted to the port of Merak on the north-western tip of Java. The Indonesians obliged, but a six-month long stand-off ensued when the asylum seekers refused to disembark at Merak until they had been assured passage to Australia. At a refugee support rally in the city of Melbourne on 1 May 2010, Aboriginal Australian activists responded to the stand-off by producing Original Nation Passports for the Merak asylum seekers. This was a defiant rejoinder to the Australian government's decision a fortnight prior to freeze all Afghan and Sri Lankan refugee claims until further notice. Aboriginal activist Robbie Thorpe, flanked by other activists publicly signing stacks of passports outside the neo-classical facade of Melbourne's Trades Hall, announced: 'we want to make it clear that the Aboriginal people, the true sovereigns of this land, are offering them a passport to enter into our territorial waters, and our land', adding, 'we're the colonised refugees' (Juice Media 2010). A few months earlier, in June 2009, the New Zealand Police had charged Maori activist Gerrard Otimi with deception causing loss and giving immigration advice without a licence after he sold visas to around 100 Pacific Island (mainly Samoan) immigrants desperate to remain in Aotearoa–New Zealand after the expiry of their work visas. Otimi charged NZ$500 per visa, which consisted of a certificate and passport sticker stating that the holder was a 'whangaied' (adopted) member of Otimi's *hapu* (a sub-tribal grouping) and had permission to remain.

Aboriginal and Maori jurisdictions over and responsibilities toward newcomers are negotiated under the spotlight of mainstream cultural and political life as well as in fringe activism. In February 2008, an Aboriginal right to welcome was recognized at the opening of the Australian parliament, when Prime Minister Rudd delivered a speech acknowledging 'traditional' owners of the land after being presented with a message stick during a 'Welcome to Country' ceremony performed by Aboriginal people.[1] Similar rituals and statements of acknowledgement of Aboriginal custodians are relatively common at events and gatherings in Australia, but they had never been part of the opening of federal parliament until 2008. In Aotearoa–New Zealand, a *powhiri* — a welcome ceremony involving a warrior challenge, songs, dance, the laying of a peace offering, and a *hongi* (pressing of noses and exchange of *ha*, or life breath) — is customarily performed for *manuhiri* (guests). On the occasion that *manuhiri* are international dignitaries the *powhiri* becomes a high profile, mediatized event — a signifier of Aotearoa–New Zealand's unique cultural 'heritage'. Since the 1980s, *powhiri* has been part of the opening protocols of parliament in the officially bicultural (Maori and Pakeha),[2] bilingual (Maori and English) nation. What seems to have emerged in both national contexts is a performative, civic acknowledgement of indigenous sovereign territoriality that inheres in the right to welcome, or presumably reject, the newcomer.

Considered side-by-side, indigenous activism via the production of passports or visas (a reterritorialization of valorised documents of state power) and indigenous welcome protocols and ceremonies (which publicly enact the idea of an unextinguished indigenous territorial authority) suggest something of the schizoid cultural conditions under which Aboriginal and Maori status claims exist in Australia and Aotearoa–New Zealand today. The juxtaposition draws attention, ultimately, to contested ontologies of sovereignty. In Aotearoa–New Zealand, the Treaty of Waitangi (1840) between several Maori tribes and the British Crown,

---

[1] The following morning, as the first item of Parliamentary business, Rudd delivered a landmark formal apology to the Aboriginal Stolen Generations.

[2] A 'Pakeha' is a New Zealander of European ethnic origins, although the term is occasionally used to refer to any non-Maori person.

while beset by historical violations and ongoing dispute over key terms relating to the relinquishment of Maori sovereignty,[3] represents at least a structural basis upon which Maori self-determination or self-governance may be negotiated. In Australia, where British sovereignty was founded in the absence of any such treaty, the symbolism of the 'Welcome to Country' does not cohere with recognizable historical or political reality. This underpinned a recent flurry of debate in Australia over the welcome ritual and acknowledgement of traditional owners, prompted by the conservative opposition leader Tony Abbott's suggestion in March 2010 that both are often 'out-of-place tokenism' (quoted in Maiden 2010: 1). The main fault-line of the debate traced the role of symbolic thought and action in organizing human affairs generally, and specifically, the issue of whether Australians should be explicitly reminded of the unceded, unresolved sovereignty of Aboriginal people — in other words, of unfinished business.

In this chapter, I aim to examine what happens when we take indigenous rights and responsibilities regarding newcomers/strangers as an analytical framework, or point of departure, for understanding transnational positionalities (asylum seekers, refugees and visa overstayers) and local positionalities (Aboriginal Australians and Maori), and indeed, for perceiving the synthesis of the two. I trace recent contexts of engagement, including protest, activism, social contact, and performance between Aboriginal Australians and Maori, and asylum seekers, refugees and overstayers. These represent certain contingent spaces for belonging (and less frequently, non-belonging) for people who are barred from both political and imagined national community. They also offer a picture of indigeneity as a complex and ambivalent identification, explicating some of the conflicted allegiances aroused by the citizen–non-citizen dichotomy, while foregrounding indigenous authority and knowledge as lived practice, and perhaps, alternative sovereignty.

The term 'alternative sovereignty' is a hazy one, affixing to juridico-political, philosophical and affective meanings that can be contiguous or at odds; to be sure, the term runs into difficulty in its implication of

---

[3] The key dispute surrounding the Treaty of Waitangi (1840) relates to the words used to represent the concept of sovereignty. The Treaty guarantees that Maori tribes retain *tino rangatiratanga*, which translates to 'self-determination', or arguably, 'sovereignty'. The Maori version of the Treaty states that *kawanatanga*, or governorship, is to be ceded to the British Crown, while in the English version, the term 'sovereignty' is used. For in-depth analysis, see Orange (1987).

a paradoxical condition, that is, two absolute authorities co-existing in one political community. With reference to Australia, Aileen Moreton-Robinson argues that an understanding of indigenous rights (central among which is recognition of prior possession or sovereignty) must take into account the ways in which its inverse, 'White possession', functions as a 'regime of truth' (2006: 389); she makes the point, via Michel Foucault, that 'rights should not be understood as the establishment of legitimacy but rather the method by which subjugation is carried out' (ibid.: 390). One way of understanding these methods is to look at the ways in which indigenous peoples influence, or do not influence, national juridico-political mechanisms. For the present purposes, this requires that geo-culturally specific attention be paid to what indigenous rights and practices might look like.

Whatever form of Aboriginal sovereignty Welcome to Country rituals and activist statements signify or articulate, its structural difference from executive, legislative and judicial powers — what Moreton-Robinson terms 'patriarchal white sovereignty' (Moreton-Robinson 2007: 87) — is vast in a nation that has only in the most recent election seen the first Aboriginal person elected to the Federal House of Representatives. Aboriginal political participation at the state and federal level is low. Moreton-Robinson pinpoints the ambivalence of ceremonial recognition in Australia, arguing that it is 'simultaneously a reminder and a denial of the existence of Indigenous sovereignty. The reminder is evidenced by the presence of Indigenous bodies, but its denial is contained in the words "traditional lands", which transports ownership back into the past not the continuing present' (ibid.: 98). The gap between material sovereignty and what might be called affective sovereignty is conspicuous.

In Aotearoa–New Zealand, Maori political representation in the national parliament has been ensured since 1867 via the Maori electorates (originally numbering four, and currently seven) that exist in addition to the general electorates. Maori voters may choose to register for either the general electoral roll or the Maori roll. Maori politicians have been a significant force in national politics since the 1980s and the Maori Party, founded in 2004, has a specific platform for Maori concerns and issues. One of the key areas of Maori juridico-political influence is in relation to the Treaty of Waitangi. In addition to continued possession of lands and waters, the preservation of Maori language and other *taonga* (treasures) is guaranteed in the Treaty (or in modern practice, in accordance with 'Treaty principles'), and since the 1980s action in these areas has been relatively robust: the *Kohanga Reo* (Maori language immersion) pre-school programme has flourished (despite changes in the regulatory environment in the 1990s) and Maori radio and television stations are commercially viable. This is not to say that indigenous sovereignty has greater materiality in Aotearoa–New Zealand than in Australia: the power that articulates to sovereignty — in particular, for the current purposes, territorial authority over who may enter and live in the country — remains centralized, and centrally Pakeha.

Aboriginal Australians, Asylum Seekers and Refugees[4]

Asylum seekers who attempt to reach Australia by unauthorized means (especially those arriving by boat) have been the subject of extraordinarily high profile, controversial debates for more or less the last decade. Since the passing of the Migration Amendment Act, 1992, most unauthorised asylum seekers have been placed in immigration detention centres in remote mainland or offshore island locations until their refugee claim is processed. Particularly from 2001, when security discourse centred on the threat of militant Islam was intensified in Australia as in other liberal democracies worldwide, asylum seekers have represented a battleground for major party politicians who lay claim to resolute toughness on border protection, on stopping boat people and the smugglers who transport them. The national policy on asylum seekers has proven both contentious and protean, readily conscripted into discourses of national identity, belonging and morality across the political and ideological spectrum. I will concentrate for the next few paragraphs on a particular dimension of this contention, one that articulates to indigenous Australian concerns and activist struggles.

The tiny Aboriginal township of Ampilatwatja, 320 kilometres northeast of Alice Springs in Australia's Northern Territory, is one of the 'prescribed' townships that were acquired by the federal government in 2007 for a five-year lease under the terms of the Northern Territory National Emergency Response. This controversial 'intervention' was implemented via a 'special measures' exemption from the Racial Discrimination Act, 1975 to address child sexual abuse and neglect in Aboriginal communities. In August 2009, a group from Ampilatwatja, who had walked off

---

[4] Parts of this discussion of Aboriginal Australian responses to asylum are developed from Cox (2011).

their dilapidated town in protest the month before, took advantage of a visit to Australia by James Anaya, United Nations Special Rapporteur on the Situation of Human Rights and Fundamental Freedoms of Indigenous Peoples, to lodge a formal request that they be classified as refugees. Spokesperson Richard Downs's letter reads: 'The current status of Aboriginal people is that we are refugees in a Country we have called our own since time immemorial' and requests that the United Nations '[e]nsure that the Australian government is aware of, and fulfils, its obligations under the International Refugee Convention, the UN Charter for Human Rights, the Declaration on the Rights of Indigenous Peoples, and other international human rights covenants' (Downs 2009).

While the Ampilatwatja people's invocation of the international discourse of asylum is intended to situate their own position — and dispossession — the reactions of a number of other Aboriginal activists, elders and scholars to asylum seekers and refugees constitute quite a cohesive statement of responsibility for and hospitality toward the dispossessed other. But like the Ampilatwatja action, these responses also seem to be propelled by an expressed understanding of experiences of displacement and oppression, and in this capacity they strategically underscore a politicized Aboriginal identity, even as they communicate a humanitarian concern for the non-citizen stranger.

The Aboriginal Tent Embassy has been at the forefront of this (indeed, it endorsed the Original Nation passports cited at the beginning of this chapter). The Tent Embassy has stood on the lawn of Old Parliament House in Australia's capital city, Canberra, intermittently since 1972 and continuously since 1992. It is an enduring nexus of activist struggles, especially regarding indigenous sovereignty and land rights. At a community event in 2000 to welcome refugees who had been resettled in Canberra, embassy activist Robert Craigie drew a connection between them and Aboriginal people, who, he asserted, had become refugees within their own country (Griffiths 2000). Sam Watson, Queensland activist and founding member of the Tent Embassy in 1972, has been a vocal advocate for asylum seekers and refugees for several years. In 2001, when Australia was redefining the limits of its sovereign power and redrawing its maritime borders in the wake of the infamous MV *Tampa* crisis,[5] Watson made a statement of mutually-constitutive solidarity:

---

[5] This incident involved the rescue at sea of more than 400 mainly Afghan asylum seekers by a Norwegian freighter ship, the MV *Tampa*, and the Australian government's refusal to allow the ship to enter Australian territorial waters. This

'The government is scapegoating refugees in the same way as they scapegoat indigenous people' (quoted in Mason 2001). In 2002, when mass hunger strikes and self-harm at the remote Woomera detention centre were making headlines, activist Pat Eatock extended an offer of asylum to detainees on behalf of the Tent Embassy. In doing so, she harnessed the prominence of the detainees' plight (the Tent Embassy's offer was reported in the national and international news media), denouncing 'callous and inhumane' (quoted in Barkham 2002: 18) treatment at the same time as she explicated the claim to indigenous sovereignty that is at the forefront of the Embassy's activism. The following year, a representative from the Tent Embassy joined elders from the Bungala (Port Augusta), Kokatha (northern South Australia) and Adnyamathanya (Flinders Ranges) nations at a large rally at the (now closed) Baxter detention centre, near Port Augusta (Murphy 2003).

More recently, in November 2009, Watson, Eatock and Natasha Moore released a statement on behalf of the Socialist Alliance Indigenous Rights collective, asserting: 'While Prime Minister Kevin Rudd increasingly resembles previous Coalition PM John Howard — the arrogantly inflexible and hard-line political "leader" who could never admit to an error of judgment or say sorry — he forgets that 98 [per cent] of Australians are "boat people", the descendants of boat people or, more recently, "plane people"' (quoted in *Green Left Weekly* 2009). South Australian Aboriginal activists Noeleen Ryan-Lester and Linda Dare have articulated the same line of connection at rallies and in media interviews. Dare asserts: 'Everyone in Parliament [has] got to realise that we are the first people of this country ... what right have they got to lock up other people? They got off a bloody boat, or their ancestors did' (quoted in *Socialist Alternative* 2005). These statements draw a line of continuity between successive histories of exclusion and what William E. Connolly terms a 'politics of forgetting' (1995: 138).

Another key touchstone for Aboriginal supporters of asylum seekers is a concept of moral duty. Gungalidda (Gulf of Carpentaria) elder and Aboriginal Tent Embassy member Wadjularbinna Nulyarimma (writing on behalf of Gungalidda elders) articulates a duty of responsibility understood in terms of spiritual and ecological knowledges: 'Before Europeans came here, (illegally), in the Aboriginal world, we were all different,

---

prompted Australia's territorial excision legislation, and its offshore detention and processing of asylum seekers has been extensively discussed in journalistic and scholarly forums.

speaking different languages, but we all had the same kinship system for all human beings ... everyone is part of us and we should care about them. We can't separate ourselves from other human beings — it's a duty' (2002). Attempting to respond to state power on its terms *and* with reference to paradigms that exceed it, Nulyarimma negotiates an indistinct terrain between the rationalist epistemologies of legality and illegality that frame the government treatment of, and discourse on, asylum seekers and Aboriginal knowledge systems that fundamentally eschew these. And undoubtedly, discourses of morality and immorality are a central problem in this negotiation. Even as Nulyarimma summons morality, she enters once more into the epistemological bind she seeks to challenge (ibid.). Discourse on asylum in Australia and abroad has, in recent years, insistently pitted the illegality of the undocumented person against moral ideas: domestic *security* and the *integrity* of borders. Scholar Tony Birch also articulates a moral view of duty to the stranger, asserting that Aboriginal people 'must ... assert more moral authority and ownership of this country. Our legitimacy does not lie within the legal system and is not dependent on state recognition ... we need to claim and legitimate our authority by speaking out for, and protecting the rights of others, who live in, or visit *our* country' (2000: 5). This comment highlights the close (perhaps constitutive) relationship between morality and authority, and seeks a radical reorientation of the relation; Birch writes in part as a call to activism to Aboriginal people 'to speak, to write, to march, to protest, to be angry and put that anger into expression and action' (ibid.: 7).

It should be said that responses to asylum seekers and refugees by Aboriginal commentators are not all supportive. Indigenous family and health policy worker Marion Hansen has identified asylum seekers as competing marginalized figures that detract from social, political and economic focus on Aborigines. At a National Press Club of Australia seminar in September 2001, Hansen expressed support for government policies and voiced concerns that the economic cost of detaining asylum seekers and subsequently assisting their resettlement in Australia threatens the employment prospects of Aboriginal people and comes at the expense of funds for Aboriginal support and benefit programmes. Hansen professed to speak on behalf of indigenous people around Australia (Wright 2001: 3). But as far as the mobilization of support is concerned, three key tropes seem to emerge: Aboriginal identification with people who are seen to be systematically oppressed by Australian powers, a duty of hospitality based upon essentialist Aboriginal values, and an identified commensurability between the Anglo-Celtic right to belong in Australia and the rights of more recent arrivals. These tropes reinforce Aboriginal identity in terms of oppression in the midst of belonging; dispossession in the midst of legitimacy; moral duty in the midst of lost authority.

What does it mean for Aboriginal people to articulate their support for asylum seekers in these ways? What is the psychological structure of this activist support and how does it construct or configure Aboriginal identities? James Goodman argues that Australia's refugee support movements are bifurcated in terms of national and global preoccupations; the former, he argues, 'is broadly instrumental, geared to national policy change, effectively to remaking "the nation", and reclaiming national pride against the shame of refugee detention' while the latter 'is more expressive, in demonstrating anger and outrage in the name of human empathy and dignity' (2009: 270–71). Both, he maintains, are underpinned by deep emotional responses to the other, which provide the necessary impetus for cross-cultural compassion and solidarity. I would argue that Aboriginal activist support for asylum seekers functions in a way that is related to, but distinct from, these modes. Aboriginal support for asylum seekers tends to not attempt to reclaim national identity, to reassert 'Australianness' as a compassionate and hospitable identity; nor does it seek to advocate for asylum seekers on the basis of values of global interconnection or cosmopolitanism. On the contrary, indigenous activists identify themselves very much in localized, territorialized terms, strategically maintaining their essential difference from other Australians. Their outrage on behalf of asylum seekers is, I want to suggest, subtly but crucially different from that expressed by other activists; it is the difference between saying *these are not Australian values* and *Australian values are not our values*.

But if one of the consequences of emphasizing, through activism, an affinity with asylum and oppression is to demarcate a politicized Aboriginal self-identification, Aboriginal activists may risk underscoring the powerlessness that they seek to challenge, reinforcing the cultural and racial hierarchies that relegate them, along with asylum seekers, to a position that is starved of hope. Australian cultural scholar Ghassan Hage reminds us that 'hope' is not a soft or whimsical idea but is vital to social success; he observes: 'once one has hope within one's field of vision, one discovers the astounding degree to which the constellations of feelings, discourses and practices articulated to hope permeate social life' (2003: 9). Hage argues that Australian society is organized in terms of an affective economy where there is 'deep inequality' in the 'distribution of hope' (Hage 2003: 17).

I argue that it is, crucially, in clusters of interpersonal contact (which are often counterparts to activism) that a redistribution of hope takes place. Anecdotal evidence gleaned from my interviews with refugees points to the importance of face-to-face contact. Iranian artist and refugee Ardeshir Gholipour proudly describes being welcomed to Australia by occupants of the Canberra Aboriginal Tent Embassy; this welcome was deeply significant for Gholipour, whose detention for five years and prolonged battle to avoid deportation took a psychological toll (interview with Ardeshir Gholipour, Canberra, 24 July 2008). The alternative authority of Aboriginal sovereignty offered similar affects of belonging in Australia for Iranian theatre practitioner Shahin Shafaei when, following his release after almost two years in detention, he was, in his words, 'adopted' by an indigenous community in North Queensland. Shafaei possesses a carved pendant given to him by this community (interview with Shahin Shafei, Melbourne, 19 July 2008). In these instances, an intimate experience of Aboriginal welcome was a crucial aspect of the affective work of belonging in a new country.

The importance of face-to-face welcome and support is understood by indigenous elder and former public administrator Lowitja O'Donoghue. O'Donoghue has spoken out regularly in support of asylum seekers. She expresses a particular sense of affinity with Afghans, citing the Afghan heritage of many of the indigenous people of her South Australian region as a result of colonial-era contact with cameleers. In recent years, O'Donoghue has taught English classes at her local church, and has been a regular presence at the so-called 'Afghan room' established in the home of her friend, broadcaster Stephen Watkins. Here, young refugees, having spent various periods in immigration detention centres, have been able to cultivate a sense of belonging. One declared to a reporter who visited the 'Afghan room': 'This is our territory' (quoted in Jopson 2003: 33). For O'Donoghue, the act of welcoming refugees must be performed in a personal as well as political capacity; in a speech she states, 'I have welcomed them. They are here. They are part of us. They are grafted into my ancestry and my country' (2003). The image of 'grafting' is a striking one, invoking an irreversible blood link; it performs precisely the opposite function of another biological metaphor for unauthorized migration, that of contamination. O'Donoghue's idea of intergenerational 'grafting' is intertwined with her private role as, in her words, 'a mother figure' (quoted in Jopson 2003: 33) to young individuals.

Of course, other face-to-face encounters between Aboriginal people and asylum seekers have manifested quite differently to this. The ambivalence that can underpin territorial, embodied proximity is illustrated well by the indigenous Tiwi Islanders' relationship with uninvited boat arrivals to their land in recent years. The Tiwi Islands are situated 80 kilometres from the Northern Territory's capital city, Darwin, and within the regulated zone of the Australian Defence Force Border Protection activities in the Arafura and Timor Seas. In November 2003, the arrival of a group of 14 Turkish Kurds and four Indonesian crew members at Melville Island led to the Australian government excising the Tiwi Islands from the migration zone and thus from Australian legal obligations pertaining to migration. A number of Tiwi people were reportedly dismayed at the government's exertion of extraordinary powers and vowed not to assist Defence Force operations in future (Hodson 2003). But in April 2009, Tiwi Land Council executive and ranger, Andrew Tipungwuti, made a request to the government for greater powers to patrol the coastline, stating: 'Our marine rangers don't have adequate powers to help and secure these people until the right authorities arrive' (quoted in Toohey 2009b: 2). Head marine ranger on the Tiwis, Jack Long, articulated how a fear of contagion can exist alongside a sense of kinship: 'I'm Stolen Generation — my mother was full-blood and my father was an Afghan, so of course I've got some sympathy for them ... The real question is about disease. We don't know what's coming in on these boats' (quoted in Toohey 2009a). In November 2009, Tiwi Land Council Chairman Robert Tipungwuti made an offer to the government for Bathurst Island to become a site for a new immigration detention centre. The Tiwi community's position at the maritime vanguard of unauthorized arrivals offers an alternative perspective on indigenous and asylum seeker engagement, reminding us that indigenous sovereignty can articulate as readily to defence of country as to solidarity and welcome.

Maori Activism, Pacific Island Overstayers and Refugees

When Gerrard Otimi's sale of Maori visas to Pacific peoples was first investigated by New Zealand Police in June 2009 it generated something of a media furore. Undaunted, Otimi articulated his position to the assembled journalists covering the story: 'We give them a certificate to say you are now part of our *tino rangitanga* ...'[6] They've been whangaied into my *hapu*. Bye, see you later 'cause you cannot take my *whanau* [family] away' (quoted in *OneNews* 2010). Perhaps not surprisingly, Otimi attracted a loyal following from his new *hapu whangai* (adopted members) and several hundred other Pacific Island visa overstayers who attended community meetings addressed by him. In a report by *Tangata Pasifika*, Aotearoa–New Zealand's long-running, state-funded news and current affairs television programme targeted at Pacific peoples, one of the Pacific Islanders says of the visa, 'this is from god'. Afakasi Slade, a Pentecostal Church Minister who was one of the first people to purchase a visa from Otimi, recounts that when he was issued with a deportation notice, Otimi 'came along and said to the Immigration, "back off, I'm *whanau* to these people"' (TVNZ). Slade explains that Otimi also gave him a new Maori name — Hohepa Otimi te Awhetu — and maintains, 'I'm now a free man because I know that I'm being adopted by the Maori' (ibid.). For Slade, or 'Awhetu', Otimi's visa offers an integration of personal and political identities, and his own Samoan name is something he is willing to surrender in order to obtain this integration — something that he articulates in terms of 'freedom'.

Unlike the Original Nation Passports produced by Aboriginal Australian activists in support of and solidarity with asylum seekers, Otimi's activism — for certainly, his *hapu* visa is, whatever else it might be, a statement of Maori sovereignty — constitutes an economic as well as political transaction: Otimi made a large sum of money from the enterprise. His use (perhaps mimicry, perhaps reterritorialization) of the western-derived model of documentation to validate political belonging — the visa and the passport — includes an appropriation of the economics imbricated in this classification and documentation system. Anyone who has applied for a passport or settlement visa will know that the financial costs (not to mention the emotional investment) are high — for many, prohibitively so. In other words, political belonging, within the terms of citizenship or residency of the modern nation-state, comes at a premium. Otimi provokes the question of what happens when a right of settlement granted by a Maori sovereign authority operates according to a similar

---

[6] Otimi is referring to *tino rangatiratanga*, by which he means 'absolute sovereignty'. See Note 3 for further information on the contention surrounding this term in relation to interpretations of the Treaty of Waitangi.

rubric of value and exchange as a right of settlement sold by a state sovereign immigration authority. Undoubtedly, the status of *hapu whangai* for the Pacific Islanders came, quite literally, at a cost.

Of course, the question of Otimi's fraudulence — something we might assess by weighing his knowledge that financial payment would not produce the kind of recognized legal status the Pacific migrants presumably believed they were purchasing, against his cultural and political convictions regarding the legal status that Maori sovereignty *should* hold — is complicated and fraught. The case brings issues of indigenous sovereignty, hospitality, political integrity, and capitalism into uneasy convergence, and raises several problems for our understanding of how indigeneity functions, and for whom, in contemporary contexts. Otimi's use of his indigenous identity to exert power over vulnerable people, his brazen assertion of right without obligation, disrupts and reorients simplistic lines of association between indigeneity, ethical hospitality, anti-capitalism, and anti-exploitation. Otimi's motives were, we can say with some certainty, at least partly financial and exploitative. Nevertheless, his actions demand a reappraisal of the ontology of sovereignty — *how* Maori sovereignty may be said to exist, *what* the consequences of this existence are and *where* they become consequent. In addition, they focus an inherent problem with an individual vindicating his or her actions with reference to collective (in this case, indigenous) values; in all likelihood, for every Maori person who supports Otimi's activism, there will be another who, like prominent Maori politician Pita Sharples, likens it to 'theft' (quoted in *OneNews* 2010).

The affair also draws attention to the geo-culturally specific issue of the relationship between different Pacific indigeneities. Otimi sold passports to Pacific peoples, in other words, peoples who share his own Polynesian ancestry. Aotearoa–New Zealand's post-settlement bicultural (Maori–Pakeha) paradigm — which, starting in the late 1970s, has come to inflect the nation's executive, legislative and judicial structures as well as cultural identifications — positions Maori in relation to the European-origin New Zealander, and vice-versa. Importantly, the bicultural paradigm is crucial for the Maori as far as the Treaty of Waitangi settlement claims to the British Crown are concerned. But it arguably marginalizes other alignments and affiliations. It permits two privileged spaces of belonging, Maori and Pakeha, and in legal terms, the Polynesian indigeneity of most other Pacific peoples does not confer them access to either. The Pacific peoples whom Otimi purported to bring into his *hapu* can be said to have some relationship with it on the basis of Polynesian kinship links, however distant, but in legal terms, their right to belong is no different from that of any other non-citizen (indeed, their legitimacy is less than that of Australians, who hold reciprocal residency rights with Aotearoa–New Zealand). If Otimi, as self-proclaimed representative of his *hapu*, or any of the individuals he sold visas to — or both — professes the sorts of affective sentiments that Benedict Anderson (1991) identifies as the basis of imagined communities (and the fervent group following Otimi inspired in many of the Pacific Islanders indicates that attachments were formulated, either with Otimi himself or with the idea of belonging that he represents) then it must be said that Otimi's actions lay bare the aporia of imagined communities vis-à-vis political belonging (citizenship). It is within this zone of misalignment that the meanings, the very ontology, of sovereignty and citizenship as well as kinship and belonging are shown as radically ambivalent political and affective ideas/ideals.

The bicultural paradigm does not, it should be said, sufficiently encompass Aotearoa–New Zealand's contemporary cultural, social, economic, and political positionings. Indeed, the nation's relationship with the Pacific articulates to post-colonial Pakeha paradigms as well as to indigenous kinship links. Mark Williams notes that many of Aotearoa–New Zealand's key cultural, social and diplomatic relations, if not its economic ties, are situated in the South Pacific, unlike in Australia, where economic and even cultural focus is increasingly directed at that nation's proximity to (or as some argue, belonging to) Asia (1996: 635). Aotearoa–New Zealand's relationship with Asia has been influenced since the mid-1990s by prominent Maori politicians Winston Peters and Tau Henare, who have become known for their vitriolic, populist opposition to mainly Asian immigration (Ip 2003: 244, 246). This context, in combination with the Polynesian indigenous connections I have discussed, highlights another important difference between the meanings and implications of Otimi's Maori visas and the Aboriginal passports for asylum seekers. Although the unauthorized migrant's vulnerability to state power is central to both, in the Australian case support is offered by Aboriginal activists in the face of explicit alterity, while in the Aotearoa–New Zealand case certain ties already bind the parties.

It is difficult to draw out the various threads of what, precisely, the Maori visa might mean for Slade/Awhetu and others like him. The possession of an indigenous identity — that is, Otimi's purchasable version of it — seems genuinely to have produced certain affects of belonging.

The term 'possession' should not be glossed over: the visas are not merely owned as commodities in a materialist mode, but are assimilated into the buyers' identities. It is surprising, to say the least, that a Samoan person would be willing to 'become' Maori in order achieve an integrated personal and political identity — a dubious one at that. The economic and ontological aspects of the visas might be drawn together if we consider how they create conditions for performative utterances. On the one hand, Otimi's indigenous commodities enable him to articulate, under the glare of national media and face-to-face with juridico-political authorities (the police, immigration officials, judges, politicians) his conviction regarding Maori sovereignty. And on the other, Slade/Awhetu is able to name, before his local community and to a community of citizens via the news media, his legitimacy (and freedom). Marina Sbisà (2006) examines the communication of citizenship with reference to speech act theory, recognizing the way relations of power inflect this communication. She argues: 'Communicating citizenship cannot be reduced to transmission of information, let alone mental content, but consists also or even primarily of ways of acting by which participants recognize or attribute to each other the rights, obligations, expectations etc. that citizenship involves, therefore affecting their actual possession of these' (ibid.: 151). The economic expense and cultural renunciation that Slade/Awhetu's transaction with Otimi entails might be the very obligations that, for him, endow it with legitimacy: he has paid the price for indigenous citizenship, and as such, may communicate it.

But the communication of citizenship is an intersubjective act, requiring the transmission of similar understandings between interlocutors, or as Sbisà argues more precisely, 'transmission of information can be described as the production of an entitlement to assert' (ibid.: 158). Whichever way Otimi's Pacific Island clients might understand the legal (non-) status of their visas, and whatever kind of illocutionary force might accompany their assertions of indigenous belonging, their transactions as a whole underscore the dialectics between the state and the individual, assertion and belief, performative utterance and ontological change, that underpin the positionalities of citizen and alien, belonging and non-belonging, indigenous and non-indigenous.

In the final part of this chapter, I want to look at a rather different kind of performative engagement between indigenous people and non-citizens. Moana and the Tribe, a band led by Moana Maniapoto — one of Aotearoa–New Zealand's most successful musicians — performs four times a year for refugees at the Mangere Refugee Resettlement Centre in the city of Auckland.[7] The band's music fuses traditional and contemporary Maori performance forms and their work is underpinned by explicit political engagement — their commercial success sits alongside and promotes their commitment to Maori cultural representation and social development. Maniapoto describes the band's regular performances at the Mangere Refugee Resettlement Centre in terms of affective cultural transactions. In April 2009, she stated on her website:

> Next week, we head out to the Refugee centre, me and the gals to do our regular concert for the next incoming group of refugees from Afghanistan, Congo, Rwanda, Iraq etc. It's something we got into a year ago — just warbling a few songs and teaching some Maori to the refugees. We really enjoy it — especially the bit where we get to cuddle the gorgeous babies!! And, we get entertained by the refugees because we make each group sing a song from their homeland. It gets positively party-like sometimes! (Maniapoto 2009).

The band's visits to the centre, this comment seems to suggest, are cultural-artistic interactions between performers and spectators that produce event-based multicultural communities. Teaching Maori to the refugees and having the refugees perform songs from their homelands, Maniapoto and her fellow artists instigate exchanges of cultural knowledge and a mutually affective reciprocity.

Like many of the Aboriginal supporters of asylum seekers and refugees that I have discussed, Maniapoto contextualizes her band's presence at the centre with reference to an indigenous morality, specifically here, the Maori value of *manaakitanga*, or hospitality and generosity: 'If you look at our culture, we have a history of *manaakitanga*, of looking after visitors. Refugees, there are only 750 a year. I think New Zealand could up that quota, double it at least' (quoted in Gifford 2009). Maniapoto interpolates an indigenous moral history into the executive operations of the sovereign state. A practical dimension of this interpolation is the linguistic and cultural exchanges that her band generates. If language is an absolutely paramount means by which newcomers orient or position spaces of belonging within the community in which they arrive,

---

[7] The Mangere Refugee Resettlement Centre is a former New Zealand Army base, and the central processing and assessment location for all refugees who arrive in New Zealand. Refugees undergo a six-week period of assessment and orientation prior to resettlement. As a consequence of its remote geography, New Zealand does not receive even a fraction of the number of unauthorized asylum seekers that Australia does.

Moana and the Tribe work to ensure that Maori language is part of that orientation.

The activism, social interaction and performance that I have discussed here are in many ways marginal; they remind us that the implications and meanings of the explicitly global or transnational phenomena of asylum and migration are negotiated and contested within communities and between individuals, as much as through legislation and state biopolitics. At the same time, they instantiate indigenous concerns and interests as global, and not just local, concerns and interests. Through their engagements with asylum and illegal immigration, and with the people bound to these descriptors, Aboriginal Australians and Maori (re)position themselves in the face of postcolonial governmental, legislative and cultural paradigms — which to some extent, it may be said, many indigenous peoples are in, but not of. And inasmuch as they are publicly enacted, these engagements invite citizen-spectators to examine their practical, conceptual and even ethical understandings of the conditions that impinge upon amorphous citizenships — and sovereignties — in the 21st century.

References

Anderson, Benedict. 1991. *Imagined Communities: Reflections on the Origin and Spread of Nationalism*. London and New York: Verso.

Barkham, Patrick. 2002. 'PM Calls Asylum Protest Blackmail: Aborigines Throw Their Weight behind Afghan Hunger Strikers'. *The Guardian*, 26 January, p. 18.

Birch, Tony. 2000. 'The Last Refuge of the "Un-Australian"', *UTS Review*, 7(1): 17–22. http://www.transforming.cultures.uts.edu.au/pdfs/last_refuge_birch.pdf (accessed 20 May 2009).

Connolly, William E. 1995. *The Ethos of Pluralization*. Minneapolis and London: University of Minnesota Press.

Cox, Emma. 2011. 'Welcome to Country? Aboriginal Sovereignties and Asylum Seekers', *Australian Studies*, 3. http://www.nla.gov.au/openpublish/index.php/australian-studies/article/view/2100/2491 (accessed 11 March 2013).

Downs, Richard. 2009. 'Letter to Professor James Anaya'.Intervention Walkoff's Blog, 20 August. http://interventionwalkoff.wordpress.com/statements/ (accessed 23 April 2010).

Gifford, Adam. 2009. 'Refugees Need Support from Maori'. *Waatea News Update*, 20 June. http://waatea.blogspot.com/2008_06_15_archive.html (accessed 4 November 2010).

Goodman, James. 2009. 'Refugee Solidarity: Between National Shame and Global Outrage', in Debra Hopkins, Jochen Kleres, Helena Flam, and Helmut Kuzmics (eds), *Theorizing Emotions: Sociological Explorations and Applications*, pp. 269–89. Frankfurt and New York: Campus Verlag.

Green Left Weekly. 2009. 'Aboriginal Leaders: "Rudd Must Change Refugee Policy"', 817, 11 November. http://www.greenleft.org.au/node/42721 (accessed 9 November 2010).

Griffiths, Phil. 2000. 'LL: Art: Canberra Welcomes Refugees'. 30 August. http://www.mail-archive.com/leftlink@vicnet.net.au/msg03494.html (accessed 6 February 2009).

Hage, Ghassan. 2003. *Against Paranoid Nationalism: Searching for Hope in a Shrinking Society*. Sydney: Pluto Press.

Hodson, Michael. 2003. 'Tiwi Islanders: "We're all Non-Australians"', *Green Left Weekly*, 562, 19 November. http://www.greenleft.org.au/2003/562/29197 (accessed 20 May 2009).

Ip, Manying. 2003. 'Maori–Chinese Encounters: Indigene–Immigrant Interaction in New Zealand', *Asian Studies Review*, 27(2): 227–52.

Jopson, Debra. 2003. 'The Barefoot Regent in her Afghan Court', *Sydney Morning Herald*, 8 March, p. 33.

Juice Media. 2010. 'Aboriginal Passports Issued to Asylum Seekers Prevented from Entering Australia', 25 May. http://www.youtube.com/watch?v=XkjJpz7nxwM (accessed 4 November 2010).

Maiden, Samantha. 2010. 'Abbott Reopens Culture Wars Over Nods to Aborigines', *The Australian*, 15 March, p. 1.

Maniapoto, Moana. 2009. 'Archived News'. *Moana*, 19 April. http://www.moananz.com/archived_news.php?Page=4 (accessed 4 November 2010).

Mason, Bill. 2001. 'Treatment of Refugees "Heartless"'. *Green Left* Weekly, 463, 5 September. http://www.greenleft.org.au/2001/463/25312 (accessed 6 February 2009).

Moreton-Robinson, Aileen. 2007. 'Writing off Indigenous Sovereignty: The Discourse of Security and Patriarchal White Sovereignty', in Aileen Moreton-Robinson (ed.), *Sovereign Subjects: Indigenous Sovereignty Matters*, pp. 86–102. Crows Nest, New South Wales: Allen & Unwin.

———. 2006. 'Towards a New Research Agenda?: Foucault, Whiteness and Indigenous Sovereignty', *Journal of Sociology*, 42(4): 383–95.

Murphy, Emma. 2003. 'Solidarity and Defiance in the Desert'. *Green Left Weekly*, 535, 23 April. http://www.greenleft.org.au/2003/535/30437 (accessed 9 July 2009).

Nulyarimma, Wadjularbinna. 2002. 'A Gungalidda Grassroots Perspective on Refugees and the Recent Events in the US', *Borderlands: e-journal*, 1(1). http://www.borderlands.net.au/vol1no1_2002/wadjularbinna.html (accessed 8 July 2009).

O'Donoghue, Lowitja. 2003. 'Return to Afghanistan: Resettlement or Refoulment?', Speech, Adelaide, 27 February. http://www.safecom.org.au/lowitja.htm (accessed 10 February 2009).

Orange, Claudia. 1987. *The Treaty of Waitangi*. Wellington: Allen & Unwin/Port Nicholson Press.

One News. 2010. 'Police Probe Fake Visa Scam', 18 June. http://tvnz.co.nz/national-news/police-probe-fake-visa-scam-2789352 (accessed 3 November 2010).

Sbisà, Marina. 2006. 'Communicating Citizenship in Verbal Interaction: Principles of a Speech Act Oriented Discourse Analysis', in Heiko Hausendorf and Alfons Bora (eds), *Analyzing Citizenship Talk*, pp. 151–80. Amsterdam and Philadelphia: John Benjamins.

Socialist Alternative. 2005. 'Interview: Refugee Activists Support Aboriginal Rights—Interview with Noeleen Ryan-Lester and Linda Dare', 90, April–May. http://ur.lc/iui (accessed 20 April 2010).

Sunday Territorian. 2010. 'Seeking Asylum in Tiwis', 17 January, p. 16.

Television New Zealand (TVNZ). 2009. 'Passport Scam Otimi', *Tangata Pasifika*, broadcast 25 June.

Toohey, Paul. 2009a. 'Save us from Boatpeople, say Tiwi Islanders'. *Australian*, 13 May. http://www.theaustralian.com.au/news/save-us-from-boatpeople-tiwis/story-e6frg6po-1225711584007 (accessed 28 January 2013).

———. 2009b. 'Tiwi Islanders Want More Power to Stop Boatpeople'. *Australian*, 1 May.

Williams, Mark. 1996. 'Immigrants and Indigenes: The Politics of Pluralism in Australia and New Zealand', *Meanjin*, 55(4): 635–50.

Wright, Lincoln. 2001. 'Asylum-Seekers "Affect Aborigines' Prospects"'. *The Canberra Times*, 22 September, p. 3.

9 Indigenous Worldviews and Environmental Footprints

The Case of Prometheus vs Hermes

A. O. Balcomb

We do not need to be reminded of the pending environmental disaster that awaits us as a planet. The causes of this disaster are also fairly universally accepted. They are to do with the way in which we are exploiting our natural resources and what we are doing, as a result, to the earth and the atmosphere. It is common knowledge too that many kinds of modern technologies — for example, those that are dependent on fossil fuel — are contributing to this crisis. What is not often spoken about, however, are the kinds of attitudes that have given rise to this crisis. What is behind the modern worldview that shapes these attitudes? What are the postures towards the world, or what Heidegger calls our way of being-in-the-world (1996: 88), that causes us to use it in such a way that simply extracts, denudes and pollutes without offering anything in return? And what is the difference between this way of being in the world and an anti-modern, pre-modern or primordial way of being in the world which leaves a lighter footprint on the environment? And if so what are the implications of this on our philosophies of life?

One way to characterize the western tradition is through Prometheus of Greek legend who stole the fire from the Gods, (and) has always been the classical hero of Western civilization which bases itself on a set of values that are typical of the Promethean story — the heroism of progress through sleight of hand and hardship, production through labour and the possibility of endless victories over new kinds of obstacles. The main thesis of the Promethean view is that the human being can only realize him or herself through the domination of nature. He has to objectify, appropriate and exploit nature, which he constructs basically as 'other' to himself (Van Niekerk 1998: 56).

The Promethean nature of the Western project of control and domination demands trenchant critique. The crisis of Western civilization could be connected with a crisis in Western rationality. It is a crisis based on the desire for control and autonomy. Further critique of the Western worldview is offered by Western scholars themselves. The Frankfurt School of philosophical thought asserts that the kind of rationality serving Western industrial civilization is responsible for the profound sense of alienation experienced in the West. This is due to its obsession with means and its loss of certainty with regards to the value of the aims that these means are meant to achieve.

> In other words, it does not serve, as reason did from Plato to Hegel, to direct the human being to his/her goals and to his/her proper place in reality. In the end, this amputation of reason leads to irrationality of the overall direction of social life. Capitalism, for one, promotes the instrumentalisation of reason to obscure the irrational desire for more and more possessions; it does this by means of a rational process of quantification and formalisation of nature and human relations (ibid.: 65).

The process of rationalization leads to the subjugation of nature. 'Nature mediated by technology creates a culture that is a kind of second objective nature that dominates the human being' (ibid.: 65). This leads to the domination of the human being in the endless cycles of production and consumption and the merry-go-round of people serving these cycles and repeating them.

An even more trenchant critique has come from a most unlikely source, from one of the best known capitalists in the world. In 'The Crisis of Global Capitalism: Open Society Endangered' George Soros defines 'market fundamentalism' as a belief that 'all social activities and human interactions should be looked at as transaction, contract based relationships and value in terms of a single common denominator, money' (2010: 10). Soros also echoes the nature of consumerism as a vicious circle, but in more frightful terms: 'The promotion of self-interest to a moral principle has corrupted politics and the failure of politics has become the strongest argument in favour of giving markets an even freer reign' (ibid.).

This mentality permeates the entire way of life in the West and raises the question as to whether a pre-modern or primordial worldview can offer a different understanding of the human's way of being in the world, more specifically one that does not pit the human being as imperious subject against nature as object. Attempts to characterize a primal way of being in the world have been made ever since the encounter between North and South, or West and East, going back to the early ethnographers of the last century, notably E. B. Tylor, Lucien Lévy-Bruhl and Claude Lévi-Strauss. In post-colonial discourse these attempts have been ruthlessly critiqued. Jacques Derrida, for example, has attempted to demonstrate that the search for a primordial way of being in the world is indicative of a misplaced nostalgic yearning for a kind of lost paradise, the roots of which are to be found in the Christian myth of a state of original innocence. According to this myth '[t]he simple condition of humankind must be returned to in order to re-unite with presence' (quoted in Wessels 2010: 52). To begin the march towards civilization is to precipitate a fall away from presence. This leads to a situation in which the '[t]he primitive human can never be allowed to exist as a reciprocating, self-representing, contemporary individual' (ibid.).

The problem with this argument lies in the fact that it presupposes the terms on which the reciprocation between the so-called primitive and the so-called civilized must take place — that is precisely as a 'self-representing, contemporary individual' (ibid.). These descriptions are already loaded with a predetermined agenda. Why should the 'primitive' want to reciprocate in contemporary, read 'modern', terms, let alone as an individual, read 'autonomously'? Indeed why should the 'primitive' want to reciprocate at all? In fact, one of the most common and arguably effective ways of reciprocation between 'primitive' and 'civilized' seems to have been through mimicry by the former of the latter, and this usually of the non-flattering variety, that is non-flattering of the so-called civilized side of the relationship. In this case Hermes, the trickster, trumps Prometheus the conqueror.

It is appropriate at this stage to try to essentialize what has been called by some African scholars a primal worldview (see Bediako 1995).

Harold Turner has characterized the primal worldview in terms of six features:

> First, a sense of kinship with nature, in which animals and plants, no less than human beings, have their own spiritual existence and place in the universe, as interdependent parts of the whole.
>
> Second, the deep sense that humankind is finite and weak and in need of a supernatural power.
>
> Third, that humankind is not alone in the universe, that there is a spiritual world of powers and beings more ultimate than itself. This is a personalized

universe where the appropriate question is not *what* causes things to happen but *who* causes things to happen.

Fourth, that human beings can enter into relationships with the benevolent spirit world.

Fifth, an acute sense of the afterlife usually expressed in belief in and respect for the ancestors who may be referred to as the 'living dead'.

Sixth, that humans live in a sacramental universe where there is no dichotomy between the physical and spiritual and that the physical can act as a vehicle for the spiritual (quoted in ibid.: 93–94).

A variety of descriptions come to mind when considering such a worldview. It is inter-subjective rather than objective (for example it views the environment as a being not a thing), it is relational rather than autonomous, it emphasizes kinship with nature rather than mastery of nature, it is spiritual rather than material, and it emphasizes the weakness rather than the strength of the human being.

If Prometheus is the figure that correctly symbolizes the attitude of the modern, according to this critique, then it is Hermes the trickster that typifies the attitude of the pre-modern. Instead of pitting yourself as imperious subject against nature as object and overcoming it by sheer will to power, you conjure the notion of nature itself as subject with whom you negotiate both identity and survival. This posture is spoken of in various ways by different anthropologists and philosophers. Lévi-Strauss, for example, speaks of the 'savage' mentality as being one that seeks not to change the world or to interpret it in radically new ways but to come to a kind of *quid pro quo* with it through a process of transformation that re-orders the symbolic system in which one conceives it (Lévi-Strauss 1976: 20). Such a transformation, in other words, is not so much of nature as one's attitude towards nature. For the modern this may mean a revaluation of myth as a vital means of understanding the self as well as recovering a sense of the numinous. Mythical arrangement of the world is the personification, anthropomorphization and spiritualization of things in the world. This leads to the development of stories about the world that are accessible to us and our post-mythic consciousness.

At an epistemological level the paradigm needs to shift from disengagement and separation to engagement and participation. Lévy-Bruhl, who is enjoying something of a comeback in some circles, having been thoroughly trashed in postcolonial discourse — he is dubbed by the environmental philosopher David Abram as the 'brilliant forerunner of today's "cognitive" and "symbolic" schools of anthropology' (Abram 2003: 57) — coined the term 'participation' to characterize the animistic logic of indigenous oral peoples. The notion of participatory consciousness has been developed as the essential characteristic of primal epistemology. For Lévy-Bruhl

> ostensibly 'inanimate' objects like stones or mountains are often thought to be alive, for whom certain names, spoken aloud, may be felt to influence at a distance the things or beings that they name, for whom particular plants, particular animals, particular places, persons and powers may all be felt to participate in one another's existence, influencing each other and being influenced in turn (ibid.: 57)

The notion of participation has also been used by African scholars such as Léopold Senghor, Alexis Kagame, and Edward Kanyike to describe African epistemology. In his monumental *La Philosophie Bantu-Rwandaise de l'Être* (1956), Kagame linguistically analyzes the term *ntu* which is roughly translated as 'being'. His findings led him to the conclusion that African cosmology was characterized by a universal similitude of being that Mudimbe describes in the following way:

> In sum, the *ntu* is somehow a sign of a universal similitude. Its presence in beings brings them to life and attests to both their individual value and to the measure of their integration in the dialectic of vital energy. *Ntu* is both a uniting and a differentiating vital norm which explains the powers of vital inequality in terms of difference between beings. It is a sign that God, father of all beings ... has put a stamp on the universe, thus making it transparent in a hierarchy of sympathy. Upwards one would read the vitality which, from minerals through vegetables, animals and humans, links stones to the departed and God himself. Downwards, it is a genealogical filiation of forms of beings, engendering or relating to one another, all of them witnessing to the original source that made them possible (1985: 189–90).

One of the most graphic descriptions of the principle of participation in the primal worldview is given by John V. Taylor in his book *The Primal Vision* (1963). He describes an experience he had on Lake Victoria where he assisted some fishermen to bring in their nets. As the fishermen draw in the two ends of the net to enclose the fish, and themselves, within it the net becomes a metaphor of the primal universe which Taylor calls the 'unbroken circle'. He feels 'the edges of separateness evaporating' as he experiences the one-ness of this universe in the one-ness of all things in and around him. His graphic account of this experience ends with the following description of what he calls the 'primal vision':

> Not only is there less separation between subject and object, between self and not-self, but fundamentally all things share the same nature and the same interaction one upon another — rocks and forest trees, beasts and serpents, the power of the wind and waves upon a ship, the power of a drum over a dancer's body, the power in the mysterious caves of Kokola, the living, the dead and the first ancestors, from the stone to the divinities an hierarchy of power but not of being, for all are one, all are here, all are now (1963: 64).

The experience that Taylor was trying to articulate here was one of the wholeness of reality. For the phenomenologist Maurice Merleau-Ponty this kind of experience is not unique to people living within a primal culture but is what all of us are having all the time, but have become unaware of through the conditioning towards objectification that we have undergone in the Western paradigm (Kwant 1966: 43). Merleau-Ponty was a psychologist and philosopher whose thinking bears extraordinary resemblance to the African ethnophilosophers and the idea of vital participation. He did not reject the Cartesian rationalist paradigm of the subject–object relationship as such but maintained that it is preceded by a deeper order of being which is defined by intersubjectivity, that, is by a world which is shaped by relationships between subjects, not between subject and object. The state that best apprehends this is one which he calls the 'savage being' by which he means the human mind in its most original life. The essence of Merleau-Ponty's philosophy lies in the simple statement *J'en suis*, meaning 'I belong to it' or 'I belong to Being'. 'He came to realize that our human existence is not separated from nature or Being, that we are not opposed to it as subjects who know, but that we belong to it' (ibid.: 44). In a paragraph entitled 'primordial unity' Kwant describes how Maurice Merleau-Ponty in his final writings accuses himself in his original work, *Phenomenology of Perception* (2002), of maintaining the Cartesian cogito which hypothesized that the primordial state of being was one in which consciousness was in opposition to object. Instead, in the book published posthumously entitled *The Visible and the Invisible* (Merleau-Ponty 1968), he posits that a primordial unity exists at the base of the distinction between consciousness and object, spirit and matter, the invisible and the visible. Commenting on the book that was published after his death Kwant maintains that

> Merleau-Ponty would have written the entire book in the perspective of primordial unity. It would have been a commentary of the words *j'en suis*.

He intended to show how visible nature manifests itself as a body which feels itself and which actualizes the hidden sensitivity of nature, how visible nature becomes a seeing body, how in this body all the conditions are there for speaking and for other forms of expression, how the speaking body is a thinking body. He would have described all these developments as the manifestations of the intrinsic possibilities of visible nature. He would have shown that on all the levels of the human development it remains true that "I belong to it". There can hardly be any doubt that this would have been the fundamental thesis of his book (Kwant 1966: 45).

Merleau-Ponty is one of a triumvirate of philosophers in the phenomenologist tradition — the other two being Edmund Husserl and Martin Heidegger. I cite them in this context because they are heavyweight representatives of an established alternative to the Cartesian tradition in the European context that resonates strongly with primordial concepts of being that, in turn, are associated with indigenous worldviews. The purpose is not to attempt to validate these worldviews but to give another perspective to the post-colonial position articulated by scholars such as Derrida, Gayatri Chakravorty Spivak, and others who have relegated the search for metaphysical presence in indigenous cultures to unrequited longings of disenchanted westerners who are singing the tune of an imperialist agenda. One of the problems with the deconstructive approach of such scholars, however intriguing, is that in exposing the alleged ideological basis of such ideas they put these ideas out of the reach of even a modicum of credibility.

A completely different approach to the primordial worldview and philosophy of indigenous cultures has been taken by environmental philosopher David Abrams, who uses both Merleau-Ponty and Lévy-Bruhl to demonstrate the participatory nature of all human engagement with the world but expressed most acutely in cultures whose worldviews can be described as animistic. His thesis is that lessons can be learned from such cultures with regard to human impact on the environment. Interaction with the world in such cultures is profoundly and consciously a matter of intersubjectivity. A classic example of such interaction is to be found in hunter-gatherer societies such as that of the Bushmen who believed themselves to be so intimately connected to the environment around them that their interactions with it were constantly a matter of negotiation and compromise, rather than conquest and dominion. The protocols around hunting among the !Xam, for example, necessitate the presence of the trickster !Kaggen to act as agent on behalf of hunted animals. To perform this role !Kaggen makes use of the fact that the hunter feels in his body what the hunted animal is experiencing after being shot by his poisoned arrow. Michael Wessels describes what happens between the time that the poisoned arrow enters the animal and its death thus:

> During this time, a sympathetic bond (is) established between the hunter and the animal. The condition of the hunter paralleled that of the dying animal. !Kaggen exploited this relationship in order to enable the animal to fight off the effects of the poison and recover. He might, for example, become a louse and bite the hunter. As the hunter fidgeted and scratched, the eland would become more active and regain its life force. Or he might startle the hunter by becoming a puff adder. The shot animal would feel the infusion of energy as the hunter reacted to the snake's presence. If the hunter shot a gemsbok, !Kaggen became a hare and placed himself in the way of the hunter. If the hunter shot the hare, the gemsbok would recover. The man who had shot an eland had to return home as if wounded himself. He was then confined to a special hut, where he lay in agony while the old man who looked after him made a fire to drive !Kaggen away. The other men would track the dying eland and bring the meat home. *To a considerable degree, the hunter and his wounded prey became a single organism* (2010: 111; emphasis added).

Wessels goes on to describe how, in !Xam discourse, !Kaggen

> makes use of a network of signifying relationships that have a wider reach than hunting or the figure of !Kaggen himself ... Broadly speaking, the materials present the body as a discursive space in its own right, one that is continuous with the world rather than separate from it (ibid.: 112).

A more graphic example of Merleau-Ponty's *J'en suis*, I belong to it, could hardly be found. Neither could there be found a better example of Placide Tempels' assertion, writing not about the Bushman but the Bantu, that

> [the] concept of separate beings which find themselves side by side, entirely independent one of another, is foreign to Bantu thought. Bantu hold that created beings preserve a bond one of another, an intimate ontological relationship, comparable with the causal tie which binds creature and Creator. For the Bantu there is interaction of being with being, that is to say, of force with force. Transcending the mechanical, chemical and psychological interactions, they see a relationship of forces which we should call ontological (1953: 58).

That all this has significance for our environmental footprint is obvious. Tim Ingold covers numerous studies of indigenous communities' relationship with their environment in his book *The Perception of the Environment: Essays in Livelihood, Dwelling, and Skill* (Ingold 2000). For hunter-gatherers such as the Kuyokon of Alaska there are not two separate worlds of humanity and nature but one world of which the human being plays rather a small part. 'Caring for the environment' in such a culture, he says, 'is like caring for people: it requires a deep, personal and affectionate involvement, an involvement not just of mind or body but of one's entire, undivided being' (ibid.: 69). Ingold characterizes this attitude to the environment as one of trust as opposed to that of domination. Once again this is highlighted in the hunt which depends not on superior cunning, speed or force but on the relationship between the hunter and the hunted where the former draws the latter into the ambit of social being in order to 'establish a working basis for mutuality and coexistence' (ibid.). This trust, argues Ingold, is a combination of autonomy and dependency.

> To trust someone is to act with that person in mind, in the hope and expectation that she will do likewise — responding in ways favourable to you — so long as you do nothing to curb her autonomy to act otherwise. Although you depend on a favourable response, that response comes entirely on the initiative and volition of the other party. Any attempt to impose a response, to lay down conditions or obligations that the other is bound to follow, would represent a betrayal of trust and a negation of the relationship ... Trust ... always involves an element of risk — the risk that the other on whose actions I depend, but which I cannot in any way control, may act contrary to my expectations ... Trust presupposes an active, prior engagement with the agencies and entities of the environment on which we depend; it is an inherent quality of our relationships towards them (ibid.: 70).

It is precisely this aspect of granting the environment agency that distinguishes this way of being in the world from a mechanistic one. To live in the world as if the world were a living being is to live a fundamentally different kind of qualitative existence than if one perceives the world as inanimate. To see the issue of causation in the world not as mechanical but personal is to ask not what causes things to happen and how they happen but who causes things to happen and why they happen. It is to seek not domination but revelation.

To conclude it is obvious that the Promethean project is in crisis. There is a growing realization that conquest is not the answer to our problems. And if it is not then what is, and where do we look to find answers? Prometheus and Hermes present to us essentially different ways of confronting the human condition. One exaggerates with increasing intensity and sophistication the illusion of human invulnerability and the other allows this vulnerability to insinuate itself into our very way of being in the world.

References

Abram, David. 2003. *The Spell of the Sensuous*. New York: Vintage.
Bediako, Kwame. 1995. *Christianity in Africa: The Renewal of a Non-Western Religion*. Edinburgh: Edinburgh University Press.
Heidegger, Martin. 1996. *Being and Time: A Translation of Sein und Zeit*, trans. Joan Stambaugh. New York: New York: State University of New York Press.
Ingold, Tim. 2000. *The Perception of the Environment: Essays in Livelihood, Dwelling, and Skill*. London and New York: Routledge.
Kagame, Alexis. 1956. *La philosophie bantu-rwandaise de l'être*. Brussels: Académie Royale des Sciences d'Outre-Mer.
Kwant, Remigius C. 1966. *From Phenomenology to Metaphysics: An Inquiry into the Last Period of Merleau-Ponty's Philosophical Life*. Pittsburgh: Duquesne University Press.
Lévi-Strauss, Claude. 1976. *The Savage Mind*. London: Weidenfeld & Nicolson.
Merleau-Ponty, Maurice. 1968. *The Visible and the Invisible: Working Notes*. Evanston: Northwestern University Press.
———. 2002. *Phenomenology of Perception*. London: Routledge.
Mudimbe, V. Y. 1985. 'African Gnosis Philosophy and the Order of Being: An Introduction', *African Studies Review*, 28(2/3): 189–233.
Soros, George. 2010. 'The Crisis of Global Capitalism: Open Society Endangered'. *Sunday Independent*, 15 August.
Taylor, John V. 1963. *The Primal Vision: Christian Presence amid African Religion*. London: SCM Press.
Tempels, Placide F. 1953. *La philosophie bantoue*. Paris: Présence Africaine.
Van Niekerk, Marlene. 1998. 'Understanding Trends in African Thinking—A Critical Discussion', in Pieter H. Coetzee and Abraham P. J. Roux (eds), *The African Philosophy Reader*, pp. 52–98. London and New York: Routledge.
Wessels, Michael. 2010. *Bushman Letters: Interpreting! Xam Narrative*. Johannesburg: Wits University Press.

10 Folk Heritage and Classical Lore

The Grand Narratives from the Aegean Archipelago and Derek Walcott's Caribbean Creole Readings

Eckhard Breitinger

In the Caribbean, the truly indigenous peoples had been exterminated by the early 18th century. The Caribbean peoples today are the descendents of involuntary migrants, who came to the Caribbean by 'fatality' rather than of their own will. They are descendents of African slaves, Indian indentured labourers, Chinese contract workers, deportees for religious reasons, or poverty migrants from the British Isles, Western Europe and the Levant/Middle East. In sum, West Indians are in a way 'neo-indigenes'.

Their culture consists of the remnants of a variety of African traditions that survived the Middle Passage, or the other sea routes from Asia or the Levant. Caribbean cultures grew into revivals and re-inventions of those cultural overseas traditions, particularly after the 1950s when the Independence Movement, the Black Consciousness Movement and the Black Personality gained momentum.

At that time when Derek Walcott started his writing career, the Caribbean figured mainly as an exotic backdrop for London West End melodramas. Characters from the West Indian plantocracy served in society melos: the docile (or rebellious) African field slave was a stock character in farces as was the seductively exotic 'negress'.

At the same time, the later Prime Minister of Trinidad and Tobago Eric Williams — 'the Doctor' — had published his seminal work *Capitalism and Slavery* (1964) in which he claims that the immense profits earned by the West Indian plantation (and slave) economy were reinvested in the mother country for the development of new technologies. James Watts's experimental research that resulted in the invention and construction of the steam engine, for instance — the key invention for the first Industrial Revolution in Europe — was funded by West Indian planters' risk capital.

Vidia S. Naipaul, like Walcott one of the West Indian Nobel laureates, complained in his book *The Middle Passage* (1962) that the West Indies completely lacked originality, that nothing of value had been invented in the Caribbean. He described — or rather defamed — the West Indians as 'mimic men' (after the title of his second novel) (Naipaul 1967). In that context of depreciation of West Indian culture, by intellectuals at home but even more so by the 'cultural customs officers' in the mother country, Derek Walcott started to write about Caribbean history, valorizing national heroes and heroes of folk culture. His first play, *Henri Christophe*, was first performed on his native island of St Lucia in 1950. A radio drama production for BBC West Indian Voices, directed by Erroll Hill, then the most influential Caribbean director and dramatist, it brought international approval.[1]

At the time, the trade union-supported movement for self-rule and independence had gathered momentum in the British Caribbean. In the neighbouring islands and territories of Martinique and Cayenne/French Guyana, officially *départements et territoires d'outre-mer* (DOM-TOM), Léon Damas and Aimé Césaire propagated their psycho-socio-cultural theories of Négritude. It was the common goal of both movements to reinstate the 'neo-indigenous' Afro-Caribbean peoples in a position of self-articulation and cultural self-appreciation.

In the socio-cultural domain, Walcott faced a situation where the Caribbean figured as a topic for light entertainment, for boulevard comedies and farces with stereotyped characters like the rich planter, the tragic mulatto, the dancing and singing negro, and the seductive shine-eye girls: 'The shine-eye girl is the trouble for a man' is a popular folk song in the Eastern Caribbean (Taylor 2002: 9–21). In this situation Walcott chose as his model the Shakespearean/Elizabethan history play (Innes 2000: 22–29), i.e., the very genre that England instrumentalized to boost the formation of its national identity at the period when European 'modern' nation states were in their *status nascendi* (nascent state). Walcott had opted for an analogous approach for a parallel historical situation in the Caribbean when the islands were striving for political self-determination. This inevitably required the formation of a regional or national identity.

---

[1] Walcott revived *Henri Christophe* in 1984 as *The Haitian Earth* (unpublished), this time with his own set and costume designs. See De Lima (1991: 174).

Imperial cultural policies of the 1950s maintained that serious dramatic forms like tragedy portraying high ethical values and deep moral dilemmas were the prerogative of the European cultural scene, while the regions on the margins of the empire had to be satisfied with topics without any moral consequence or any really touching emotional impact. Thus, Walcott's subtitle 'A Caribbean Tragedy' becomes a highly political statement. When catharsis and the noble feelings of empathy are reserved for Europeans, while laughter and merriment — i.e., light and slight entertainment — remain the prerogative of the colonials, then to claim the right to present Caribbean history and heroic historical figures from a distinctly Caribbean perspective with a distinctly Caribbean voice challenges the conventional Euro-centric pattern of historical thought with a superordinate metropolitan culture and a subordinate, subaltern peripheral culture. The subtitle 'A Caribbean Tragedy' expresses Walcott's conviction that the popular culture on the islands and the 'high' culture in the metropolis are of equal status.

The Haitian revolution and the establishment of the first Negro republic in world history on Haiti, formely Saint Domingue, was an important historic event in a period of dramatic political change in the wake of the French and the American Revolutions. The Haitian Revolution developed tremendous symbolic importance for all the African–American cultural and political movements from the Harlem Renaissance, through Indigensimo and Négritude to Black Consciousness. Walcott shows that he is fully aware of the symbolic value of his topic, but he is also aware of the specific situation of a historic watershed at the time of writing. The end of World War II and the independence of India suggested that Harold Macmillan's 'Wind of Change' (1960) was about to blow away colonialism as part of the old world order.

While Walcott confirms the historical importance of the Haitian revolution and the revolutionary leaders, he is also very much aware of the deficiencies of the revolutionary personnel (Jean-Jacques Dessalines, Henri Christophe, Alexandre Sabès Pétion, not so much Toussaint L'Ouverture) and the failures of the Haitian political élite to achieve the revolutionary goals. This was true for the entire 19th century, for the time of Walcott's writing when Papa Doc Duvalier established his terror regime (cf. Greene 1966), but it was also true in 2010, when another presidential election failed to bring stability and reconciliation to the devastated island.

Henri Christophe, who betrayed Toussaint l'Ouverture and declared himself emperor, is not the shining historical hero suitable for national myth-making, but rather a shady hero who exemplifies the duplicities in all colonial and postcolonial situations: 'one may see such heroes as squalid fascists who chained their own people, but they had size, mania, the fire of great heretics. Dessaline and Christophe were our only noble ruins' (Walcott 1970d: 12–13) .

As an act of repossession and reappropriation of one's history and one's cultural and literary expression *Henri Christophe* has been a revelation and initiation for Caribbean literature. Walcott's historical consciousness, his veneration of the past but also his dedication to the present is strongly testified in the play *Drums and Colours* (1961), a commissioned work for the independence of the West Indian Federation. *Drums and Colours* takes the form of a pageant play — the tradition of European religious drama — that highlights key events and key personalities of West Indian history.

Together with his twin brother Roderick, Walcott set up the Trinidad Theatre Workshop, where he produced most of his early plays. Trinidad is the most cosmopolitan of the West Indian islands. Besides the descendants of African slaves and East Indian indentured labourers, it boasts of pockets of population of Irish and Scottish descent whose ancestors had been deported under Cromwell, of French people whose ancestors had fled the Haitian Revolution, of Sephardic Jews who had fled from the Inquisition in Spain and Portugal, of Madeira Portugese who had fled the poverty of their islands, but also Chinese, Syrians, Lebanese, and Greeks. Orient and Occident, Africa, Asia, the Middle East, and the West are contained in one island; Christianity and Islam, Hinduism, Buddhism, and African syncretistic religions meet and merge into the uniquely Trinidadian cultural phenomenon of Carnival and its major literary form, the Calypso. With the initiation of the Trinidad Theatre Workshop, the Walcott twins intended to create a platform 'where someone can do Shakespeare or sing a calypso with equal conviction' (Walcott 1970b: 306). They intended to position the culture of 'the motherland' and the culture of the island on the same level.

Walcott and the African Caribbean Oral Tradition

Compared to the early plays, *Ti-Jean and his Brothers* (Walcott 1970c) appears to be exclusively African-Caribbean, although critics have traced inspirations from Kabuki in the controlled movements of the dances. Walcott merges two different strands of African-Caribbean oral tradition:

the animal story and the trickster tales. When the curtain rises, we see Frog, Cricket, Firefly, and Bird on the stage — an emblematic set of figures from the animal stories. They remain visible throughout the play, Frog being the Master of Ceremonies and Narrator. They warn and advise the characters in the play, comment on the action and the actors, and pronounce general value judgements like the Greek chorus. Frog opens the play with 'Greek croak, greek croak ... Aeschelus me. All that rain and no moon tonight' (Walcott 1970: 85) thus alluding to Aristophanes' comedy *The Frogs* (405 BCE). But 'Crick crack' is also the opening and closing formula for a West Indian animal story. Classical Greek and local West Indian tradition are practically merged into one. The play *Ti-Jean* is structured as a serial quest-and-test tale, where a number of persons have to undergo an identical set of tests. Here, Papa Bois/Papa Diable puts Ti-Jean and his brothers to the test and promises them all the riches, if they succeed in making him feel angry, i.e., show human emotions. The first one to try his luck is Gros-Jean, who relies on his physical strength. He does not heed the advice from his mother nor the warnings from the animals of the forest. His task is to herd a very unruly billy goat and to count the leaves in a field of sugar cane. The muscular Gros-Jean fails dismally. And so does his brother Mi-Jean, who relies on book learning. His colonial education does not help him in outwitting Papa Bois. So both of the brothers are killed. Only Ti-Jean, the youngest, the weakest, who has just let go his mother's apron strings, succeeds in passing all the tests. He listens to the advice of his mother — experience — and heeds the warnings of the animals of the forest — instinct. Ti-Jean goes about the tasks he is set subtly and cunningly. He simply castrates the billy goat, which takes all the fire out of that animal. The problem with the leaves of the sugar cane field is solved even more pragmatically but also in a revolutionary manner: he sets the field on fire — the *cannes brûlées* is an action of revolt. Maureen Warner-Lewis (1991: 188) explains *cannes brûlées* or *canboulay* as 'unseasonal burning of unmature fields of sugar cane by slaves ... This was, and still is, an act of sabotage against the estate's owner'.

When Ti-Jean realizes that Papa Bois, Papa Diable and the white plantation owner are one and the same person, he sets fire to the Great House as well, and while all is burning down, he gleefully roasts the goat. What Ti-Jean is really doing is to trigger off a slave revolt, and that is seen as an action against the devil. Both the internal plot about the three brothers and the frame with Frog, Cricket and Firefly are distinctly oral and African in origin. By merging them into one, Walcott created from the mono-directional and mono-causal tales a new, extended, complex, and multilayered dramatic narrative. (Louis MacNeice's *The Dark Tower* (1947), a radioplay from 1944, deals with an almost identical folk motif from the European tradition.)

'Crick crack' and 'Greek croak', Aeschylus and Caribbean oral narration, Calypso and Shakespeare, the Caribbean and the Elizabethan history plays, Walcott's topics and his comments strongly emphasize his belief in the equal validity of Caribbean folk culture and metropolitan high culture.

As diverse as the ethnic, cultural and religious origins of the people in the Caribbean might be, they share one common destiny: a history of displacement, of forced migration, of being castaways (the title of Walcott's first major collection of poems [1965b]) stranded 'by fatality' on the shores of the Caribbean islands. They all look for their cultural sources, for their spiritual, ancestral homes to somewhere beyond the seclusion of their island homes. The multiplicity and diversity of cultural origins has brought universality into the narrow confines of the islands, it has condensed the world in the insularity of the Caribbean archipelago. Separation from the sources and isolation from the great centres of the world are crucial to the West Indian experience: Walcott dealt with this isolating quality of the sea in his poems in *The Gulf* (1969). The sea is, however, also a connecting element, that invites one to leave behind the limitations of the shoreline, that invites one to cross beyond and link up with other parts of the world. Walcott had looked at the classical archipelago of the Ionian islands as a bridge between Asia and Europe. The Homeric Tales travelled over the seas and through the islands to the West, as he has described it in *Omeros* (1990) and the most recent play *The Odyssey* (1993). In Walcott's view, the Caribbean archipelago is for the modern world what the Ionian Archipelago was for classical antiquity: it bridges the gulf between the old and the new world, between East and West, North and South. The Caribbean is where neo-Homeric yarns are spun in tales of loss, alienation, dislocation and in tales of re-identification, home-coming and acculturation (Figueroa 1991; Hamner 1986). Insularity and universality, centrifugal and centripetal movements, looking inside and reaching beyond, all these are essentials of West Indian experience and as such at the heart of much of Walcott's writings.

Walcott and the American Tradition

Dream on Monkey Mountain (1970a) is Walcott's most successful play. It won the Obi-Award as the best foreign play in the United States (US) in

1970 and it was performed as part of the cultural programme of the 1972 Olympic Games in Munich. It deals with racial and individual identity and the question of how to come into one's own. Its structure is that of a procession play. The plot itself and the temporal structure relate to the stations of the cross. The Passion of Christ obviously provides the subtext when Makak, the hero of the play, descends from Monkey Mountain, performs miraculous healings, triumphantly rides on his mule into the town of Quatre Chemins, where he is arrested and brought before the market inspector Caiphas Pamphilion — even the names match the Biblical story.

Makak is put into prison and tried together with the two felons, Souris (mouse) and Tigre, and eventually resurrected as king of the African tribes, where he sits in court to pass judgement over the White Goddess. The character of the passion play appears to be of lesser importance on the level of construction of meanings. But the structure of the passion play and its popularity relate *Dream on Monkey Mountain* to theatrical folk traditions and popular religious practices. For the constitution of meaning Walcott relates to another model of greater importance, i.e., *A Dream Play* (2005) by August Strindberg. Through the revelation of the dream passages, the sub-conscious of the individual and the entire race are laid open and brought to the forefront on the level of consciousness. That is the process that brings Makak back from his elementary consciousness and reinstates him in his individual identity of Felix Hubain. Finally the play is also an endeavour to regain control over the discourse about race, racial consciousness and identity, particularly in relation to another play that also cites Strindberg's *A Dream Play* as its model for inspiration, namely Eugene O'Neill's *The Emperor Jones* (1969[1922]).

The Emperor Jones, particularly in the famous production with Charles Gilpin in the lead role, had tremendous influence on the image of the Negro at the very outset of the Harlem Renaissance (ibid.). O'Neill's *The Emperor Jones* is informed by the most recent reception of psychoanalysis in the Jungian archetypal version. Jones's journey from his imperial palace on an 'island in the West Indies as yet not self-determined by White Marines' (ibid.: 146) to the hut of the Congo Witch priest, where he finally surrenders to the power of an African river god in the form of a crocodile, is presented as a journey into the individual and the collective subconscious.

The play is loaded with settings symbolic of psychoanalytical concepts: the jungle, the night as spatial and temporal locations of the *Nachtbewußtsein*, i.e., the darker side of the human subconscious. The dream concept and the iconic presentation of such archetypal situations as the slave market (Scene Five), the slave ship on the Middle Passage (Scene Six) stand for the re-surfacing of the subconscious to the level of the *Tagesbewußtsein* (consciousness). O'Neill structured his play about the degradation of an apparently outstanding human personality to a figure of merest animal existence through six stations of a journey downward from bright broad daylight into the dusk and the dark night of the jungle, or from an ostentatiously self-conscious emperor down into the abyss of absolute natural primitivism (ibid.).

Jones re-experiences in his dream vision stations of his individual history that constitute his individual identity: the killing of Jep for playing with loaded dice (Scene Three) and the killing of the road gang warden (Scene Four). This is followed by stations that constitute the collective history of the race — the collective sub-conscious — in the scene of the slave auction and aboard the slave ship on the Middle Passage from Africa to the Americas, quite in line with the teaching of psychoanalysis, where individual consciousness and identity develop on the basis of collective and racial consciousness.

O'Neill gives three recurring signals that underline the schematism of the plot structure, and thereby help to construct the meaning of the play (ibid.). He times each of his stations precisely by spelling out the exact hour of the day in his stage directions. We first see Emperor Jones in his palace at three o'clock in the afternoon, he enters the jungle at nightfall — six o'clock in the evening — and his dead body is brought back from the jungles onto centre-stage just after six o'clock the following morning. Linear chronology is strongly emphasized, also to underline the fatality and the inevitablity of Jones's fate (ibid.). On the visual level, O'Neill repeats the degradation motif by way of costume use. In the opening scene at the imperial palace, we see Jones in his full and gaudy operatic uniform. From scene to scene, he is stripped of these outward signs of a preposterously assumed status and in the last scene, we see him clad just in a loin cloth. We are clearly made to understand that the uniform in which we first encounter Jones in his palace is covering up his true identity and that the gradual stripping of the uniform reveals his animal identity. On the aural level O'Neill repeats the same message by the iconic sound of tomtom drumming (ibid.). Drumming is, of course, the most common icon for the Africanness in the stereotyped white vision of African-Americans. O'Neill's dramatic use of tomtom drumming echoes one of the most popular ballads of the Harlem Renaissance, Langston Hughes' *Danse Africaine* (1989[1922]):

> The low beating of the tom-toms,
>   The slow beating of the tom-toms,
>   Low ... slow
> Slow ... low
> Stirs your blood.
>   Dance!
> A night veiled girl
> Whirles softly into a
> Circle of light,
> Whirls softly ... slowly
>   Like a wisp of smoke around the fire
>   And the tom-toms beat,
>   And the tom-toms beat
> And the low beating of the tom-toms
>   Stirs your blood (Hughes 1989[1922]: 7).

The growing intensity and volume, but also the increasing rhythmic speed of the drumming represents the increasing impact of Africanness while the gradual discarding of bits and pieces of Jones's uniform stands for the decrease in his assumed whiteness. O'Neill's play presents exclusively external ascriptions of identity (O'Neill 1969). The description of what constitutes Black identity rests exclusively on the white concept of Jungian psychoanalysis and a purely Western structure, that of the linear plot development.

Dream on Monkey Mountain (Walcott 1970a) is quite obviously a direct answer to O'Neill's *The Emperor Jones*. Although the structure, the setting, the characters appear to be quite different, many scenes in the two plays directly contrast with each other: Makak in his charcoal burner's cabin as opposed to Jones in his palace; Makak's triumphant entry into Quatre Chemins market as opposed to Jones's slave market; Makak's sailing back to Africa to claim his royal ancestral throne as opposed to Jones's slave ship; Makak's sitting in state on the throne, ruling over the African tribes and finally executing the White Goddess as opposed to Jones prostrating himself in front of the witch doctor's cabin, the river god and being finally killed by Jep's warriors. *Dream on Monkey Mountain* has a circular structure as opposed to *The Emperor Jones*'s strictly linear structure. Consequently, the play is also vague in its temporal structure as opposed to O'Neill's exact clocking of each and every scene. As every dream-play of necessity must do, *Dream on Monkey Mountain* starts out in a space that is clearly defined as 'real', and then dives into the realms of the imaginary spaces of the dream allegory. Real space is the cabin on Monkey Mountain and the prison cell in Quatre Chemins police station. It is from the charcoal burner's cabin and the prison cell that Makak forages out onto his dream excursions.

The play opens with a mock trial (after a dream-like dance and mime prelude) that establishes Makak's non-identity. Makak answers the police officer's question 'What is your name?' with 'I have forgotten'. To the question 'What is your tribe?' the answer is 'Tired'. This tiredness is seen as specifically West Indian. When Makak tries his miraculous healing powers and the crowd fails to respond, he comments: 'They are too tired to believe anything' (ibid.: 219–20). None of the questions that Corporal Lestrade asks concerning his personal status are answered satisfactorily by Makak., i.e., in terms of civil administration, Makak is a non-identifiable person. Walcott underlines this aspect of non-identity of the Caribbean peasant population by his naming of characters. It is only the representatives of state authority who have proper names: Corporal Lestrade as police officer and Caiphas Pamphilion as the market inspector. With the name Caiphas another association with the passion sub-plot is constituted. The other characters are given de-individualizing generic names like Makak the monkey, Tigre, Souris the mouse, Moustique the fly. The characters are thereby associated to the African-Caribbean tradition of the animal tale. Walcott reveals how the annihilation of West Indian personality operates on the two levels: the private and the public. On the public level, it is the police officer Lestrade (who straddles the black and the white world) who submits Makak to a degrading routine that is meant to demonstrate Makak's absolute lack of power and lack of will power, and his complete domination by the concepts of civilization as represented by the rules and the rulers of the colonial regime.

On the private level, it is the white goddess whose mask Makak hides under his bed, who instills in him the misconceptions about his African ancestry — it is the white goddess who generates in him the dream of Africa as his home. The degradation as a second-class citizen on the formal plane and the psychic dislocation in the yearning for Africa on the private informal level, are the conditions for the prevailing West Indian identity of externally prescribed values and concepts. It allows for the islands to function only as an accidental physical or geographical home, while it refers the West Indian to other spiritual and cultural homes that are fabrications of the imagination and lie beyond the space occupied in real life.

O'Neill had based his psycho-drama about Emperor Jones on the Jungian version of psychoanalysis, Walcott arranges his play around Frantz Fanon's theories about colonial psychopathology. Fanon's seminal *Black Skin, White Masks* (1967) and in particular Chapter VII on 'Colonial Psychopathology' provide the basis for an understanding of Makak's original psychic disposition (as monkey) and his psychic growth and liberation through the dream experience that finally makes him accept his subject position, his individuality as Felix Hubain. Like the tom-tom drumming in *The Emperor Jones* (O'Neill 1969), the mask of the white goddess is a recurring motif in *Dream on Monkey Mountain* that emphasizes the Fanonean inspiration of the play. The black skin-white masks-syndrome manifests itself differently with the different characters. This is visualized on stage in that Makak sees the white apparition while Corporal Lestrade and the others see nothing; later, it is the police corporal and his entourage who stare at the white apparition while Makak has already gone beyond the recognition of that symbol of mental bondage. It is also revealing that the mulatto Lestrade switches chameleon-like between aping the white value world and becoming the firebrand of a black consciousness movement that has arisen around Makak at his royal court in Africa. Lestrade is the one who upholds unthinkingly the order of the colonial master and submits Makak to that humiliating monkey routine and to the mock trial that establishes Makak's non-identity.

In the second mock trial in the African dream palace, it is Lestrade who pleads mercilessly for the death sentence and the immediate execution of the white goddess. It is the task of Makak, the African dream king and spiritual leader of the tribes, to perform the ritual killing of the white goddess and thereby liberate himself and his people from her psychic despotism. After beheading the goddess, Makak says: 'Now, I am free!' (Walcott 1970a: 320).

In the final scene, back on the 'reality level' of the prison cell in Quatre Chemins and up on Monkey Mountain, we encounter a completely changed Makak, who suddenly remembers his 'real' name, Felix Hubain. Thus, he is reinstated in his civil identity. When he returns to his cabin on the mountain top, he concludes 'This is where I belong', thereby affirming his Caribbean social and cultural identity (ibid.: 326). The resistance against the colonial administrative monkeyism and the rejection of the African dream *à la* Négritude lead Makak to a realization of his true West Indian identity and to a positive identification with the place in which he lives.

Walcott and the Great Tradition

In his collections of poems *The Castaway and Other Poems* (1965b), Walcott concentrated for the first time on the figure of Robinson Crusoe as a symbol of human existence in general and of West Indian experience in particular. Being shipwrecked, being stranded, being a castaway who has to gain control over his own insular individual existence became his metaphor for human existence. Walcott alludes to the debate carried on in the field of the history of mentality that associated the discovery of the New World with the Renaissance longing for a second Eden, for Renaissance man to act as second Adam, for Renaissance utopian redemption myths as, for example, the myth of El Dorado. Walcott packed all these late medieval and Renaissance myths into the figure of Robinson Crusoe, that epitome of Protestant rationalism and enlightenment. These spiritual and emotive undercurrents in the character of Crusoe provide a new dimension for that personality that in the British tradition has assumed such an elevated status as a hero of religious dedication and colonial expansion. In 'Crusoe's Island' Walcott writes:

> Upon this rock the bearded hermit built
> His Eden:
> Goats, corn-crop, fort, parasol, garden,
> Bible for Sabbath, all the joys
> But one
> Which sent him howling for a human voice.
> ....
> The second Adam since the fall,
> His germinal
> Corruption held the seed
> Of that congenital heresy that men fail
> According to their creed.
> Craftsman and castaway
> All heaven in his head,
> He watched his shadow pray
> Not for God's love but human love instead (ibid.: 55).

Walcott sees Crusoe as a human being with emotional needs and a longing for human closeness and personal attachment rather than abstract religiosity. In 'Crusoe's Journal' (1965a: 51–53), Walcott further emphasizes the humanity of Robinson Crusoe as opposed to the virulent interpretations of the famous journal passage in Daniel Defoe's novel, that was taken as an affirmation of Puritan rightousness and Calvinist pre-determination. While Defoe's Crusoe gives the daily account of his religious and ethical assets on his way to heaven by stating his good deeds in relation to the goals he set himself, Walcott's Crusoe is more governed by accidence, by fatality, than by premeditation and predetermination. This is so because Walcott's Crusoe is a composite character comprising many different trends of the Occidental history of mentalities, while Defoe's Crusoe — at least in the most generally accepted interpretations of the Great Tradition — is more of a mono-directional, monochrome, singly motivated character. Walcott explains his concept in his essay 'The Figure of Crusoe' (1965c):

> My Crusoe, then, is Adam, Christopher Columbus, God, a missionary, a beachcomber, and his interpreter, Daniel Defoe. He is Adam because he is the first inhabitant of a second paradise. He is Columbus because he has discovered this new world, by accident, by fatality. He is God because he teaches himself to control his creation, he rules the world he has made, and also, because he is to Friday, a white concept of Godhead. He is a missionary because he instructs Friday in the uses of religion ... He is a beachcomber because I have imagined him as one of those figures of adolescent literature, some derelict out of Conrad and Stevenson ... and finally, he is also Daniel Defoe, because the Journal of Crusoe, which is Defoe's journal, was written in prose, not in poetry, and our literature, the pioneers of public literature have expressed themselves in prose (ibid.).

Next to William Shakespeare's *The Tempest* (1610–11), Defoe's novel became a key text for post-colonial intertextual writing. It was not the straightforward narrative of conquest of *Captain Singleton* (Defoe 1720), that induced the South African writer J. M. Coetzee (*Foe* [1986]) or Walcott to respond with their own re-creations, but it is the more subtle tale about the solitary colonizer Crusoe who inspired them.

Walcott came back to his favourite theme of Robinson Crusoe again in his play *Pantomime* (1980). Here, the duplicity of meanings is already injected into the title. In the British understanding, pantomime is a light Christmas entertainment of a fairytale character, a type of theatrical performance that was made popular in the West Indies by the Theatre Company of the Naval Officers, stationed at Port Royal (Hill 1992: 41).

With the 1948 pantomime 'Anancy', the pantomime became radically West-Indianized. It drew on motives from folklore — Anancy, the trickster from Akan oral tradition, always caused roars of laughter — where the sweet pill of oral lore was seasoned with spicy social and political comment. The West-Indianized pantomime has become the popularly accepted medium of resistance, of talking back to, of rejecting official views and official values. In this capacity, the pantomime in the West Indian understanding is an unruly folk opera, a typical form of cultural expression in the final years of the colonial era.

Walcott's *Pantomime* (1980) is a play about a play that never came onto the stage. But it is also a play about a misunderstanding — deliberately or inadvertently — of the generic properties of pantomime. Harry Trewe, a one-time English actor, has retired to the island of Tobago — generally considered as Crusoe's island — where he is running a ramshackle hotel. The only hand to assist him is the ex-Calypsonian Jackson Phillip. Both characters have their background in the performing arts, though, of course, in very different traditions. It is Harry Trewe, who has the splendid idea of welcoming his guests for the opening of the tourist season with a little pantomime. And what could be more appropriate for Tobago than to perform a play about Crusoe and Friday. Jackson Phillip is not so taken by his master's idea. He agrees to take part in the performance only on the condition that he is playing the part of Crusoe. Thus, the white Harry Trewe has to take the part of the black cannibal Friday.

Jackson Phillip takes his role very seriously, also within the West Indian concept of pantomime. He obviously feels that he has to reconquer and reappropriate his own cultural space, which is most effectively achieved through a Bakhtinian Carnevalesque inversion of world views and heavenly values. Above all, Jackson Phillip excels in the art of re-reading the Great Tradition text, which Harry Trewe in his British admiration has over-stylized into iconic proportions. Harry Trewe conceived a bombastic opening monologue for Crusoe in a style that Walcott decried in another context as 'postcard poetry'. Jackson Phillip mercilessly tears Harry Trewe's text to pieces by insisting on his interpretation of the figure of Crusoe as a pragmatic West Indian.

> Jackson: He not sitting on his shipwrecked arse bawling out ... "O silent sea, O wondrous sunset," and all that shit. No. He shipwrecked. He desperate, he hungry. He look up and he see this fucking goat with its fucking beard watching him and smiling, this goat with its forked fucking beard and square yellow eye just like the fucking devil standing up there ...
>
> (*Pantomimes the goat and Crusoe in turn*)
>
> smiling at him, and putting out its tongue and letting go one fucking bleeeeeeh! And Robbie ent thinking 'bout his wife and son and O silent sea

and O wondrous sunset; no, Robbie is the First True Creole, so he watching the goat with his eyes narrow, narrow, and he say: *blehhh*, eh? You motherfucker, I go show you *blehhh* in your goat-ass, and vam, vam, next thing is Robbie and goat, *mano a mano*, man to man, man to goat, goat to man, wrestling on the sand, and next thing we know we hearing one last faint, feeble *bleeeeeehhhhhhhhhhhh*, and Robbie is next seen walking up the beach with a goatskin hat and a goatskin umbrella, feeling like a million dollars because he *have faith* (Walcott 1980: 148).

Jackson Phillip sees in the West Indies not the second Eden, but a place of enslavement, violence, cheating, and bloodshed, and his Crusoe is part of that historical tradition. Walcott's play operates on three different levels in its effort to deconstruct the hallowed 'Great Tradition' and reconstruct a truly West Indian text. The most obvious level is that of the carnevalesque inversion on the level of themes. The second level is that of physical acting and mime, where Jackson Phillip mimes all the parts — Crusoe, Friday — but also the parts of the animals, the sea and the natural environment, thus visually supplementing the stage directions. The third level is that of language. Jackson Phillip recites the words of Harry Trewe's text in an immaculately formal English. But at the same time, he enacts Harry Trewe's vision by overdone mime, and on top of that, he comments on his own acting and on Trewe's wording in his informal West Indian Creole. Jackson Phillip is also insistent on taking his acting very seriously, for example when he uses an upturned table as Crusoe's raft and mimes the landing on the shores of Tobago. When Harry Trewe impatiently interferes, Phillip insists on completing the action in which he is in at the moment: letting himself carefully down from the raft, wading through the shallow water to the shore, and only when he is mimetically on firm ground again, does he accept to respond to Harry Trewe's objections.

> I think it's a matter of prejudice. I think that you cannot believe ... that any black man should play Robinson Crusoe. A little while aback, I came out here ... with the breakfast things and find you almost stark naked, kneeling down and you told me you were getting into your part. Here am I getting into *my* part and you object. This is the story ... this is history. This moment that we are now acting here is the history of imperialism; it's nothing less than that ... I could go down to that beach ... and I could play Robinson Crusoe, I could play Columbus, I could play Sir Francis Drake, I could play anybody discovering anywhere, but I don't want you to tell me ... what to discover and when to discover it, All right? (ibid.: 125)

The determination with which Jackson Phillip insists on playing Crusoe the way he sees him, makes Trewe gradually realize how dubious his perspective of history has been. And when Jackson, in his capacity as second Adam, even insists on his right to name things and persons, when he decides to name that 'white cannibal' played by Harry Trewe — not Friday, but Thursday, it suddenly dawns on Harry Trewe that his little pantomime has been changed into a fully-fledged drama on the philosophy of history:

> *Harry*: All right, so it's . . . Thursday. He comes across this naked white cannibal called Thursday, you know. And then, look at what would happen. He would have to start to . . . well, he'd have to, sorry . . . This cannibal, who is a Christian, would have to start unlearning his Christianity. He would have to be taught . . . I mean . . . he'd have to be taught by this — African — that everything was wrong, that what he was doing . . . I mean, for nearly two thousand years . . . was wrong. That his civilization, his culture, his whatever, was . . . *horrible*. Was all . . . wrong. Barbarous, I mean, you know. And Crusoe would then have to teach him things like, you know, about . . . Africa, his Gods, patamba, and so on . . . and it would get very, very complicated, and I suppose ultimately it would be very boring, and what we'd have on our hands would be . . . would be a play and not a little pantomime . . . (ibid.: 126).

With 'Dream on Monkey Mountain' (1970a), Walcott seemed entirely 'original', strictly Caribbean in setting and atmosphere. Our analysis however showed, that Walcott engaged in a confrontational debate with Eugene O'Neill's *The Emperor Jones* (1969), another seminal dramatic text on African-American identity. Walcott's counter-discourse from the 1960s, when the atmosphere was dominated by the Civil Rights and Black Consciousness movements, reveals O'Neill's dramatic text as condescendingly paternalistic. The Harlem Renaissance, the Jazz Age style, the agencies of the West Indians Claude MacKay and Marcus Garvey, and the benevolent support from whites like Carl van Vechten obviously gave preference to an imagology based on racial stereotypes, on archetypal structures that claimed to be colour blind but weren't. Jung's archetypal psychoanalysis, that informs much of the writing in and about Black America shortly before and after 1930, still maintains the white Western norm as the baseline for character constellation and interaction.

Walcott's story of Makak's homecoming to Monkey Mountain from an imagined journey to an African kingdom (cf. Soyinka 1963) in his regained identity as Felix Hubain establishes his Caribbean hero in his subject position. Although Walcott never mentioned O'Neill as a pretext, it is pretty obvious that he means to respond to that text. Walcott clearly intends to set the record on West Indian identity straight. It also appears that Walcott's *Dream on Monkey Mountain* in its reaction/relation to *The Emperor Jones* is aiming and achieving very much the same for the Caribbean as Chinua Achebe aspired to with *Things Fall Apart* (1958) in relation to Joseph Conrad's *Heart of Darkness* (1899) or Joyce Cary's *Mister Johnson* (1939).

Walcott dismisses white paternalists and Black Negritudinists as false prophets when it comes to the role of the true and truthful spokesperson on West Indian-ness, on West Indian identity. The Caribbean writers have the right and the duty to speak for themselves.

With *Pantomime* (1980), Walcott's strategy of adaptation changes drastically. He actually made adaptation, the mechanisms, the strategies and processes of adapting one 'canonical' imperial text to a post-colonial situation, the major topic of his play. Adaptation became the key issue on all levels of presentation. On the level of genre he negotiates the West Indian pantomime *vs* the British panto tradition on the level of different performance traditions, on the level of language (Creole *vs* Standard English) and particularly on the level of characterization. Walcott thematizes the issue of a post-colonial reading when he brings in the incidental issue of 'racial casting' (Black actor playing a white character and vice versa) which creates a total change of perspective that gives birth to a debate on cultural relativism.

Walcott and the Greek Classics

Time and again Walcott had drawn on his education in classics and played on the similarities of the Caribbean and the Ionian island worlds. The Homeric tales stand at the very beginning of Western literary history. They appear apparently out of nowhere, without precedent and yet already right from the beginning perfect in theme, style and form, and thus became the model for the literary tradition of the heroic tale, the grand narrative, the narration that generates cultural identities. The *Iliad* (Schrott 2008b) (which Walcott had touched on in *Ione* [1957]), celebrates the victory of the Occident — the new up and coming cultural and military power — over the Orient that had apparently existed for a long time, but had not found artistic and cultural expression in a written national narrative (the *Epic of Gilgamesh* being the exception). This at least was the allegation, carefully tended to and maintained by the academic discipline of classics. Cultural, ethnic, linguistic purity as the essence of those Homeric tales of cultural origin, this myth of the Greek classical ideal became the foundation myth of Western aesthetics from the 18th century on, as propagated by German classics scholar Winkelmann on the Continent or Lord Elgin in Britain (the most unrestrained, large-scale pirate of classical sculpture).

Walcott's approach differs from this in the sense in that he looks at the classical Ionian archipelago with the sensibility of the 20th-century islander in the West Indies. For Walcott the islands are stations on the transitory routes of migration for people, goods, material and symbolic cultural values. Islands can function as stages of solidification for these migrant ideas, but they can also be stages of transition and transformation. Thus the ideas of the 'old Orient' impact on their transit route the new developing ideas of the Occident and merge into a new hybrid form of cultural development — this process of creolization obviously originated at the very beginning of classical antiquity. Being from the West Indies, where hybridization is the order of the day in religion, music, oral traditions, languages and even food and dress, Walcott was obviously particularly receptive to that classical model of a creolization process way back at the hour of the birth of the Western cultural tradition. Walcott thereby conforms to more recent findings in Classical literary studies but above all the more recent exploration in archaeology which prove beyond doubt that the purity of classical Greek culture and art is fake, and that Homer's tales do not document the immaculate birth of cultural purity or even the result of the victory of one culture over another, but are the result of an amalgamation of pre-Homeric tales, of Hetitian stories and myths, i.e., old Oriental tales that were cast in a new and modern (Greek) form. This ties in nicely with the recent debate about the originality of the Homeric tales generally. There has always been the saying that we know what Homer looked like and what he wrote, but we were never sure whether he actually lived. A new dimension in the debate about the person of the author was advanced in 2008 when the Austrian writer/critic Raoul Schrott published *Homers Heimat* (2008a) in which he claimed that Homer really hailed from Kilikia (not Greece or the Greek coastline of Anatolia) and wrote in the service of Assyrian authorities. At the time of writing *Omeros* (1990) and *The Odyssey* (1993), Walcott could not have known about these latest results of an ongoing debate about Homer's true identity, but it is significant to see that Walcott adopts a post-colonial perspective similar to that of Wole Soyinka in his adaptation (*The Bacchae of Euripides* [1973]) of Euripides'

The Bacchae (405 BCE). Soyinka too, strongly emphasizes the mixed qualities of the central character of Dionysos, not as a pure figure of Greek rationality, but as the wild hybrid character that incorporates the irrational and ecstatic qualities and rituals of the oriental deity rather than the more utilitarian aspects of Dionysos as god of spring, rebirth, regeneration, and in essence as god of production and productivity.

Walcott's *Odyssey* pursues yet another strategy of adaptation (Hardwick 2004: 19–241). He calls the play 'a stage version', suggesting a 'true' translation from the epic narrative representation to the dramatic presentation on stage (ibid.). Very much like Soyinka's adaptation of Euripides' *The Bacchae*, Walcott's *Odyssey* appears absolutely faithful to the original. The original locations were maintained: the beach at Troy with the departing ships of the Greek army of invasion, the various islands visited by Odysseus, the island of Aeolos and his daughter Nausicaa, Polyphemus/Cyclops' islands, the island of Circe, the straits of Scylla and Charybdis, the shallows and cliffs of the Sirens, the pillars of Hercules (the Straits of Gibraltar) figuring significantly to indicate the limits of classical Greek geography. Walcott also maintains the major characters in their classical functions: Odysseus, Menelaus, Agamemnon, and Nestor as Greek commanders; Penelope and Telemachus, the wife and son of the Greek knight errant Odysseus; Eurycleia the nurse; and Eumaeus the swineherd; Elpenor the helmsman; and Stratis, Costa, Stavros, and Tasso from Odysseus' crew who were drowned in the shipwreck (Walcott 1993). But the repetition and pretended sameness of plot, episode and character is deceptive. We soon realize that this play has a completely different ring to it, that it is not an Elgin Marbles or Lord Byron-style veneration of an idealized classical Greece, but a recreation that is distinctly West Indian in tone.

The major vehicle for this West-Indianization is again language. Walcott plays on a range of linguistic variants, from the moderately West Indian accent as the idiom of the Trojan heroes to a deep Creole spoken by the indigenous islanders or sailors. The blind singer Billie Blue exploits the full range of linguistic variations in his speech. When Walcott leaves behind the Western tradition of the high-pitched tone imitating the classical Greek poetic diction, when he brings down the language from the heights of hero worship to the pragmatic language usage of commoners, he also changes the quality of the characters and redesigns the heroic profile.

Walcott's *Odyssey* (ibid.) opens with a scene on the beach where the Greek generals assemble around the funeral pyre of Achilles, the last of the great Greek heroes to lose his life in the war against Troy, with the smoke of the smoldering ruins of Troy, the greatest city of the Orient in the background. The assembly on the beach acquires the character of an official declaration of the end of the war. It took the Greeks 10 years before Menelaus, Nestor and Agamemnon could solemnly declare their 'Mission Accomplished'.

Celebrating their victory and the restitution of their national pride as the official part of the celebration recedes immediately vis-à-vis the still unsettled issue of the private profits and gains from this war. The Greek war heroes without exception prove to be rapacious and profit-oriented warlords, filling their ships to capacity with the booty of defeated Troy before embarking to sail back to Greece. The distribution of the spoils becomes the most important issue and from the beginning we see Odysseus as the most rapacious and acquisitive of the Greek generals.

Odysseus is the last to join the group of Greek commanders and the first to state his claims. He even insists on taking Achilles' shield, forged by Zeus's son Hephaistos — God of metalworking and technology. Achilles had willed this shield to Ajax, the young warrior hero of the Greeks. Achilles' shield is charged with extreme symbolic value since it protected him in his famous fight with Troy's greatest hero, Hector. The shield will protect Odysseus' life in the course of the play, but Odysseus uses the shield to hide instead of fight. He hides under the shield like a tortoise in its shell — the exact opposite of classical heroism. Here Walcott links up again to the Afro-Caribbean oral tradition where Tortoise is — next to spider/man Anancy — the most famous trickster hero on both sides of the Black Atlantic.

Odysseus' insistence marks him out as a war profiteer, not a hero in pursuit of classical ideals. When the other commanders leave, he 'retrieves more souvenirs from the funeral mound' (ibid.: 4). This image of an aggressive entrepreneurship in the martial business world is repeated throughout the play, in Odysseus's own actions, in the assessment by others, in reported speech. Nestor, Menelaus and even the staff of his home base in Ithaca refer to Odysseus as '[t]oo smart. Too acquisitive' (ibid.: 32). Walcott has Menelaus referring to him as '[t]hat sacker of cities? He'd say "Kings have to live" ... He took his share ... he's coming back well-loaded, you can be sure' (ibid.: 32–33). Odysseus' son Telemachus, hearing about the deeds of his father ('He did well from the war? ... That's why Troy burned ...' [ibid.: 32] shakes his head in disbelief: 'He sounds like a rug seller, not a warrior' (ibid.). Even Odysseus's crew discuss the rapaciousness of their captain: 'Done all right by the war, din't he? Looting, sacking ... He's made his fortune ... No sharing the swag ... He's made a pile from the war. Gold cups, coins, that shield' (Walcott 1993: 38, 42). Sacker of cities, fighting for booty, stealing substantial treasures, all this sounds very familiar in the Caribbean context, because that is the essence of the many pirate stories and the pirate lore in the Caribbean.

Even at his last stop at the Aeolian Island, we see how Odysseus' crew members Stavros, Tasso and Costa bring additional booty on board. Aeolos, god of the winds, suspecting that Odysseus abused his hospitality makes Odysseus a present with the distinct qualities of the Trojan horse: a huge bag with allegedly invaluable treasures. Aeolos seems to have speculated on the rapaciousness of Odysseus and his crew, that they would disregard his strict instructions not to open the bags before reaching home. The crew opens the bags and out come the adverse winds that blow Odysseus and his ship off their course into more dangerous adventures: the cliffs and shallows of Scylla and Charybdis, the Sirens, and eventually end with the loss of ship and crew.

All these descriptions undermine the image of the celebrated Greek hero and replace it by the typical West Indian hero: the buccaneer, the freebooter, the martial entrepreneur who has taken over at his own risk and his own cost the business of 'Her Majesty's' naval warfare. Sir Henry Morgan, 'the most notorious buccaneer ... and his capture of Panama City in 1670 in a furious battle followed by twenty-eight days of fire, pillage and violence before Morgan withdrew with £10,000 worth of spoils' (Augier et al. 1960: 54), as a true West Indian hero could have stood as model for the figure of Odysseus as violent, brutal and profit-oriented.

Each episode of Odysseus' quest journey concentrates on one particular feature of the West Indian hero in a rather mixed and composite, even contradictory set of characterstics. This creates an opaque and multifarious quality of the hero, trickster, villain. The Nausicaa episode gives us a glimpse of the womanizer, the playboy that haunts the beaches of the Caribbean islands. The Polyphemus and Circe episodes are most explicit. The episode on Cyclops/Polyphemus's islands reflects the political atmosphere in the Caribbean in the 1950s and 1960s. On landing on Polyphemus' island, Odysseus and his crew are captured. Polyphemus invites Odysseus to dinner, an invitation that must not be ignored. Polyphemus, seemingly soft-mouthed, interrogates Odysseus about his intentions, his crew and his stories. He proves to be a shrewd and brutal dictator, who pursues intellectuals, suppresses freedom of expression and alternative ideas. He obviously commands a sophisticated machinery of secret police, surveillance and suppression, where torture, murder, even cannibalism occurs. Odysseus sits at Polyphemus' table, wondering whether the meat on his plate is the meat of his crew members, murdered by Polyphemus and his men. Thus, Polyphemus reveals all the characteristics of the most infamous Caribbean dictators at the time, of Papa Doc Duvalier in Haiti, of Trujillo in the Dominican Republic, or Batista in Cuba.

Odysseus cheats Polyphemus in the manner of the trickster hero. He plays on Polyphemus one of the oldest trickster tricks, playing on the old linguistic riddle tradition of wrong, misleading names. He tells Polyphemus, who is brutal, cruel, but not particularly bright, that his name is 'Nobody', that he is on 'his way home to Nowhere' — an old Tortoise story. So when Odysseus manages to escape and Polyphemus calls for help shouting 'Nobody blinded me, he has escaped to Nowhere' (Walcott 1993: 71), none of his underlings will come to help him. Consequently, Odysseus manages to escape hiding under Achilles' shield which the enraged monster mistakes for the shell of a tortoise. (In the original Odysseus and his men are hiding under the bellies of sheep.)

In his poem about his West Indian identity, Walcott had concluded: 'I am either nobody, or I am a whole Nation' (Walcott 1977). Vis-à-vis Polyphemus he exploits the nonentity of his Caribbean identity. Sailing away from Cyclops' island, Odysseus teases the defeated monster once more by revealing his real identity:

"Son of Poseidon, you obscene octopus ... my name is not Nobody! It is Odysseus ..."

(The Cyclops picks up an oil drum and hurls it at the retreating Odysseus ...)" (Walcott 1993: 72).

The oil drum also reclassifies the episode as West Indian rather than classical Greek. Trinidad was one of the major fuelling ports for the US navy during World War II and Trinidad's contribution to world music the steelband, consisting of tuned petrol drums — testifies to the iconic quality of the oil drum in the Caribbean.

The barbecue skewer instead of the wooden pole hardened in fire as the instrument for the blinding, hiding under Achilles' shield as a tortoise shell instead of under Polyphemus' sheep, the petrol drum instead of the rock — these paraphernalia establish the Caribbean atmosphere and suggest a Caribbean scenario in which Polyphemus acts as one of the Caribbean dictators and/or as another version of Papa Diable/Papa Bois, to be outwitted by the Anancy and Tortoise trickster. Walcott successfully relocated the Cyclops episode not geographically, but definitely in atmosphere and character profile from the Ionian islands to the Caribbean.

The most drastic adaptation to the Caribbean scenario appears in the Circe episode where Odysseus' crew dance across the stage as carnival revellers. Sexually dehydrated, having been onboard ship for years, the men assault the women on Circe's island. This is of course what Circe had practically arranged to happen, namely to expose men as swine in their relationship to women. In Walcott's version, there is a touch of masquerade and carnevalesque performance; it appears as if the sailors are 'playing mass', that they are just part of a wild carnival ritual (Balme 1999: 128).

> Aeaea
> Aeaea ......
> Ai-ee-o
> Bacchanal
> And Carnival
> Is the place to go ...
>
> O Lord have mercy
> On all me sins, is true
> But when Circe spell fell on me
> I turn beast too (Walcott 1993: 75)

They celebrate the licentiousness, the obscenity and the violation of the rules of everyday life as the essence of carnival. Walcott gradually transforms this bacchanalian ecstasy into a religious ritual, where Zeus and Athena, the Yoruba gods Shango, Ogun, Erzulie, and the Caribbean Maman de l'Eau join in an ecstatic performance of religious trance and spirit possession (ibid.: 87) such as are practiced in the Pocomania or Camboulaye rituals. Walcott retained the classical Greek localities and names, but he models his characters clearly according to popular figures of West Indian folklore.

Athena, daughter of Zeus, who protected Odysseus against the wrath of Poseidon, bears witness to the creolized mythological heritage in the

Caribbean. Athena deviates significantly from the classical norm. In the Greek original, she is the goddess of the arts, invention and wisdom; in Walcott's version she becomes a much more pragmatic deity standing for 'applied wisdom', for sagacity, cleverness and expediency. In this capacity she is at par with Odysseus. With Walcott she assumes the qualities and appearance of a *Madame (Maman) de l'Eau* — a close relative to the Caribbean *Mammy Wata*. But she also changes into other characters: into Captain Mentes, into Circe's maid and then she assumes the qualities of the *obeah*[2] woman, the Voudoun priestess. She protects Odysseus against the charms of Circe, whose magic potion makes men fall for her. To counter Circe's charm, Athena draws a flour circle around Circe's bed. Magical signs and a protective circle drawn in flour that keeps out the evil spirits that might harm the worshipper belong to the essence of Voudoun rituals.

Walcott not only adapts the scenario, the locations to the Caribbean environment, he also plays strongly on the commonalities and differences in the narrative and performative traditions between the classical Homeric and modern Caribbean orality. With the figure of Blind Billie Blue, Walcott presents us with a character that represents the various narrative traditions of classic and Caribbean lore. Blind Billie Blue functions as narrator, stage manager, the omniscient persona who links the various locations, connects the scenes and confirms the continuity in plot development across different time layers. He links the episodes of Odysseus at sea, of his wife Penelope and son Telemachus on Ithaca, or Menelaus in Sparta.

The figure of Blind Billie Blue recalls the figure of Homer, the blind poet, singer who according to classicist literary tradition created the first and the real original specimen of the western heroic tale, the 'Urbild', the model of the grand narrative to which all later writers will be indebted. Billie Blue/Homer also stands for the transition from oral tradition to written transmission, the narrator who shifted the tone and location from the original Oriental setting to the archipelegan settings of the Greek classics. Billie Blue also functions as satirical commentator, a character carved in the shape of the West Indian Calypsonian, the Chantewell, the 'Crick-Crack' storyteller of the animal folktale, and he thus closes the circle of narrative traditions from pre-classical orality through classical literacy to academic literary traditionalism and the post-colonial re-oralization of the classical Greek tales.

---

[2] Healer, witch doctor, soothsayer, sorcerer.

Euryclea, the nurse of both Odysseus and his son Telemachus, in this function responsible for the informal oral literary education of her disciples, refers to the 'Nancy stories me tell you and Hodysseus' (Walcott 1993: 8) (thus imitating the West Indian speech habit of adding an aspirated 'h' to words beginning with a vowel). We have seen how characteristic motifs and episodes of Anancy stories have been applied, the same with Tortoise and other animal stories ('Nancy stories me tell you' [ibid.]) — through the voice/mouth of the naïve narrator Euryclea — Walcott points to African-Caribbean folk stories as an influential narrative genre on which he will draw as a model. Members of the crew and Odysseus himself (in disguise), speak of '[t]hat liar Odysseus ... tell[ing] us his stories ... in a sailor's prose' (ibid.: 54). Sailor's prose stands for the colonial tradition of popular culture in Caribbean narratives like Captain Flin in Robert Louis Stevenson's *Treasure Island* (1883), the buccaneer and pirate adventure stories or the Maroon stories (Black 1966: 62–77) that circulate in the islands. Thus, Walcott refers to old and new orality, classical and colonial literacy, pre-classical and post-colonial oralities, and he confirms that his inspiration and his creative impetus arises from that mix of cultural and literary traditions.

Joseph Brodsky, Walcott's close friend and fellow Nobel laureate, commented on the hybridity inherent in the postcolonial situation generally. In his essay 'The Sound of the Tide' (Brodsky 1986), he speaks about the spirit of empires — of classical antiquity and modern empires — and highlights the linguistic continuity even after empires have ceased to exist as a political force:

> Because civilizations are finite, in the life of each of them comes a moment when centers cease to hold. What keeps them at such times from disintegration is not legions but languages. Such was the case with Rome, and before that, with Hellenic Greece. The job of holding at such times is done by the men from the provinces, from the outskirts. Contrary to popular belief, the outskirts are not where the world ends — they are precisely where it unravels. That affects language no less than the eye (ibid.: 164).

That this spirit of transition is rarely shared by the guardians of the imperial cultural spirit — the literary critics — is what Brodsky complained about when he wrote that 'the establishment in literary criticism simply cannot accept the fact that the major poet of present day English is a black man' (Brodsky 1983: 39). In a poem in celebration of John

Donne, Brodsky cites Donne's 'metaphysical conceit' of the insularity or totality of human existence:

> No man is an *Iland* [island], intire of it selfe; every man is a peece [piece] of the *Continent*, a part of the *maine*, if a *Clod* bee washed away by the *Sea*, *Europe* is the lesse, as well as if a *Promontorie* were … any mans *death* diminishes *me*, because I am involved in *Mankinde* (Donne 2003: 127).

Brodsky cites John Donne from the motto of Ernest Hemingway's *For Whom the Bell Tolls* (1940) and thus establishes a 'pedigree' of literary pamlimpsests, a continuity in the imagology of the Caribbean — islands and people — from the early 17th century through Hemingway's 20th-century America to the Caribbean present of the 1980s. Walcott himself talked about what constituted his own identity as a West Indian in an astonishingly parallel concept of ideas and images as John Donne did in his sermon:

> I'm just a red nigger who love the sea,
>   I had a sound colonial education,
>   I have Dutch, nigger, and English in me,
> and either I'm nobody, or I'm a nation.
> ('The Schooner Flight', in Walcott [1986: 346])

The ethnic diversity of his 'pedigree' and the diversity of his formal and informal education is what determines his status, either as an islander or a citizen of the world. Walcott's definition of his West Indian identity determines how he relates to the literary traditions in a chronology of intertextualities.

References

Augier, Fitzroy R., Shirley C. Gordon, D. G. Hall, and M. Reckord. 1960. *The Making of the West Indies*. London: Longmans.

Balme, Christopher B. 1999. *Decolonising the Stage: Theatrical Syncretism and Postcolonial Drama*. Oxford: Oxford University Press.

Black, Clinton. 1966. *Tales of Old Jamaica*. London: Collins.

Brodsky, Joseph. 1983. 'On Derek Walcott'. *New York Review of Books*, 10 November, p. 39.

Brodsky, Joseph. 1986. 'The Sound of the Tide', in *Less than One: Selected Essays*, pp. 164–75. New York: Farrah, Straus & Giroux.

Coetzee, J. M. 1986. *Foe*. London: Viking.

De Lima, Clara Rosa. 1991. 'Walcott, Painting and the Shadow of van Gogh', in Stewart Brown (ed.), *The Art of Derek Walcott*, pp. 171–90. Bridgend: Poetry Wales Press.

Defoe, Daniel. 1720. *Captain Singleton*. London: Printed for J. Brotherton, at the Black Bull in Cornhill, J. Graves in St. James's Street, A. Dodd, at the Peacock without Temple bar, and T. Warner, at the Black Bay in Pater-Noster-Row.

Donne, John. 2003. *One Equall Light: An Anthology of the Writings of John Donne*, ed. John Moses. Norwich: Canterbury Press.

Fanon, Frantz. 1967. *Black Skin, White Masks*. New York: Grove Press.

Figueroa, John. 1991. 'Omeros', in Stewart Brown (ed.), *The Art of Derek Walcott*, pp. 192–213. Bridgend: Poetry Wales Press.

Greene, Graham. 1966. *The Comedians*. London: Bodley Head.

Hamner, Robert D. 1986. *Derek Walcott*. Boston and New York: Twayne.

Hardwick, Lorna. 2004. 'Greek Drama and Anti-Colonialism: De-Colonising the Classics', in Edith Hall, Fiona Macintosh and Amanda Wrigley (eds), *Dionysus Since 69: Greek Tragedy at the Dawn of the Third Millenium*, pp. 219–42. New York and Oxford: Oxford University Press.

Hill, Errol. 1992. *The Jamaican Stage 1655–1900: Profile of a Colonial Theatre*. Amherst: University of Massachusetts Press.

Hughes, Langston. 1989[1922]. *Danse Africaine* (*Selected Poems of Langston Hughes*), ed. E. McKnight Kauffer. New York: A. Knopf.

Innes, Christopher. 2000. 'Staging Black History: Re-imagining Culture', in Yvette Hutchison and Eckhard Breitinger (eds), *History and Theatre in Africa*, pp. 21–29. Bayreuth: Bayreuth African Studies.

Macmillan, Harold. 1960. 'Wind of Change'. Prime Minister's Speech at the joint meeting of both Houses of Parliament, 3 February, Cape Town. http://www.africanrhetoric.org/pdf/J%20%20%20Macmillan%20-%20%20the%20wind%20of%20change.pdf (accessed 11 March 2013).

MacNeice, Louis. 1947. *The Dark Tower and Other Radio Scripts*. London: Faber and Faber.

Naipaul, Vidia S. 1962. *The Middle Passage*. London: André Deutsch.

———. 1967. *The Mimic Men*. London: André Deutsch.

O'Neill, Eugene. 1969 [1922]. *The Emperor Jones*. London: Jonathan Cape.

Schrott, Raoul. 2008a. *Homers Heimat: der Kampf um Troia und seine realen Hintergründe*. Munich: Hanser Verlag.

——— (trans.). 2008b. *Iliad*. Munich: Carl Hanser Verlag.

Soyinka, Wole. 1963. *A Dance of the Forests*. London: Oxford University Press.

———. 1973. *The Bacchae of Euripides*, London: Eyre Methuen.

Strindberg, August. 2005 [1907]. *A Dream Play*, ed. Carol Churchill. London: Nick Hern Books.
Taylor, George. 2002. 'Anti-Slave Trade Drama in England:1786–1808', in Yvette Hutchison and Eckhard Breitinger (eds), *History and Theatre in Africa*, pp. 9–20. Bayreuth: Bayreuth African Studies.
Walcott, Derek. 1950. *Henri Christophe*. Bridgetown, Barbados: Advocate Publishers.
———. 1957. *Ione: A Play with Music*. Caribbean Plays no. 8. Mona, Jamaica: Gleaner for Extra-Mural Department, University College of the West Indies.
———. 1961. 'Drums and Colours: An Epic Drama', *Caribbean Quarterly*, 7(1–2): 1–104.
———. 1965a. 'Crusoe's Journal', in *The Castaway and Other Poems*, pp. 51–53. London: Jonathan Cape.
———. 1965b. *The Castaway and Other Poems*. London: Jonathan Cape.
———. 1965c. 'The Figure of Crusoe'. Paper presented at University of the West Indies, St. Augustine, Trinidad, 27 October.
———. 1969. *The Gulf and Other Poems*. London: Jonathan Cape.
———. 1970a. 'Dream on Monkey Mountain', in *Dream on Monkey Mountain and Other Plays*. New York: Farrar, Straus and Giroux.
———. 1970b. 'Meanings', *Savacou*, 2: 45–51.
———. 1970c. 'Ti-Jean and his Brothers', in *Dream on Monkey Mountain and Other Plays*, pp. 3–40. New York: Farrar, Straus and Giroux.
———. 1970d. 'What the Twilight Says: An Overture', in *Dream on Monkey Mountain and Other Plays*, pp. 3–40. New York: Farrar, Straus and Giroux.
———. 1977. 'From The Schooner Flight', *Massachusetts Review*, 18(4): 795–800.
———. 1980. 'Pantomime', in *Remembrance & Pantomime: Two Plays*. New York: Farrar, Straus and Giroux.
———. 1986. *Collected Poems 1948–1984*. New York: Farrar, Straus and Giroux.
———. 1990. *Omeros*. New York: Farrar, Straus and Giroux.
———. 1993. *The Odyssey: A Stage Version*. New York: Farrar, Straus and Giroux.
Warner-Lewis, Maureen. 1991. *Guinea's Other Suns: The African Dynamic in Trinidad Culture*. Dover MA: The Majority Press.
Williams, Eric. 1964 [1944]. *Capitalism and Slavery*. London: André Deutsch.

Appendix

Figure 10A: Linear Plot Development in Eugene O'Neill's *The Emperor Jones*

Eugene O'Neill: Emperor Jones

time:	🕒 3 p.m.	🕒 6.30 p.m.	🕒 9 p.m.	🕒 11 p.m.	🕒 1 a.m.	🕒 3 a.m.	🕒 5 a.m.	dawn
costume:	parade uniform	hat lost	tattered uniform	stripped to waist	tattered trousers	loin cloth	practically naked	
location:	palace	fringe of forest	forest	forest	forest clearing	clearing	under tree	fringe of forest
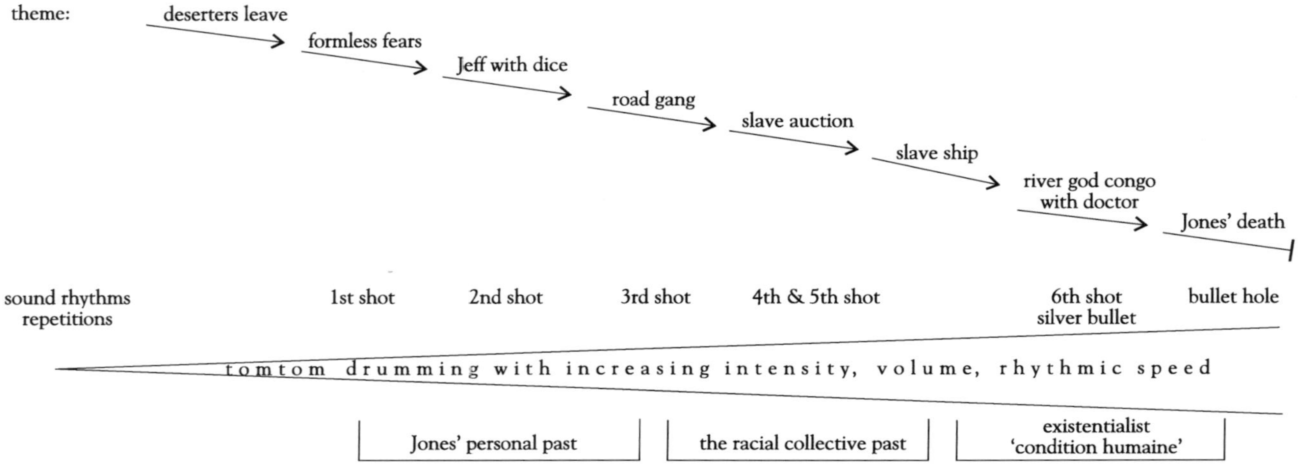 theme:								

deserters leave
formless fears
Jeff with dice
road gang
slave auction
slave ship
river god congo with doctor
Jones' death
bullet hole

1st shot   2nd shot   3rd shot   4th & 5th shot   6th shot silver bullet

sound rhythms repetitions

t o m t o m   d r u m m i n g   w i t h   i n c r e a s i n g   i n t e n s i t y, v o l u m e, r h y t h m i c   s p e e d

| Jones' personal past | the racial collective past | existentialist 'condition humaine' |

Source: Prepared by the author.

Figure 10B: Circular Plot Development in Derek Walcott's *Dream on Monkey Mountain*

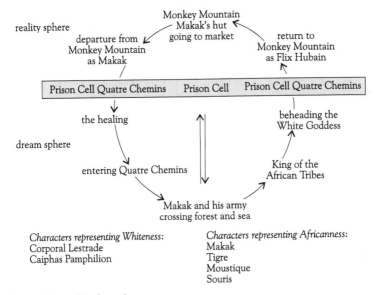

Source: Prepared by the author.

11 Conceptualizing Space and Indigenous Knowledge

Articulations and Considerations for Natural Resource Management in the Himalayas

Seema M. Parihar, P. K. Parihar, Soma Sarkar and Shilpy Sharma

I

Space and indigenous knowledge are complementary phenomena essential to environmental protection along with human development. Conceptualizing space and indigenous knowledge together through the articulations and considerations of a section of the Himalayan community is the premise of this chapter. The relevance of space — physical, social, cultural or mental — cannot be omitted from the sphere of indigenous knowledge. Although very little of this knowledge is systematically recorded, it offers rich insights into how communities negotiate space with respect to their natural resources. 'If indigenous knowledge has not been documented and compiled, doing so should be a research priority of the highest order. Indigenous knowledge is being lost at an unprecedented rate, and its preservation, preferably in data base form, must take place as quickly as possible' (National Research Council 1992: 45). Elders in the village are also very worried about this. Rama Devi (female, 67 years old) states: 'It is only the selection of the right kind of wood that enables me to use it for longer period in the winter ... today's girls are not knowing the correct wood to be used as a fuelwood or otherwise' (interview, Gangi Village, Tehri Garhwal, June 2008). A similar opinion is echoed by a native Shyam (male, 63 years old, Ayurvedic physician; interview, Ghansali, Tehri Garhwal, June 2008): 'We are going through a phase of transition, where on one hand natives are losing their traditional knowledge and practices, and on the other they are failing to adopt the modern scientific techniques due to lack of training'.

Over the space it is the indigenous knowledge that distinguishes one community from the other. Thus, how communities perceive space through and within their indigenous knowledge is a matter of concern. The point about grappling with space as a key concept in our study is an effort to identify how this concept might be better integrated into the existing social, literary and cultural outlay of indigenous knowledge and with what effects to our study area. According to scholars, it is part of the general cultural web, and like any cultural entity space is formed and changed, accepted or rejected. There are many indigenous practices in the study area, but this chapter is restricted to the practices which are related to natural resource management only. The article revisits the traditional practices followed in the Garhwal and Kumaon region of the state of Uttarakhand in the Himalayas and documents the resource base and processes practiced over the years; it further conceptualizes the possibility of their being regarded as suitable technology for the management of natural resources in particular climatic and living conditions. Sometimes, owing to the integration of traditional societies with the mainstream society and market economy, indigenous knowledge and traditional practices for resource extraction, utilization and management are on the verge of extinction. Through this study, an attempt has been made to revisit them, to scrutinize their relevance in present times, and to comprehend whether the intrusion of modern science-based knowledge in the livelihood of the indigenous people has changed their perception of space or not. We also examine whether through community participation and the co-operation of the local community it would be easy to document indigenous practices and also to understand the processes followed in blending contemporary resource management practices using geospatial tools with the traditional practices in a particular ecology to benefit the subsequent livelihood of the local community.

A few studies have countered the view that indigenous people can live in harmony with their surroundings while managing their natural resources; they have called them primitive and regarded as simple and static a knowledge system that is complex. But we must always remember that the benefits of the indigenous knowledge system can be shared when there is respect, understanding and the recognition of traditional rights and the existing indigenous stewardship. This chapter takes this view forward and presents a case through visualization and articulations rendered by the indigenous community about the importance of knowledge, innovations and sustainable practices tracked by them.

Moreover, this documentation will be helpful for the future course of research in this field, as owing to the integration of their traditional society with the mainstream society and the market economy, their indigenous knowledge and traditional practices for resource extraction, utilization and management are on the verge of extinction. Further, it will also direct us towards redefining/rethinking the Geographical Indications (GIs) in a community.[1] What is to be noted is that till March 2009, none of the GIs have a bearing on the Uttarakhand space (GIs registry, Chennai, 2009). With this view in mind while conceptualizing the space, we have attempted to review the indigenous knowledge related to the natural resource management of the Garhwal and Kumaon region of the Himalaya using traditional methods and, in addition, we have experimented with the use of contemporary geospatial tools and technologies with the local people of the study area.

Though the indigenous people are identified as 'tribals', 'adivasi', 'ethnic minorities', 'natives', 'local inhabitants', 'aborigines', or 'Indians' and the Government of India refers to indigenous peoples as 'scheduled tribes', in our study, we have taken the term 'natives' to describe the indigenous people of our study area.

Study Area

The Garhwal and Kumaon Himalayan region, as a part of Uttarakhand in India, is rich in biodiversity and anthropology as a result of which it has become a storehouse of nature-based indigenous knowledge and traditional practices. Uttarakhand is the catchment area of the Indo-Gangetic plain. It is divided into two commissionaires: Garhwal and Kumaon. The Garhwal Himalaya, the westernmost part of the Central Himalaya, lies between latitudes 29°26′ to 31°28′ N and longitudes 77°49′ to 80°06′ E, whereas Kumaon lies between latitudes 28°44′ to 30°49′ N and longitudes 78°45′ to 81°05′ E (Map 11.1).

---

[1] Trade-Related Intellectual Property Rights (TRIPS) of the World Trade Organization (WTO) define 'GI' as any indication that identifies a good as originating from a particular place, 'where a given quality, reputation or other characteristics of the good' are 'essentially attributable to its geographic origin' (WTO n.d.).

Map 11.1: The Study Area

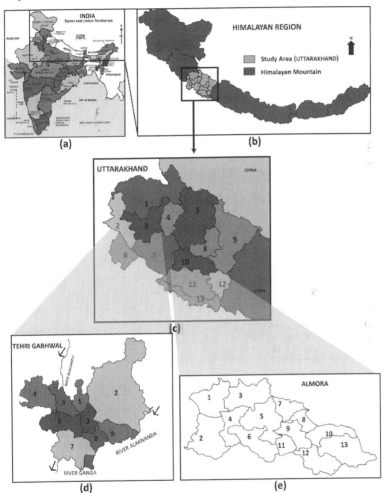

Map not to scale

Source: Prepared by the authors.
Note: In **(a) India**; in **(b) Himalayan Region**; in **(c) Uttarakhand:** (1) Uttarkashi, (2) Dehradun, (3) Tehri Garhwal, (4) Rudraprayag, (5) Chamoli, (6) Haridwar, (7) Paudi Garhwal, (8) Bageshwar, (9) Pithoragarh, (10) Almora, (11) Nainital, (12) Champawat, (13) Udhamsingh Nagar; in **(d) Tehri Garhwal:** (1) Pratapnagar, (2) Bhilangana, (3) Jhakhnidhar, (4) Jaunpur, (5) Thauldhar, (6) Chamba, (7) Narendranagar, (8) Devprayag, (9) Kirtinagar; in **(e) Almora:** (1) Syalde, (2) Salt, (3) Chaukhutia, (4) Bhikyasain, (5) Bamapur, (6) Tarikher, (7) Someshwar, (8) Taluka, (9) Hawalbagh, (10) Bhainsiya Channa, (11) Almora, (12) Lamgarha, (13) Dhauladevi.

Since the Mesolithic age (5000 BCE), it has been the home for various races (Kole, Kirata, Khasas, Sakas, Huns, and Bhotia) and for tribes and communities (Garhwalis, Kumaonies, Gujjars, Bhoxas, Tharus, Koltas, Kinnauries, Junsaris, etc.). Each group has their own wisdom about the ethnic use of the natural resources of the region. In this region some of the practices are open-pit manure decomposition, constructing brushwood or longwood check dams across the drainage channels for controlling soil loss, the use of tree trunks as rainwater irrigation channels for checking seepage, and water harvesting systems, to mention just some.

Methodology

Natural resource management involves evaluation, deliberation, dialogue, and negotiation. So whether and to what extent the indigenous people follow these methods is also a matter of concern. Through this study, the objective is to gain an insight into the local dwellers'/natives' perceptions of what is called nature in *modern scientific discourse*; what resource and resource management mean to them; what their ideas of a good life are; and what, if any, are their notions of sustainability as they live through a transitional phase. By following a community-centric approach in an emerging paradigm of participatory learning, the answers to the following five *whether* questions are established and tested in the study:

(a) Whether indigenous practices are closely entwined with the surrounding space through the indigenous people?
(b) Whether indigenous practices are relevant for natural resource management in the present scenario?
(c) Whether indigenous practices involve the components of natural resource management that include evaluation, deliberation, dialogue, and negotiation?
(d) Whether enough importance is given to GIs for each natural resource practice (appraisal, management and development) in the study area?
(e) Whether, when and how blending contemporary resource management practices using geospatial tools and technologies with the traditional practices will benefit the ecology and livelihood of the local community?

The answers to these questions were found by using various methodologies — starting with the collection of secondary data by investigating various archives, databases and other written materials available from local libraries, local traditional practitioners, web search engines, and government offices. All this was followed by close primary interaction with the indigenous people and indigenous spaces in the study area — ranging from interviewing 'key respondents' or people who are especially knowledgeable about the traditional practices of the region to conducting a systematic survey to obtain a range of information and responses using either a set of open-ended questions (a 'protocol') for discussion or a more formal written set of questions with more directed responses (a 'questionnaire'), where applicable. Beyond the primary and secondary data collection, observations, articulations and considerations experienced during field visits to communities and their activities and visiting sites with knowledgeable people enriched the learning as well. Studying the impact of external interventions through geospatial tools and technologies on and through local community members and documenting the process involved in capacity building of the local community further provided an insight into the possibilities of external intercessions within the indigenous driven framework.

II

Understanding Basics

Conceptualizing Space

Space has been a subject of study for a long time. The point about grappling with space as a keyword in our study is to identify how this concept might be better integrated into the existing social, literary and cultural outlay of indigenous knowledge and with what impact. Conceptualizing space from the perception of various thinkers and philosophers brings us closer to our understanding of various interactions within spaces.

For Gottfried Wilhelm Leibniz (1646–1716), a German rationalist philosopher and one of the great Renaissance men of Western thought, space was only the collection of spatial relations between objects on earth that could not be continuous but must be discrete (Vailati 1997). However, the German philosopher Immanuel Kant rejected the view that it should be either a substance or relation. Instead, he stated that it can be both *a priori* and 'synthetic', which is a part of an unavoidable systematic framework for structuring human experiences (Carnap 1974). Another German philosopher, Martin Heidegger, referred to space, whether of external environment, or of the body, as man's relation to locations in terms of his dwelling place (Heidegger 1971). The idea of '[s]pace as a product of heterogeneous, historically specific social practices' has been put forward by French sociologist Henri Lefebvre (Stanek 2008: 67). While rejecting Heidegger's ontological valuation of space as a site of dwelling, Lefebvre speaks about different forms of production of space from natural space ('absolute space') to more complex, socially produced space (i.e., social space) (Lefebvre 1991). While describing the concept of 'heterotopia', French philosopher Michel Foucault elaborated on spaces as consisting of more levels of meaning or relationships to other places than what immediately meets the eye, which are the spaces of *otherness*.

David Harvey, a Marxist theorist, also tried to search for the ontological answer to the question whether 'space' is absolute, relative or relational in itself. He felt that it is none of these, but can become one or all simultaneously depending on the circumstances (Harvey 1973). Thus, he writes:

> there are no philosophical answers to the philosophical questions that arise over the nature of space — the answers lie in human practices. The question 'what is space?' is therefore replaced by the question 'how is it that different human practices create and make use of different conceptualizations of space?' The property relationship, for example, creates absolute spaces within which monopoly control can operate (ibid.: 13).

According to Ernst Cassirer, a German philosopher, space can be 'organic', 'perceptual' and 'symbolic', all represented through linguistic, scientific, scholarly, or artistic symbols. Edward W. Soja, a postmodernist thinker, puts forward the view that space is never given and not an 'empty box' to be filled, but always a culturally constructed entity. He introduced the concept of 'Thirdspace', i.e., perceived space, conceived space, and lived space. 'Perceived' space is one that consists mainly of concrete spatial forms, things that can be empirically mapped, but are also socially produced with respect to human activity, behaviour and experience. 'Conceived' space is space that is constructed in mental or cognitive forms (or, as Lefebvre puts it, it is 'imagined' [1991: 10]). And 'lived' space consists of actual social and spatial practices, the immediate material world of experience and realization (Soja 1996). In his book *Space and Place: The Perspective of Experience* (2006), the eminent geographer Yi-Fu Tuan suggests that place is security and space is freedom. For his thoughtful and insightful analysis, he explored various modes of space, whether sacred versus biased space, mythical space and place, time in experiential space, or cultural attachments to space (ibid.).

Thus, while dealing with the indigenous knowledge and indigenous people, the role of space becomes important not only because it is their home (sphere of interaction with their natural environment) but also because it has faced a paradigm shift with time.

Indigenous Knowledge and Indigenous People

The adjective 'indigenous' has the common meaning of 'from' or 'of the original origin'. Various scholars have given their views on the meaning of the indigenous knowledge and its system. D. M. Warren (1989) defined 'indigenous knowledge' as knowledge that is local and 'unique to a given culture or society' (cited in CIESIN n.d.). R. Basanta (1990) argued that since knowledge originates in and characterizes a particular community, region or country it varies across space and time. However, Bertus Haverkort (1993), widens the definition of indigenous knowledge by including both 'the experiences based on traditions' and 'more recent experiences with modern technologies' (cited in CIESIN n.d.). B. Rajasekaran (1993) views indigenous knowledge as the product of 'accumulation of experiences, informal experiments and intimate understanding of the environment' by local people of a given culture (ibid.). Thus, in simple words, 'indigenous knowledge' refers to the long-standing beliefs, customs and traditions of certain regional, indigenous, or local communities which are expressed through their various traditional practices — an actual knowledge practised to achieve stable livelihoods.

Over the space it is indigenous knowledge that distinguishes one community from the other. Thus, the indigenous people are identified by various terms as previously discussed. While the government of India refers to indigenous peoples as 'scheduled tribes', they are popularly known as 'adivasi', which in Sanskrit means 'original people'. For our study, we have considered the 'natives' of our study area as indigenous people. All others have been referred to as 'external persons'.

Although there are exceptions, as always, to any generalization, there still are recognized characteristics of indigenous people and their knowledge. For them the land is the basis of all realities — human selfhood and identity. The earth is the focal point of reference and all religious activities are centred on the soil, and not on any historical idol. Though it is the oldest religion, there is no scripture or creed. They are morally and spiritually linked to the earth as sacred and central for life. They are holistic in thinking, because there is no clear-cut distinction between sacred and secular, religion and non-religion, and thus there is no sharp dualism (recognition of two independent principles). As an intuitive component, the self of the Supreme Being is seen in creation and an inseparable relationship is maintained. Thus, they perceive all realities from the creation perspective. Community participation and activities are highly group-oriented and based on mutual well-being and sharing. Beside this, it also has a personal orientation, where the relationship between individuals in society is more important than the simple performance of tasks; cooperation is valued more, and they value giving over saving. Their practices are based on empirical observations and accumulation of facts by trial-and-error. Thus, they are adapted to the environment and believe the world to be sacred with a motto: 'It is our mother. How can we sell and exploit our mother!' (interview with Shiv Juyal, 52 years old, Jakholi village, July 2009)

III
Contextualizing Traditional Natural Resource Practices of the Study Area

Natural resources available in the Tehri Garhwal and Almora region and their use by the native communities through their traditional practices have both direct and/or indirect influence on their culture, customs, ethos, religious rites, socio-cultural beliefs, craftsmanship, food habits, settlement patterns, and various other resource-based practices. Moreover, the native practices through their utilization of the resources have demonstrated their impact on the surrounding spaces as well.

Water is apparently the most important resource of the region. A dense network of rivers is found in the Tehri Garhwal and Almora districts of Uttarakhand (Map 11.2). Owing to the rugged topography, first-, second- and third-order drainage with trellis, rectangular and radial patterns can be seen in this region. Some of the major streams of Tehri Garhwal are Bhilangna River, Algar *nadi* (river), Mandakini River, Bal Ganga River, Dharm Ganga River, Hanval River, Hiyunil River, and Bandal River. Major rivers of Almora district are Ramganga River, Bino River, Nayer nadi, Naurar Gadhera nadi, Kach Gad, Gagas nadi, Sarod Gad, Kosi River, Swal nadi, Kali Rao, Panar Nadi, Sidya Gad, Sarju River and Kutar Gad.

Beside these streams, there are numerous bodies of water comprising springs, seepages, natural and man-made lakes and ponds called *tal, khal, nala, dhara, choyas, daan* serving the region. Dyodital, Deoriatal, Nachiketatal, Mashartal, Chirbatiatal, Vasukital, Khedatal, and Mashartal

Map 11.2: Drainage Network of Tehri Garhwal and Almora

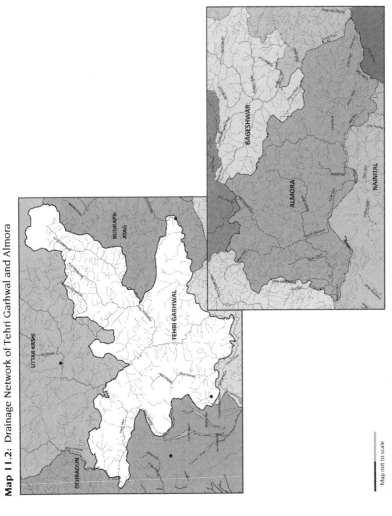

Map not to scale

Source: Prepared by the authors.

are some of the big natural bodies of water referred to as *tals*. Ajit (male, 51 years old, Gangi Village, Vikas Khand Bhilangana) remembers the importance of *khals*, man-made water pounding structures. 'The usefulness of *khals* cannot be ignored any time and I remember when we were young all of us had a sense of pride towards them and the tasks entrusted towards it involved many members of the our community' (interview with Krishna Negi, 52 years old, Briha village, 17 June 2008). Jamnikhal, Nagchulakhal, Paukhal, Kandikhal, Gumkhal, Rikhnikhal Ghodikhal, Buwakhal, Phedikhal, Acherikhal, Dandakahal, and Agrakhal are some examples of man-made water pounding structures in the region. *Chals*, as referred to by Ramphal Negi (male, 31 years old), are man-made water recharge zones (interview, Bhatgaon, 11 June 2009). These typical water pounding structures are also referred to as *rou* by Jai Pal Bandooni. 'We cannot even think of overusing our *rous*, it is the outsiders who are just spoiling everything' (interview, Seela Malla, 7 April 2010). Geeta (female, 38 years old) describes her almost daily travel to *nalas*, the tanks, to collect water from subterranean springs as an outing and a necessary chore: 'I look forward to go to our neighboring *nala* as that is a place where I meet my friends . . . in my young days however, it was a great fun as at a fixed time along with doing work for my mother we were getting a chance to meet our friends and play, sing to' (interview, Thakulsari Badi, 9 April 2010). Equal exuberance is showcased by Saroj (37 years old) of Thakulsari Choti village when she reminiscences about her visits to neighbouring *dhara* (stream) that yields a perennial clear and perpetual water source to be used for drinking and other household purposes, and retting fibre plants (interview, Seela Malla, 7 April 2010). The spaces appear well-defined. *Dhaans* are ponds used for bathing animals and irrigation. They are also found largely in the outskirts of most living spaces in each village.

The natives carry out a number of water management practices too. Radhakrishan (male, 75 years old, farmer) says: 'We get water for agriculture from *gadera* (gully). There is *panta* (taking turns) for that and then we can sow our field. Next day it is done for the next village. There is a common *saira* (water source, a tank) for four to five villages. The water supply is just enough for us' (interview, Khwada village, Tehri Garhwal, 16 April 2009). Another native Sukhi (female, 44 years old) said: 'There was and still is a *ghul* (canal) for irrigation and its water is distributed through *panta* by different villages. The water would go to this village until this time, and then to the next. We have our own spring for drinking water in the village' (interview, Dargi village, Tehri Garhwal, 16 June 2010). *Gools*, as described by Suresh (male, 61 years old), 'are a network of channels to divert water from small rivers to agricultural fields . . . Help of the elders is always taken into consideration while designing the channels ... as *gools* enable flow along gravity and the experience positively lend a hand towards it' (interview, Dangi village, Tehri Garhwal, 16 June 2010).

The importance of rain water, too, is well understood by the natives through the various practices followed by them. As seen during our visit the natives manage rainwater through their indigenous creation of *nalas* and *pusata* (embankment). These are small dug-out ponds in and around their villages that enable rainwater harvesting. Ram Bandhooni (male, 61 years old) was enthusiastic to share the use of tree trunks as rainwater irrigation channels. 'During heavy rains, the tree trunks guide the flow of rain water ... many a times their placing takes days together and involves many of us ... few do it eagerly like me, but many detest it as the importance is not understood by them' (interview, Thakulsar Choti village, 8 April 2010). Brushwood or longwood check dams too are constructed by the local community for checking floods in the region.

As the topography is rugged, the farmers work hard to manage and maintain the land and soil through their traditional practices. For instance, for slope stabilization and soil conservation, they practice terrace farming with *nalas* and *pusata* to manage rainwater. Shivprasad (male, 49 years old) speaks about the value of *mole*: ' we do not waste anything ... take too much care in protecting organic matter of livestock dung, straw, grasses, left over feed ... even today it is the most important manure ... we do not like depending on artificial, *shahri* (urban) products' (interview, Thakulsar Choti village, 8 April 2010). Application of Farm Yard Manure (FYM), locally called *mole*, is a practice which involves using fully-decomposed organic matter. Open-pit manure decomposition is another common practice followed for enhancing the fertility of the soil. Many natives deeply recognize the importance of faunal diversity too. Sanjeev (male, 35 years old) of Tehri Garhwal says, 'I have learned from my elders the caring that we need to bestow on earthworms, ants, arthropods, nematodes, mycorrhiza ... their presence in our fields readily enables maintaining soil fertility' (interview, Beironkhal, 10 April 2010). Spraying of ash is another practice shared by Sanjeev, which is undertaken by the natives for enhancing the fertility of the various crops like onion, garlic, coriander, and spinach, as is growing grasses such as *Eulaliopsis binnata*, *Chrysopogun fulvus* and agave sps for ground cover. Jamuna Das (male, 34 years old), an educated youth, shared the use of biological fencing by plants like bans keora, pangar, rambans, bankhor, etc. in the region for checking soil erosion and landslides (interview, Beironkhal, 10 April 2010). He further guided the use of longwood check dams by the local community for controlling soil loss during flood.

Most of the natives have displayed extensive awareness about the vegetation surrounding them and their varied uses. They have also displayed concerns related to various supply and demand issues. Sanjay Negi (male, 61 years old) says that 'today's forests are different than the forest of yesteryear. They were rich, luscious with spaces for everybody... they looked ours. Today the species have reduced, we do not have a say in its planting' (interview, Bhatgaon, 11 June 2009). Not many knew about the Indian Forest Act, 1927, but they were all certainly concerned about the reduction of their local forest on different pretexts.

The indigenous knowledge about the forest species is so immense that its deep penetration in the knowledge base across hierarchies is well spread and locally practised too. Though the scale is limited, their usefulness appears accurate and well-tested. For medication, the popular species include: *Acacia pennata*, chilla, chillaka, chihlak, tirvengadum, maindul, mainfal, madanfal, sulla, surai, schund, akhrot, akhror, akshor, mahwa, madhuca, *Sapindus mukorossi*, reetha, arishthak, kala jamun, phalend, jambu, timroo, tejbal, timbur, andhaka, and tumbak. Ethnomedicinal value is attached to individual species too, and every elder woman of the house has a story to share about it like Damyanti (female, 61 years old) of Balganga range *gaon* (village), who remembers her interaction with the group of foreigners who were moving uphill towards the snow-bound upper reaches:

> The foreigners were very tired and three of them very unwell too, I remember the small baby who was unwell too and with a deep wound... their own medicines were not providing relief... when they stopped for tea, I offered them our local medicine and added them in our tea... they profusely thanked us and gave us lot of gifts... I still have that blanket (interview with Shivprasad, male, 56 years old, Reh, 11 October 2010).

Some common species with medicinal relief in the study area include tirvengadum, maindul, mainfal, madanfal, dolu, and pangar as antibiotic and antiseptic; vantulsi, chilla, chillaka, chihlak, atibish, genthi, van ajwain for coughs and colds; barmoola, gurjar gudchi, atibish, kutki for relief during fever; *Casearia elliptica*, kalihari, salampanja for healing wounds and dhavephul, dudhibari, kapoorkachri for piles. Other medicinal referrals of the indigenous community included species like jatamanshi for arthritis; dhatura kala for asthma; kins or kinjadi for constipation; goochi, atibish for improving the digestive system; satuwa for gastric problems; mamira for jaundice; paashan bhed, shilpari for kidney stones; kutki for malaria; and dolu for skin diseases.

Even for handicrafts the knowledge the local people have is immense and useful too, like deodar (*Cedrus deodara*), thuner (*Taxus baccata*), deo-ringal (*Arundinaria spathiflora*) for boxes and furniture; gol-ringal (*Arundinaria falcate*), tham (*Dendrocalamus strictus*), belkarm (*Ichnocarpus frutescens*), deo-ringal for baskets; pangar (*Aesculus indicus*) and burans (*Rhododendron arboreum*) for cooperages; bhangla (*Cannabis sativa*), vimal (*Grewia optiva*), cantala (*Agave cantala*), kandali, pani bel, singhi, safed bel, singori for ropes and cordage; and pangar, papri (*Buxus sempervirons*) for toys; agali, rigad, sulla, surai, schund, akhrot, akhror, akshor, anyar, aiyaar, mahwa, madhuca, Sapindus mukorossi, reetha, arishthak, kinna, khindra, khinna, jamun, phalend, jambu are some of the other species recognized by the indigenous community as to be used for furniture and woodwork like toys, and construction.

Instead of changes in agriculture, the natives prefer to maintain their traditional farming practices and are strongly in favour of reviving and maintaining their traditional approach. According to Mahender (male, 44 years old, farmer, Sabli village, Tehri Garhwal, June 2010):

> Our traditional agriculture was fully self-reliant. The seeds, the manure and the bullock, everything was personal, only seeds were exchanged by farmers. But the farmer today is totally dependent on the government machinery ... and has become a slave to multinational seeds and fertilizer.

Most of the farmers practice sustainable agriculture, with mixed cropping for minimizing risks under rain-fed conditions. The local communities grow a variety of crops. These crops are used in various ways like urd or kali dhal (*Vigna mungo*), nanni dhal (*Vigna angularis*), soyabean (*Glycine max*), gehet (*Macrotyloma Uniflorum*), sonta (*Vigna unguiculata*), tor (*Cajanus cajan*), chhemi (*Phaseolus vulgaris*), matar (*Pisum sativum*), shivchana (*Vicia faba*), and masoor (*Pisum arvense*) to be cooked as local dishes; urd or kali dhal as an adhesive in the past of colouring and housing materials; and urd or kali dhal, nanni dhal, soyabean, tor for husks and/or cattle feed. Various traditional landraces of paddy (*Oryza sativa*) like bhabri, ghyasu, jolya, kalon kala, kalon safed, khagola, khullu kala, khullu safed, kimoli, and lal sati have ethno-medicinal uses like in cases of stomach ache and shivering, loose motion, constipation, leucorrhoea, dysentery, delivery, pimples, wounds, internal injury, and many more.

Livestock has great relevance in the life of the local communities as they serve a number of purposes, like yak (*Bos grunniens*) for breeding; cow (*Bos indicus*), jumo (fertile), garmo (fertile), *talbuni* (cross-breed) for milk; sheep (*Ovis aries*), goats (*Capra hirtus*), Tibetan sheep, Tibetan goats for meat; and local hens for eggs. Sheep, goats, Tibetan sheep, and

Tibetan goats appear popular for wool with the local people, whereas pack animals include *jhupu* (sterile), *garu* (sterile), *talbuni*, sheep and goats; and drought animals are oxen (*Bos indicus*), *jhupu*, *garu* and *talbuni*. Local horses and mules are common with the natives for transportation. Tibetan dogs and local cats are useful as watch-guards and for keeping a check on rodents. However, in higher reaches, with the development imperative the scale is reducing, as most say they keep far fewer animals now due to the loss of grazing land to cultivated fields, and the loss of fodder because of deforestation. According to Bhuvan (male, 49 years old, farmer; interview, Jakhanidhar Vikas Khand, Tehri Garhwal, June 2009):

> Earlier we had our own wool ... but now the produce is too little. It is cheaper and practical to get from Tibetan people. Even the number of goats with us has reduced, because there is no one to look after them. Big children are in *shahar* (cities) for work, whereas younger ones are studying. Even the grazing land has got reduced.

Shamsher (male, 52 years old), a Gaddi community member met at Pawali Kantha, says:

> I take my sheep on a fixed path ... but over the years, I am finding it difficult to maintain them ... my community is having a tough time ... children are not wanting to stay with us as their aspirations are different ... the respect too is diminishing. We wonder if we all will stay along to keep the tradition (interview, Pawali Kantha, 7 June 2009).

The development models created by local natives emphasize the possibilities of the indigenous solutions. One such solution is a fixed-forest, farming-based model village demonstrated by Jagat Singh Chaudhary who is called *Junglee* (inhabitant of the forest) because of his activities in Kot Malla village in Rudra Pryag district of the Uttarakhand at an altitude of 3000 m. Covering 1.5 hectares of land, *Junglee* demonstrated the immense scope of the sustenance of his model, which he started working on 40 years back in 1971. Another successful indigenous model is the creation of a water management-based model by Sachidanand Bharti in an Uffrainkhal village in Pauri Garhwal district in 2004–5. This model village covers 5 hectares of land at an altitude of 2500 m. Whereas the former was self-driven, the latter is facilitated through the resources of the non-governmental organization Doodhatoli Lok Vikas Sansthan. The suitability of the models is evident on rugged and steep slopes. Whereas in the former model, adequate seasonal rainfall is required, in the second even the spaces with water scarcity — with low to medium rainfall — can follow the model. As Jagat Singh Choudhary (male, 55 years old) emphasized, 'there are two things most required for the success of my model, with one being the need or the requirement and the second being a sense of belongingness' (interview, Junglee Gaon, 10 April 2010).

The spiritual values of the local communities are the core to all their beliefs. These are characterized by their sense of the sacredness of their mountain surroundings. Many prominent peaks and geographical features, as well as the streams, trees, plants, and seeds that sustain communities, have been infused with religious significance. There are well-marked spaces, occupied by the local forest species, which are deeply protected by native communities because of their belief in them as gods and deities. If for Damyanti (female, 43 years old), *Parima* (fairy mother) is living in the large patch of oak trees, for *Falhari Baba* (spiritual master who only eats fruits) (male, 70 years old), a forest patch of deodar (as a higher Himalayan species) is protected by the community as the property of God. *Kalpavriksha* is another species of banyan protected as a religious tree. Nagdev and Tadkeshwar is a long stretch of forested area protected by the forestry department and the local community, since it is believed to be the forest of *Nag* (serpentine god). As these are protected by the famous belief in Goddess trees, villagers perform rituals on an annual basis in the forest and protect them as sacred spaces. This belief confers natural protection and ensures continuity of these natural resources.

So there are innumerable beliefs and indigenous practices that protect natural resources in the study area. However, they largely appeared isolated, *ad hoc* and with a general lack of awareness about the need for conservation and subsequent natural resource management and development. For the natives, the framework of the interrelationships between basic natural processes and the man–nature inter-relationship appeared largely random and disorganized. Indigenous communities, albeit following many *ad hoc* resource-use practices, had little access to the collective database about their surrounding resources. Puran Singh (male, 70 years old), an elder of the village, recognizes the need for conservation of resources as he says: 'my community recognizes water availability as their primary concern but they have made no concerted effort towards ensuring its security; neither do the development bodies feel the need' (interview, Thakulsari Badi, 9 April 2010). Therefore, in addition to the community's indifference to this issue of conservation of their resources and noting their traditional practices, even the development bodies lacked alertness to the issue and are not organizing efforts to resolve it.

IV

Assessing the Introduction of Geospatial Tools in the Study Area

Understanding the context and comprehending the urgent need to do something for the indigenous community, an experiment using geospatial tools was conducted (Parihar and Parihar 2008). One is aware of the presence of high-resolution data and technology for comprehending remote-sensing technology, and above all the ready availability of Geographic Information Science; but would that be of any use to the indigenous community? Given the resources, will the introduction of Personal Digital Assistants (PDAs) coupled with the Global Positioning System (GPS) make any addition to the learning curve of the community? Recognizing the importance of indigenous knowledge, it became more important that their space be respected with an assured access to information for the communities and that, most importantly, an effective utilization of the existing information be assured. One way to do this was to allow the communities to generate and manage geospatial information on their locality. Community-generated information will result in dual benefits; first, it will assure common access to information; and second, it will create spatial data infrastructure that can support community goals.

As in recent years, Geographical Information System (GIS) applications and information management systems are emerging as the most dominant tools for decision-making for resource management. So *Mapping with Belongingness*[2] was conducted in Bhilangana basin taking into consideration the community practices of resource use and indigenous knowledge of resource management. The methodology followed was the same as that followed in Thakkarwal village (Parihar and Parihar 2008), thereby facilitating the community's access to knowledge, information and new techniques by generating the maps. The assumption was that the concrete applications of geo-information technologies would provoke change and therefore have an impact on behaviour. Technology policy statements since the 1980s too have been emphasizing technological self-reliance and development and the adaptation of suitable technologies for local needs to make an impact on the lives of ordinary citizens. The focus in the present experiment was sustainable

---

[2] 'Mapping with Belongingness' can be interpreted as mapping the neighbourhood — the space where you have a feeling of belongingness.

development of water with community participation for resource management. As depicted previously, the main sources of water are *nalas* and *dharas* — the springs that are fast depleting. As shared by Gopinath (male, 43 years old, scientist): 'Springs are colluvial-related and fracture/joint-related water discharge points in the region; *dhara* are in *situ* springs[3] and *nalas* are shallow tanks to collect water from subterranean springs'. Jagdamba (female, 61 years old) shares the urgency for doing something: 'the *nalas* and *dharas* are changing ... it seems that in the years to come they will not be there ... they will just disappear' (interview, Gangi village, 16 June 2010).

With the aim of creating 'Maps with Belongingness', the school children with their teacher from the village mapped their locality through the use of indigenously developed GIS software running on a PDA coupled with the GPS. While mapping (as well as surveying), the students recorded valuable geospatial information (on resources, *nalas*, springs, community demographics, livelihood information, land use, infrastructure, etc.) about their village and the community. The data collected and the map prepared in the PDA is transferred to and processed in desktop GIS software and thematic maps are created. Technical capacity building was carried out for students, teachers and select community members. Students and the others were trained and learnt the need and uses of maps along with the basic concepts of GIS and thematic maps and the use of such maps for effective decision-making through awareness workshops on 'Mapping and Map Use' as a basic theme. There were two related workshops held in the village for understanding space through maps, one on maps as a tool for spatial planning — to understand the concepts of time, distance, topology, service area and pattern, as they are the building blocks of any spatial planning (mapping their natural resources, indigenous knowledge, locations, resources, etc.) — and the other on the utility and application of geospatial tools for local problem-solving.

The students generated the village maps, and collected and marked the GPS location for all nature-related relevant sites. The location of each household was marked and linked to GIS in order to be able to reassess the need and supply situation. Other built structures (temples, roads and pathways, shops, community centres, etc.) were also mapped. The GPS mapping started with points being collected using the GPS equipment in the Tehri Garhwal region.

---

[3] The natural water oozing out of the permeable rocks in the form of small streams.

Subsequent open forums definitely sensitized the community on the importance of information about water supply and delivery, water management, water quality, and water use issues. It also highlighted the sense of belongingness to the region and the pride that emanated also brought the wish to conserve resources to the surface. At the same time, the acceptance level for the exercise encouraged the hope that given the resources, the scope for blended technologies within the indigenous community would be immense, if done with sensitivity. There are many assessment tools available for mapping human competencies. The index evolved for assessing the Geospatial Capacity Building Initiative conducted at the Thakarwal Village (Parihar and Parihar 2008) was replicated. The assessment illustrated that the Geospatial Capacity Building Initiative Index (GCBII) was definitely different in the pre-assessment phase than in the post-assessment phase. The most favourable impact was on the outlook towards capacity building, which clearly reminded us of the fact that young people (girls and boys) were enthusiastic and ready to learn and even teachers demonstrated some interest. But the sad part was that monitoring after three months indicated a decline by one level, that is with an index of 0.74 (high impact), and after six months registered almost nil impact. In almost all others (understanding maps, awareness level, perception about decision-making, and knowledge about geospatial tools) there was a high impact and most people showed high learning ability in the beginning, and the adaptability after six months also showed promise. But very few decision-makers appeared to be in favour of actual implementation. That means actual practitioners still shied away from using maps and information collected by the members of the community in decision-making or solving any problem when they come across one.

V

Contextualizing Relationships

Contextualizing relationships between space, indigenous knowledge and resource management illustrates the concern over how different communities observe the interactions. Perceptions vary and what emerges is a space redefined as isolated, discrete and detached at micro level, an idealized abstraction as followed for generations, generally without a question (Table 11.1). The space produced by the indigenous community certainly serves as a tool of thought and of action.

Table 11.1: Evolved Relationship of Indigenous Knowledge with Space

Contextual Emerging Questions?	Yes (in per cent)	No (in per cent)	Evolved Relationship of Indigenous Knowledge (IK) with Space
Are spaces occupied or interacted with by the indigenous community discrete?	82	18	Space is isolated, discrete and detached at micro level; sphere of influence is limited.
Is the space an idealized abstraction from the relations between indigenous people and their geographical bearings?	95	5	Space is an idealized abstraction as followed by generations, generally without a question.
Are spaces discovered by indigenous people to be objective features of the world?	24	76	Indigenous people are not much concerned about the intention or recognition given to their space by others.
Are spaces an unavoidable systematic framework for organizing the experiences of the indigenous community?	68	32	Spaces cannot be ignored while formulating a framework for organizing the experiences of the indigenous community.
Whether true nature of space occupied by the indigenous community is conditioned by the existential experience of dwelling.	86	14	True nature of the space occupied by the indigenous community is certainly conditioned by the existential experience of dwelling.
Whether indigenous driven space is a (social) product.	15	85	Indigenous driven space is not a social product, but largely guided by the individual.
Whether the space produced by the indigenous community serves as a tool of thought and of action or not.	95	5	The space produced by the indigenous community certainly serves as a tool of thought and of action.
Whether indigenous driven space is a means of production, . . . a means of control, and hence of domination, of power.	58	42	Though indigenous driven spaces guide towards the means of production, they do not necessarily become the means of control or power.

(Continued)

Whether the space produced by the indigenous community has more layers of meaning or relationships to other places than immediately meets the eye.	93	7	Deep down, the space produced by the indigenous community has more layers of meaning or relationships to other places than immediately meets the eye.
Can perceived space, conceived space, and lived space of the indigenous people be mapped differentially?	64	36	To a certain extent, the perceived space, conceived space, and lived space of the indigenous people can be mapped differentially.
How do indigenous people feel and think about space, how do they form attachments to home, neighbourhood, and nation, and how are feelings about space and place affected by the sense of time?	34	66	Impact of changing time has slowly started affecting the indigenous people too, and in turn, the indigenous knowledge systems.

Source: Prepared by the authors.

In the Himalayas, as depicted here, space can be perceived at three levels: macro, meso and micro. As understood here, macro space relates to the concept of understanding or visualizing the whole world as a single entity. Micro space, on the other hand, designates the local sphere where the maximum interaction of a human being with his surrounding environment takes place. The meso space lies in between the above two, i.e., it is neither complex like macro space nor constricted or narrow like the micro region. As shown in Table 11.2, the concept of space varies between an external person and an indigenous person. In other words, an external person interacts with the macro or meso space, while the indigenous person interacts with the micro.

Table 11.2: The Meaning of Space as Perceived by an External Person and an Indigenous Person

Conceptualizing Space	*External Person*	*Indigenous Person*
Area	Larger	Micro
Vision	Broader	Narrow
Training	Formal	Inherited
Processes	Complex	Simple

Source: Prepared by the authors.

The intrusion of modern science-based knowledge into the livelihood of the indigenous people has changed the concept of space from a sphere of community participation and co-operation to isolation. It is significant that several respondents said that the greater the proximity to roads and 'modern' practices, the weaker the community spirit. Jagat (male, 44 years old, self-taught forester and farmer, Kot Malla village, Alaknanda Valley, Chamoli) cites a general rise in individualism — and this is one of the main social changes identified by the respondents:

> Today each person is isolated and wants to depend on his own resources. All that talk of community is over. It was not like this earlier. For example, for canals and *ghul* [embankment] there is the irrigation department, but earlier everyone went and did the work without wages.[4]

This sense that these societies are in a transition stage is echoed by another respondent, Mohan (male, 60 years old, Ayurvedic physician, Chamba, Henval valley, Tehri Garhwal):

> This is the transition period. On the one hand people are losing their traditional knowledge and means, and on the other hand they are not getting adequate training in modern scientific techniques. As a result of it they are losing all their assets. That's why I advocate the revival of traditional occupations, measures and methods.[5]

A paradigm shift in the vision of space from a place of community participation and co-operation to a place of isolation is visible in the traditional societies, and this has disintegrated and hollowed their faiths, beliefs and knowledge. The reasons behind this setback, as some respondents say, are the changing behaviour of people, lack of interest among the younger generations in preserving and carrying on their heritages, the changing economic structure of the region from a subsistence economy to a money-order economy (as most of the educated and skilled people of the region move to the nearby towns or cities for higher earning and send money home), and the intrusion of modern scientific knowledge in their traditional practices. From this discussion on contexualizing space a three-tier Indigenous Knowledge WEB model therefore emerges.

Figure 11.1 shows the space of indigenous knowledge system that has developed due to the interaction between experienced and practiced knowledge, acquired knowledge and the physical environment, and inside

---

[4] http://www.mountainvoices.org/i_th_community_activities.asp.html (accessed 22 January 2013).

[5] Ibid.

Figure 11.1: Space of Indigenous Knowledge

Source: Prepared by the authors.

that space the spirituality core is well-guarded. The spirituality core in the centre is an important component of the first stage, untouched by the externalities and the external pulls and pressures. It is a pure form with indigenous people not much concerned about the intention or recognition given to their space by others (Figure 11.1).

When in this balanced space the modern scientific knowledge system is inserted forcefully, a situation of unrest develops, where the modern scientific knowledge system engulfs some of the indigenous practices and directly affects the three components of the indigenous knowledge. This leads to the formation of a conflict zone (as shown in Figure 11.2). The spirituality core struggles within itself to remain away from the change, making the situation more difficult. One way to remove the conflict zone that evolves is to document the indigenous knowledge properly before merging it with contemporary knowledge.

One can find a number of such instances where environmental planners have neglected indigenous knowledge since they lacked patience to regulate it at the local level and favoured quick gains, which led to long-term damage. Moreover, planners or implementers do not recognize different requirements for the capacity building of the native people. According to a respondent named Jampa (female, 43 years old), 'I also got into the trap of spoiling my field ... In the first year use of chemical fertilizers yielded positive results, but in the subsequent second and third year, I regretted that I bought them and used them in my field ... the

Conceptualizing Space and Indigenous Knowledge 221

Figure 11.2: Intrusion of Modern Scientific Knowledge System into the Sphere of Indigenous Knowledge System

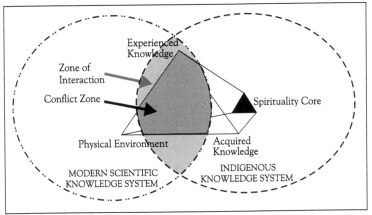

Source: Prepared by the authors.

yield fell ... in the fourth year the output appeared even less than when I had started' (interview, Rampur village, 11 June 2010).

Furthermore, indigenous knowledge is not sufficiently taken into account in the design and implementation of conservation and development schemes in which the government is involved too. Most of the time, the role of indigenous knowledge is sidelined because local people's objectives are ignored. Despite the fact that local users have the developed traditional knowledge to manage their own resources, policies and regulations are made to favour the objectives and interests of the state. By privileging state objectives, local objectives, such as subsistence and resource-based commerce — the space in which indigenous knowledge can be exercised — are limited and indigenous knowledge is marginalized.

Thus, with few exceptions, most respondents are strongly in favour of reviving and maintaining their traditional approach. One explains, 'For us, our ancestors' methods alone were right. We are sowing the same seeds' (interview with Radhe, female, 39 years old, Rampur village, 11 June 2010).

Figure 11.3 shows the relation between indigenous knowledge and space in a hexagonal web space. At the centre is the 'spirituality core' of the indigenous person protected by the Zone of Acquired Knowledge, the Zone of Experienced Knowledge and the physical environment. If it is intended to introduce Modern Scientific Knowledge tools of resource

Figure 11.3: Indigenous Knowledge Web and Space

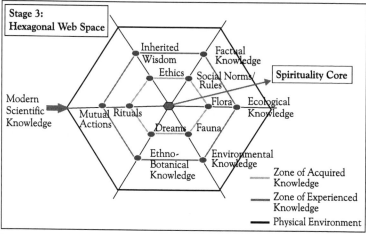

Source: Prepared by the authors.

development and management and to change the thoughts or practices of the natives, then these zones have to be intercepted to reach the core. Any forceful intrusion will only scramble the web, leading to annihilation of both natives and their ecosystem.

Conclusion

The indigenous knowledge and spaces created by the native people are closely related. There is so much of the cumulative body of knowledge generated through generations in them that we have not even recorded a fraction of it. They are not recorded even in the latest GI list in India. The knowledge generated through generations in the form of indigenous knowledge and disseminated through various cultural transmissions by local people in Uttarakhand Himalaya reveals the formidable scope to be practised. There is a need to create a blend between the spiritual core, the line of acquired knowledge and experienced knowledge. What emerges is that the local-level indigenous knowledge held by the natives, rooted in an intimate and long-term involvement in local ecosystems, can be a crucial tool and source of knowledge for long-term sustainability and immediate resource conservation. It is not the physical but the mental space that binds and preserves indigenous knowledge and practices within the communities. So mapping different spaces and recording their importance with the blended geospatial tools and technologies is required. While considering whether modern technology should become a part of the indigenous system, there is a call for the diffusion of both the systems. However, the urgent need is to be cautious before introducing any new technology depicting concerns, false or real, for sustainable livelihood of local communities.

References

Basanta, R. 1990. 'Documentation of Indigenous Knowledge in Gujarat Agriculture'. Paper presented at 'International Workshop on Sustainability through Farmers Involvement in Technology Generation and Diffusion in Indian Society of Agronomy', 9 February, New Delhi.

Carnap, Rudolf. 1974. *Philosophical Foundations of Physics: An Introduction to the Philosophy of Science*, ed. Martin Gardner. New York: Basic Books.

Castree, Noel and Derek Gregory (ed.). 2006. *David Harvey: A Critical Reader*. Malden MA and Oxford: Wiley-Blackwell.

Center for International Earth Science Information Network (CIESIN), n.d. 'A Framework for Incorporating Indigenous Knowledge Systems into Agricultural Research, Extension and NGOs for Sustainable Agricultural Development'. http://ciesin.org/docs/004-201/004-201.html (accessed 22 May 2013).

Copleston, Frederick C. 2003. *A History of Philosophy: the Enlightenment — Voltaire to Kant*, vol. 6. London and New York: Continuum.

Gibbons, Sahara, L. 1994. *Kant's Theory of Imagination: Bridging Gaps in Judgement and Experience*. Oxford: Oxford University Press.

Harvey, David. 1973. *Social Justice and the City*. London: Edward Arnold.

Haverkort, Bertus. 1993. 'Agricultural Development with a Focus on Local Resources: ILEIA's View on Indigenous Knowledge', in Leendert Jan Slikkerveer, Dennis M. Warren and David Brokensha (eds), *Indigenous Knowledge Systems: The Cultural Dimensions of Development*. London: Kegan Paul International.

Heidegger, Martin. 1971. 'Building, Dwelling, Thinking', in Albert Hofstadter (trans.), *Poetry, Language, Thought*, pp. 156–60. New York: New Directions.

Lefebvre, Henri. 1991. *The Production of Space*, trans. Donald Nicholson-Smith. Oxford: Blackwell.

National Research Council. 1992. *Toward Sustainability: A Plan for Collaborative Research on Agriculture and Natural Resource Management*. Washington DC: National Academy Press.

Parihar, Seema M. and P. K. Parihar. 2008. 'Evolving Web Based Geospatial Capacity Building Infrastructure (WGCBI) for Map Use Research'. Project Report submitted to the University Grants Commission (unpublished).

Pretty, Jules and Richard Sandbrook. 1991. 'Operationalising Sustainable Development at the Community Level: Primary Environmental Care'. Paper presented at the Development Assistance Committee (DAC) Working Party on Development Assistance and the Environment, October, London.

Rajasekaran, B. 1993. 'A Framework for Incorporating Indigenous Knowledge Systems into Agricultural Research and Extension Organizations for Sustainable Agricultural Development in India'. PhD Dissertation, Iowa State University, Ames.

Röling, Niels G. and Paul G. H. Engel. 1991. 'Information Technology from a Knowledge Systems Perspective: Concepts and Issues', *Society: the International Journal of Knowledge Transfer*, 3(3): 6–18.

Soja, Edward W. 1996. *Thirdspace: Journeys to Los Angeles and Other Real-and-Imagined Places*. Oxford: Blackwell.

Stanek, Lukasz. 2008. 'Space as Concrete Abstraction: Hegel, Marx, and Modern Urbanism in Henri Lefebvre', in Kanishka Goonawardena, Stefan Kipfer, Richard Milgrom, and Christian Schmid (eds), *Space, Difference, Everyday Life: Reading Henri Lefebvre*, pp. 62–79. New York: Routledge.

Thrupp, L. 1989. 'Legitimizing Local Knowledge: Scientized Packages or Empowerment for Third World People', in Dennis M. Warren, Leendert Jan Slikkerveer and Sunday O. Titilola (eds), *Indigenous Knowledge Systems: Implications for Agriculture and International Development*, pp. 138–53. Ames: Iowa State University.

Tuan, Yi-Fu. 2001. *Space and Place: The Perspective of Experience*. Minneapolis: University of Minnesota Press.

Vailati, Ezio. 1997. *Leibniz & Clarke: A Study of Their Correspondence*. Oxford: Oxford University Press.

Venkataratnam, L. 1990. 'Farmers' Wisdom for a Sustainable Agriculture', *Kisanworld*, 7(12): 22.

Warren, D. M. 1989. 'Linking Scientific and Indigenous Agricultural Systems', in J. Lin Compton (ed.), *The Transformation of International Agricultural Research and Development*, pp. 153–70. Boulder CO: Lynne Rienner.

World Trade Organisation (WTO). n.d. 'Overview: The TRIPS Agreement'. http://www.wto.org/english/tratop_e/trips_e/intel2_e.htm (accessed 21 January 2013).

12 Breaking the Power of Patriarchy

Unity Dow's Novel
The Screaming of the Innocent

Geoffrey V. Davis*

Such familiarity as most older readers may have gained with Botswana through fiction will probably have been gleaned from the writings of the exiled South African writer Bessie Head, who moved to the country in 1964, two years before it won its independence from Britain, and remained there for the rest of her life. Head not only set novels like *Maru* (1971) and *When Rain Clouds Gather* (1969) and short stories such as those in *The Collector of Treasures, and Other Botswana Village Tales* (1977) in her country of exile, she also documented her commitment to her adopted country and its traditional way of life through important non-fictional texts such as her volume of social anthropology *Serowe: Village of the Rain Wind* (1981) and her historical study, *A Bewitched Crossroad* (1984a). As an exile, what Head sought was an alternative to the South Africa of the apartheid era she had escaped, a place where she could, as she phrased it, 'put down some roots in the African soil and ... find a sense of peace about the future' (Head 1984b: 280). She thought that in Botswana enough of African life and tradition had survived to make that possible. Accordingly the picture of life in Botswana that emerges from her published work is largely a positive one.

In recent years attention has once again been drawn to Botswana as a locus of literary fiction through the success of a series of popular novels by Alexander McCall Smith. Books such as *The No. 1 Ladies' Detective*

---

* This is a considerably revised version of a text first published in memory of Michel Fuchs as 'Confronting the Demons: Ritual Murder, Detection and Activism in Unity Dow's *The Screaming of the Innocent*', *Cycnos*, vol. 24, 2007, pp. 183–98. All translations in the chapter, unless otherwise mentioned, are the author's own.

Agency (1998), *Morality for Beautiful Girls* (2001) and *The Kalahari Typing School for Men* (2002) have achieved international bestseller status. This is due not only to his creation of an appealingly homespun lady detective, Precious Ramotswe, who rarely has to deal with crimes of any great moment and is greatly given to drinking bush tea, but no doubt also to his appealing, if somewhat sentimental, portrayal of Botswana as a largely unsullied place of peace and solidarity where basic human values have been meaningfully preserved, a society quite at variance with the image of the African continent all too frequently purveyed in the press.

Neither of these two writers, however, is Botswanan and Unity Dow, my subject in this essay, is thus quite correct to state that in her country 'there's no history of writing fiction' (Daymond and Lenta 2004: 54). In that sense she is indeed a newcomer to the scene. And, one might add, she is one who paints a portrait of her society, which is in some ways both more directly related to immediate social issues and more critical than anything to be found in the work of her two predecessors.

*

Since Unity Dow's life and work are not yet well-known and since her fiction is in significant ways related to her profession, it is worth looking briefly at her career. Born in a rural village in Botswana in 1959, she went on to read law at the universities of Swaziland and Edinburgh. She has since had a distinguished career in the legal profession. She has been a prosecutor in the Attorney-General's office, a partner in the first all-female private law practice in the country, and an activist with a particular interest in women's and human rights issues. One of her central concerns has always been what she terms 'the participation of women in the public space' (Dow 2011). Indeed, she has worked consistently for the empowerment of women in many areas of Botswana society.

An early initiative of hers was the establishment of the Metlhaetsile Women's Information Centre in her home village. Dow herself recalls how the initial impact of the centre was due not least to the fact that it had come into existence at all; that alone was sufficient to cause discussion and give the place publicity. At first women were reluctant to utilize its services because they were so unused to seeing such an institution in Botswana. An early tangible measure of its success was that the police agreed to set up a task force on violence against women.

In 1998 Unity Dow was appointed to a life-time position as the country's first female High Court judge, a position in which she served for a period of some 10 years. She had been appointed in succession to a series of white males in a country which 'had never hired a female police officer' (ibid.). As the first female to be named to the High Court, she regarded the appointment as having more general significance for women in Botswana. As she put it in an interview, there are many women in the country who think women *should* hold such positions: 'it meant more than just me' (Dow 2002). In the same interview she discounted any notion that her appointment might have been a government manoeuvre to silence an outspoken critic: 'If you don't trust somebody', she said, 'you don't make them a judge' (ibid.).

As a judge Dow placed great emphasis on talking with people at the grassroots, aware as she was of the disparity between what the law says and the reality on the ground. She proved a forceful advocate of reforming the laws on child support. She coordinated a research project on Women and Law in Southern Africa focusing on human rights for women in six countries and was elected to the International Commission of Jurists. Currently she is a judge of the Interim Constitutional Court of Kenya. Recently she was one of the three judges presiding over 'the most expensive and longest-running law trial this country has ever dealt with' (Beresford 2006). This was a remarkable case in which Bushmen were fighting for the right to remain on their reserve in the central Kalahari and to preserve their ancient way of life as hunter-gatherers rather than be forcibly relocated by the government. Ruling in favour of the Bushmen, Dow commented that the case was 'ultimately about a people demanding dignity and respect. It is a people saying in essence: "our way of life may be different, but it is worthy of respect. We may be changing and getting closer to your way of life, but give us a chance to decide what we want to carry with us into the future"' (ibid.). That statement alone gives some idea of the principles which inform Dow's legal judgements.

*

It is, however, not only such enlightened legal judgements that are making Unity Dow known beyond her native Botswana. She is also increasingly making a name for herself as an author whose writings, fictional and non-fictional, provide ample evidence of the way she has successfully integrated such social and legal concerns into her literary activities, particularly as far as gender issues are concerned. Her most recent work, the non-fictional *Saturday is for Funerals* (2010), written together with Max Essex, Lasker Professor of Health Sciences at Harvard University, offers a fine example. It is at once an emotionally harrowing and a scientifically authoritative study of the AIDS pandemic, which juxtaposes Dow's perceptive and empathetic accounts of how the illness has impacted on the people of Botswana with Essex's lucid explanations of the medical implications. What emerges is a uniquely informative volume on the pandemic, whose powerful impact on the reader derives from Dow's gift as a storyteller and Essex's informed commitment as a medical researcher who has long devoted himself to AIDS research, specifically in Botswana. Their joint account of personal courage and medical progress in a country whose government has with exemplary awareness gone beyond denial to positive response provides encouragement to other African countries that have not yet achieved so much and a considerable measure of hope that the HIV/AIDS crisis may yet be overcome.

*

It is, of course, not particularly usual for a practising judge to follow a second career as a writer of fiction. Dow has stated that one reason why she did so, apart from the fact that it enabled her to reach a wider audience, was as 'a way to reclaim the voice I lost as an activist' (Dow 2011). Accordingly, all of the four novels Dow has written and published to date — *Far and Beyon'* (2000), *The Screaming of the Innocent* (2001), *Juggling Truths* (2003b), and *The Heavens May Fall* (2007) — powerfully address social concerns, gender issues and the clash of tradition and modernity she sees as a fundamental feature of modern Botswana society. Thus, *Far and Beyon'* tackles the AIDS crisis; *The Screaming of the Innocent* confronts *muti* killing; *Juggling Truths* is a memoir of a rural Botswana childhood; and *The Heavens May Fall* addresses rape and sexual abuse, while taking a critical look at the legal profession itself. It is probably fair to say that, of these, *The Screaming of the Innocent* has attracted most attention so far;[1] it has now also been translated into German and French.[2] And it is to that work that I should now like to turn.

---

[1] There is not, however, as yet much critical writing on Dow's work. I have discovered only two critical articles. See Lenta (2004); Bettinger (2006). For a useful brief discussion of *The Screaming of the Innocent*, see Gagiano (2006).

[2] It has been translated into German as *Die Beichte* (Dow 2003a) and into French as *Les cris de l'innocente* (Dow 2006). The German title refers to Rra-Naso's confession in the final chapter of the book.

*

In September 2001, the body of a Nigerian boy was found in the River Thames. It had been severely mutilated in such a way that the police concluded that he had been the victim of a ritual murder. Such crimes are thankfully rare in Europe and knowledge of them is scant.[3] In basing her novel *The Screaming of the Innocent* on a crime of ritual murder Unity Dow is focusing the reader's attention on a crime whose frequency is thought to be increasing in southern Africa. In South Africa where there has been much concern about the rise of such crimes, so much so that one of the first post-liberation tasks of the African National Congress was to establish a Commission of Inquiry into Witchcraft Violence and Ritual Murder in the Northern Province (Comaroff and Comaroff 2004: 513),[4] the crime of ritual murder is also known as *muti* killing. It is worth citing a definition of what the Zulu word *muti* (or the Setswana equivalent *dipheko*, which Dow uses) means. The *Dictionary of South African English on Historical Principles* defines it as

> a substance or object which has or is believed to have curative, preventive, protective or harmful powers of a medicinal or supernatural kind; esp. medicines or charms traditionally used among the black peoples of Africa, made usu. of plants or animal parts, and sometimes, reportedly, of parts of the human body (Silva 1996: 484).

Accordingly, ritual murder is 'a murder carried out for the purpose of obtaining body parts to be used in the making of *muti*' (ibid.: 598).

The belief behind the practice of ritual murder is that a person who can obtain the relevant body parts — those parts normally being, to quote the dreadful verb used in the novel, 'harvested' from a girl who is ideally about 14 years old and being obtained while the child is still alive — can have them used by a traditional bush doctor or witchdoctor in the preparation of a potion that will strengthen him, for instance, in achieving political office or obtaining a better social status or business advantage. Occult crimes of this sort are always related to power in this way.

---

[3] Terence Ranger (2007) refers to this incident.

[4] The Comaroffs' absorbing article is primarily concerned with what they term 'the incommensurability between a European national law founded on liberal principles and vernacular African beliefs in the occult, beliefs that defy investigation or interrogation under the usual terms of Western legal reason' (Comaroff and Comaroff 2004: 530).

It is important to note some of the accompanying features common to such murders. Most of the cases generally do not come to court and thus remain unsolved. It has been suggested that 'the police, far from working hard to get to the bottom of the ritual murder cases seem to be putting every effort at protecting the perpetrators of the crimes' (Mathokgwane 1997). There is also a widespread belief that the perpetrators of such crimes are to be found amongst the richer members of society.[5] The fact that traditional healers or diviners are presumed to be involved is significant. Recourse to them has long been normal social practice in southern African society; they are consulted by rural people 'to divine the cause of affliction, to guard against attack, to give a competitive edge over rivals and to ensure their own well-being' (Comaroff and Comaroff 2004: 519).[6] At the same time their involvement generates fear of their supposedly supernatural powers. Such fears are sometimes shared by the police themselves. The South African inquiry into ritual murder found for example that 'the majority of black police believe in witchcraft and are reluctant to intervene' (ibid.: 524). Dow herself referred to this aspect when she remarked in an interview that 'it would take a very brave police officer to go and arrest a very prominent traditional doctor' (Dow 2002). Elsewhere she has expressed her scepticism about their role and the beliefs which lead people to consult them.[7]

Asked about her accusation that ritual murder is a crime everyone knows about but nobody does anything about, Dow responded:

> Of course everyone knows that it happens, as everyone knows that traffic accidents happen. It happens. Kids disappear all the time — everyone knows it happens. It's in the papers that a child disappeared, and then when the body is found it's reported that the genitalia were missing and the tongue was missing, and that the police suspect ritual killing; but that's the end. It's not as though it's kept a secret that a child has disappeared — it's very obvious (Daymond and Lenta 2004: 53).

---

[5] Both points are made by James Mathokgwane (1997) among others.

[6] In the novel Dow shows the degree of acceptance traditional healers enjoy. They are consulted even by the police, but they are also shown as abusing their position, as Mma-Neo's experience of being raped by one shows (Dow 2001).

[7] For example, in her interview with Astrid Reinberger, where she stated: 'There are some very good herbal specialists among them, who know a lot about roots and their use in healing methods. And there are a very few psychologists amongst them. In general, however, I have a problem with a belief system which makes others responsible for one's own illness or one's own misfortune' (Reinberger 2003: 496–97).

Speaking about such cases in her Cincinnati interview Dow recalled that in 1984 she was herself present in court when such a case was tried and she also referred to a conviction handed down in 1996, when an uncle, who had taken body parts from his own niece, was sentenced to death (Dow 2002). In discussing ritual murder in Botswana several commentators refer to the particular case of the 14-year-old Segametsi Mogotsi who was killed in Mochudi in 1994, an incident that provoked riots on the part of her fellow students.[8] Elfi Bettinger thinks that Dow is consciously taking up this specific case in *The Screaming of the Innocent* (Bettinger 2006: 177).

Although Dow stresses that the vast majority of people in Botswana forthrightly condemn such practices, her concern is the degree of toleration on the part of Botswana society that allows such things to happen (Reinberger 2003: 495).[9] And that is of course one reason why she wrote the novel.

*

The story the novel has to tell is a little complicated. The time is 1994; the place is a small village in northern Botswana on the edge of the Okavango. As the story opens, we are introduced to three men. They have in common that, although they have achieved a measure of success in their chosen careers, each of them desires to further enhance his position in society. The businessman, Mr Disanka, wants to expand his butcher's business; the headman of Diphukwi village, Mothlababusa Bokae, longs to become chief; the deputy headmaster Mr Molatedi Sebaki, wishes to succeed to the headmastership of his school. None of them appears to have any moral qualms about the methods he is prepared to resort to in order to achieve his aim. So together they conspire to commit what in the Setswana language is known as *dipheko* and in English as 'ritual murder'. In the belief that the removal of body parts such as the breasts, the genitalia and the anus of a young girl who is a virgin and still alive during the mutilation will, when used in the preparation of a medical potion by a traditional doctor, strengthen them in their endeavours, they enlist through bribery and coercion the unwilling aid of an impoverished elderly man, Rra-Naso, to identify a potential victim, Neo Kakang. After they have performed the deed, Rra-Naso, on the spur

---

[8] Mpho G. Molomo (2001) gives a brief account of this.
[9] The original text of the interview is in German.

of the moment and undetected by the others, takes Neo's clothes and, equally spontaneously, later throws them away in the bush. The perpetrators take the body parts to Mr Disanka's butchery, where on their arrival in the dead of night they are accidentally witnessed unbeknownst to them by Mr Disanka's teenage daughter, Lesego. Her worst suspicions as to her father's complicity in the crime are confirmed by television reports on the disappearance of the girl from the village. Revolted by her father's deed, Lesego requests her parents to send her away to boarding school far to the south. The clothes that Rra-Naso has thrown away are later found and handed over to the police, but when Neo's mother, Mma-Neo, arrives to identify them they are found to have vanished. Two weeks later a poorly briefed detective sergeant (Senai) comes to the village to report that the police are assuming that Neo was taken by lions and that the case is being closed. He has no knowledge of any clothes, is seriously embarrassed by the villagers' questions about them and returns to the police station incensed that he has not been provided with full information. These contradictions in the behaviour of the police lead the villagers to suspect that the police are guilty of attempting to cover up a killing, and angry that they no longer have any means of proving it since the clothes are lost, they resort to violence, which is suppressed by paramilitaries. No further action is taken, no arrests are made and no one is ever brought to trial. The case is never resolved to the villagers' satisfaction (Dow 2001).

Five years later, a bright young woman from Gaborone, Amantle Bokaa, is sent to do her national service (known in Botswana as *Tirelo Sechaba*) at the health clinic in the same remote village in the northern part of the country where the girl had disappeared. When given the task of cleaning out a long neglected storeroom at the clinic, a box marked 'Neo Kakang CRB 45/94' comes to light. As it turns out, it contains the missing girl's blood-stained clothing. The angry villagers demand explanations from the police. Amantle is summoned to the police station to explain what has happened and subsequently acts as a go-between between the villagers and the police. She enlists the aid of a young female lawyer, Boitumelo Kukama from Gaborone, in whose practice she had previously spent some time as a student gaining work experience. The two nurses who had first instructed Amantle to clean out the storeroom, and for whom in the light of their high-handed treatment of the villagers the latter feel nothing but disdain, are as government employees effectively held hostage by the village community. Police efforts to persuade the head of the national service organization, Mrs Molapo, to have

Amantle transferred out of their district raise her suspicions. The villagers decide to address a petition to the Minister for Safety and Security Mr Mading. In the meantime, he calls a high-level conference on their course of action with the chief of police, the deputy attorney-general and the director of *Tirelo Sechaba*, Mrs Molapo, in the capital. The outcome of the conference is a proposal from the minister that a *kgotla* or community meeting be held at the village, but he fails to mention that the proposal does not originate with him but from a demand made by the villagers.

Meanwhile in the northern bush Amantle meets the lawyer from Gaborone, who has been joined at some risk to her career by a young state counsel from the attorney-general's office, Naledi Binang. Camped out in the bush some miles from the village they debate their strategy for the *kgotla* on the following day. They are firmly convinced, as are the villagers, that they are dealing with a case of ritual murder and that the police must have connived in a cover-up.

The village meeting is attended by the villagers themselves, by Amantle in company with her legal friends, and by government officials, including the minister himself. Also on the Very Important Person (VIP) stand are Mr Disanka the businessman and headman Bokae. Almost hidden in the crowd of villagers, but noticeable because of her city clothes, is Lesego who has returned to the village for the meeting. In his speech the minister concedes that the police had made mistakes in their handling of the case, but he attributes these to the kind of fear all of them feel in alleged cases of ritual murder rather than to any desire on the part of the police to conceal what had actually happened. He asks the villagers to hand over the new evidence in the form of the girl's clothes (which they do), to cooperate in the renewed investigation, and to release the nurses. Boitumelo responds by articulating the villagers' demands: how did it come about that the clothes were in the clinic? Where were they before then? Which police officers had falsified the records and lied to Mma-Neo about the fate of her daughter? The minister then produces the officers who were involved in the investigation at the time, but again excuses their actions on the grounds of the fear they had felt. He promises that he will personally oversee the renewed investigation.

Naledi, who meanwhile has become curious about Lesego's evidently emotional reaction to all of this, approaches her in the crowd and tries to find out who she is and what her interest in the case is — without success.

As the group of young women debate the events of the day later on, Rra-Naso appears. Throughout the years since Neo's 'disappearance' he has acted as a stalwart friend to Mma-Neo, providing moral support and sharing her pain. Now he asks them to listen to his story, which takes the form of a confession. Rra-Naso reveals his own participation in the ritual murder, relating in gruesome detail how he was pressurized into becoming an accomplice and how Neo met her death. He tells how unnoticed by the others he took her clothes and later threw them away in the bush. He also describes the trauma which the event has induced in his mind; ever since he has been haunted by Neo's screaming. And finally he reveals the names of the culprits, astonishing the group when he names as the one who arrived at the scene after the murder to be given a piece of the body parts the Minister of Safety and Security himself. The next day the body of the old man is discovered hanging from a tree and Amantle faces the task of telling Mma-Neo and the villagers why he has committed suicide. She also has to admit that she has failed in her task since they have been tricked by the minister and are no longer in possession of the evidence.

*

Some reviewers have had difficulty in deciding what type of novel *The Screaming of the Innocent* (Dow 2001) actually is. A review of the French edition by Diane Saint-Réquier (2006) puts the problem succinctly: *Le roman de Unity Dow est un inclassable. S'il s'agit assurément d'un roman policier de qualité avec suspense, rebondissements et personnages hauts en couleur, il s'agit aussi d'un portrait du Botswana* (Unity Dow's novel cannot be classified. It's certainly a crime novel of quality, with suspense, twists in the plot and colourful characters, but at the same time it is a portrait of Botswana). That tends to suggest that, as in all good fiction, the novel invites several ways of interpreting it. As a judge Dow was able to bring to her fiction an exhaustive knowledge of legal process and great familiarity with all manner of crimes, including ritual murder, so it should not surprise us that the novel displays features that we normally expect to encounter in the genre of crime or detective fiction. So let us begin by examining them.

First, of course, we have a murder of a particularly gruesome sort committed in mysterious circumstances. Since there is no body and no evidence, it is also one that has remained unsolved for years. We also have a degree of suspense since we follow a process of detection which proceeds from the discovery of evidence and — initially at least — holds out hope that the mystery may finally be explained. In this case we know from the start who three of the culprits are since we witness the conspiracy that sets events in motion; we know that they will stop at nothing to achieve their aims and we also see them using bribery and intimidation to secure their reluctant accomplice's co-operation. The fact that we do know who they are serves to focus our attention on the process of detection itself and to suggest that there is more at stake than the mere revelation of the identity of the killers. We do not, however, suspect until the end that two other people are involved and in both cases the revelation of identity is wholly unexpected and quite shocking. We also have a corrupt police force, who we readily suspect of some degree of complicity in the crime; in this instance their incompetence is compounded by their fear of the supposed powers of traditional healers. There is corruption in high places, too: those involved in the crime are people of reputation and authority in society; the nature of the crime is evidently not one usually committed by people in poor circumstances. In many crime fictions where the police are shown to be inadequate to their task, there is frequently a person, often a private detective, operating independently and it is usually he — or she — who arrives at the solution. Here this role is taken by Amantle and her associates. And finally we have a confession in the final chapter: Rra-Naso confesses that he has been an accomplice to the murder, informs us in detail how the crime was committed and supplements information we have already gained from Lesego's eyewitness account of the murderers' return to her father's butchery.

All these elements are, of course, staples of detective fiction which Dow has used to good effect in structuring the story she has to tell. There are, however, also a number of significant ways in which she breaks with the conventions of the genre. Prime among them is the fact that here justice is *not* seen to be done. Dow cleverly contrives the end of the novel to disappoint the reader's expectation, doubly so in fact, since no accusation is forthcoming from Lesego, who would be in a position to denounce her father and reveal what happened to the *kgotla*, and the criminals are not brought to trial or punished. Indeed, the final scenes of the novel hold out little hope that they ever will be. Only Mr Disanka, who forfeits the respect of his daughter and the unity of his family, and Rra-Naso, who commits suicide because he sees no other way to atone for what he has been a party to, pay the price of their deeds.

*

The Screaming of the Innocent (Dow 2001) is more than just crime fiction: not only does it use elements of criminal investigation to explore a broad social issue, it also interrogates belief systems and explores gender relations. As this account of Unity Dow's legal career has indicated, she has always been much concerned with gender issues. This broadly feminist perspective is evident in many different aspects of her fiction as well. In her Cincinnati interview Dow spoke of her desire to orient her fiction to the lives and concerns of women and to show women acting in the public arena. In the figure of the teenage Mosa in *Far and Beyon'*, for example, she felt she had 'created a role model for other girls', who could demonstrate that 'you can create spaces' and that 'change is possible' (Dow 2002). That is a fundamental dictum of her writing. The reader of *The Screaming of the Innocent* will detect similar principles informing the actions of Amantle (Dow 2001).

The novel is thus particularly concerned with revealing the kind of problems the women have to face in Botswana society: a traditionally patriarchal social order; deep class divisions between rich and poor; widespread corruption in the administration and the police; victimization and marginalization of women throughout society; an absence of morality; the persistence of ancient superstitions even into the higher echelons of power; inadequate protection for children; and a degree of tolerance and passivity, which brings about a collapse of the moral order and facilitates sexual abuse and heinous crimes such as ritual murder. In such a society traditional virtues such as children's obedience to their elders can lead to death.

The men portrayed in this novel emerge from it extremely badly. Dow proves a shrewd observer of patriarchal abuse and a bitter critic of the passivity which facilitates it. The first chapter, for instance, is a bitterly satirical portrait of Rra-Lesego. Regarded by one and all as 'a good man', 'a good lover' and 'a good father' (ibid.: 1–3), who 'lived within society's boundaries' (ibid.: 3), his reputation for good works is such that when a committee is set up to investigate a murder the police are stalling over, he is 'naturally selected' (ibid.) as a member of it, even though, as it later turns out, he was one of those who actually committed the crime. The people of the village, who suspect he has acquired wealth and success 'by devilish means' (ibid.: 5), have done nothing to stop him. It is such toleration, such passivity which enables him to pursue his initially voyeuristic and later murderous activities.

Of those who participate in the ritual murder, Rra-Lesego is a businessman who professes to love his family while openly maintaining a mistress; the second is a headman who flagrantly abuses his administrative position and frequently helps himself to schoolgirls for his sexual pleasure; and the third is a school teacher who schemes to bring about his headmaster's downfall and rejoices over his supposedly successful use of witchcraft when the latter is killed in a car crash. The traditional healer abuses his position to commit rape; the police are shown to be incompetent, corrupt and superstitious; the politicians seek only their own betterment. Only the old and terminally ill Rra-Naso stands out as a tragic figure.

In exposing the gender conflict (which is also a generational conflict) at the heart of Botswana society, Dow places great emphasis on the need for women to overcome their traditionally prescribed — and circumscribed — gender roles. She shows how Amantle, Boitumelo and Naledi as activists oppose the patriarchal system and resolve, even when at the end they do not fully succeed in their endeavour, to continue their struggle. She insists on the importance of education in producing young women who are capable of prosecuting the cause of female empowerment. On occasion, the reader may feel that the character of Amantle is somewhat overdrawn. As Dow remarked, some people in Botswana thought that 'she's an impossible character ... she's too strong for a Motswana woman' (Daymond and Lenta 2004: 51). But that, it would seem, was her intention. Amantle, with her education and her previous experience of student demonstrations and oppositional activity, is intended to demonstrate to young women readers that they can be like her, that 'she is possible' (ibid.). Naledi, Boitumelo and Mma Malopi are significant figures in this connection too. Naledi, having spontaneously decided to join the others on their journey to the north, thus risking her career as an employee in the attorney-general's office, draws the lessons from her experience and changes sides, as it were, by accepting a job with Boitumelo. She, for her part, will continue to run a lawyer's practice that takes on cases that do not make much money but do serve the community. And Mma Malopo serves the community by running the national service programme while rejecting the corruption of administrative structures. If these are women in the process of successfully overcoming imposed gender roles, it is perhaps worth pointing out that in her portrayal of the two nurses who deride their jobs Unity Dow also provides an example of how some women are manifestly failing in their task of serving the village community and exercising their responsibilities.

*

As Diane Saint-Réquier pointed out, in *The Screaming of the Innocent* (2001) Unity Dow paints a portrait of Botswana society. Comprehensively depicting rural and urban settings and different social groupings in interaction with one another, she provides a critical survey of a whole society, its institutions and its social ills (Lenta 2004: 35). In bringing together the concerns of Dow's professional life and her literary career, in giving literary expression to the professional concerns that have occupied her in her earlier legal career and latterly as a judge, whether these be women's issues, human rights or the protection of children, the novel not only addresses important social issues but also indicates some solutions to the problems it perceives.

Chief among these is the question of female empowerment. The novel demonstrates the need for women to break the power of a corrupt patriarchy, to begin to take power into their own hands, and to assume positive roles in society. The actions of Amantle and her friends illustrate how such a process might begin. Amantle herself is shown as a role model in the struggle for gender equality, as an activist who resolves to continue the struggle for justice she began as a student.

If the potential for change is seen to lie largely with young people, the villagers also represent hope for the future. The institutions of the rural community such as the *kgotla* hold up; they overcome their passivity, their mutual solidarity binds them, even where their poverty and lack of real power circumscribe their possibilities of action.

This novel is driven by the powerful convictions of an activist. It must be read as a warning, as a call to action in the cause of social reform. In a society where crimes such as ritual murder occur and justice is *not* seen to be done, the search for justice must continue. Fear and intimidation must be overcome; toleration of violent crimes and a culture of silence must be ended.

Finally, in any assessment of this novel the role of Rra-Naso is particularly important. This is not only because of the key he holds to the unravelling of the plot but also to the tragic stature he assumes at the end. Regarded by one and all as 'kind' and 'gentle' he emerges as an accomplice to the crime. His reluctant complicity, born of fear, weakness and poverty, raises the larger question about human kind's capability to commit such deeds. As he concludes his confession, Amantle ponders the ambivalence of the man:

> [she] looked at the gentle old face before her: was it the face of a man full of compassion and love? the face of a brutal killer? the face of a brave man? the

face of a coward? ... Was he a monster? ... Is there a monster lurking in all of us? And if we're so paralysed by fear, if we don't dare face this evil, who will heed the screams of the innocent?' (Dow 2001: 214).

References

Beresford, David. 2006. 'Judge Unity Dow on Botswana's Most Expensive Trial'. *The Observer*, 17 December.

Bettinger, Elfi. 2006. 'Riddles in the Sands of the Kalahari: Detectives at Work in Botswana', in Christine Matzke and Susanne Mühleisen (eds), *Postcolonial Postmortems: Crime Fiction from a Transcultural Perspective*, pp. 161–79. Amsterdam and New York: Rodopi.

Comaroff, John and Jean Comaroff. 2004. 'Policing Culture, Cultural Policing: Law and Social Order in Postcolonial South Africa', *Law and Social Inquiry*, 29(3): 513–45.

Daymond, Margaret J. and Margaret Lenta. 2004. '"It was like singing in the wilderness": An Interview with Unity Dow', *Kunapipi*, 26(2): 47–60.

Dow, Unity. 2000. *Far and Beyon'*. North Melbourne: Spinifex Press.

———. 2001. *The Screaming of the Innocent*. North Melbourne: Spinifex Press.

———. 2002. 'An Interview with the Hon. Ms Unity Dow, Justice of the High Court of Botswana', interview by Bert Lockwood, Faculty Library, College of Law, The Urban Morgan Institute for Human Rights, 15 May. http://stremedia.uc.edu/law/urban_morgan/2002/morgan_20020515/index.html (accessed 23 January 2013).

———. 2003a. *Die Beichte*. Munich: Goldman.

———. 2003b. *Juggling Truths*. North Melbourne: Spinifex Press.

———. 2006. *Les cris de l'innocente*. Arles: Editions Actes Sud.

———. 2007. *The Heavens May Fall*. North Melbourne: Spinifex Press.

———. 2011. *Life Matters*. Interview by Richard Aedy, Radio National, Australian Broadcasting Corporation, 7 March.

Dow, Unity and Max Essex. 2010. *Saturday is for Funerals*. Cambridge MA and London: Harvard University Press.

Gagiano, Annie. 2006. 'The Screaming of the Innocent'. http://www.litnet.co.za/africanlib/innocent.asp (accessed 7 May 2006).

Head, Bessie. 1969. *When Rain Clouds Gather*. London: Gollancz.

———. 1971. *Maru*. London: Gollancz.

———. 1977. *The Collector of Treasures, and Other Botswana Village Tales*. Cape Town: David Philip.

———. 1981. *Serowe: Village of the Rain Wind*. London: Heinemann.

———. 1984a. *A Bewitched Crossroad: An African Saga*. Craighall: Ad Donker.

Head, Bessie. 1984b. 'A Search for Historical Continuity and Roots', in Margaret J. Daymond, Johan U. Jacobs and Margaret Lenta (eds), *Momentum: On Recent South African Writing*, pp. 278–80. Pietermaritzburg: University of Natal Press.

Lenta, Margaret. 2004. 'Postcolonialism in an Anti-Colonial State: Unity Dow and Botswana', *Kunapipi*, 26(2): 34–46.

McCall Smith, Alexander. 1998. *The No. 1 Ladies' Detective Agency*. Edinburgh: Polygon.

———. 2001. *Morality for Beautiful Girls*. Edinburgh: Polygon.

———. 2002. *The Kalahari Typing School for Men*. Edinburgh: Polygon.

Mathokgwane, James. 1997. 'Where is Justice?', *AfricaNews*, May. http://web.peacelink.it/afrinews/14_issue/p4.html (accessed 8 February 2007).

Molomo, Mpho G. 2001. 'Civil–Military Relations in Botswana's Developmental State', *African Studies Quarterly*, 5(2): 3. http://www.africa.ufl.edu/asq/v5/v5i2a3.htm (accessed 8 February 2007).

Ranger, Terence. 2007. 'Scotland Yard in the Bush: Medicine Murders, Child Witches and the Construction of the Occult: A Literature Review', *Africa*, 77(2): 272–83.

Reinberger, Von Astrid. 2003. 'Von Überlebensstrategien im Alltag und der Ankunft in der Informationsgesellschaft', pp. 494–97. http://www.heinz-kuehn-stiftung.de/pdf.jahrb18_16.pdf (accessed 3 February 2013).

Saint-Réquier, Diane. 2006. 'Les cris de l'innocente de Unity Dow: Justice contre tradition', *l'œil de l'exilé*. http://www.maisondesjournalistes.org/lire_cris_innocente.php (accessed 29 January 2007).

Silva, Penny (ed.). 1996. *A Dictionary of South African English on Historical Principles*. Oxford: Oxford University Press and Dictionary Unit for South African English, Rhodes University.

13 The National, the Indian, and Empowering Performance

Festive Practices in the Highlands (Bolivia)

Ximena Córdova

The city of Oruro, the fifth city of Bolivia, planted in the highlands at almost 4000 m of altitude, sits quietly most of the year by the side of the mineral-rich mountain that promoted its foundation in 1606 as a Spanish colonial mining settlement.

However, between the months of November and March, its quiet buzz is transformed into a momentous crescendo of activity leading up to the most renown of festive practices of the region — the Oruro Carnival parade.

The carnival is celebrated around February or March as a Christian festivity in Oruro (as in many other locations in the continent) with public entertainment, food, a variety of public rituals, and dance performances in the streets. In Oruro, at its centre-stage is the carnival parade, with around 16,000 dancers performing 18 types of folkloric dances (Lara Barrientos 2008). The parade is attended by an audience of 400,000 (ACFO 2000: 6), via paid seats along its route across the city, and is broadcast nationally to millions of people. The Oruro Carnival parade is Bolivia's officially most prominent folkloric expression, attended by the country's authorities and mediatized all over the world as a source of Bolivian national pride.

I conducted fieldwork in Oruro between 2007 and 2008, returning to my own country after having left Bolivia as a young child in 1979, as a cultural researcher based at a United Kingdom (UK) institution to study festive practices in the Andes. This long hiatus, despite shorter visits in between, had certainly reflected on my own identity as a Bolivian without the experience of everyday Bolivianness. Therefore, as I prepared to encounter my home country and to embark on fieldwork, I was able to realize that — to a large extent — I was returning to Bolivia wanting to understand something about my own identity, and how identities, rather than acting as fixities in time and space, become shaped by the context from which they emerge, borrowing Judith Butler's notions around performance and subjectivity. Maybe to try to understand what it was that I had lost, by not being there all those years.

Using ideas of performativity by Butler (1999) as point of departure, whereby we understand the subject ('the doer') as not *per se* but as the result of becoming ('the deeds'), I was intrigued by the powers of the festive in playing a part in performing and projecting imaginaries of national and individual subjectivities through dance and music, articulated into particular ideas of national heritage at the site of the Oruro Carnival — in its status as Bolivia's most recognized festive and folkloric event.

It must be made clear that 'heritage' in this context refers to 'intangible' cultural legacy. However, when dealing with 'cultural heritage' one is working with a concept of numerous ramifications, basically involving communities, their past and ideas of transmission, charged with values that are significant for those communities. Heritage scholars have grappled with these ideas for long periods, looking at the practice of heritage, and the professionals and disciplines (i.e., archaeology, museumology, folklore, etc.) dedicated to it (Fairclough et al. 2008).

It has been established, that in its primarily communicative and representative role, the praxis of heritage involves an element of editing from a wealth of random experiences channelled into a single coherent narrative — a 'storying' (Hall 2008: 221) — that links a community to accounts of an earlier period and helps to shape ideas of identity (Appadurai et al. 2008; Hall 2008). These edited narratives of identity operate among symbolically distinctive signs — for instance, the symbolic distinctions between good and evil, proper and improper behaviour, higher and lower status — which organize society as a hierarchical whole (Bourdieu 2000: 34), whilst at the same time, being constitutive of ideas of belonging and social identity.

These connections between the festive, ideas of the past and processes of identity construction are at the bottom of this enquiry, as they are particularly relevant in official discourses around the carnival parade. The transmission of heritage is largely promoted as the most important aspect of knowledge transfer taking place in the performance of the danced procession and the rites associated to it. In the application that was presented by Oruro's cultural authorities to the United Nations Educational, Scientific and Cultural Organization (UNESCO) to be included in the list of World Intangible Heritage, the first justification for the application (that went to win a place for the Oruro Carnival on the list since 2001) is that

> [t]he Oruro Carnival is a cultural process that features a high degree of interculturality and intangibility, dating back more than 2000 years. It is carried out in a cultural space that obeys to processes of accumulation and selection of cultural expressions (ACFO 2000: 6).[1]

In other words, the emphasis is placed on the antiquity and the accumulative powers of the celebration, and its ability to transmit images, ways and values from the past, onto the present, as a sort of repository of culture, all linked to the 'cultural space' of Oruro. Clearly this idea that the parade is more than just a contemporary visual display of dance and music is worth pursuing. The text emphasizes that the parade reaches far back and establishes clear connections between past and present, suggesting it has 'mediatic' capabilities. But I would add that that which is transmitted has not been left untouched by each passing performance, as the performance of danced parades in Oruro also constitutes a space for cultural production, and the 'condensation and intersection' of multiple power networks (Martín-Barbero 2003: xxi). The polyphonic character of cultural performance is not alluded to in the text, but I would add that it could not be taken out of the analysis because there is not just one narrative at play given the performative nature of the celebration. The understanding of performance employed here takes up from Diana Taylor's proposition of focusing on embodied practices as an act of learning, storing and transmitting knowledge. Diana Taylor, among others, has argued that knowledge is the result of performed practices whereby 'slips, misses, new interpretations' in the transmission of the original are constantly rendering a new original (Taylor 2003: xx).

The rest of the text implies that it is thanks to a variety of identities coming together for the event, that a sense of the cultural diversity of the nation is achieved:

> [The celebration] is a display that allow[s] for the affirmation of the cultural identity and diversity of the peoples that take part in it, and it constitutes a privileged way to bring closer together these participating peoples and communities, willing to share the heritage of their ancestors, all in a spirit of respect in the presence of differences, and the recognition of other expressions of spirituality (ACFO 2000: 6).

---

[1] All translations in the chapter, unless otherwise mentioned, are the author's own.

Departing from Stuart Hall's assertion that heritage is a discursive practice: 'It is one of the ways in which the nation slowly constructs for itself a sort of collective social memory' (2008: 221), there is no doubt that the 'language' of nation-making is at play ('affirmation of cultural identity', 'diversity among the peoples in it', 'heritage of their ancestors', 'respecting and recognition of differences'). This is particularly significant in light of the adoption of the parade by the Bolivian official authorities as a metaphor for the nation since the 1970s declaration of Oruro City as the Folkloric Capital of the nation, which gave Oruro's cultural manifestations (centred mainly around the carnival parade) a higher status over cultural expressions of other locations in the nation.

However, if so called national traditions, are spaces 'of dispute as much as of consensus, of discord as much as accord' (Scott 1999, quoted in Hall 2008: 221), this brings into question the principles of selectiveness in the establishing of expressive or modes of behaviour as 'tradition', both conferring authority and status to it whilst making it hard to shift or to review.

In the UNESCO application for Oruro, which represents the view of many cultural and political authorities, for instance, it is implied that religiosity is embedded in universal conceptions of a Bolivian subjectivity:

> The religious behaviour of the native population is one of the basic components derived from human creation. This represents immediate layers of Oruro's society, such as socio-cultural urban groups. The hierarchical position of this religiosity is constantly increasing, to the extent that it is now a universal phenomenon of social integration (ACFO 2000: 6).

It is implied in the two extracts here that the parade and associated rites generate a larger sense of identity by channelling the diversity of identities and past memories that compose it, which is glued together by the (Catholic) religiosity that was first generated among urban Orureños — but now reaches everyone, 'universally'.

However, regional and national identities are by no means uniform. There are 'fissures' along the lines of race, class and location, and it is interesting to question how these are voiced into the national narrative (Hall 2008: 222). The case of religion is one that merits attention given the historical relationship between the Spanish colonialism and Catholicism in the Andes.

The main issue generated in this analysis is to determine the coherence of the official discourse, which is supported by the management of the parade by the Asociación de Conjuntos Folkóricos de Oruro (the Oruro's Association of Folkloric Troupes, or ACFO) which runs the parade, and the work of the cultural authorities in the region, against the polyphony of actors in the festive space provided by carnival in Oruro. In terms of this journey, I would like to explore the possibilities of counter-arguments to the official view that the carnival represents a sort of homogenized mix of the religious and cultural hybridity of Bolivians as a whole, in particular such as is offered by the performance of alternative rural parades in the city of Oruro during the larger framework of carnival festivities.

Particularly, I would like to explore how the most prominent of these rural parades, the Anata Andina, could be seen as a political option for indigenous Aymara in Bolivia by looking at the use of the festive space of Oruro as a platform for national identity discourses.

I also plan to look at the how the Anata Andina emerged in response to the appropriation of the carnival parade — a previously subaltern phenomenon up to the 1940s in Oruro — by hegemonic forces. I will attempt to establish a relationship between understandings of cultural heritage and political exclusion, in particular in reference to the negligence to include indigenous histories in national constructions of cultural heritage mentioned in post-coloniality discussions.

The study of performed and embodied practices is relevant in the context of Latin America in that an exploration of the communicative powers of the performative decentres the fixity of writing and literacy 'as knowledge' above all other forms of transmission, which is a tenet of Western epistemology (Taylor 2003: 16). Therefore, I also propose that performative practices such as ritual danced parades constitute a way to make visible, and further develop previously excluded practices. The Anata parade will serve as case-study for this postulate.

Oruro's Festive Framework

At this point it is important to establish the relationship between the carnival parade and the Anata Andina, because the position of each with regard to the other is an important part of the identity of both festivities.

The Anata

The Anata is a festivity celebrated since the early 1990s in the city of Oruro, but it is linked to pre-Hispanic agricultural practices in the rural highlands related to fertility. The most public expression of the Anata in

Oruro is a danced parade that is performed mainly by rural communities from around the outskirts of the city. Preparations starts with the launch of the *jallupacha* (rainy season, in Aymara) in November, the time of growth for crops and also the time of the dead, which are considered as helpers in the development of the produce, in Aymara cosmology (Téllez Nava 2003: 19). Along with the making of the costumes to be worn by all the performers, and the creation and selection of the music and dances to be executed from a repertoire of ritual dance and music associated with the rainy season which goes on from November to March in the highlands, ritual activity is directed from communities to the deities in charge of the fertility of the land. Offerings and ceremonies accompany the 'ways and customs' of indigenous Aymara of the *jallupacha* period, including danced parades where a community may participate in its entirety, some as dancers, others as musician/dancers, and some as sponsors of the event.

However, from the start, the Anata has to be considered alongside the more prominent Oruro Carnival. In its shape, the Anata parade is similar to the carnival parade, in that it is a danced procession that crosses the city centre. The Anata dances performed are sometimes called 'autochthonous': played to the tune of hand-made traditional instruments such as the *pinkillos* or the *tarka*,[2] to make them differ from 'folkloric' dances which are urban and are performed to music from brass or modern electronic instruments. The clothes worn in Anata *comparsas* (carnival dancing troupes) are uniform across each of the dancing troupes, and traditionally hand-made using animal products and mechanical tools — as opposed to the folkloric costumes of the *fraternidades* ('brotherhoods') and *conjuntos* (the 'dancing troupes') of the parade which are made using man-made materials (such as sequins or synthetics,) and massive manufacturing technology, as well as being more attuned to modern ideas of spectacle, centred on the visual and linked to globalized ideas of beauty. The date of the Anata performance is contingent on the celebration of the carnival parade. It takes place two days before the official carnival parade, which is a moving Christian festivity between February and March, amidst the rainy season in the highlands.

Indeed, the relational dynamics between the Anata and the carnival Parade are not fortuitous. The Anata emerged, as we will see later, as an indigenous response to the official carnival parade, so it is worth

---

[2] These are traditional wind instruments of the highlands in the region, of pre-Hispanic origin.

establishing what takes place in the official parade in order to understand what the Anata is responding to.

The urban festive space of Oruro at this time of the year is heavily loaded with demonstrations of devotion to Christian as well as pre-colonial Andean deities. The proliferation of festive activity in the region attracts a lot of attention from authorities, the media and people in general, both locals and visitors. It is a high profile period (in the case of the folkloric carnival parade in particular), attended by the country's leading figures, and broadcast nationally and internationally. It also attracts tourism in large numbers. The carnival parade is at its centre (Plate 13.1).

Plate 13.1: The *Gran Tradicional y Auténtica Diablada Oruro* (GTADO) Perform the Devil Dance at the Oruro Carnival Parade, 2008

Source: Photographed by the author.

The Carnival Parade

The carnival parade is danced over two days, crossing the city centre along the streets of Oruro and finishing inside the Church of the Mineshaft, Oruro's most prominent religious temple, at the feet of the sacred painting of the Virgin. There are 48 dancing troupes that vary in numbers of participants from a few dozens to 1,500. Prospective carnival participants must join a carnival troupe to perform in the parade, which incurs paying troupe fees and preparing in all sorts of ways during several months — financially, physically and religiously.

Live brass bands accompany the dancers, and there is an army of artisans that make the costumes, wigs, masks, and accessories of the dancers. The dances performed — all 18 of them — are called folkloric dances, which in this case means standarized expressions of national culture that mix indigenous culture with the non-indigenous, as opposed to 'autochthonous' dances which is how public authorities call the Anata dances given their independence from intervention from national authorities and their links to rural indigenous communities and their pre-Hispanic traditions. The two most representative among the 18 dance styles of the carnival parade are the Devil Dance (the *Diablada*) and the Moreno Dance (the *Morenada*). Each dance style has its own choreographic patterns and characters, which are personalized and interpreted by each of the comparsas. For instance, there are five *Diablada* troupes, and they vary enormously in terms of aesthetics approaches, number of dancers and even variations of the movements, all developed from a basic pattern and a general 'plot' of the dance (shared by all *diablada* troupes), which shows a troupe of devils, Lucifers and other biblical characters and their female companions, complemented by the Condor and the Andean bear, all of whom are escorted into the church by the figure of a single angel dancing to the tune of the brass bands.

The carnival is organized by dancing troupes' authorities, together with cultural and religious authorities. Financially, it represents a huge opportunity for economic exchange. Dancers are the main financers, as they must get a costume and pay fees to the organizers. As part of my methodological approach to collect empirical data, I joined one of the dancing troupes at a cost of US$ 240.30[3] — with the oldest Devil Dance troupe, the *Diablada Auténtica*.[4] Tickets are sold for seats along the route of the parade, which becomes a 3-km long spectacle of dance, music

---

[3] A figure that must be considered alongside other general economic statistics in the region. It is necessary to calibrate the cost of the participation in the Carnival parade and the position of the Oruro's festivity as Bolivia's most celebrated folkloric and religious spectacle, against average annual income per capita of just US$ 1,512 (just US$ 126 a month [INE 2009: 29]). The cost of being a participant in this most important demonstration is out of the question for many.

[4] The official name of the *Diablada Auténtica* is the *Gran Tradicional Diablada Auténtica de Oruro*. I will use the more familiar name, *Diablada Auténtica*, because it is shorter.

and amazing costumes, alongside which commerce and trade flourish in the shape of food and drink stalls, tourist accommodation and bars and restaurants.

The Festive Actors

The actors of the festive period in Oruro represent a good sample of the population: a mix of urban and rural, native and global, Indians (or first nation citizens), Criollos ('Creoles', people of European descent) and Mestizos (mixed descent) all sharing time and space in celebrations. Not in vain is Oruro used as an official reference in national identity constructions.

On the one hand, Anata participants are not 'dancers' (*danzarines*) but belong to 'peasant' (another word for indigenous) ethnic groups, most of whom are rural agricultural workers who live and work in *ayllus*,[5] although most spend some time of the year doing manual work in urban centres. This fact, rarely acknowledged in the omnipresent dichotomy rural/urban maintained by the status quo, places an insurmountable gap between the two realms, and a hierarchy that places urban above rural values, whereas in reality (at least in the case of Oruro) most 'rural' people have become intercultural between countryside and urban lifestyles due to their working arrangements around agricultural cycles, thus subverting the view that there are two separate and opposing identities at play.

The Anata music is played using traditional instruments (Plate 13.2), manually constructed, and agricultural rituals are performed not just in preparation but also during the parade; like, for instance, animal sacrifices which always seem to cause some shock among the urban Orureños who see these 'rural' practices as 'barbaric'.

Carnival dancers, on the other hand, are mostly ethnically mixed (also called *mestizos*) of urban-descent, from students to professionals, authori-

---

[5] The term *ayllu* does not refer only to territory-based indigenous communities, but must be understood as a denomination for an 'autonomous space for the continuation of Aymara knowledge' (Fernández-Osco 2006: 82). In Western academia, anthropologists Tristan Platt (1982) and Olivia Harris (1978, 1995, 2000), among others, have written extensively about the *ayllu* as territory-based networks linked by production needs and kin. A generation of Aymara and Bolivian intellectuals have also started to conceptualize the *ayllu* as a depository of traditional knowledge and indigenous political teachings (see the work of Fernández Osco [2006], for example).

Plate 13.2: Playing the *Tarka* at the Anata Parade, 2008

Source: Courtesy of Yuvel Soria.

ties and those running informal businesses. There are also many young people (Plate 13.3). Given the cost of taking part in the celebration, the majority of them lead a fairly comfortable lifestyle for local standards, although many low-paid manual workers and service providers (miners, lorry drivers, meat sellers, office clerks, etc.) find ways of supporting their participation in the less expensive troupes.

Having established the festive framework and actors of Oruro, and the spaces occupied by the carnival parade and the Anata Andino, we will now look at the historical emergence of the parade as a symbol of national identity, and the counter-emergence of the Anata Andina as a response to official and elite attempts to homogenize the cultural identity of the region.

Carnival and the Making of the National Subject

Oral accounts documented in written legends date the start of the celebration of carnival in Oruro to 1789 inside the mines (Villarroel 1999). However, there are links to earlier pre-Hispanic practices, as pointed out by several local researchers (Beltrán Heredia [1962, 2004]; Condarco Santillán [1995, 1999, 2007]; Murillo Vacarreza [1999], among others).

Plate 13.3: The Caporal Dance is Popular among the Youth and the Middle and Upper Classes in Oruro

Source: Courtesy of Yuvel Soria.

The first official records of a carnival parade date back to 1904 with the foundation of the *Diablada Auténtica* (GTADO n.d.) describing primarily a marginal and urban-indigenous (*cholo*)[6] parade structured around kin and trade networks. According to some dancers, this consisted of unchoreographed dances inherited from colonial miners performed in reciprocity towards The Virgin, mining deities, in a ritual parade that crossed from the one of the poorer quarters of the city towards the Church of the Mineshaft. Pancho Corrales, one of the great grandchildren of a founder of the *Diablada Auténtica*, describes it thus:

> Originally, it was a heterogeneous group, without choreographies. People jumping up and down the Avenida Cívica [one of the main streets is still runs along] (interview, 28 January 2008, Oruro).

---

[6] The term *cholo* is a significant pointer to the ethnic and racial constitutions of the highlands. It denotes someone who is of indigenous descent but based in an urban setting. It is often used pejoratively but it has recently been claimed as a source of pride in terms of acknowledging one's indigenous roots, making them visible, and following certain traditions clearly linked to rural practices, despite being able to adhere to ideas of modernity and global aesthetics. Ximena Soruco Solonguren (2006) has written about the 'unintelligibility of the cholo' in terms of the historical roles attributed to the term as a definer of ethnic identities.

This first period lasts up to the 1940s. In social terms, Bolivia was a racially segregated society, as indigenous people did not have the right to vote, or access to education like the rest of the population. It is commonly said of this period that Indians were banned from certain main squares, and were systematically excluded from entering the financial market (Bautista 2010: 130). The economy of the nation was rural and behind the rest of the region, as Bolivia did not yet operate as a nation after its independence from Spain in 1825, unlike some of its richer neighbours, i.e., Brazil and Argentina. Things changed with the painful defeat of the Chaco War to Paraguay in the 1930s, which led to important territory loss and, eventually, the rise of a Bolivian national consciousness (Klein 2003; Zavaleta Mercado 1986).

The second period of significance for the Oruro Carnival started in the 1940s, and is linked to the awakening of the national character orchestrated by the authorities who saw an opportunity in the event to conjure up ideas of hybridity and social and ethnic equilibrium to counteract social (and racial) segregation, and 'the oligarchic nature of its political and economic life' that had reigned in the country until then (Klein 2003: 184), stopping it from performing as a collectivity united in the defence of public interests, as demonstrated by the Chaco defeat. In 1944 was the first performance of Carnival folkloric dances for national authorities — as other Bolivians became interested in the symbols and elements of the parade, particularly its links to an earlier period depicted in the dances and symbols of pre-Hispanic significance. This first presentation to the larger community and the authorities also marked the start of an introductory period of the middle classes into dance troupes, and the split of initial dance group structures. This marked the end of the 'marginal period'.

The 1950s was the decade of the 1952 Revolution and the configuration of Bolivia as a nation-state. The 1952 Revolution brought the expropriation of natural resources, universal voting and education and land reform, and the assimilation of indigenous identity into the national — with the hope of turning a backward Bolivia into a 'progressive' and unified nation, able to compete and deal as part of the global market. However, the cost, documented by historians of the region (Bautista 2007, 2010; Klein 2003; Zavaleta Mercado 1986), was the negligence of indigenous histories and indigenous collective identities in the construction of a national project, as defined by the non-indigenous elite who led the Revolution, who did not understand indigenous experiences or epistemologies. Instead, we witness the appropriation of selected elements of indigenous culture and spaces through the practice of folklore that served the nation-making production of imaginaries for the creation of an 'imagined community' (Anderson 1991), which included selected, sanitized and simplified images of the 'Indian', that did not portray the experiences of discrimination, theft and extermination suffered by indigenous peoples for centuries as a result of Spanish colonialism, and then neo-colonialism at the hands of the Creole elite, but one placid assimilation. During this period, the Oruro Carnival — a previously subaltern, indigenous event — became populated by the non-indigenous and elites who mixed the use of indigenous symbols, such as indigenous clothes or danced parading for religious purposes, with a concern for homogenizing the diversity of cultures and bodies that had now to be recognized as part of the national.

During the 1960s and 1970s, the appropriation of the celebration by the elites became officialized and reached new dimensions, as Catholicism became a requirement for participation, being enforced in many dancing troupes. Also, the then president named Oruro the Folkloric Capital of Bolivia by national decree in 1970, raising the profile of the city and its celebration to the level of the national. At the same time, new dances were created in imitation of indigenous practices[7] decontextualizing certain traditions and inserting them into the realm of the folkloric. The ACFO was created to safeguard the 'interests' of the dancing troupes. Since then, the organization and management of the festivities is run by this institution leading to the standarization of many elements of the event.

In the following decades, money entered the scene significantly as dancers were asked to pay fees and acquire uniformed costumes in order to increase the spectacular potential of the parade, which became increasingly more expensive. The event became massively mediatized, and sponsorship deals became players in the look and management of the festivity, just as warned by anthropologists John Comaroff and Jean Comaroff, and their study of cases when an ethnicity or cultural identity with a sense of 'authenticity' or 'uniqueness' becomes commodified: 'identity is increasingly claimed as *property* by its living heirs, who proceed

---

[7] The Tinku dance is a good example of this case. It is based on warring indigenous dances celebrated in May in North Potosí, whereby two partitions of a community come together to engage in ritual fighting and music. The Tinku dance depicts dancers wearing clothes similar to those worn in Potosí, and its choreography is based on movements around simulated kicks and punches. This dance is popular among university students in Oruro and La Paz.

to manage it by palpably corporate means: to brand it and sell it, even to anthropologists, in self-consciously consumable forms' (2009: 29). Just as processes of commodification and spectacularization gained a firm grasp of the event, to coincide with the 500-year remembrance of the arrival of Spanish colonization to the continent in 1992, a year later, the Anata was first launched in 1993 in the city of Oruro: with Indians entering the Capital City of Folklore with dances and practices that had been relegated to the rural.

By 2001, the carnival parade was inscribed in the list of World Intangible Heritage by UNESCO. This marked a new era of global projection of Bolivian national cultural heritage. As a result of the inscription, the issue of change and innovation to carnival practices became problematic as many questions are raised each time an innovation or evolution looks imminent, seen as a threat to the veil of 'authenticity' of the parade. Cultural authorities became the gate-keepers of the cultural content, the management, and the finances; they started to determine the limits of the celebration in accordance with UNESCO's priorities around 'safeguarding the authenticity', 'documentation' and 'promotion' of intangible cultural heritage (UNESCO n.d.) — leading somewhat to a process of 'fossilization' of the expressions performed, in particular of the indigenous elements of the parade.

The last of the events I documented during my fieldwork between 2007 and 2008, showed a globally mediatized and highly choreographed event led by the Church. The carnival parade is now ruled by strict governance of innovations, and a strict Catholic focus (albeit with an Andean twist), including the action of a 'guard' whose members will pull out a dancer performing a character that is not 'scientifically documented' to be an 'authentic' component of the tradition of any particular dance (interview with Ascanio Nava, Oruro, 12 December 2007); as well as several clauses in the regulating documents that allude to the mandate of Catholicism for the performers. Also, dancers nowadays require very considerable amounts of funds to take part, whereas a larger number of international performers are present, as visitors come in to dance in the parade sometimes after their first visit, attracted by the popularity and exuberance of the event.

In the development of the event in the course of the century, nation-making and racial politics can still be discerned. To a large extent, despite some improvement led by the inclusive policies of Bolivia's first indigenous present since 2005, Evo Morales, Bolivia still operates on the colonial racial categories that were inherited from colonial times and valid in 1904 (when the parade is first officially recorded), based on 'racialised biopolitics of white supremacy and brown subalternity' at the level of mentality (Cadena and Starn 2007: 12). Although the elites, in today's Andean hybrid society, look phenotypically similar to Indians, their background, cultural values and aspirations are the markers of the differences. As Ximena Soruco Solonguren, Bolivian race scholar, says, nation-making discourses are built over the basis that the indigenous is the alter ego of the 'white', where 'the indigenous could be thought of as inhabiting a symbolic far space and time (pre-Spanish, rural, refractive to civilisation)' (2006: 82). I found that this was still valid to a large extent in 2008, as accounts of discrimination and racism abound in contemporary Bolivia.

In the dichotomy of Indian backwardness/white supremacy in nation-making discourses, the Mestizo (or person of mixed descent) appears as the only possibility of national unification, which is why the 1952 Revolution tried to establish Mestizo identity as part of the national project, doing away with the racial differences although placing the loyalties still within 'white' subjectivity. In her historical account of a fluctuating Mestizo identity, Soruco Solonguren concludes that at present,

> '*mestizo*' denotes the search for western assimilation and the negation of any indigenous or *cholo* past and it soon imitates the [Creole] (ibid.).

Using what Homi Bhabha calls the 'pedagogical plenitude' of unilinear historicism (Bhabha 1990, quoted in Radhakrishnan 2003: 314), Mestizo culture is presented as the only alternative to the 'backwardness' and 'otherness' of the Indian, and a reconciliation with the fact that although the aspirations of the elite may be 'white', our shared indigenous past cannot be denied: it is imprinted on our faces, on our take on Catholicism, on the foods we eat and our intonation when we speak Spanish.

In short, through its historical developments, the high profiling of carnival as a symbol for national identity, and its appropriation by the elite, have managed to help define the boundaries of modern Bolivian subjectivity: placing Mestizo-Whiteness, Catholicism and European 'modern' aspirations in the foreground, and indigeneity in the background (Bautista 2010: 127–29). Significantly, the interconnection between ethnicity and religion in the making of the national subject has a highly political charge, as we shall see further in the chapter.

Festive Practices on the Boundaries of National Politics

Although not overtly political, the festive arena of Oruro allows for certain discourses to be highlighted above others. One of the consequences of this discourse of homogenization is that undeniable existing differences have had to be glossed over, and gaps refilled, with a tendency to overlook subalternity and indigeneity.

Some Questions around National Homogeneity: Religion and Ethnicity

First, there are a number of counter-arguments for the idea that there is a sense of universal integration among the different religions that are followed or professed in Bolivia, as stated by the ACFO in their UNESCO application. The nation is rich not only in different approaches to Christianity (i.e., Protestantism, Catholicism, Evangelism) but also has significant numbers of groups that have understandings of divinity altogether different from Christianity.[8] One such alternative religiosity is offered by the performance of the Anata Andina parade, which although following the same route and similar structure as the carnival parade, does not enter the Church as its conclusion. It is organized by the Federación Sindical Única de Trabajadores Campesinos de Oruro (FSUTCO), the local branch of the national confederation of peasants and rural workers which represents the interests of many of the rural indigenous groups of the region, and according to the founder and Aymara thinker and activist Irineo Zuna, who was the cultural secretary of the FSUTCO, the Anata represents a different type of spirituality, in stark opposition to the 'evangelizing' and 'mercantilist' message of the carnival parade, in his own words (interview, 25 March 2008, Oruro). The reciprocity rites

---

[8] A United States Agency for International Development (USAID) survey indicates that Bolivia has a percentage of 81.8 per cent of its population as Catholics, with the rest divided among Protestant (2.7 per cent), Evangelical (10.7 per cent), Mormon or Jehovah's Witnesses (0.7 per cent), Non-Christian (0.4 per cent), Atheists (3.3 per cent), and 'traditional' religions (0.1 per cent). I am not aware of how this data was collected, or how the categories were created (particularly in terms of 'traditional religions' which would be relevant for this enquiry), but even so, it is interesting that a significant close to 20 per cent of the population does not classify as Catholics according to this survey (Díaz-Domínguez 2009: 11).

that are performed during the Anata are aimed at pre-colonial deities found in nature. In the words of one of the organizers:

> The Anata is an expression of reciprocity towards the Pachamama for the help received in agriculture and animal rearing, it is also a sort of permanent link between the men and women from the countryside and the Mother Earth [or Pachamama] (Huanaco 2010).

The *Pachamama* is one of the main deities in Andean and Aymara cosmovision. It is matched to the nurturing power of the Earth and nature to give life to humans, animals and all other forms of life.[9] The Anata is part of a series of agriculture-related rituals of reciprocity that allows people to think of life as part of a larger network that sustains several forms of life, not only human and certainly not individualistic, all of which are deserving of respect, promotion, nourishment, and consideration (Fernández-Osco 2006: 83).

The performance of an alternative religiosity in the national and mediatized space of Oruro presents a challenge to the discourse that national heritage is homogenous, and consequently that national identity can be simplified into the 'harmonious' and depoliticized Mestizo voice — precisely what Radhakrishnan calls 'metropolitan hybridity' (Radhakrishnan 2003: 316).

By contrast, the Church has long been associated with the parade. Many local carnival researchers speak of how 'the Virgin presides a sacred Carnival' (Murillo Vacarreza 1999: 35); the ACFO regulating documents call the parade a 'pilgrimage' and dictate that each dancing troupe must be preceded by a *cargamento* (decorated vehicle used to identify each troupe) carrying an image of the Virgin of the Mineshaft along the parade (ACFO 2008: 8). Church representatives visit and speak in *veladas* (weekly gatherings around the Virgin in preparation for the parade), some even participate dancing in some of the carnival troupes. In fact, one of the most senior of representatives of the Church told me that even today the official carnival parade presents an opportunity for indoctrination. In the words of Fray Jairo, the oldest serving member of the Church of the Mineshaft, the 'buzz word' at the then most recent (2008) Catholic council in Bolivia had been 'inculturation' (interview, 25 March 2008,

---

[9] Olivia Harris has written significantly about Andean ideas around the significance of the *pachamama* in agricultural cycles in Bolivia (Bouysee-Cassagne and Harris 1987; Harris 2000, among others).

Oruro). He emphasized the importance of learning from local traditions, even if they were sometimes regarded as 'sentimental' or not entirely compatible with Christian principles, in order to use this vehicle for the indoctrination of people into Christianity. However, in cultural events that are less (or not at all) controlled by the church, such as the Anata Andina, the attitude of the Church officials changes. When I enquired about the reasons for this distance from the Anata celebrations, I was told that from the perspective of the Church, there is 'nothing that can be rescued', in other words, nothing fit for inculturation from this type of event. As a result, the doors of the Church are closed on the day of the Anata parade, probably the only day in the year when the Church closes. By contrast, carnival dancers end the parade inside the Church where each dancing group is received by the priest, and a mass offered (see Plate 13.4).

Plate 13.4: At the End of the Parade Dancers Enter the Church and Meet the Image of the Virgin at the End

Source: Courtesy of Yuvel Soria.

When I enquired why that was, Fray Jairo said that in previous versions of the Anata people had drunk too much, urinated outside the temple's door and things had got out of hand. The issue of street urination is a problem for all of the celebrations around carnival time, including the main parade, given that the infrastructure is lacking to accommodate a population that almost doubles the population of the city over the festive period, but it is only for the Anata parade that the church closes its doors. The installation of removable public toilets around the city by the authorities might solve this, but instead the guilt is placed on the inherent 'backwardness' and 'alterity' of Indians.

From the Catholic Mestizo-white perspective, the Anata is the embodiment and performance of 'alterity', therefore the closed Church for the Anata could not be more loaded with actively constructing and excluding otherness (Gupta and Ferguson 1997). The parade is filled with indigeneity symbols: in the outfits of the dancers that resemble the clothes worn by indigenous people who live in the countryside and in the cities, the ceremonial chewing of coca leaves (or *akullikus*) performed in the weekly gatherings to honour the Virgin even among upper-class people who would never perform this tradition outside of the carnival environment, in the lyrics of the music alluding to the lifestyle of Indians in rural Bolivia who still live in mud-brick (*adobe*) houses and cross the highlands by foot, as they have done since before the arrival of the Spanish:

> Soy un hombre solitario, que camina por el mundo, en busca de un gran amor. Y si la encuentro mañana, me la llevare a Oruro, a mi chocita de paja, rinconcito del amor.
>
> English translation:
>
> I am a solitary man, walking across the world, looking for a great love. And if I find her tomorrow, I will take her to Oruro, to my straw hut, our little love nest (Flores n.d.).

The 'Hombre Solitario' is one of the most famous Morenada songs, and the Morenada dance in the context of Oruro is favoured among the elite.[10] In the parade, it is sung by the Morenada dancers at the top of their voices as they parade and accompany the brass bands eliciting the emotion of the audience on hearing such a classic piece accompanied by live dance and live music. This is usually a point of high emotion in the parade.

However, when the 'true' Indians enter the festive arena via the Anata or any other of the rural parades performed around the same time, the

---

[10] This varies from location to location. In La Paz, the Morenada is the dance favoured among Aymara-descent people who live in the city. There it has become a symbol of the powerful masses of indigenous women dancing in their traditional outfits, overpowering the streets with their presence.

Church closes its doors (despite the fact that there are many Catholics among indigenous Aymara), and the cultural authorities deem that although they are welcome to use the festive space of Oruro they must not be perceived as part of a whole, according to Carlos Delgado, Tourism and Heritage Office for the Mayor's Office in Oruro (interview, March 2008, Oruro). This is partly why the rural parades were not included in the application to UNESCO for a place in the list of World Intangible Heritage, which receives not just international recognition but also financial help towards 'preservation' and 'dissemination' programmes. Enrique Dussel (1992) noted that 1492 marked the start of European modernity and the imposition of a modern European worldview as 'universal', leading to the 'eclipse' of the Americas, its peoples and knowledges. I would argue that the colonial 'eclipse' of the Indian continues to be a strategy used among the managers of the festivity in Oruro, despite claims that the period represents a coming together of the multiculturalism of the nation.

In the absence of acknowledgment of the multivocality of the nation by the Church and cultural authorities that manage the festive space of Oruro, and in the face of the 'eclipse' of the Indian by 'predatory heritage practices' (term coined by Appadurai et al. [2008]) from elite groups to subaltern groups, the alternative taken by local indigenous people — as previously indiscernible subjects of the nation — was to invade the performative space (the streets of Oruro) with signs and symbols of indigeneity. Their aim being, I would argue, to become visible as national subjects with a sense of historical, cultural and political trajectory of their own that differs from the official narrative of the *mestizaje* — as a homogenous Eurocentric and Catholic monoperspective on national identity — at the most high-profile site of performance and representation of the 'national' (see Plate 13.5).

Festive Challenges and the Politics of Recognition

The origin, or rather, the urban re-emergence of the Anata Andina in the city of Oruro in the 1990s is clearly linked to a post-colonial response.

During an interview, Irineo Zuna, who was among the founders of the Anata Andina explained the emergence of the parade in terms of a process of self-discovery. He recalled attending a political meeting with other indigenous activists and returning political exiles in 1982. This was in the context of the short-lived left-wing government of President Hernán Siles Suazo (1982–85) and the opportunity it provided for the

Plate 13.5: An Aymara Priest Performing Reciprocity Rites at the Sacred Sites (Wak'as) in Advance of the Anata Parade

Source: Courtesy of Yuvel Soria.
Note: Interestingly, there is a modern reproduction of the image of the Virgin in the background, placed there by cultural authorities.

reorganization of resistance against the series of mostly right-wing military dictatorships of the 1970s and 1980s. Zuna narrated how at the end of the meeting, many of the left-wing urban returnees turned to him and his commission to ask who they were and what they were, referring to their ethnicity, or indigenous ethnic group. Zuna said that at the time he had not been able to offer a reply to 'what' they were any more than by mentioning the name of the hamlet (*ayllu*) of their provenance. The episode followed thus:

> 'But what language do you speak?'
> 'I speak Castellano'.
> 'What else?'
> 'English, a little'.
> When it was our time to leave, the men asked again, 'but what else do you speak?'
> 'Aymara!' (interview with Irineo Zuna, Oruro, August 2008).

According to Zuna, this was the moment when he and many of his companions developed a clearer sense of their own identity as Aymaras.

The episode, he said, had brought home to him that they spoke a distinct language, had their own territory, and practised their own *usos y costumbres* (ways and customs). He said that 10 years later the Anata Andina was launched to *lo que pasa en el campo con los indios* ('show the nation what goes on in the countryside with the Indians') (interview with Irineo Zuna, Oruro, August 2008). I would argue that in those terms it was also an Indianista response to the carnival parade's depiction of folkloric Indians looking to assert instead a 'true' indigenous voice to speak to the nation about indigeneity.

The Anata Andina was launched despite strong opposition from the Church, organized by the Oruro Peasant Federation (FSUTCO) as Zuna and others decided that it was time to show the nation — through the invasion of the national festive space provided by Oruro — what goes on in the countryside, and what it meant to be an Indian (ibid.). This led to the emergence of an ever-increasing arena where identity can be debated and mediated and self-reflexivity may lead to change (Radhakrishnan 2003: 17).

> The Catholic Church didn't want the Anata Andina parade to take place... Because by 1991 when we remembered with force the 500 years of resistance, the Spanish invasion. So at that time there was a powerful confrontation with the Church [by] the Aymaras and the Quechuas. We advanced with force since 1993, we made our own priests. We researched and we have our own Aymara priests now. That's how we had our first Anata on 1993. Thanks to the impetus of those who lived in exile abroad, we were able to identify our identity and see that we had been confused by the Spanish evangelizing invasions (interview with Irineo Zuna, Oruro, August 2008).

This was an attempt to rescue and enrich their own body of knowledge of their ways and customs (*usos y costumbres*) inherited from their *abuelos* (another word for 'ancestors') — which he referred to as *cosmovisión andina* (Andean cosmovision) — by the performance of danced rituals to the Pachamama, inside the urban environment of Oruro. These rites had always been performed in rural *ayllus*, where the technology more readily available was the knowledge inherited from other generations, as the State, despite reforms, had gone a long way to disengage socially from those communities.

Authorities in Oruro (cultural, religious, municipal) and the troupes made up of elite people all continue to praise Mestizo culture, based on a Eurocentric discourse of progress, as the culmination of a great process of cultural enrichment product of the 'encounter of cultures' since 1492. They ignored the perspective of Anata organizers that after 500 years of exploitation and theft of local resources, there was a real need to promote their own 'ways and customs' and the scientific knowledge of their ancestors, by continuing to delve into a more 'native' way to understand the universe and humanity, an Andean epistemology. The Anata signified the performance of these principles inherited from previous generations (to 'live well' and under the rules of the Andean concept of *ayni*, or 'in reciprocity with nature and others') that survived in hiding from the oppressor. The possibility, as suggested by Gramsci, of an 'inventory of oneself':

> to know oneself means to be oneself, to be master of oneself, to distinguish oneself, to free oneself from a state of chaos, to exist as an element of order — but of one's own order and one's own discipline in striving for an ideal. And we cannot be successful in this unless we also know others, their history, the successive efforts they have made to be what they are, to create the civilization they have created which we seek to replace with our own ... And we must learn all this without losing sight of the ultimate aim: to know oneself better through others and to know others better through oneself (Gramsci 1988 [1916]: 59).

In this view, the best-placed option for resistance and power reconfigurations is rearticulation: between 'imposed' self and inner self, between self and other, between an own history and the history of the other. Gustafson (2009) has correctly pointed out that cultural heritage intersects with the area of indigenous knowledges and its relationship to learning and knowledge transfer. Nowadays, though, rather than a 'symbolic or textual corpus', such as is imprinted on the figure of the *indio permitido* (docile, acculturated Indian) versus *indio salvaje* (savage Indian), indigenous knowledges are a 'hybrid, networked form of socio-political and cultural practice that articulates with other forms of knowledge production and practices' (ibid.: 23–24). As Gustafson observed in his analysis of discourses and practices associated with policies of interculturality in education in eastern Bolivia, different identities and dynamics enter processes of articulation in an attempt by indigenous peoples to create power reconfigurations leading to the emphasis of 'struggles over epistemic (i.e. political) authority and legitimacy, rather than debates over purism, identity, authenticity, or essentialism' (Gustafson 2009: 24).

In my view, the best approach to more fully interpret the issues raised by the emergence of the Anata is a focus on the politics of recognition, as proposed by Taylor (1992). The incursion of the Anata in the area reserved for carnival celebrations in the 1990s served to challenge the view that Mestizo heritage contains all the voices, or the view promoted by the ACFO — *todos hacen el Carnaval* ('we all make Carnival') — that carnival represents the true multiplicity of all Bolivians (Nava 2004: 80). It contests the notion that national heritage (inherited values, selected traditions and beliefs promoted as the embodiment of the nation) can be homogenously represented by the performative actions and symbols of an increasingly exclusive group.

Concluding Remarks

In fixing national heritage through institutional management of Bolivian folklore, particular versions of national identity are projected nationally and globally — Mestizoness, Catholicism, homogeneity, the 'folkloric' Indian — and become validated in festivals at home and cultural events abroad. More than a nostalgic revisit of the past, the Anata offers the possibility of agency: envisioning a future in accordance to an own subjectivity which, as a work-in-progress, lends the possibility of authentic self-representation and past-contingency, rather than the imposed celebration of a false and decontextualized self.

Parallel in time to the emergence of the Anata in 1993, to mark the 500 years of colonial history, the words of Rigoberta Menchú, Nobel Peace Prize Winner, resonate with a similarly powerful message: 'We are not myths of the past, ruins in the jungle, or zoos. We are people and we want to be respected, not to be victims of intolerance and racism' (Menchú 1992, in Porras and Riis-Hansen n.d.).[11]

Direct associations of indigeneity with misery and poverty have been challenged with the emergence of powerful indigenous figures in many areas of the globe, from Evo Morales (see Plate 13.6)[12] in South American

---

[11] This interview with Rigoberta Menchú Tum, Mayan refugee from Guatemala, had been conducted shortly before she received the Nobel Peace Prize.

[12] Morales emerged as a serious political contender only in 2002 breaking through a wall of very traditional Latin American politicians: educated abroad, from elite families accustomed to political roles, versed in liberalism, and quite partial to European or American business models. By contrast, Morales was born in a small locality in the Bolivian highlands — Orinoca — and followed the path of many among the poor rural indigenous. As a young man, he emigrated to the urban centres to work mainly in manual labour or to serve as domestic helps in wealthy family houses. His rise to political power took place through the indigenous trade union movement in the coca-growing lowlands of El Chapare rather than through traditional party politics. His win in 2005 was not just a

Plate 13.6: Huge Poster of Evo Morales outside the Presidential Palace on the Main Square in La Paz

Source: Photographed by the author.
Note: This photograph was taken during the celebration for the approval for the new political constitution of 2008, which was considered a political victory for indigenous peoples across the Americas.

politics to the rise of Maoris in the arts, sports and national New Zealand life (Smith 2007). Indigeneity has moved out of the world of 'culture' and

---

presidential victory but earned the highest percentage of electoral support in history, and all without the backing of an established political party. His campaign was basically a poor man's campaign, using taxis and tennis shoes rather than chauffeur-driven luxury. The documentary film *Cocalero* (Landes 2007) shows the campaign as it was coming to its last few weeks before the election.

'language' into other contemporarily significant arenas, such as global circulations of indigeneity in politics, indigenous self-representation and the politics of knowledge.

For Zuna, the Oruro Anata is what has promoted the identity of first nations in Bolivia, and ultimately the structural changes of the country that led to an Aymara Indian becoming the nation's president (interview with Irineo Zuna, Oruro, August 2008). The visibility of Aymaras in Bolivia and the powerful emergence of Evo Morales, an *ayllu*-born Aymara, as a Latin American political leader, confirm new understandings of indigeneity whereby indigeneity is no longer assumed as relating to something intrinsic (race, religion, subalternity, or other) but has to be looked at amidst the changing political, cultural, national, territorial, and epistemological boundaries (Cadena and Starn 2007: 3).

For indigenous and colonized people in Bolivia and the world over, the struggle for self-representation, and the visibility of indigenous histories is also a struggle for a new epistemology, in which new is not forward but different (ibid.: 25). It is a decolonizing 'return' that need not be based on ontological or epistemological purity but engages with the past with an intention to reclaim it, as R. Radhakrishnan has suggested (2003: 318).

This is when I enter the debate, as a researcher but also as a Bolivian member of my generation, to try to fix some of the decisions made by our parents and grandparents: i.e., that to be brought up in indigenous ways, for instance, using Aymara instead of Spanish, would hinder our possibilities of success in life.

I am also here to reclaim the heritage that is not too distant (only two or three generations behind) but has been denied through an upbringing charged with Western values and the contempt for anything that acted as reminder of the nearness of our indigenous legacy.

References

Anderson, Benedict. 1991. *Imagined Communities: Reflections of the Origin and Spread of Nationalism*. London: Verso.

Appadurai, Arjun, Ashish Chadha, Ian Hodder, Trinity Jackman, and Chris Witmore. 2008. 'The Globalisation of Archaeology and Heritage: A Discussion with Arjun Appadurai', in Graham Fairclough, R. Harrison, J. H. Jameson, and J. Schofield, *The Heritage Reader*, pp. 209–18. Abingdon: Routledge.

Asociación de Conjuntos Folkóricos de Oruro (ACFO). 2000. 'Formulario para la candidatura UNESCO'. Asociación de Conjuntos Folkóricos de Oruro. http://docs.google.com/viewer?a=v&q=cache:VrPsa49hZlgJ:www.carnavaldeoruroacfo.com/documentos/FORMULARIO%2520DE%2520CANDIDATURA.pdf+acfo+formulario+para+la+candidatura&hl=en&gl=uk&pid=bl&srcid=ADGEEShZ-FJp3j0DnorJPLefli2Ma-V0yy4AUiVPlL_dsdOnK_IB-HSt6PwQWJ0WqEMC1jxUq_MGOv6FVT2E8im8NiUEvmY6I7Y8wu7qboaiKrLnnbWKjf91DUJbVGW2MfvDaq PP69w-&sig=AHIEtbTuibp3-2F9iETAQnqpXZ6hkSpXlA (accessed 2 September 2010).
―――. 2008. 'Reglamento Carnaval Oruro 2008'. Asociación de Conjuntos del Folklore Oruro.
Bautista, Juan José. 2007. *Crítica de la razón boliviana: elementos para una crítica de la subjetividad del boliviano con conciencia colonial, moderna y latino-americana*. La Paz: Editorial Tercera Piel.
―――. 2010. *Crítica de la razón boliviana: elementos para una crítica de la subjetividad del boliviano con conciencia colonial, moderna y latino-americana*. La Paz: Rincón Editores.
Beltrán Heredia, Augusto. 1962. *El Carnaval de Oruro y Proceso Ideológico e Historia de los Grupos Floklóricos*. Oruro: Edición del Comité Departamental de Folklore.
―――. 2004. *El Carnaval de Oruro Bolivia*. Oruro: Latinas.
Bhabha, Homi K. 1990. 'DissemiNation: Time, Narrative, and the Margins of the Modern Nation', in Homi K. Bhabha (ed.), *Nation and Narration*, pp. 291–322. London: Routledge.
Bourdieu, Pierre. 2000. *Capital cultural, escuela y espacio social*. Delegación Coyoacán: Siglo Veintiuno Editores.
Bouysee-Cassagne, Thérèse and Olivia Harris. 1987. *Tres reflexiones sobre el pensamiento andino*. La Paz: Hisbol.
Butler, Judith. 1999. *Gender Trouble: Feminism and the Subversion of Identity*. New York: Routledge.
Cadena, Marisol de la and Orin Starn. 2007. 'Introduction', in Marisol de la Cadena and Orin Starn (eds), *Indigenous Experience Today*, pp. 1–30. Oxford: Berg.
Comaroff, John and Jean Comaroff. 2009. *Ethnicity, Inc*. Chicago: University of Chicago Press.
Condarco Santillán, Carlos. 1999. *La serranía sagrada de los Urus*. Oruro: Latinas.
―――. 2007. *"Uru-Uru": Espacio y Tiempo Sagrados*. Oruro: Latinas.
Díaz-Domínguez, Alejandro. 2009. 'Nota metodológica: Midiendo religion en encuestas de Latinoamérica', *Perspectivas desde el Barómetro de las Américas*, 29: 1–13. http://sitemason.vanderbilt.edu/files/bVWgP6/I0829 Midiendo%20religion%20en%20encuestas%20de%20Latinoamrica.pdf (accessed 29 January 2011).

Dussel, Enrique. 1992. *El encubrimiento del Otro: Hacia el orígen del mito de la Modernidad*. La Paz: Plural Editores.
Fairclough, Graham, R. Harrison, J. H. Jameson, and J. Schofield (eds). 2008. *The Heritage Reader*. Abingdon: Routledge.
Fernández-Osco, Marcelo. 2006. 'Pachakuti: Pensamiento crítico descolonial aymara frente a epistemes opresores', in Mario Yapu (ed.), *Modernidad y pensamiento descolonizador: Memoria seminario internacional*, pp. 79–102. La Paz: Universidad para la Investigación Estratégica en Bolivia and Instituto Francés de Estudios Andinos.
Flores, Jose (J'acha). n.d. 'Hombre Solitario'.
Gramsci, Antonio. 1988 [1916]. 'Socialism and Culture', in David Forgacs (ed.), *An Antonio Gramsci Reader: Selected Writings 1916–1935*, pp. 56–95. New York: Schcken Books, p. 56-59.
Gran Tradicional y Auténtica Diablada Oruro (GTADO). n.d. Foundation documents, unpublished.
Gupta, Akhil and James Ferguson. 1997. 'Culture, Power, Place: Ethnography at the End of an Era', in Akhil Gupta and James Ferguson (eds), *Culture, Power, Place: Explorations in Critical Anthropology*, pp. 1–32. Durham: Duke University Press.
Gustafson, Bret. 2009. *New Languages of the State: Indigenous Resurgence and the Politics of Knowledge in Bolivia*. Durham: Duke University Press.
Hall, Stuart. 2008. 'Whose Heritage? Unsettling "The Heritage", Re-imagining the Post-Nation', in Graham Fairclough, R. Harrison, J. H. Jameson, and J. Schofield (eds), *The Heritage Reader*, pp. 219–28. Abingdon: Routledge.
Harris, Olivia. 1978. *Kinship and Vertical Economy of the Laymi Ayllu, Norte de Potosí*. Proceedings of the 42nd International Congress of Americanists, vol. 4, pp. 165–77.
———. 1995. 'Ethnic Identity and Market Relations: Indians and Mestizos in the Andes', in Olivia Harris and Brooke Larson (eds), *Ethnicity, Markets, and Migration in the Andes: At the Crossroads of History and Anthropology*, pp. 351–90. London: Duke University Press.
———. 2000. *To Make the Earth Bear Fruit: Ethnographic Essays on Fertility, Work and Gender in Highland Bolivia*. London: Institute of Latin American Studies.
Huanaco, Félix. 2010. 'Convocan a la Anata Andina con dos meses de anticipación'. http://www.eabolivia.com/social/2751-convocan-a-anata-andina-de-oruro-con-dos-meses-de-anticipacion.html (accessed 20 January 2011).
Instituto Nacional de Estadística (INE). 2009. 'Actualidad Estadística Departamental: Estadísticas Socioeconómicas del Departamento de Oruro'. http://www.ine.gov.bo/pdf/Est_Dptales/EN_2010_1.pdf (accessed 5 February 2010).
Klein, Herbert. 2003. *A Concise History of Bolivia*. Cambridge: Cambridge University Press.

Landes, Alejandro. 2007. *Cocalero*. DVD. New York: First Run Features.
Lara Barrientos, Marcelo. 2008. 'Las dimensiones económicas del Carnaval de Oruro'. *Revista Cultura y Desarrollo*, United Nations Educational, Scientific and Cultural Organization. http://www.unesco.org.cu/culturaydesarrollo/pdf_nros/nro5art1.pdf (accessed 28 April 2008).
Martín-Barbero, Jesús. 2003. *De los medios a las mediaciones*. Bogotá: Convenio Andrés Bello.
Murillo Vacarreza, Josermo. 1999. 'Intento para una historia de la Virgen del Socavón de Oruro', in Josermo Murillo Vacarreza and Antonio Revollo Fernández (eds), *La Vírgen del Socavón y su Carnaval*, pp. 7–38. Oruro: Cedipas.
Nava, Ascanio. 2004. *Referencias sobre el Carnaval de Oruro*. Oruro: Latinas.
Platt, Tristan. 1982. 'The Rôle of the Andean *Ayllu* in the Reproduction of the Petty Commodity Régime in Northern Potosí (Bolivia)', in David Lehmann (ed.), *Ecology and Exchange in the Andes*, pp. 27–69. Cambridge: Cambridge University Press.
Porras, Silvia and Anders Riis-Hansen. n.d. 'Interview with Rigoberta Menchu Tum: Five Hundred Years of Sacrifice Before the Alien Gods'. Race & Ethnicity. http://race.eserver.org/rigoberta-menchu-tum.html (1 September 2010).
Radhakrishnan, R. 2003. 'Postcoloniality and the Boundaries of Identity', in Linda Martín Alcoff and Eduardo Mendieta (eds), *Identities: Race, Class, Gender and Nationalities*, pp. 312–30. Oxford: Blackwell Publishing.
Smith, Linda-Tuhiwai. 2007. 'The Native and the Neoliberal Down Under: Neoliberalism and "Endangered Authenticities"', in Marisol de la Cadena and Orin Starn (eds), *Indigenous Experience Today*, pp. 333–52. Oxford: Berg.
Soruco Solonguren, Ximena. 2006. 'The Unintelligibility of the Cholo in Bolivia', *T'inkazos*, 2(21): 77–96.
Taylor, Charles. 1992. 'The Politics of Recognition', in Amy Gutman (ed.), *Multiculturalism*, pp. 25–73. Princeton, New Jersey: Princeton University Press.
Taylor, Diana. 2003. *The Archive and the Repertoire: Performing Cultural Memory in the Americas*. London: Duke University Press.
Téllez Nava, Félix. 2003. 'Anata: Expresión cultural del mundo andino en el contexto del Carnaval de Oruro', in Carlos Condarco Santillán (ed), *El Carnaval de Oruro III: Aproximaciones*, pp. 9–34. Oruro: Latinas.
United Nations Educational, Scientific and Cultural Organization (UNESCO). n.d. 'What is Intangible Cultural Heritage?'. http://www.unesco.org/culture/ich/index.php?pg=00002 (accessed 3 March 2010).
Villarroel, Emeterio. 1999 [1908]. 'Novena de la Virgen del Socavón', in Josermo Murillo Vacarreza and Antonio Revollo Fernández (eds), *La Vírgen del Socavón y su Carnaval*, pp. 40–48. Oruro: Cedipas.
Zavaleta Mercado, René. 1986. *Lo nacional-popular en Bolivia*. México: Siglo XXI Editores.

14 Contemporary Maori Painting

Pictorial Representation of Land and Landscape

Dieter Riemenschneider

Landscape and Land

During the years my wife and I lived in New Zealand we travelled quite often and virtually covered the two islands from north to south, from Cape Rainga to Bluff, and enjoyed the often spectacular scenery of the country. Not only was I impressed by the volcanoes in the centre of the North Island and the almost perfectly shaped cone of Mt Taranaki, the glaciers and mountain ranges of the Southern Alps including Mt Cook, but also by the breathtaking views of the large lakes in Southland, the rolling hillsides of Northland and the huge basin-like valleys of Central Otago, the vast outlook across Banks Peninsula or the intricately shaped Otago Peninsula. Having experienced these sights, I realized how attractive the New Zealand scenery must always have been to artists, poets as well as painters, and I began to visit art galleries and museums and started buying books on landscape painting. Their number and the variety of thematic approaches chosen to present the abundant richness of New Zealand scenery testifies to the sheer pleasure of artists in sketching or painting — either on the spot or from memory — the details of a scene that had evoked their aesthetic pleasure and triggered their artistic sensibility and execution. As David Filer pertinently observed in the introduction to his richly illustrated book, *Painting the Frontier — The Art of New Zealand's Pioneers*:

> When European explorers and settlers arrived in New Zealand, they immediately began recording this unique country with pen, pencil and paint brush [because they] were fascinated by the dramatic landscape (2009: 7).

And I should add, this enchantment for the newcomer has remained ever since.

At the same time I was struck by never having come across even one landscape painting by a Maori artist, and I began wondering whether any existed or whether galleries only cared for Pakeha (New Zealander of European descent) artists — which would not have surprised me since the very idea of exhibiting art objects of indigenous people appeared to be the concern solely of ethnological collections in museums. Yet even here Maori landscape paintings seemed not to exist, and I met with the same blank in art publications until I happened to discover *Mataora: The Living Face — Contemporary Maori Art: Te Waka Toi* (Adsett et al. 1996), a collection of essays and pictorial representations of paintings, sculptures, installations, and mixed media 'objects' created by a whole range of Maori artists during the previous three decades. This book, edited by the leading Maori writer and committed art expert Witi Ihimaera under the general editorship of two Maori artists, Sandy Adsett and Cliff Whiting, proved an eye-opener to me since it offered a wealth of information on Maori artists and their work. In particular, an essay by Robert Jahnke and Witi Ihimaera held a lot of answers to my question about the absence of Maori landscape painting. Entitled 'Te Whenua — The Land', its first sentences offer the following explanation:

> Perhaps because Maori have always had an intimate relationship with the land, and because this relationship was regulated by tapu [sacred, forbidden, taboo] and whakapapa [genealogy], Maori of the past could not distance themselves sufficiently to be able to define — as Western traditions of landscape painting did — what that relationship was. It just was. It just is (Jahnke and Ihimaera 1996b: 86).

Paying attention to 'customary carving', the preferred traditional artistic expression of Maori people, the essay then points towards the architectural features of the *pataka*, or storehouse, and the *whare whakairo*, or meeting house, as symbolizing and thus celebrating 'the tribe's relationship with its Gods, its ancestors, *land, sea, rivers and mountains*', which express the idea of 'a living relationship with the land [which is] as alive today as it was in the past' (ibid.: 86; emphasis added). As both critics add, 'one of the ironies, of course, is that this relationship was illustrated in the abstract, way before the Western Impressionist movement overturned Realism in landscape painting' (ibid.). It is no wonder then that neither the concept nor the various styles and periods of European landscape painting took hold of Maori artistic sensibility — which, however, would not necessarily mean that the practice of traditional forms of representing *te whenua*, or the land, would exclude the use of visual artistic forms such as paintings for representation. Indeed, Jahnke and Ihimaera argue that 'today, representation of the land is a major theme of Maori artists and Papatuanuku [Earth Mother] has become a principal visual concept' (Jahnke and Ihimaera 1996b).

Probing into Maori art history, David Filer in a sense concurs with the two critics' words in his brief study of early European painters' relationship with Maori, where he comments, with great care, that 'most nineteenth-century Maori artists did not work in a European format or style' (Filer 2009: 8). He refers to the only examples he has come to know of — of drawings — 'by an early Maori artist' whose name is not known. These pictorial representations are 'detailed drawings in a naïve style... showing the players in the drama, village life and emotion [and] not following the rules of proportion or perspective' (ibid.: 38) (Plate 14.1).[1]

Plate 14.1: *Sketches of a Maori muru at Parawera*

Source: Artist unknown [A-081-004; A-081-005], pencil on paper, Alexander Turnbull Library, Wellington, New Zealand. Reproduced in David Filer, *Painting the Frontier: The Art of New Zealand's Pioneers*, Auckland: David Bateman, 2009, p. 39.

Of additional interest in this context proves the discourse on modern Maori art and where this is pursued by Maori art critics. In an essay contributing to the catalogue of a New Zealand art exhibition in Sydney in 1992, Rangihiroa Panoho argues about the flexibility of Maori art which points at the culture's adaptability. 'Borrowings', he says, 'and appropriations have become part of our culture, our identity' (Panoho 1992: 123); which, of course, raises the question as to the Maoriness of Maori art works. While a Pakeha like Robert Leonhard is of the opinion that

---

[1] *Sketches of a Maori muru at Parawera*. A-081-004; A-081-005, Alexander Turnbull Library, Wellington; in Filer (2009: 39).

'"contemporary Maori art" [is] a contested term' (1991: 52), one of the leading Maori art critics, Jonathan Mané-Wheoki, disagrees with Leonhard and differentiates Panoho's generalizing sentiment by laying down 'that contemporary Maori art must be defined culturally and holistically in terms of comprehensiveness and inclusiveness, within the Maori conceptual framework' (Mané-Wheoki 1995: 12).

It is a claim that does not overlook the presence of a '"Maoriness" spectrum' in art that takes into account cultural and psychological differences between, for example, urbanized and de-tribalized artists, many of whom went through Western-type art schools in New Zealand, and those who have a 'standing on any *marae*[2] "tribal home base"' (ibid.: 15). Mané-Wheoki agrees with other Maori critics that their own culture is complex and dynamic because of the manifold interrelations and interactions with Pakeha in particular and the world at large so that it

> constitutes a pluralistic subset of a global pluralist culture, a subset of extraordinary diversity, which encompasses westernisation and internationalisation, on the one hand, and neotraditionalism, ethnocentrism and interculturalism, on the other (ibid.: 16).

Indeed, the translation of culture is not a phenomenon unknown to contemporary Maori artists as we will discover when we look at visual representations of *te whenua*. For one, Maori painters have adopted the technique of picture painting with the concept of painting as 'a window to the world' (Pound 1983: 12); further, with the frame as 'one of those declared qualities of painting' (ibid.: 13); and finally, with the painted product's 'posings, symmetries, signature, unities of tone, etc.' (ibid.). Second, Maori painters have adopted the use of painterly means and material, of 'pen, pencil and paint brush' (Filer 2009: 7), as well as of other tools, and the use of chemical colours replacing natural ones, used for example in painting their wooden carvings or decorating their meeting houses. Yet, they have not adopted the convention of sketching or painting a *lantskaf* (landscape) that represents a section of geographical space framed by a horizon and looked at from a chosen viewpoint; in other words, the convention of 'seeing the land as *picture*' (Pound 1983: 23) as in Western (art) tradition: a concept and a practice that emerged 'around the turn of the sixteenth century to denote a painting whose primary subject matter was natural scenery' (Cosgrove 1993: 9, quoted in DeLue and Elkins 2008: 168).

---

[2] (Ceremonial) meeting area of a village.

Though he does not conceive of the '"region" or the "prospect of a country"', as Samuel Johnson defines 'landscape' in his dictionary (1755), Francesco Petrarca's letter *ad Dionysium de Burgo Sancti Sepulchri* (Sadlon n.d.) has often been referred to as one of the first, if not the first, written documentations of the experience of land as landscape. Describing his ascent of Mount Ventoux on 26 April 1336, Petrarca explains that '[m]y only motive was the wish to see what so great an elevation had to offer', and further, that he 'was bent on pleasure and anxious that my enjoyment should be unalloyed' (Robinson 1898: 307). Curiosity and aesthetic pleasure characterize this 14th-century poet as the spectator of 'the prospect of a country' viewed from the summit of Mount Ventoux and framed on the right by 'the mountains of the region about Lyons, and to the left the Bay of Marseille and the waters that lash the shores of Aigues Mortes, altho' these places were so distant' (Robinson 1898: 307) (Plate 14.2).[3]

Petrarca then continues by saying that after having looked at the 'terrestrial object' he then raised his soul 'to higher planes' and looks at the copy of St. Augustine's *Confessiones* (397–398 CE) he was carrying with him.

Inserting a few quotes here from Petrarca's letter is not just meant to remind us of the long history of the discourse on landscape as 'the prospect of the country — the actual landscape', as James Elkins calls it (DeLue and Elkins 2008: 150) — but to draw attention to two aspects of the discourse that are of immediate concern for my topic: either an approach to landscape as foregrounding a viewer's subjective experience or one mediated by the culture he relates to. In her comments on a

---

[3] Robinson's translation (1898) differs from the German translation of the original Latin text by Hans Nachod and Paul Stern in 1931 (see Petrarca 1996), much to the neglect of an awareness of the aesthetic experience of landscape. The German word *Begierde* (desire/avidity; in the Latin original *cupiditate* from *cupiditas*) expresses a much stronger emotional drive than does the flatter 'wish'. Also, '[t]o see what so great an elevation had to offer' (Robinson 1898) does not only sound cool and detached but leaves out 'this spot of the earth', as in *die ungewöhnliche Höhe* dieses Flecks Erde *durch Augenschein kennenzulernen* ('to come to know the unusual/exceptional elevation/altitude of this spot of the Earth by having a close look' [emphasis added]; in the original: *sola videndi insignem loci altitudinem*) (ibid.). And it is precisely this reference to the viewer's marked spot that establishes a relationship between subject and object, between viewer and (framed) view — or the experience of land as landscape — that the English translation misses out on.

Plate 14.2: 'Mt Ventoux as seen from Mormoiron'

Source: Photographed by the author.

seminar on landscape theory that took place in Ireland in 2006, Jennifer Jane Marshall referred to these approaches as even an 'implicit opposition between the ideological and the phenomenological dimensions of landscape ... landscape as a determined cultural production and ... as an indeterminate subjective experience' (ibid.: 196).

Such an assessment raises the question about the attitude of Maori paintings to land and landscape within the spectrum of Maori art touched upon by Mané-Wheoki. In other words, what artistic response(s) do we ascribe to them? A subjective one, perhaps entirely aesthetic or even deeply romantic as it characterised much of Western landscape painting in the 19th century and even Pakeha New Zealand paintings of the same period?[4] Or a spiritual, mystifying, mythologizing response, which has its aesthetic side too but is, partly or wholly, culturally grounded? And further, is it possible then to discover a tendency, a trend or perhaps even

---

[4] Francis Pound comments upon Augustus Earle's painting *Distant View of the Bay of Islands* (1827) as an example of a European pictorial attitude to nature, of contemplating it, which became a 'stock pathos formula' found in many 19th-century New Zealand landscape paintings. It indicates a subjective response to nature as well as to its visual representation (Pound 1983: 12ff.).

a 'movement' foregrounding a more aesthetic or a more culture-bound inspiration on the part of Maori artists? I shall attempt to offer a tentative answer by commenting on a few examples — tentative because a more insightful presentation and persuasive argumentation presupposes the kind of comprehensive study that cannot be undertaken here.

Western perceptions of landscape and its pictorial representation were introduced to New Zealand first by William Hodges (1744–97), a professional British painter who accompanied James Cook on his second journey from 1773–75: a pictorial attitude to land as *nature*, followed up and expanded in the 19th century by future generations of painters like Augustus Earle (1793–1838), William Fox (1812–93) or Charles Heaphy (1820–81).[5] In contrast to the views held by many of them and following generations of New Zealand landscape painters as well as critics such as Gordon Brown, Hamish Keith or E. H. McCormick,[6] Jahnke and Ihimaera's words tell us that the Maori conception of landscape painting is based on looking at land as *cultural*.[7] It is a view commonly shared among Maori as a 'central component of Maoridom [as it links] people to the land and to their kinfolk' (Sims and Thompson-Fawcett 2002: 260). In other words,

> spirituality and the relationship between people and the gods is an integral part of how Maori view the landscape. The relationship is seen as a two-way

---

[5] According to Francis Pound, an interesting aspect of early European painters' perception of the New Zealand scenery as picturesque or sublime is grounded in their reaction to the country's wilderness as ugly, 'gloomy' and even evil: an emotional response reinforced by the presence of pagan inhabitants. Nature experienced as 'Nature untouched by Grace' needed to be redeemed through a model: 'the English landscape, its villages, greenswards and trees' (Pound 2009: 197).

[6] Pound (1983) refers to Brown and Keith (1969) and McCormick (1940).

[7] We should take note though of the change problematic terms like 'landscape' or 'perception' have undergone. Art critic Christopher Johnstone concedes that it 'is easy enough to confuse landscape with the land itself, the countryside ... [as] landscape is a concept, a loaded term, and implies a certain significance; it means different things to different people ... The same can be said of perception. No two people will perceive something in the same way. How does an artist pin down perception? ... And what is perception anyway ... For many painters the process of drawing in front of the motif ... is about knowledge, not copying' (2008: 7). And finally, talking about his selection of landscape paintings, he calls them 'man-made images ... one person's selection of paintings, viewed largely through the tradition in which they were made' (ibid.: 13).

process. If the gods sustain and protect people and the environment, people reciprocate the links by means of ritual (ibid.: 261).

As the Maori adage puts it: *Te toto o te tangata, he kai; to oranga o te tangata, he whenua* (The blood of people: food; the sustenance of people: land) (ibid.).[8]

Maori Land Paintings

When I talked to the art critic David Eggleton about contemporary Maori art, he confirmed Jahnke and Ihimaera's view that 'Maori culture did not include landscape painting as such; their genius went into carving, deriving from myths' (personal communication). 'However', he added:

> there are of course the ancient and mysterious limestone cave paintings of the South Island's east coast, which were photographed by Theo Schoon, and which were the basis of early paintings by Gordon Walters, and also inspired paintings by Toni Fomison. More recently Shane Cotton and other artists of Maori heritage have made direct or indirect references to these 'drawings' (ibid.).[9]

Yet, here we can speak as little of landscape paintings as with modern Maori examples, the first of which chosen by me was painted by Darcy Nicholas. He began painting in 1974 and has held a number of positions in the art world. In his almost haunting image, *Te Kotuku's Bush* (1983), part of a face in the upper right corner and the outline of a standing figure in white near the centre and under a tree emerge respectively from behind a hillside and tufted ground. Both create a surreal effect that is heightened by the blurred, almost faded representation of bushes, trees

---

[8] See also David Eggleton's statement: '*Manawhenua* is that sense of belonging that connects people and land. The landscape of Aotearoa New Zealand is our cultural centre of gravity, our leading literary theme, our dominant metaphor ... the land is our *waka*, our location beacon, a site of layered history. Landscape is a state of mind: the environment that determines the character of the people' (Eggleton 2001: 7).

[9] In his comprehensive 2009 study, *The Invention of New Zealand: Art and National Identity 1930–1970*, Francis Pound discusses the connection between the limestone paintings and modernist Pakeha art in some detail ('Maori rock art and ultra-modernist primitivism' [2009: 282–97]). I will not go into it here, as Pound's reading touches only slightly on my topic.

and tufts of grass and suffused by an unearthly looking bright light that seems to stream in from a hidden source above. It interrelates with the reddish-brown colours of the vegetation and highlights the figure, obviously a Maori warrior with three feathers rising from the back of his head. Darcy himself commented on 'the faces in my painting [as] a reminder of the great spiritual strength that made us warriors of the land and the sea' (Adsett et al. 1996: 94], and thus emphasized the link between *iwi*, Maori people, and the land as their *turangawaewae* (their home) (literally, 'place to stand'). *Te Kutu's Bush* clearly conveys its being grounded in Maori culture. At the same time the spectator cannot resist the aesthetic appeal of an almost mystifying representation of man's relationship with his surroundings.

It is an impression we come across again in *Papatuanuku* by Robyn Kahukiwa (1984, in Kahukiwa and Grace [2000: 23]) who began painting in 1967, has been one of the most frequently exhibited Maori painters and has also worked as a book illustrator; for example, for *Wahine Toa: Women of Maori Myth* (Kahukiwa and Grace 2000), to which the well-known Maori writer Patricia Grace contributed the texts. *Papatuanuku* (Kahukiwa 1984), the mythical figure of Earth Mother, is shown here as 'womanland' lying on her side with her head in the left lower corner and her body stretching diagonally across on a dark blue surface that is separated by a sharply drawn horizontal line (Plate V, colour plate section). Above, a concentric spiral rises that expands in colours changing from white at the *koru* (coiled leaf; here, spiral pattern) centre to yellow, orange and red in the outer spheres. The *koru* is a traditional motif used in Maori carving and scroll painting (and incidentally also used as a logo by Air New Zealand), a symbol of life. Earth Mother's head, arms, upper body, haunches, and thighs, all painted in shades of green are represented as stylized land features, as hills, valleys and wooded regions. Her ochre face stands for the blood she shed when she was severed from Rangi, the Sky Father, whose blood has flowed into the heavens and turned into the colours of sunsets (Kahukiwa and Grace 2000: 66). On either side of Papatuanuku, who was turned over so she could not see Rangi any longer, two carved poles or *toko* painted in light blue, composed of stylized ancestral figures and topped by the similarly stylized figure of Rangi, border the painting and relate to their erection by Rangi and Papatuanuku's son Tane. Sky Father now merges with the blue of the sky in the upper left and right corners while the clouds drifting across the sunset-coloured sky stand for Earth Mother's morning sighs/mists rising and mixing with Sky Father's night-dew tears. The six pegs arranged in a half circle at the centre bottom and next to Earth Mother's head represent the other important sons, each peg shaped differently according to the sons' attributes and functions in the world. Kahukiwa's explanation that 'I do not see my paintings as illustrations of the myths but rather the myths in painted form' (Kahukiwa and Grace 2000: 10) departs radically from viewing a painting as representation: here the object painted is meant to be identical with the object.[10] The viewer, nonetheless, is drawn in by the carefully considered composition of a painting that 'translates' a myth into a symbolically executed and aesthetically appealing representation of land.

In a sense *Te Whenua Te Whenua Engari Kaore He Turangawaewae*, or 'Placenta, Land, but Nowhere to Stand' (1988), again by Robyn Kahukiwa, complements *Papatuanuku*. Two standing female figures, modelled after the traditional carving style of *pou* (pole) images, are modified as a pregnant woman bordering the left of the painting and the other on the right who drops her placenta, symbolized as a red tube, arching onto the land below — placenta and land are both named *whenua* in Maori.

Both figures are set in rectangular 'boxes' bordering on the upper edge and left and right edges of the painting, respectively and stand on a clearly demarcated red space. Painted in colours ranging from red to light brown and black, they are separated by a white square box that borders on the upper edge and contains a red cross shaped as an x. This left-to-right sequence of the three 'boxes' reminds us of a narrated text that affirms the history of the intimate relationship between *iwi* and *whenua*, with the crossed-out white square between the two figures relating to an episode of the past: temporarily Pakeha forbade Maori to carry out their custom of burying the placenta. While the left woman raises her arms and shows an embryo in her belly, the female figure's action on the right represents the assertion of her culture and *turangawaewae*, 'a place to stand for ever' (Auckland Art Gallery Toi o Tāmaki 2001: 130).

---

[10] Roma Potiki's poem 'Papatūānuku' (1992) offers more proof of the central meaning of land for Maori as Earth Mother: 'I am Papatuanuku / giving completely I hold strength in its upright / form — / my base maps the pattern of mottled life, / rain and rivers. / When the rest is gone / you will know me — / you who press on my skin / tread the body you do not recognise. / With my face made of bones / my stomach eternally stretching / I need no definition / I am Papatuanuku, the land' (Riemenschneider 2010: 146). A further remark: One can of course object by arguing the fact that what we see is painted on a metaphorical glass, a 'window to the world', and thus, 'we look *at* it, not *through* it — [because] the painted surface is a system of signs, not a transparent medium' (Pound 1983: 12).

Again, Robyn Kahukiwa resorts to objects of the Maori traditional visual arts but now in a more conventional manner than in *Papatuanuku*. The painted sculpted figures and colours are clear symbolic markers of the intimate coherence of life, birth, land, and culture. At the same time, the geometrical arrangement of the single parts of the painting combined with its stark red and white colouring clearly convey the feeling of strong satisfaction felt at setting right a colonial injustice.

Ka Awatea (1991) by Emare Karaka, whose works have been exhibited very often and who has created large paintings, takes us a step further in the process of representing Maori people reappropriating their land. As she stated,

> my work is centred around the Treaty of Waitangi. It's to do with rangatiratanga, our atua, our taonga, land rights, living rights, arts and cultural rights (Adsett et al. 1996: 24).[11]

Here we have a huge board (241 x 239 cm) onto which the artist has drawn an almost overwhelming number of diversely coloured signs, shapes and figures, letters and words. Besides, we recognize fish swimming in and outside fish traps, an eel, plants, hills and, at the centre in the foreground, a four-headed and red painted *kaitiaki*, or guardian. He resembles a *pou* carving with his uplifted arms ending in three 'fingers' and embraces the upper and lower parts of the painting that is hinged by a horizontal yellow line creating a diptych turned on its side by 90 degrees. Below it is the land and its resources and above are the people, symbolized as ever so many, tiny, two-eyed ovals. At the far and straight-lined horizon the blue underground indicates the land suffused with thickly painted black lines and rows of drawing pins. In front of it, as it were, are two circles coloured in red and black and filled in with a figure and the painting's title and, respectively, twelve stars. They are balanced on top of the three stumped fingers of the guardian's arm to the left and a triangle on top of his head. A rainbow is balanced on the fingers of his arm to his right, symbol of the 19th-century religious Ringatu movement.[12]

---

[11] The words *rangatiratanga, atua* and *taonga* mean 'sovereignty', 'gods' and 'treasures' respectively.

[12] The Ringatu movement, a syncretic politico-religious movement, was founded by Te Kooti Arikirangi in 1867 while he was banned to the Chatham Islands by the colonial government. *Ringatu* means 'upraised hand', the greeting (and the movement's symbol) of its followers.

My brief description can hardly do justice to Karaka's huge and intricately composed painting that draws our attention to *taonga*, the treasures of the land; treasures claimed and to be returned in the course of the settlement process between the government and Maori with the help of the Waitangi Tribunal that was set up in 1975. By freely drawing on traditional visual objects, painted as well as carved, by repeatedly inserting the title *ka awatea*, words like *iwi* and the letter 'k', she relates to a painting practice very frequently employed by the Pakeha painter Colin McCahon, but also by contemporary Maori artists like Ralph Hotere or Peter Robinson.[13] Combining visual representations of Maori culture with individually expressive modern painting practices not only lends *Ka Awatea* the status of a glocal art work but reveals a skill of execution evoking aesthetic pleasure.

Among contemporary Maori painters Shane Cotton has made a name for himself since the early 1990s as an impressive, versatile and challenging artist. I have chosen two of his works, with the first one marking Cotton's early style, which he turned away from in the mid-1990s (Cotton and Strongman 2004: 2). *Whakapiri Atu te Whenua* ('Retention of the land' or 'Remain close to the land') (Cotton 1993), is a painting commented upon by the editors of *Dream Collectors: One Hundred Years of Art in New Zealand* (Te Papa Press, Museum of New Zealand Te Papa Tongarewa 1998) as one of 'a potted history' (Cotton and Strongman 2004: 140). Land is potted, or soil (invisible though) is contained in five dissimilarly sized and shaped pots positioned along the base line of the painting as if on a window sill. The largest pot at the centre is the only one with a plant in it that stretches not only right up but its leaves and flowers are spread all across the upper part of the painting. Smaller in size and flanking this pot on both sides we recognize fence posts and flags fixed to poles stuck in the pots. The use of the colour ochre, now darker, now lighter, against a shaded yellowish background, separates and identifies the painting's objects: the plant's stalk, its leaves and flowers, the pots and flagged poles, lending them a near-naive naturalistic expressiveness. Even though the minutely drawn title can be deciphered in its upper left corner, the painting's reference to Pakeha ownership of the land, indicated by the potted flags and fence posts, will not be missed. However, their comparative smallness and marginal position directs attention to

---

[13] For instance, 'Are there not twelve hours of daylight' (McCahon 1970) and 'Boy am I scared, eh!' (Robinson 1997), cited in McAloon (1991: 41, 53). Also, see Hotere (1971–72).

the flowering centre plant with its big leaves, a hint at the Tree of Life, that affirms the regaining and retaining of Maori land. Stylistically totally different because of Cotton's use of decorative motifs from depictions of meeting houses in the 19th century, when Te Kooti and his followers peacefully though unsuccessfully protested against the alienation of their land (Cotton and Strongman 2004), *Whakapiri Atu te Whenua* finds its place, politically speaking, next to Karaka's *Ka Awatea* (1991).

Undoubtedly, the obvious alliance between Maori land painting and politics is a distinct characteristic of contemporary Maori art and, as installations and sculptures demonstrate,[14] this is not confined to painting. The final two examples corroborate this. Emare Karaka's *Te Uri o Te Ao Manawhenua Hapu o Tamakimakaurau* (1995) — literally, 'The Descendants of the People of Tamakimakaurau' (a part of Auckland) — is even more densely painted and larger (300 x 380cm) than her *Ka Awatea* (1991). It signals that the contracts on land earlier agreed upon by the government and her *hapu*, or clan, in Auckland[15] were broken and refers to registered land claim numbers for compensation before the Waitangi Tribunal, for example, WAI 423, WAI 357 or 27.

At the top, the stylized raised head of a *ruru*, or owl, 'often a bearer of ill omen' (Auckland Art Gallery Toi o Tāmaki 2001: 133),[16] faces the viewer and the figure stands with wide-spread wings on land divided into small plots that are marked by claim numbers and letters that partly spell out the title of the painting and partly words like *waka* (canoe), *wai* (water),[17] 'Tainui',[18] and others. Under the *ruru*'s wings on the right we recognize the shape of a heart with the figure '27' and 'TE AO uri' inserted, and on the left the symbol of peace and nuclear disarmament.

---

[14] See, for example, works by Sandy Adsett, Jacqueline Fraser, Paratene Matchitt, Michael Parekowhai, Peter Robinson, or Cliff Whiting (McAloon 1999; Te Papa Press, Museum of New Zealand Te Papa Tongarewa 1998).

[15] Specifically referred to are the State Owned Enterprises Act, 1986 and the Resource Management Act, 1991 to which Maori objected because they did not redress broken contracts but perpetuated or even strengthened the government position vis-à-vis Maori claims for compensation.

[16] The owl, *ruru*, also stands as a sentry or *kaitiaki*, as an angry defender, and as the god of peace depending on the meaning attributed to it by different Maori painters (Jahnke and Ihimaera 1996b: 87–88).

[17] Here *wai* refers to Waitangi — 'wai 423' and 'wai35' — which means the claim numbers registered with the Waitangi Tribunal.

[18] This is the name of one of the first Polynesian canoes arriving in Aotearoa/ New Zealand.

More letters like 'S', 'e', 'M', and 'A' in blue and red and made up of minute dots and lines create a canvas held in front of itself by the *ruru*'s wings. All in all, we look at an impressive panorama of shapes, figures, words, and colours — the yellow *ruru* contrasting with the green patches of land, as with white, red, purple, and black letters — that is topped by the phrase 'THIS LAND IS MAORI LAND'. Though Karaka's extraordinary painting reminds us of Colin McCahon's technique of combining text and image in his more abstract landscape paintings,[19] it also shows influences of modern painting from outside New Zealand — I am, for instance, reminded of Jackson Pollock's vibrantly colourful works. The Maori artist Karaka translates visual representation of her own culture into an individual language that can be approached from a phenomenological and a cultural angle.

My last example is Shane Cotton's *View* (1995), also a large oil painting (1827 × 1675 cm) belonging to the artist's second period when he returned, again and again, to a kind of cartographic representation of Northland where his family comes from. Divided into 18 almost equally sized and closely resembling horizontal segments that alternate between dark sepia-coloured ones — a few of them showing cone-shaped small mountains at the centre, and lighter-coloured ones, at times bare, at others, containing very small constructions (a bridge, a barge, a raft) or lines indicating paths — these images are stacked on top of each other: a technique that echoes the layered 'landscapes' of Charles Heaphy, for example in his six-tiered *Coastal Profiles from Mt. Egmont to Queen Charlotte Sound* (1842). It is a painting technique which in turn relates to 'maritime traditions of charting and map-making' (Pound 1983: 56).[20]

In *View* (Cotton 1995) the larger mountain cones in its lower half differ from smaller ones towards the top — and their final disappearance. By contrast, the 'higher' the layers the more they are 'crowded' — with tiny objects as have already been mentioned — with letter-shapes ('a b c d') arranged along the horizontal lines that separate the layers and, almost at the top, a row of vertical lines balancing tiny letters or zeroes. Finally, we read the spelt out year 'n i n e t e e n n i n e t y f i v e' at the very bottom

---

[19] See, for instance, *Northland Panels* (McCahon 1958). A large number of reproductions are to be found in Auckland City Art Gallery (1988).

[20] Among Colin McCahon's work we also find works of this technique that make the viewer move from one 'scene' to the next and at the same time to imagine the totality of the segmented parts. See Auckland City Art Gallery (1988: 116).

of the painting and moving up, 'BLUFF', '1969', '199', and '1907', all ranging across from left to right. At the top we read, also spread across, 'A F E', a letter sequence, the meaning of which I have been unable to understand, while Heaphy's technique, based on the painter moving on board a ship along the coast of New Zealand, may offer an answer to Cotton's layered landscapes.

They suggest the painter's similarly moving from place to place though his interest is not directed at topographical accuracy but at the land in its historical perspective. By letting our eye wander from the top to the bottom of *View* (Cotton 1995), we move from the past towards the present: from 1907 to 1995, or from the year when the Tohunga Suppression Act, 1907 was passed by Parliament, which outlawed Maori seers and medical practitioners,[21] to the one when *View* (ibid.) was painted. The gradual growth of the mountain as well as the clearance of barges, fence posts (as the vertical lines could be read) and pathways indicate the clearing of the land of its colonial traces[22] and the growing hope of owning the land again, symbolized by the mountain whose shape is identical to Heaphy's Mt. Egmont, now known by its original naming, Mount Taranaki. Looked at from this angle, *View* can be compared to a scroll that is gradually unrolled telling a story that ends here and now once we have unscrolled it totally. The lowest layer can be interpreted as *turangawaewae*, or the essence of land, which to some degree relates Cotton's perception to Colin McCahon's and his generation's idea of grasping the meaning of the New Zealand landscape, its essence, by stripping it, by 'removing the merely contingent, the accidental garment, with all its embroidery of detail, to get at the underlying and naked truth, the land's essence beneath', as Francis Pound has put it (2009: 126). The Maori artist though reads the stripped landscape and its essence differently. As Blair French has said,

> Cotton's paintings are fundamentally iconological assemblages of figures, objects, colours and texts — they do not represent or embody a singular moment or space, even when place is iconographically evoked (2004: 104).

---

[21] The Act was repealed only in 1962.

[22] See also Robert Jahnke's interpretation of paintings like *View* calling them representations of the colonial era and the land 'strewn with the bric-a-brac of cultural capture' that evidences 'the alienation of mana Māori and Māori land' (Jahnke 2004: 10).

But, we should add, like Karaka's two art works, View is representative of Maori land painting by its not merely combining 'the experience of the local within the global; of the global destabilized within local frameworks' (ibid.: 105), but by fusing the ideological and the phenomenological dimensions (Marshall 2008: 196) of land, the painting's 'Maori message' with its aesthetically rendered individual artistic execution. We have come full circle, starting with Nicholas Darcy's *Te Kotuku's Bush* (1983) as an example of a near-realistic visualization of landscape, to Shane Cotton's assemblage of landscape elements which nonetheless foregrounds the land and not an 'embroidered' presentation of a chosen 'view'.*

References

Adsett, Sandy, Chris Whiting and Witi Ihimaera (eds). 1996. *Mataora: The Living Face — Contemporary Maori Art: Te aka Toi*. Albany, Auckland: David Bateman.
Auckland Art Gallery Toi o Tāmaki. 2001. *The Guide*. London: Scala Publishers.
Auckland City Art Gallery. 1988. *Colin McCahon: Gates and Journeys*. Auckland: Auckland City Art Gallery.
Brown, Gordon and Hamish Keith. 1969. *An Introduction to New Zealand Painting 1839–1980*. Auckland: Collins.
Cotton, Shane, Lara Strongman and City Gallery Wellington. 2004. *Shane Cotton*. Wellington: City Gallery Wellington and Victoria University Press.
DeLue, Rachael Ziady and James Elkins (eds). 2008. *Landscape Theory*. London and New York: Routledge.
Eggleton, David. 2001. 'Introduction', in David Eggleton (ed.), *Here on Earth: The Landscape in New Zealand Literature*, pp. 6–23. Wellington: Craig Potton Publishing.
Filer, David. 2009. *Painting the Frontier: The Art of New Zealand's Pioneers*. Auckland: David Bateman.
French, Blair. 2004. 'Shane Cotton: Painting, Postcolonial-ism and the Age of Globalisation', in Shane Cotton, Lara Strongman and City Gallery Wellington, *Shane Cotton*, pp. 97–107. Wellington: City Gallery Wellington and Victoria University Press.

---

* Reproductions of the paintings discussed in this chapter could not be included owing to certain institutional and financial limitations.

Jahnke, Robert 2004. 'Voices Beyond the Pae', in Shane Cotton, Lara Strongman and City Gallery Wellington, *Shane Cotton*, pp. 10–13. Wellington: City Gallery Wellington and Victoria University Press.

Jahnke, Robert and Witi Ihimaera. 1996a. 'Mataora: The Living Face', in Sandy Adsett, Chris Whiting and Witi Ihimaera (eds), *Mataora: The Living Face — Contemporary Maori Art: Te aka Toi*, pp. 17–19. Albany, Auckland: David Bateman.

———. 1996b. 'Te Whenua — The Land', in Sandy Adsett, Chris Whiting and Witi Ihimaera (eds), *Mataora: The Living Face — Contemporary Maori Art: Te aka Toi*, pp. 86–89. Albany, Auckland: David Bateman.

Johnson, Samuel. 1755. *A Dictionary of the English Language*. London: Richard Bentley.

Johnstone, Christopher. 2008. *Landscape Paintings of New Zealand: A Journey from North to South*. Auckland: Random House.

Kahukiwa, Robyn and Patricia Grace. 2000 [1980]. *Wahine Toa: Women of Maori Myth*. Auckland: Penguin Books.

Leonard, Robert. 1991. 'Against Purity: Three Wood Sculptures by Michael Parekowhai', *Art New Zealand*, 59: 52–54.

Mané-Wheoki, Jonathan. 1995. 'The Resurgence of Maori Art: Conflicts and Continuities in the Eighties', *The Contemporary Pacific*, 7(1): 1–19.

Marshall, Jennifer Jane. 2008. 'Toward Phenomenology: A Material Culture Studies Approach to Landscape Theory', Rachael Ziady DeLue and James Elkins (eds), *Landscape Theory*, pp. 195–203. London and New York: Routledge.

McAloon, William. 1999. *Home and Away: Contemporary Australian and New Zealand Art from the Chartwell Collection*. Auckland: Auckland Art Gallery Toi o Tāmaki in Association with David Bateman.

McCormick, E. H. 1940. *Letters and Art in New Zealand*. Wellington: Department of Internal Affairs.

Panoho, Rangihiroa. 1992. 'Maori: At the Centre, On the Margins', in Mary Barr (ed.), *Headlands: Thinking through New Zealand Art*, pp. 123–34. Sydney: Museum of Contemporary Art.

Petrarca, Franceso. 1996 [1931]. *Die Besteigung des Mont Ventoux*, trans. Hans Nachod and Paul Stern. Frankfurt and Leipzig: Insel Verlag.

Potiki, Roma. 1992. 'Papatūānuku', in *Stones in Her Mouth*. Auckland: IWA Associates.

Pound, Francis. 1983. *Frames on the Land: Early Landscape Paintings in New Zealand*. Auckland: Collins.

———. 2009. *The Invention of New Zealand: Art and National Identity 1930–1970*. Auckland: Auckland University Press.

Riemenschneider, Dieter (ed. and trans.). 2010. *Wildes Licht: Gedichte aus Aotearoa Neuseeland*. Christchurch and Kronberg im Taunus: Tranzlit.

Robinson, James Harvey (ed. and trans.). 1898. 'The Ascent of Mount Ventoux', in Francesco Petrarca, James Harvey Robinson, Henry Winchester Rolfe,

Petrarch: *The First Modern Scholar and Man of Letters*, p. 308. New York: G. P. Putnam. http://history.hanover.edu/texts.petrarch/pet17.html.
Sadlon, Peter. n.d. *epistola ad Dionysium de Burgo Sancti Sepulcri*. http://petrarch.petersadlon.com/read_letters.html?s=_f_04_01.html (accessed 11 April 2013).
Sims, Miranda and Michelle Thompson-Fawcett. 2002. 'Planning for the Cultural Landscape', in Merata Kawharu (ed.), *Whenua: Managing Our Resources*, pp. 252–71. Auckland: Reed.
Strongman, Lara. 2004. 'Rurangi: The Meeting Place between Sea and Sky', in Shane Cotton, Lara Strongman and City Gallery Wellington, *Shane Cotton*, pp. 15–31. Wellington: City Gallery Wellington and Victoria University Press.
Wedde, Ian, John Walsh and Alexa Johnston. 1998. *Dream Collectors: One Hundred Years of Art in New Zealand*. Wellington: Te Papa Press.

Paintings/Illustrations

Cotton, Shane. 1993. *Whakapiri Atu te Whenua*. Oil on canvas, 1780 x 1600 mm, Museum of New Zealand Te Papa Tongarewa, Wellington. Reproduced in Shane Cotton and Lara Strongman, *Shane Cotton*, Wellington: City Gallery Wellington in conjunction with Victoria University Press, 2004, p. 41
———. 1995. *View*. Oil on canvas, 1827 x 1675 mm, College House, Christchurch. Reproduced in Sandy Adsett, Chris Whiting and Witi Ihimaera (eds), *Mataora: The Living Face — Contemporary Maori Art: Te aka Toi*, Albany, Auckland: David Bateman, 1996, p. 55.
Earle, Augustus. 1827. *Distant View of the Bay of Islands*. Watercolour on paper, 226 x 448 mm, Rex Nan Kivell Collection, National Library of Australia. Reproduced in Francis Pound, *Frames on the Land: Early Landscape Paintings in New Zealand*, Auckland: Collins, 1983, p. 41.
Heaphy, Charles. 1842. *Coastal Profiles from Mt. Egmont to Queen Charlotte Sound*. Watercolour on paper, 385 x 495 mm, Alexander Turnbull Library, Wellington. Reproduced in Francis Pound, *Frames on the Land: Early Landscape Paintings in New Zealand*, Auckland: Collins, 1983, p. 57
Hotere, Ralph. 1971–72. 'Untitled 1971–72'. Reproduced in Ian Wedde, John Walsh and Alexa Johnston, *Dream Collectors: One Hundred Years of Art in New Zealand*, Wellington: Te Papa Press, 1998, p. 76.
Kahukiwa, Robyn. 1984. *Papatuanuku*. Oil on hardboard, 1180 × 1180 mm. Reproduced in Robyn Kahukiwa and Patricia Grace, *Wahine Toa: Women of Maori Myth*, Auckland: Penguin Books, 2000 [1980], p. 23.
———. 1988. *Te Whenua Te Whenua Engari Kāore He Tūrangawaewae* [Placenta, Land, but Nowhere to Stand]. Oil on canvas, 2085 x 2960 mm, Auckland Art Gallery Toi o Tāmaki, Auckland. Reproduced in Auckland Art Gallery, *The Guide*. Auckland: Auckland Art Gallery Toi o Tāmaki in association with Scala Publishers, London, 2001, p. 130.

Karaka, Emare. 1991. *Ka Awatea*. Oil and mixed media on board, 2410 × 2390 mm, Museum of New Zealand Te Papa Tongarewa, Wellington. Reproduced in Sandy Adsett, Chris Whiting and Witi Ihimaera (eds), *Mataora: The Living Face — Contemporary Maori Art: Te aka Toi*, Albany, Auckland: David Bateman, 1996, p. 25.

———. 1995. *Te Uri o Te Ao Manawhenua Hapu o Tamakimakaurau*. Oil on canvas, 3000 x 3800 mm, Auckland Art Gallery Toi o Tāmaki, Auckland. Reproduced in Auckland Art Gallery, *The Guide*. Auckland: Auckland Art Gallery Toi o Tāmaki in association with Scala Publishers, London, 2001, p. 133.

McCahon, Colin. 1958. *Northland Panels*. Enamel on unstretched canvas (8 panels A–H), National Gallery New Zealand. Reproduced in Colin McCahon, *Colin McCahon Gates and journeys : Auckland City Art Gallery Centenary Exhibition*, Auckland: Auckland City Art Gallery, 1988, pp. 120–21.

Nicholas, Darcy. 1983. *Te Kotuku's Bush*. Acrylic on board, 1220 x 915 mm, Private collection. Reproduced in Sandy Adsett, Chris Whiting and Witi Ihimaera (eds), *Mataora: The Living Face — Contemporary Maori Art: Te aka Toi*, Albany, Auckland: David Bateman, 1996, p. 96.

15 Art, Landscape, and Identity in *She Plays with the Darkness*, *The Madonna of Excelsior* and *Cion*

Gail Fincham

In this chapter I investigate the imbrication of Zakes Mda's texts with the visual arts. In an article on Mda, I had traced the relationship between his story-worlds in *The Madonna of Excelsior* (2002) and the story-worlds depicted in Frans Claerhout's paintings (Fincham 2009). I argued that Claerhout's and Mda's refusal of hegemonic ways of seeing induct the postcolonial reader into new understandings of class, race and gender issues. In this essay I extend the examination of visual arts into the arena of landscape, looking at the ways in which *She Plays with the Darkness* (1995a), *The Madonna of Excelsior* (2002) and *Cion* (2007) link the visual in paintings and quilts with a particular understanding of the environment. As Peter J. Ucko and Robert Layton point out,

> Landscapes are ... ways of expressing conceptions of the world and they are also a means of referring to physical entities. The same physical landscape can be seen in many different ways by different people, often at the same time ... the term may refer both to an environment, generally one shaped by human action, and to a representation (particularly a painting) which signifies the meanings attributed to such a setting (Ucko and Layton 1999: 1).

Denis Cosgrove has linked the concept of landscape in the evolution of European societies to 'a way of seeing — a way in which some Europeans have represented ... the world about them and their relationships with it'. This concept of landscape implies 'an attempt to sustain the moral order [of] pre-capitalist conceptions of human relations with the land and nature against the economic order of industrial capitalism' (Cosgrove 1988: 252). After the 19th century, squeezed out by economic and technological forces, this concept of landscape could no longer be sustained.

But Mda's landscapes depict an indigenous or pre-capitalist conception of individuals in concord with their environments. This is portrayed in the healing rituals celebrated by the bushmen in the Cave of Barwa in *She Plays* (1995a),[1] in the ecological balance between the human and the natural worlds emblematized by the Free State's sunflower fields in *Madonna of Excelsior* (2002), and in the farming economies of poor Appalachian communities in *Cion* (2007). These novels connect non-commodifying environments with non-commodifying art forms,[2]

---

[1] Thomas Dowson writes about the cultural and political importance of representing Bushman art in non-commodifying ways. He is speaking about rock art imagery as it appears in the South African landscape, but his argument applies equally to the fictional representation of Bushman art undertaken by Mda in *She Plays*:

'Just as rock art had a power for the original producers and scores of subsequent and diverse consumers, so too these images have a power to transform and re-negotiate popular perceptions, not only about so-called "primitive art", but also the past, which itself is constituted in the present. Rock art need not be seen as an early stage in the origins of Western art, as it is often presented in the grand evolutionary histories of art from earliest times to the present. In its re-production and consumption today, rock art imagery can be used to challenge the prejudices of the past. The power of the images that resulted from the working of art in times past can continue to be harnessed by generations to come' (Dowson 1996: 321).

[2] Mda's linking of environmental awareness with graphic and performative arts, and the idea that art can enable psychic growth in the poorest circumstances, recalls Alice Walker's *The Color Purple* (1983).

There Celie's development is shaped by her interactions with Shug Avery, 'singer and magic-maker — a woman who has taken charge of her own destiny' (ibid.: dust jacket blurb). Living with Shug in Memphis, Celie is charmed with a house and garden full of monuments and fountains, and with Shug's bringing together of America with Africa in the 'turtles and elephants ... in the fountain ... under the trees. And all over the house' (ibid.: 188). Together, Celie and Shug draw extensions to the interior and exterior of the house — flower-beds, geraniums, stone elephants, turtles and ducks — so that the whole environment is imaginatively transformed: '[b]y the time we finish our house look like it can swim or fly' (ibid.: 189). This creativity is figured in Mda's fiction by the three novels discussed in this chapter, and prefigured in the imaginative collaborations of Toloki and Noria in *Ways of Dying* (Mda 1995b).

whether in paintings or quilts, and foreground the role of community. Gregory Bateson's remarks on the connection between art works and the environment are apposite here:

> The role of art in technological culture is to act as a corrective to our too-purposive view of the world and consciousness. Art calls attention to a systemic view of life. This means that the wisdom of art is humility: the knowledge that the human is only part of a larger system and that the part can never ultimately control the whole (Bateson, quoted in Frielick 1992: 71).[3]

An asymmetrical progression emerges when we compare *She Plays with the Darkness*, *The Madonna of Excelsior* and *Cion*. At the centre of *She Plays* (Mda 1995a) is a destroyed or extinguished imagined /Xam cave painting, *Madonna of Excelsior* (Mda 2002) is dominated by a whole array of the real paintings of Frans Claerhout, and *Cion* (Mda 2007) invites the reader to imagine an art world quite different from the traditional quilt patterns it describes in relation to escaping slaves on the Underground Railway. So we move from a destroyed art world which inspires the creativity of the artist/dreamer Dikosha, to the real paintings on which Mda builds the story-worlds of his characters Niki and Popi, to an art-world in *Cion* that though related to traditional quilting patterns must be created by the reader's imagination. What links all three novels is the relationship they create between their protagonists' performative activities and the landscapes that surround them and enable their creativity.

She Plays with the Darkness

Set in Lesotho and published in the same year as *Ways of Dying*, the opening of *She Plays* (Mda 1995a) is a *tour de force*. We are shown a vividly portrayed mountain setting, and witness the singing and dancing of the young girls who perform the songs of the pumpkin. Yet from the opening page this vibrant performance exists within a context of death

---

[3] Marita Wenzel (2009) similarly remarks:

'Zakes Mda perceives art as a form of self-expression which induces self-knowledge, acts as a survival technique ... and enables insight and transcendence through the imagination ... For Mda, all forms of art provide the necessary distance, the "liminal" space that induces change and new ways of "seeing" life as well as an alternative perspective on and interpretation of reality' (ibid.: 125–26).

and loss, for the girls fear that 'one day the great mist will rise and suffocate them all to death' (Mda 1995a: 1). The young girls' songs are full of 'lost loves and unfulfilled desires. Of husbands who have been devoured by the city of gold, never to return to their families again' (ibid.). The main protagonist, Dikosha, refuses to submit to domestic patriarchal pressures; instead of preparing and cooking the staple dish of maize porridge, she chooses to dance and sing. Instead of agreeing to marriage she chooses her own path. Dikosha is a precursor for the figure of the artist capable of transforming her society — as Niki and Popi do in *Madonna of Excelsior* (Mda 2002). This female artist figure, T. Spreelin Macdonald writes, '[provides] a vision of the role of the marginal creator in bridging the dichotomies of post-colonial existence. Asserting the vitality of the creator of non-instrumental art, Mda's Dikosha is the figure of the post-colonial cultural innovator, isolated yet vital' (2009: 114). Dikosha's creativity is stimulated by the *dikema* patterns painted by villagers on the walls of their homesteads, and finds its most powerful inspiration in

> the Cave of Barwa, which had been home to the ancient Barwa people hundreds of years before. The Barwa, or Bushmen as the white people called them, were the original inhabitants of the land. They lived here happily for centuries, hunting animals and gathering wild fruits and roots, until [Dikosha's] ancestors came and drove them away, and killed some, and married others. They left a legacy of caves with wonderful paintings on the walls, and the Cave of Barwa was the most famous of them all. It had red and black paintings of big-buttocked people chasing deer with bows and arrows, or dancing in a trancelike state. Dikosha was spellbound by one painting especially, which showed a dancer with the body of a woman and the head of a beast. It was a fierce-looking beast that no one had ever seen before. Dikosha saw herself as the monster-woman-dancer, ready to devour all the dancers of the world, imbuing herself with their strength and stamina, and then dancing for ever and ever, until the end of time (Mda 1995a: 16).

The Cave of Barwa painting teaches Dikosha not only about dancing, but about healing in the trance-states enacted by the San dancers, for whom the ancestors are all-important. The 'People of the Cave' share Dikosha's musicality and creativity (ibid.). But in Chapter 10, 'The Great Snow', the monster-woman-dancer of the Cave of Barwa is finally extinguished by the graffiti painted by tourists on the Cave walls; with her go also the other /Xam dancers. For Dikosha this is the end of 'the healing dances of the night with the people of the cave. It was not only the death of the dance, but the death of a lifestyle as well' (ibid.: 128).

From this point, halfway through the novel, Mda's attempts to render justice to the political events that keep overwhelming Lesotho cause a falling-off of intensity in the characterization of the protagonists whom we have met in an ecologically rich and challenging environment. Dikosha's twin Radisene now becomes involved in fraudulent business practices in the Lowlands, while Dikosha is reduced, after losing her connection with the Cave of Barwa, to hearing the confessions of the village men — an ambiguous role at best. Has she now become merely an instrument of patriarchy, or does her prophetic role allow her some autonomy?

In 'Twinship and Humanism in *She Plays with the Darkness*' (2009), T. Spreelin Macdonald argues that the novel, through its creation of the twin protagonists Dikosha and Radisene, undermines social binaries and '[asserts] the role of the marginalized artist' (ibid.: 173). Discussing the destructive paternalism that robs Dikosha of her creative potential, Macdonald maintains that 'the realm of privacy most closely achieved in the Cave of Barwa is the ["darkness"] of the novel's title ... In her quest for the self-contained aesthetic transcendence of her life station, Dikosha risks becoming fully enveloped by the darkness of isolation' (ibid.: 139).

Ingenious as is this reading, it leaves in my opinion certain questions unanswered. The first has to do with the power of art as a non-instrumental agent of change — which Mda will demonstrate in *Ways of Dying*, *The Madonna of Excelsior* (2002) and *Cion* (2007). Why is the desire to create art — whether in dancing, singing, painting, or storytelling — necessarily destructive of community? Even more disturbingly, why is the real power of the Bushman painting which inspires Dikosha allowed to be extinguished, given Mda's insistence throughout his fiction on the vitality of /Xam traditions?

In their remarkable book *My Heart Stands in the Hill* (2005), Janette Deacon and Craig Foster superimpose the images of the original Bushman interlocutors — /A!Kunta, //Kabbo, /Han ≠Kass/O, Dia!kwain, ≠Kasin and !Kweitan-ta — who served as interlocutors to Lucy Lloyd and William Bleek in the correspondence recorded in the 1870s called the Bleek and Lloyd Manuscripts[4] — on the landscapes which make up their

---

[4] In his recent study of the Bleek and Lloyd manuscripts entitled *Bushman Letters* (2010), Michael Wessels demonstrates the textual complexity of these tales. He rescues them from the essentializing tendencies of Western theorists who have read them as representing a stable world-view like that described by Jacques Derrida's discussion of the myth of origins. Wessels comments:

'It has been my contention that much of the interpretation of the stories reflects the intellectual tradition from which it has emerged rather than the

ancestral homes. Their images appear on cracked mud around the water hole at the Bitterpits, on grasslands stretching as far as the eye can see, on the *kokerboom* or aloe tree whose hollowed-out branches were used to store Bushman arrows, on the carapace of a tortoise, on the water falling over an upstream weir, on the rocks on which the /Xam painted lizards, buck, elephants, and elephant-shrews, onto a hillside in the Flat Bushman heartland, onto the heart of the eland which the /Xam held sacred, on the leaves and branches of a tree by the water hole, on engraved rocks, on the lichen of a dolerite boulder and the white reeds of grasslands. Accompanying these striking images is a text which records 'the rich complexity and depth of understanding of /Xam concepts and beliefs about their spirituality in relation to the land that sustained them both physically and emotionally' (Deacon and Foster 2005: 16). The authors comment:

> The/Xam who lived in /Xam-Ka! are still there in spirit, if not in person. This was the firm belief of the /Xam people themselves who relied on their ancestral spirits for help ... Our words and photographs layer past and present experiences to celebrate the intangible beliefs that sustained this landscape for millennia. In the theatre of our minds, the /Xams' words and images can still give life to the land (ibid.: 36).

Connections between individuals and their surroundings are reflected in the section headings designed by the authors. Part 1, 'A Landscape Full of Memories' is subtitled 'Landscapes are like theatres accumulating memories of performances over many years'. Part II, 'Earth', is subtitled 'The /Xam lived with the land, not simply on it/'. Part V, 'My Heart Stands in the Hill' is subtitled 'When a Bushman dies he goes to this place'. The authors comment:

> The landscape was integral to /Xam beliefs. The land itself and the things it had to offer were personified. People were buried in it. Spirits of the dead inhabited it. Breaking through, or simply transcending the imaginary barrier between the natural and the supernatural worlds, is what the /Xam beliefs were all about. Their environment provided the sensory stimuli the /Xam chose to humanise through mythology (ibid.: 54).

/Xam narratives themselves. I have followed Derrida in characterising this tradition as predicated on the myth of the lost origin and a metaphysics of presence ... the lack of attention to the detail of individual stories points to a hermeneutic practice that is more interested in overarching or underlying patterns and structures than it is in the signifying practices of the /Xam discursive tradition itself' (ibid.: 309).

In novel after novel, Mda has recorded his sense of this abiding legacy. Toloki, protagonist of *Ways of Dying* and *Cion* (2007), explains to Ruth Quigley in Ohio that 'there are strong possibilities that my ancestry is a Khoikhoi one, which is the case for many Southern Sotho and Nguni people in South Africa' (ibid.: 25). In *The Heart of Redness* (Mda 2000), Twin's marriage to Quxu, a Khoikhoi woman called Qukezwa by the amaXhosa, is repeated several generations later in the contemporary marriage between Twin, son of Zim and Qukezwa, whose son is once again given the hybridized Xhosa/Khoikhoi name Heitsi Ebib, after the son of Tsiqwa, bearer of ancient traditions. In *The Whale Caller* (Mda 2005), the protagonist imagines seeing 'before there were boats and fishermen and whalers, the Khoikhoi of old dancing around a beached whale' (2). And in *The Madonna of Excelsior* (Mda 2002), many of the people in Claerhout's paintings resemble the mixed-race 'coloured' people around whom the Miscegenation Trial revolves; they are descended from slave labourers from the East as well as from the nomadic Bushman or Hottentot people and from the indigenous African people. The Khoikhoi legacy is thus everywhere remembered and celebrated in Mda's South African fiction, in ways which marry creativity with sensitivity to the environment.

For me, therefore, *She Plays with the Darkness* (Mda 1995a) takes first steps in the directions which *Madonna of Excelsior* (Mda 2002) and *Cion* (Mda 2007) will develop. But the novel fails to sustain the momentum created by the now vanished /Xam inhabitants of the Cave of Barwa and the storyworlds of Dikosha and her twin brother collapse into incoherence. Mda, as his memoirs attest, spent many formative years in Lesotho. But its languages and culture were not the same as his own, as a Xhosa-speaking South African. Perhaps this is why it is not until Mda writes his first South African novel — *Ways of Dying* (2005) — that he is able to bring his insights into the transformative potentials of art into full relationship with the landscape.

The Madonna of Excelsior

I will start with a few remarks about the relationship between landscape and 'the Western gaze', since these concepts are so central to the setting of the *Madonna of Excelsior* (Mda 2002) in the sunflower fields of the Orange Free State and its use of the story-world of Claerhout's expressionist/symbolist paintings. Landscape has been described as 'situated on the interface between the physical and the cognitive' (Ucko and

Layton 1999: 7), and as encompassing both 'an object external to perception' and 'the expression of an idea' (ibid.: 1). The eye seeing this landscape has, in the Western tradition deriving from the Cartesian 'I', embodied surveillance. In the Enlightenment paradigm western knowledge is considered globally valid and superior to the local knowledge of indigenous cultures. Barbara Bender writes:

> 'The Western Gaze' succinctly expresses a particular, historically constituted, way of perceiving and experiencing the world. It is a gaze that skims the surface; surveys the land from an ego-centred viewpoint; and invokes an active viewer (the subject) and a passive land (object). This active viewer is equated with 'culture' and the land with 'nature', and viewer/culture are gendered male, land/nature ... female. Finally, the Western Gaze is about control (1999: 31).

I move on now to the Chapter 1 of *The Madonna of Excelsior* (Mda 2002): a little chapter of just over three pages that describes women, donkeys and sunflowers in the landscape of the Orange Free State. It is the time of the wheat harvest. As in many of the chapter openings, we start with a description of Claerhout's paintings: the vibrant, surreal world of exploding colour — green, yellow, red and blue — and the characteristic distortions of Claerhout's symbolist/expressionist vision: the boy riding the donkey backwards, people without feet or toes, skewed houses. The world of Claerhout's paintings — the story of the Catholic priest whom Mda calls the Trinity (because he is man, priest and artist, and because he paints the 'threeness' of the Free State's open skies, vastness and loneliness) — is immediately linked to, and appropriated by, Mda's story-world. This is the story of Niki and Popi, the mother and daughter Madonnas of Excelsior who will both figure in the Trinity's paintings and be at the centre of the town's notorious Miscegenation Trial.

In the opening chapter, we see the Trinity's paintings and the landscape of the Free State through the child Popi's eyes. Twenty-five years of the Mda story-world are juxtaposed against the present in a scene that fuses past and present, drawing our attention to the continuity of people living in, and working with, the landscape.[5]

---

[5] As Marita Wenzel notes, there is a close association in *Madonna of Excelsior* between art and nature:

> '[Mda] pays attention to the ... patterns of life that emulate seasonal cycles and find resonance in the depiction of human lives and their representation

What, then, attracts Mda to the Claerhout paintings around which he constructs *Madonna of Excelsior* (ibid.)? To begin with, the visual analogies that feed Mda's fictional world demonstrate an ecological symbiosis, a living in harmony with the universe, which links back to Claerhout's European ancestor Pieter Brueghel. Like Claerhout, Brueghel depicted simple people doing ordinary things, often in context of community celebration. This context is very different from the controlling, patriarchal, technological, exploitative, and instrumentalizing relationship to nature implied by the 'Western Gaze'.

The landscape of the Free State — its hills, wheatfields, sunflower fields and cosmos — falls outside the nature/culture binary created within the 'Western Gaze'. Flowers of course are natural, though sunflowers as cash crop link with the cultivated agricultural world. As a landscape, sunflower fields escape the negative associations of, let's say, sugarcane plantations in the Caribbean or cotton plantations in the American South, which destroyed indigenous vegetation and relied on slave labour to produce profit. Sunflower seeds are eaten, sunflower oil is used for frying or to produce margarine. Sunflowers are also reputed to extract toxic ingredients such as lead, arsenic and uranium from soil. (They were apparently used to remove uranium, cosium-137 and strontium-90 from the ground after the Chernobyl disaster.) Heliotropic in their budding stage, sunflowers turn towards the east at sunrise and follow the sun over the course of the day, inclining from east to west. Indigenous to the Americas, the sunflower has been 'domesticated' since around 2000 BCE. The Aztecs, Otomis of Mexico and Incas of South America venerated the sunflower as the symbol of the sun deity. Incorporating in its life cycle a particular closeness to sun and earth, the sunflower is often depicted today as a symbol of green ideology, just as the red rose is a symbol of socialism or social democracy. And of course Van Gogh immortalized sunflowers in painting after painting. In the Claerhout story-world, sunflowers are everywhere.

From the first paragraph of the opening chapter, Mda interrogates the 'Western Gaze'. 'All these things flow from the sins of our mothers.

---

in art ... The natural world is depicted in shades of vibrant colours that assume unnatural connotations when juxtaposed with violent human actions that disrupt the natural harmony ... The emphasis on colour in *The Madonna of Excelsior* results in vivid verbal images that accentuate the vibrancy of the African landscape, its inhabitants and their lack of self-consciousness and affinity to nature' (2009: 128–29)

The land that lies flat on its back for kilometre after restless kilometre ... the sunflower fields that stretch as far as the eye can see — the land that is awash with yellowness. And the brownness of the qokwa grass' (Mda 2002: 1). Here immediately we encounter Mda's deconstruction of 'the Western Gaze'. When the Bible speaks of 'the sins of our fathers' the reader connects these back to the story of the Fall — the expulsion from Eden, the story of the travails of Adam and Eve, now forced to labour by the sweat of their brows, and bear children in pain. In this story, Eve is the main culprit because she eats the forbidden fruit and tempts Adam to do so too. The misogyny of the Western tradition, which demonizes Eve and her daughters for their transgressive sexuality, is satirized by Mda. As is the trope of the land as feminized, passively awaiting the penetration of the active male explorer. Here the 'explorers' are Afrikaans farmers who rape helpless black women in the sunflower fields where they work.

Throughout the novel, Mda's imbrication of his characters' story-world with the paintings of Frans Claerhout continues to challenge the 'Western Gaze'. For instance, Chapter 6 is titled 'She is holding the Sun' and describes Claerhout's painting *Catcher of the Sun* (Plate VI, colour plate section). Here the sun is explicitly a feminine principle of life and death — although in the Western canon the Sun is usually depicted as masculine, and the Moon as feminine. You will recall Francis of Assisi's canticle 'Brother Sun and Sister Moon'. Probably the attribution of male deity to the Sun goes back to Europe's indebtedness to Roman and Hellenic mythology — for in numerous non-European cultures, sun goddesses are venerated. Certainly, the sun is all-powerful, for in this chapter the drought 'incinerating parts of the Free State' (ibid.: 25) is so severe that it makes the Afrikaans farmers forget their lust for black women in the crisis created for their crops by the scorching weather.

Another Claerhout painting that challenges the Western gaze by disrupting chronology is one which 'conveys our yesterdays in the continuing present' (ibid.: 38). In this painting, the villages are sad because the sky is 'bereft of stars' (though a lonely full moon is present). Suddenly they see 'a giant with a boyish face', dressed in 'red hat and red boots and yellow overalls' who carries over his shoulder 'a big star attached to a stick' which he brings to illuminate the village: 'The friendly giant transformed the blues and yellows into a scintillating light-filled land of promise. A world conceived of beautiful madness' (ibid.: 39) (Plate VII, colour plate section). Here Mda, shifting into the magical realist mode which occasionally interrupts his realistic depiction of individuals and communities, uses Claerhout's painterly vision to suggest the ways in which past and present, factual and fictional, individual and communal memory, fuse in the oral storytelling world of non-literate people. Their view of their own history falls outside the Western discourse of rationality but has strong resonances within oral cultures.

In the chapter 'The Pan' we are shown the Claerhout painting of the church — *Church and Parishioners* (Plate VIII, colour plate section) where, in Mda's story-world, Niki worships:

> People walk out of the skewed houses that form a circle. A blue church completes the circle. The houses are pink with cobalt blue doors. People are floating to the church. People with black faces, each holding a giant white flower ... A woman in a long white dress and white veil leads the procession into the church. The procession glides augustly on the raw sienna path. Blazing light surrounds the solemn procession. Absorbing the devout into a halo of yellowness (ibid.: 27).

This, the narrator assures us, is 'our church ... Niki's church. She belongs here' (ibid.: 28). Its congregation is very poor. The minister speaks consolingly

> ... of how the meek would inherit the earth and the poor in spirit would see the kingdom of heaven. How those who were oppressed and persecuted would get their reward in heaven. They were the salt of the earth and the light of the world. But in the meantime, he would plead, while they were still on earth preparing for their inheritance in heaven, it was necessary that the leaking roof of the house of the Lord be repaired ... How did the congregation think the Lord felt about being praised in a dilapidated building with a leaking roof and cracked walls with peeling paint? The congregation would respond with amens. But only small brown coins would find their way into the collection plate (ibid.: 29).

From the affectionate humorous focalization of the narrator we move to that of Niki. On this Sunday she is not going to her own church, but to the 'whites only' church. She will be looking after Tjaart Cronje whose parents, after the church service, will be going on to a people's congress in nearly Clocolan. Niki and Viliki, who may not enter the church, listen to the service outside the gates. Staring up at the Reverend François Bornman's 'beautiful church built of sandstone and roofed with black slate' (ibid.: 29), Niki fails to see how the shape resembles hands in prayer: 'Often she had tried to work out how exactly the strange architecture translated into hands in anything, let alone prayer' (ibid.). The reader shares in her alienated perception of this Calvinist monument to racial prejudice — so different to the vivid, scruffy, community-inspired church where the townspeople of Mahlatswetsa worship. Claerhout's painting evokes the simple church of his mission station, built by hand by fervent non-literate practitioners (Plate VIII, colour plate section). This is the church we see through the narrator's description of the painting. Bornman's affluent whites-only church is not made visible to the reader, who shares Niki's disaffection with it.

Popi's focalization, as she moves from childhood into adolescence and then early adulthood, is a striking example of rejection of the metaphysical straitjacket of the Western gaze. Initially Popi the child is ambivalent about the Trinity's paintings. Excited by their vibrancy, she is also distressed by their refusal to render physical reality recognizably:

> At five, she was precocious enough to wonder why the houses were all so skewed. And crowded together. She thought she could draw better houses. Her people, those she sketched in the sand in the backyard of her township home, were not distorted like the priest's (Mda 2002: 2).

But as a young adult, Popi's most treasured postcard is entitled 'Jesus among the flowers': 'Its celestial blue calmed her when she had had a particularly bad day' (ibid.: 139). She turns to Claerhout's paintings when overwhelmed with nostalgia. But Niki — not yet over the bitterness of her treatment during the racist and sexist Miscegenation Trial — rejects Claerhout's vision as mendacious:

> Jesus was not black. You have seen his photos in church ... And which of these women is Mary? If it's this black woman, how come she is wearing a purple hat and a red dress like the women of today? Jesus didn't live today. And if it's this white woman, how come she is a nun, and how come she is white and her child is black? (ibid.: 140).

Popi, unlike Niki, loves her three postcards of the Trinity's pictures because she unconditionally accepts their contradictions. She acknowledges an emotional power with which she challenges her mother: 'How come you remember every detail of [the painting] even when you are not looking at it ... Admit it, Niki ... it has got into you too' (ibid.: 140). The story of Popi's *bildungsroman* — her learning to accept her coloured identity and to be at peace with herself — has enabled her to accept the Trinity's imaginative transpositions as far richer and truer than realistic depictions of an unjust society.

The Madonna of Excelsior (ibid.) ends with Niki, who has come much further in her journey towards self-acceptance, under the blue-gum trees and evergreen melliodora and the black ironbark beloved of honeybees. She is arranging coloured hives for the bees, placing the wooden hives randomly because she realizes that hives in straight rows would have confused the bees who would not have known to which hive they belonged. She has learned, on a beekeeping course, that 'unlike American bees, South African bees did not know how to count' (ibid.: 228). But she assumes that they can distinguish colours — red, blue, yellow, and green — and arranges her hives in clusters, back to back and facing in different directions. Niki, who has taught Popi that 'anger eats the owner' (ibid.: 231) tells the community that rather than looking after the bees, the bees look after her, for they communicate 'calming messages to her through their airborne hormones. It was as if she shared the same pheromones with the bees' (ibid.: 229). But Niki's healing is far from passive acceptance of the injustices she has suffered: to Johannes Smit's plea for 'a truce' she replies: 'I do not understand all this nonsense about a truce. I don't remember any war between us. You, Johannes Smit, wronged me. You stole my girlhood. And now you talk of a truce?' (ibid.: 261).

On the last page of the novel, we hear the songs of Viliki and the Seller of Songs, who are making music and love in the distant sunflower fields. These fields have now come to represent the symbiotic, unexploitative relationship between human beings, non-human beings and the environment that Claerhout's paintings have depicted throughout. This celebration of the performance activities of singing and dancing demonstrates community values like those celebrated in Claerhout's paintings, a mutuality between the physical and the social environment. Mda's achievement in *Madonna of Excelsior* (ibid.) is to appropriate this non-racial, non-gendered vision for his novel, showing us how out of the sins of the mothers beautiful people flow.[6]

---

[6] Of the relationship between Claerhout's and Mda's story-worlds, Marita Wenzel remarks:

'Both [Claerhout and Mda] celebrate nature and the role of human nature. This correspondence becomes clear in an extract taken from an interview with Claerhout ... Asked whether he was "a priest who paints, or a painter who is a priest," he replied:

"I am one, a human being created to grow — the rural environment, the seasons, the human being, a smile, a curse, a prayer, love, nudity, fertility, humour; from the soil, of the soil, Christian mysticism, nature, God, the

Cion

Cion (Mda 2007) is a novel about the importance of ancestors, and the centrality of the past in shaping the future. In its Acknowledgements, Mda pays tribute to 'Sello K. Duiker, Phaswane Mpe and Yvonne Vera who continue to transmit to me buckets of inspiration from the world of the ancestors' (ibid.). The novel imbricates the story of the development of Mda's first protagonist, Toloki the Professional Mourner from *Ways of Dying* (Mda 1995b), with the quilt-making tradition and skills of a poor rural community in Appalachian America, where Toloki comes to live with the Quigley family. The Quigleys are of mixed white, Indian and Negro ancestry, and are descended from the plantation slaves of the South, whose escapes on the Underground Railroad were inspired by a matriarchal quilt-making tradition which pointed their way to freedom. Now in present-day Kilvert, Ohio, Ruth Quigley continues to produce traditional quilt patterns while her rebellious daughter Orpah plays the sitar, reads gothic novels, and draws amazing quilt designs which she refuses to constrain within traditional forms, since she wants to 'tell [her own] story' (Mda 2007: 234). Along comes Toloki the Professional Mourner. In the process of individuating himself from his creator, the Sciolist, he will learn in America new and more powerful ways of mourning, inspired by other times and other cultures. The stories of Toloki and of the quilt-makers, past and present, of Ohio and the deep South, coexist, and jointly demonstrate values of tradition, community and non-commercialism, against the consumerist, violent and militarily aggressive values of George Bush's Republican America.

I will illustrate this section by referring to some quilt designs of rural America in the 19th century. Some of the original quilt designs — the North Star, the Drunkard's Path, the Log Cabin, the Monkey Wrench, Flying Geese — have given rise to a fascinating but apocryphal body of research and writing. This links a secret system of symbols contained in the quilt designs with the Northward escape routes taken by fugitive slaves. But the overwhelming consensus amongst historians today is that the quilt code story was meant to be a mnemonic device, not an actual code placed in a quilt. We may conclude, and Mda's novel corroborates this, that early quilt designs, though they had great cultural and symbolic value — as had freedom songs in apartheid South Africa, or Negro

---

question why, are all composites of my paintings and drawings'" (Claerhout, quoted by Wenzel 2009: 144).

spirituals in slave-owning America — were never intended to provide secret maps to enable escape to the North.

I therefore move away from the traditional designs described in the novel. These were made by the slave matriarch named the 'Abyssinian Queen' for her sons, the escaping slaves Abednego and Nicodemus. Instead, I move towards the more futuristic quilt designs to which Toloki refers when he remarks that 'many modern quilt-makers create works of art that are inspired by traditional designs but that venture into new directions' (ibid.: 145) — exactly what he is trying to encourage Orpah to do. Quilt-making in this novel then encompasses not only the traditions of the past but the future potentialities of quilting as an art form. In the same way, Toloki's *professional mourning* in this novel moves into newly individuated creative and eclectic forms that are far more sophisticated than his original practice of *professional mourning* in South Africa. Quilt-making and *professional mourning* have many similarities. They celebrate memory and the past, have strong ecological or environmental connections, and affirm community values in a non-consumerist, non-capitalist ethos.

Like several of Mda's novels, *Cion* alternates two time-scales in its story-worlds: the past of the plantation slaves in the South and the present of their ancestors in Kilvert, Ohio. There are numerous cross-overs between these story-worlds. For instance, Toloki, newly arrived in Ohio, memorizes the landmarks of his route 'in case I have to return this way on my own' (ibid.: 18), just as earlier Abednego and Nicodemus were taught by their mother to notice their surroundings because their survival depended on having 'sharp ears for every sound of escape' (ibid.: 49). They had to listen for, and understand, the noises made by 'birds, frogs, and crickets' because '[a]ll these spoke the language of flight' (ibid.). Similarly, the remarkable performances of the Abyssinian Queen — quilter, singer, dancer, story-teller — are recaptured in the contemporary memory rituals enacted by the 'medium man' Mahlon Quigly, and his daughter, the 'spirit child' Orpah. From the beginning of the story, the reader is made aware of living history, unfolding in an ecological context that has many continuities with the past. Obed Quigley talks about the sycamore trees as 'carriers of memories' and tells Toloki about 'the pull of the ancestors' (ibid.: 20) which keep his people 'in villages like Stewart, Kilvert and Cutler' (ibid.: 19). This talk of ancestors resonates strongly with Toloki, since he is aware 'that there are strong possibilities that my ancestry is a Khoikhoi one, which is the case for many Southern Sotho and Nguni people in South Africa' (ibid.: 35). Ruth Quigley, making pickle, tending to her vegetable garden, and quilting, is a figure who connects with the women of the past. The worn fabric on her table is another 'carrier of memories' (Mda 2007: 30), and the ensuing story will be told 'by the quilts' earthly aroma. Quilts, Ruth tells Toloki, 'embody the life of the family [because] people were born on them, people got sick on them, people died on them' (ibid.: 30).

Moving back into the past story-world we meet the remarkable 'Abyssinian Queen', a slave in the Fairfield slave-breeding farms. A gifted storyteller, she sews and mends for the slave community, initially in a purely functional capacity — creating shirts and dresses from feed sacks — then in the decorative idiom of 'crazy' patchwork, in which she becomes expert decades before 'crazy quilts' became fashionable in Virginia (ibid.: 44). Although the Abyssinian Queen next learns 'the language of the quilts' — that is, traditional designs — she includes in the 'seemingly haphazard arrangements' (ibid.: 44) (of her 'crazy' quilt designs) certain elements which teach her children 'to identify some landmarks. A hill here ... A forest there. A creek. A river. She had painstakingly stitched and knotted the map of the plantation and beyond, using information she had gathered from those who had seen these places. Patches of different colours represented actual landmarks' (ibid.). The Abyssinian Queen's tapestries serve her boys in their escape by teaching them certain principles: how to follow the North Star, to take note of the Drunkard Path lesson 'never to take a straight route when they escape' (ibid.: 48) and to recall the Monkey Wrench's reminder that before setting off one must be equipped with essential tools and provisions to facilitate flight.

'Crazy' quilt designs like those in which the Abyssinian Queen encrypts topographical clues for her sons' escape, reflect a transition between the realistic and the symbolic. They incorporate many asymmetrically arranged elements — some natural (deer, butterfly, stork, flowers, moon, and stars) and some geometrical, in which each block exemplifies minute detail. These details are more important than overall design harmony. Similarly, 'crazy' designs may replicate features of local scenery. In *The Pieced Quilt: An American Design Tradition* (1973), a history of quilting in America, Jonathan Holstein (1973) remarks that quilts of this nature look quite like 'aerial landscapes'. 'Crazies' may also incorporate futuristic designs in which no two blocks are alike. 'Crazy' quilts, then, in which the Abyssinian Queen has expertise, anticipate the originality and unpredictability possible in drawing and painting. 'Crazy' patterns have elements of both reality and fantasy; what the Abyssinian Queen perceives as 'rudimentary maps' represents for her boys 'a world of dreams out there ... an attainable world' (Mda 2007: 44). The Abyssinian Queen's storytelling magic draws on matriarchal African folklore. She performs the stories of 'Ananse the wily spider who came with the ancestors from the old continent' (ibid.: 45) and who is capable of assuming protean forms. Quilts can also capture the intricate delicacy of gossamer and the geometrical complexity of spider web patterns, exemplifying the transgressive power of the female artist (spinning, painting, weaving) as an endlessly inventive antidote to marginalization under patriarchy. This spider-like activity engenders creativity across generations. As the Abyssinian Queen tells of Ananse's exploits, the listening children become involved in her tales and create their own stories. These African-derived stories, inspired by the originary myth of a female sun, create a cosmology and an ontology that is ecologically far richer (though the Slave Owner's wife describes them as 'voodoo') than the Bible stories of the Western tradition.

Through descriptions of orality and communal performance we move to the next stage of the story, which is told by 'ghost trees' or sycamores. Still growing in Kilvert, they were used in slave-owning times to provide refuge to runaway slaves; now Orpah deposits her transgressive drawings in them to protect them from her mother. Ruth, driven by a fundamentalist Old Testament censure of representation, demonizes and destroys Orpah's patterns. The worldview of the other Quigley family members — Ruth, Obed, Mahlon — closely resembles the worldview of the Shawnees, Pochattans, and Cherokee Indian tribes of Abednego's story, to whom the Quigleys are related. This worldview is matriarchal — the Creator is a woman. It strongly celebrates memories of the ancestors and escapes the nature/culture binary characteristic of Western patriarchy. Transcending the Christian Chain of Being, it embodies an ecological mutuality that extends to all creation.

Defending Orpah's unconventionality, Toloki draws attention to the fact that quilt-making is not just an important link with the past, but a generative art form undergoing constant transition: 'many modern quiltmakers create works of art that are inspired by traditional designs but that venture into new directions' (ibid.: 145). Deploring the lack of inventiveness that keeps the Kilvert Community Centre quilters working within traditional historical American parameters, Toloki, as he masters the art of quilt-making, wishes to create 'art quilts'. If we searched in a book like *The Pieced Quilt* (Holstein 1973) for stylized optical effects that make quilts resemble modern paintings, we could find quiltmakers contrasting inner with outer space in a manner that recalls the experimental art of the Cubists. Cézanne believed that everything in nature conformed to one of three basic shapes — the sphere, the cone and the cylinder. A painter who could draw these could draw anything. These three shapes frequently figure in art quilts, extending the challenge of creating the illusion of three-dimensionality in paint to fabric. In the preceding sections, I have sketched the ethos of quilt-making as an art form that is constantly evolving and that has strong community ties. Holstein remarks:

> Most [quilt] designs were given names meaningful to the makers and drawn from the whole realm of American experience: *nature:* Bear's Paw, Pineapple, Spider's Web; *religion:* Tree Everlasting, Jacob's Ladder, Star of Bethlehem, Job's Tears; *politics:* Whig's Defeat, Kansas Troubles, Lincoln's Platform, Jackson Star; *historical events:* Nelson's Victory, Free Trade Patch, Underground Railway, Kentucky Crossroads; *games:* Johnny-Round-the Corner, Leap Frog, Puss-in-the–Corner; places: Philadelphia Pavement, New York Beauty, Indiana Puzzle; *common objects:* Monkey Wrench, Fan, Indian Hatchet (1973: 59).

The quilt-makers' repertoire, then, fuses realistic with imaginative elements, capturing but transforming real events places and objects.

Toloki as chief protagonist of *Cion*, mounting a metafictional *tour de force* in which he supplants his author, is equally involved in dynamic aesthetic and performance practices as he brings his *professional mourning* to new heights. Where in South Africa he relied on the Nurse to provide the biographical information about the deceased required for the funeral ceremony, in America he has to find or invent individuals' life-stories before he can mourn them. With his American family, the Quigleys, he learns the importance of the past not just as nostalgia but as a psychological condition enabling engagement with the present. By finding the grave of Mahlon's mother and so facilitating the mourning that celebrates her life, Toloki releases Mahlon into a new state of being that is ecologically renewing. He now plants living things in his garden, instead of garden gnomes. Similarly, Toloki gets Ruth to reconcile her quilt-making talents with her fundamentalist religious obsessions; she is determined now to find a book that will teach her to make Bible quilts. At the end of the novel Toloki declares: 'Before I came to Kilvert I lived only in the past and in the future ... Orpah is a kindred spirit in this respect. Hopefully together we'll discover how to live in the present' (Mda 2007: 286). No less than quilt-making, Toloki's itinerant professional mourning, in which Orpah is his partner, expresses ecologically progressive and non-consumerist values, connects strongly with the past, and is both universal and rooted in *this* American time, *these* American places. It is joyfully ludic, incorporating Orpah's performing talents as singer, sitar-player and graphic artist. Together Toloki and Orpah hope to design 'performances and exhibitions with which we'll dazzle the bereaved' (ibid.), just as the quilt-makers, inspired by the past, move into new aesthetic freedoms. These not only carry memories but express a creative originality that speaks to the present and the future.

References

Bender, Barbara. 1999. 'Subverting the Western Gaze: Mapping Alternative Worlds', in Peter J. Ucko and Robert Layton (eds), *The Archaeology and Anthropology of Landscape: Shaping your Landscape*, pp. 31–45. London and New York: Routledge.

Cosgrove, Denis. 1988. *The Iconography of Landscape: Essays on the Symbolic Representation and Use of Past Environments*. Cambridge: Cambridge University Press.

Deacon, Janette and Craig Foster. 2005. *My Heart Stands in the Hill*. Cape Town and London: Struik.

Dowson, Thomas. 1996. 'Re-production and Consumption: The Use of Rock Art Imagery in Southern Africa Today', in Pippa Skotnes (ed.), *Miscast: Negotiating the Presence of the Bushman*, pp. 315–21. Cape Town: University of Cape Town Press.

Fincham, Gail. 2009. 'Zakes Mda: Towards a New Ontology of Postcolonial Vision?', *Kunapipi*, 31(1): 22–46.

Frielick, Stanley. 1992. 'Deep Ecology: The Environment and African Literature', in A. N. Bell and Meg Cowper-Lewis (eds), *Literature, Nature and the Land: Ethics and Aesthetics of the Environment*, pp. 60–74. Durban: University of Natal.

Holstein, Jonathan. 1973. *The Pieced Quilt: An American Design Tradition*. Boston MA: New York Graphic Society.

Macdonald, T. Spreelin. 2009. 'Twinship and Humanism in *She Plays With the Darkness*' in David Bell and J. U. Jacobs (eds), *Ways of Writing: Critical Essays on Zakes Mda*, pp. 133–48. Scottsville: University of Kwazulu-Natal Press.

Mda, Zakes. 1995a. *She Plays with the Darkness*. Florida Hills: Vivlia.

———. 1995b. *Ways of Dying*. Oxford: Oxford University Press.

———. 2000. *The Heart of Redness*. Oxford: Oxford University Press.

———. 2002. *The Madonna of Excelsior*. Cape Town: Oxford University Press.

Mda, Zakes. 2005. *The Whale Caller*. London: Penguin Books.
———. 2007. *Cion*. Johannesburg: Penguin Books.
Schwager, Dirk and Dominique Schwager. 1994. *Claerhout: Artist and Priest*. Maseru: Visual Publications.
Ucko, Peter J. and Robert Layton. 1999. 'Introduction: Gazing on the Landscape and Encountering the Environment', in Peter J. Ucko and Robert Layton (eds), *The Archaeology and Anthropology of Landscape: Shaping Your Landscape*, pp. 1–20. London and New York: Routledge.
Walker, Alice. 1983. *The Color Purple*. London: Phoenix.
Wenzel, Marita. 2009. 'Zakes Mda's Representation of South African Reality in *Ways of Dying*, *The Madonna of Excelsior*, and *The Whale Caller*', in Michael Meyer (ed.), *Word and Image in Colonial and Postcolonial Literatures and Cultures*, pp. 125–46. Amsterdam and New York: Rodopi.
Wessels, Michael. 2010. *Bushman Letters: Interpreting /Xam Narrative*. Johannesburg: Wits University Press.

16 Indigenous Languages in the Post-Colonial Era

Zahid Akter

In this chapter, I will examine the condition of indigenous languages in the post-colonial context taking into account two of its defining phenomena, namely, imperialism and nation-states. Where imperialism is concerned, I will discuss how it marginalizes indigenous languages through the appeal of its 'common-sensical' ideology of one world, one language. As for nation-states, I will analyze how the underlying paradigms of such states have essentially replicated and dragged on many of the discursive formations of the colonial era, and threaten numerous small, indigenous languages with extinction. In the course of my analysis, it will become clear how the workings of imperialism and nation-states, in many ways, overlap and how they collaborate with each other to marginalize indigenous people and their languages. This chapter aims to help create awareness about the impacts of imperialism and nation-states on indigenous languages in us. This should, in turn, motivate us to join the cause of indigenous peoples and their languages.

Introduction

The Third-World nationalist bourgeoisie often point to the European '21st century' with such zeal as if in this century alone the masses of the globe, irrespective of their class and ethnic identities, were heading for ultimate salvation from poverty and exploitation. In their construct of the term '21st', notions such as 'poverty', 'famine', and 'inequality' appear to be anachronistic. But even a cursory examination of the living conditions of the majority of world people does not reveal any causal relationships between the time and progress of the lives of common folks (Foucault 1980). In support of this, we find the continued invasions of territory, famine, war, and genocide. On the other hand, we find global warming, an increasing gap between the rich and poor, and loss of cultural and linguistic diversity. Against this backdrop, post-colonial (political) studies often focus on the interface between imperialism and nation-states and such macro-political aspects as the North–South conflict, territorial invasions and the war on terror. While I do not deny the importance of such correlations, I believe that the workings of imperialism and nation-states have significant ramifications for language diversity. No doubt, language diversity has received widespread attention in linguistics but much of this has evaded the interconnection between imperialism, nation-states and language in the post-colonial context. In order to redress the situation, I will relate imperialism to language endangerment to show how imperialism, by its nature, requires a condition that is hostile to pluralism of all sorts including language diversity. Similarly, I will show how nation-states, through their 'mission of nation-building', become repressive of multiple voices, which leads, among other things, to the loss of language diversity. I must point out that nation-states do not represent homogenous characteristics. For example, where language choice is concerned, the United States (US) is more assimilative in nature than India (Kachru 2002). Thereby, I will take into account the main tendencies of the majority of nation-states. I will take only indigenous languages into my consideration, as those languages predominantly constitute the list of the world's endangered languages (Hinton 2001). These languages, as opposed to migrant languages, are usually endemic to small areas and are more vulnerable to extinction.

The Current State of Indigenous Languages: An Overview

The world has now about 6,912 living languages (Grimes 2000). Of these, we stand to lose almost half in this century alone, while the remaining languages will be endangered at the end of this century (Krauss 1992). The likelihood of this linguistic catastrophe is attested by the fact that 516 world languages are now categorized as 'nearly extinct languages' (Grimes 2000). However, language extinction is not a recent phenomenon; incidences of language loss date back even to the prehistoric times. Language loss at that time, however, was rather slow and was a part of natural evolution. In contrast, language disappearance in modern times is both rapid and systematic and is triggered by human interventions. For example, European colonization alone accounts for the death of hundreds of indigenous languages around the world (Tsunoda 2005). Australia has killed at least 200 indigenous languages while the US has killed about 50 (Edwards 2004). The list can easily be expanded to include countries such as the former Union of Soviet Socialist Republics (USSR), Japan, Canada, New Zealand, Brazil, and China.

Importantly, the numerical strength of the world languages is misleading as speakers are unevenly distributed across languages. Ten big languages of the world, for instance, account for 60 per cent of the world population — about 3,019 million (Ammon 2003). Besides, the fact that the world has around 6,912 languages against 291 nation-states means most indigenous languages do not have countries of their own; most of them are not languages of government, commerce and education. Further, many of these languages do not have their own alphabets and are yet to be documented. Once these languages cease to be spoken, they will be lost forever.

Indigenous Languages in the Imperial Context

Though post-colonial countries are politically independent, they operate under the shadow of imperialism. Since its inception, imperialism has worked differently at different times. Modern imperialism is distinct from the earlier ones (i.e., Roman, Persian, Ottoman, etc.) in terms of its nature, strategy and impact. Whereas apparatuses of the earlier imperialisms were more obsessed with collecting levies and taxes, the concern of modern imperialism goes far beyond that to influence peoples' cultures and languages (Edwards 2004). Perhaps because of this, modern imperialism accounts for the highest amount of language death (Tsunoda 2005). To achieve total control over peoples' lives without territorial occupation, this imperialism requires a language to make political, economic and cultural domination possible. At present, the language that serves this purpose is English. English is now the language of commodity, knowledge, technology, and communication. In this role, it not only displaces countless small indigenous languages but marginalizes even big languages like Hindi, Bangla, Spanish, etc. The imperialist power legitimizes the hegemony of English by the so-called 'common-sense' logic that says the world requires a common language for communication. What remains implicit is that the capitalist West monopolizes both knowledge and commodity in the process and takes up the subject position in affairs regarding language and communication. The imperialist force does not see the possibility of cohabitation of languages and can envisage only a monolingual and monocultural society reflecting the Western view of them (Edwards 2004).

Similarly, in order to give English international status, the imperialist power propagates that the US or the United Kingdom (UK) no longer holds ownership of the language; English is rather owned by those who speak it. But the irony is that the Anglophone countries retain the monopoly of English by setting its norms and standards. In doing so, they make a staggering profit. Besides, they also dominate the English Language Teaching (ELT) industry. They have created a global ELT market where they sell books, materials and export 'native-speaker' teachers. In this way, the profit they make exceeds the collective budgets of a number of poor countries (Khan 2009). The US and UK monopoly over the world's English tests through the Test of English as a Foreign Language (TOEFL) and International English Language Testing System (IELTS) bears testimony to this. Another factor that reinforces the hegemony of English through its workings in areas such as aesthetics and epistemology is the omnipresence of English Literature in the Third-World countries. English Literature, in complicit role with imperialism, keeps converting the post-colonial people ideologically, aesthetically and politically which, in turn, undermines local languages and literatures.

There are also other ways in which imperialism affects indigenous languages. One such way is its 'modernist project' which attempts to transform indigenous peoples' notions of 'life' and 'development'. At present, with its superiority in technology, military and politics, imperialism is more capable than ever of converting peoples' beliefs and notions about 'progress'. This notion of 'progress' entails owning private property, earning printed money and having access to global commodity markets. The indigenous way of life cannot support and sustain this lifestyle. This results in mass migration of indigenous peoples to urban areas where they disintegrate and use other languages for cross-cultural communication.

Indigenous Languages in Nation-states

Along with imperialism, nation-states also systematically displace languages of the minority and the less powerful. What the modern nation-state does immediately upon its formation is to declare the ideology of the majority and powerful ethnic group the ideology of the state. In the process, it imposes the identity and preferences of the ruling ethnic group on all citizens. So Malaysia takes after the identity of the Malay, the majority and powerful ethnic group, Bangladesh after that of the Bangalee, Sri Lanka after that of the Sinhalese, and so on. In the process, the language of the most powerful ethnic group becomes the language of the state. This was not the case before the emergence of nation-states when a language was associated only with its speech community (Mackey 2003). Now most countries of the world, whether explicitly or implicitly, make a language their national language (e.g., Israel, Bangladesh, etc.), or some languages their official languages (e.g., India, South Africa, etc.). It is as if a country belonged to a language or vice versa. A danger of this tendency is that only about 300 languages (against about 287 nation-states) out of about 7,000 get state support and protection while the rest remain ignored and unprotected. Emulating the paradigm of imperialism, nation-states also stress the need of a common language for all to communicate. But compared to imperialism, the workings of nation-states are far more direct (though not essentially more effective) and take place under legal protection. For them, the use of official or national languages and, thus, of the language(s) of the powerful ethnic group, is an essential condition for all to be citizens. In effect, those languages become associated with one's prospects in education, job and career. Moreover, one's ability to use the language reflects one's patriotism and allegiance to one's country. In this process, by making all people believe that an official or a national language is the language of all, nation-states legitimize their patronization of the language(s) using all means and capacities. First, they formulate language policies accommodating only the language(s) of the powerful ethnic group. In policy documents, they declare a language as national or some languages as official. Second, they direct all kinds of economic and political leverage in 'developing' and disseminating the language(s). They sanction money to disseminate the language(s); they commission linguists, text-book writers and educationists to systemize and promote the language(s). In addition, they force print and electronic media to use the language(s). All these take place often with total negligence to small, indigenous languages. A direct consequence of this kind of language policy is that indigenous children fail to get education through their mother tongues. This disrupts inter-generational transmission of the language. Besides, poor utilitarian value of indigenous languages, their absence in books, media and public places generates a negative attitude to those languages even among their own speakers (Bradley 2002). Consequently, it is no wonder that sometimes they are reported to be unwilling to preserve their own languages.

Moreover, the 'development' projects that nation-states undertake often go against the interests of indigenous peoples. For example, the undertaking of dam projects (Maan Dam, Bargi Dam, Maheswar Dam, etc.) by the Madhya Pradesh government has displaced thousands of *adivasis* from their homes (Roy 2005). Likewise, the building of the Captai Dam in the core living areas of the adivasi people of Bangladesh left hundreds of them homeless. The Malaysian government, as I have seen, has undertaken a number of massive palm oil plantation projects by clearing forests where a large number indigenous people live. Similar projects are being taken by nation-states every day without their giving a thought to their impact on indigenous people. These kinds of 'development' projects usually result in mass migration of indigenous people to cities. There they assimilate with the majority and powerful ethnic group(s), abandoning their languages.

Last, I should point out that workings of imperialism and nation-states overlap in many ways in the post-colonial era. One reason for this, of course, lies in their identical interests in such matters as politics and the economy. But more precisely, their collaboration results from the fact that the rulers of nation-states are mostly represented by those who come from the majority and powerful ethnic group(s) and who have been ideologically converted by the Modernist project of imperialism. The predecessors of these few local elites from this dominant group were the main beneficiaries of imperialism during its territorial phase (Mommsen 1986). It should not then come as a surprise that these governments often divert national resources to the service of these national elites. This is evident from their enormous allocations of budget for the promotion and dissemination of the English language often by hiring foreign experts and consultants. They do so usually without sanctioning any money to ensure indigenous peoples' basic education in their mother tongues. Budgetary allocations for education of most of the Third-World countries from Asia and Africa and their contribution to the 'promotion' of the English language conform to this tendency (Mackey 2003).

Conclusion

The importance of language diversity hardly requires any justification. A myriad human wonders starting from their cognitive patterns to their evolution of knowledge and survival strategy are stored in language. Each language is unique in that each is best in its own place of birth and that each represents unique phonological, syntactic and discourse features. Besides, language is usually considered the most significant component of human identity. This shows the importance of language diversity and the significance of a large number of languages that indigenous peoples add to our language stock. At this moment, this diversity of language is seriously threatened due to multiple factors. While there is no doubt that these factors are inextricably connected and operate in a complex way, I have set aside two of them, namely imperialism and the nation-state, and have tried to examine their impacts on indigenous languages separately in a post-colonial situation. I have shown that spheres of modern imperialism, unlike its earlier counterparts, go as far as to affect language diversity through many of its advanced and sophisticated apparatuses. Specifically, I have shown that the language of modern imperialism is English and that it has vested political, economic and cultural interests in disseminating the language. In so doing, it continuously suppresses, marginalizes and displaces indigenous languages around the world. Where nation-states are concerned, I have argued that in most cases, they are governed and controlled by the majority and powerful ethnic group(s). As a result, the language policy they formulate and the way they distribute resources in the name of the state are discriminatory and serve their own purposes. In the course of my argument, I have also shown that many times imperialism and nation-states work hand-in-hand to repress indigenous people and their languages. I hope that my analysis will help us to take an informed stance regarding the issues of indigenous peoples and their languages. It should help us to raise such crucial questions as indigenous peoples' power-sharing on various levels of state mechanism and their economic, political and cultural stakes in diverse spheres of the globe. Finally, it should help us raise a consciousness of the need for collective resistance against the dual force of nation-states and imperialism so as to make it possible for us to join the cause of indigenous people and their languages.

References

Ammon, Ulrich. 2003. 'The International Standing of the German Language', in Jacques Maurais and Michael A. Morris (eds), *Languages in a Globalising World*, pp. 231–49. Cambridge: Cambridge University Press.

Bradley, David. 2002. 'Language Attitudes: The Key Factor in Language Maintenance', in David Bradley and Maya Bradley (eds), *Language Endangerment and Language Maintenance*, pp. 11–23. London: RoutledgeCurzon.

Edwards, Viv. 2004. *Multilingualism in the English Speaking World*. Oxford: Blackwell.

Foucault, Michel. 1980. 'Truth and Power', in Colin Gordon (ed.), *Power/Knowledge: Selected Interviews and Other Writings*, pp. 107–33. Brighton: Harvester.

Grimes, Barbara F. 2000. *Ethnologue: Languages of the World*, 14th edition. Dallas, Texas: SIL International. http://www.sil.org/ethnologue/ (accessed 30 May 2009).

Hinton, Leanne. 2001. 'Language Revitalization: An Overview', in Leanne Hinton and Kenneth Locke Hale (eds), *The Green Book of Language Revitalization in Practice*, pp. 3–18. Oxford: Elsevier Science.

Kachru, Yamuna. 2002. 'Language Maintenance, Shift and Accommodation: Linguistic Repertoire in South Asia', in Edward C. Dimock, Braj B. Kachru and Bhadriraju Krishnamurti (eds), *Dimensions of Sociolinguistics in South Asia: Papers in Memory of Gerald B. Kelley*, pp. 261–70. New Delhi: Oxford & IBH Publishing.

Khan, Sarah Zafar. 2009. 'Imperialism of International Tests: An EIL Perspective', in Farzad Sharifian (ed.), *English as an International Language: Perspectives and Pedagogical Issues*, pp. 190–208. Bristol: Multilingual Matters.

Krauss, Michael. 1992. 'The World's Languages in Crisis', *Language*, 68(1): 4–10.

Mackey, William F. 2003. 'Forecasting the Fate of Languages', in Jacques Maurais and Michael Morris (eds), *Languages in a Globalising World*, pp. 64–84. Cambridge: Cambridge University Press.

Mommsen, Wolfgang J. 1986. 'The End of Empire and the Continuity of Imperialism', in Wolfgang J. Mommsen and Jürgen Osterhammel (eds), *Imperialism and After*, pp. 333–58. London: Allen & Unwin.

Roy, Arundhati. 2005. *An Ordinary Person's Guide to Empire*. New Delhi: Penguin Books.

Tsunoda, Tasaku. 2005. *Language Endangerment and Language Revitalization*. Berlin: Mouton de Gruyter.

17 The Struggle for Survival
Globalization and its Impact on Tribal Women in Kerala

Lata Marina Varghese

Globalization, driven by an integrated global economy based on incentives and integration and propelled by multinational corporations and international banks, has raised fears all over the world that the market could destroy the social fabric of societies. According to Robert J. Samuelson (2000), globalization is a double-edged sword. While it creates new markets and wealth, it also causes widespread suffering, disorder and unrest. For billions of the world's people, business-driven globalization means uprooting old ways of life and threatening their livelihoods and cultures. The tidal wave of global culture is sweeping away indigenous cultures all over the world. As a result, many of the world's tribal societies have been decimated, their cultures devastated and their members enslaved. This chapter is a critique of globalization and its impact on the lives of tribal people, especially the tribal women of Kerala, whose 'economic and cultural survival is at stake' (Joshi 1998: 279).

The natural wealth of the tribal areas in Kerala, one of the southern states in India, is under new threats with the liberalization policies of the state government. Ever since it opened its doors wide to private investment and foreign capital, forest resources, minerals and the natural beauty of the region have been projected as the major vehicles of 'development'. The government having invited industries to set up tourism projects, holiday resorts and forestry/medicinal plantation projects, the future survival of the tribals depends on the effectiveness of their struggle to resist these 'development' policies of the state, which work against social justice. One example of such struggle is the agitation led by *adivasis* against multinational companies like Pepsi at Plachimeda.

The problems faced by the adivasis of Kerala are numerous, the most important being land alienation. Wayanad, which has the largest population of adivasis, is a pocket of poverty, inequality and deprivation. According to media reports, in the last 100 years, over 1 million acres of land are believed to have been grabbed from Kerala's tribal population.

Their long agitation to regain the forests and lands where their ancestors lived for generations was intensified following the unprecedented starvation deaths of 32 tribals in July–August 2001, and the subsequent 48-day agitation launched by the Adivasi-Dalit Action Council led by C. K. Janu in front of the state secretariat. In spite of land reforms and distribution elsewhere in Kerala, 30 per cent of tribal families are still landless. Over 90 per cent of Kerala's tribals live below the poverty line. Their high illiteracy levels make them vulnerable to exploitation. Land shortage is critical, forcing them into unofficial bonded labour. The forests, the mainstay of the tribal economy, have almost disappeared. A state of desperation now prevails among them as evidenced by the agitations that culminated in the Muthanga agitation in February 2003 and recently by the agitation for land at Chengara. Though the Government perpetrated a sham of distributing *pattas* (documents) of alternative lands to the tribals of Attappadi, none of the beneficiaries have occupied the land so far as the place is difficult to reach apart from being unsuitable for human habitation or cultivation. In the present confrontational phase, their struggle is to regain their lost land from those who had usurped the forests and turned the forest dwellers into bonded labourers by alienating them from their natural habitat in the name of eco-tourism and creation of national parks or plantations, and setting up of industries, construction of large reservoirs and other 'development' projects that have led to large-scale and multiple displacement of tribals. Ambiguities over boundaries have given opportunities for both the Revenue and Forest departments to implicate the tribals in false cases, making the inhabitants 'encroachers' on forest lands. The record of the government in the agency areas is dismal, whether in providing basic amenities and infrastructure, education, medical services, or in extending support and linkages to agriculture, forest produce, irrigation, and other activities. This has ensured that the tribals remain illiterate, indebted, susceptible to endemic diseases, and capable neither of protecting their traditional institutions nor of competing with the mainstream.

Tribal Education

The adivasis of India rate very low on the three most important indicators of development: health, education and income. Literacy and educational attainment are important indicators of social and economic development among the backward groups. In India, lack of education is particularly marked among Scheduled Tribe (ST) women, who have literacy rates that are among the lowest in the country. This trend reflects the social and cultural trends and degrees of gender inequality in India.

But the state of Kerala shows relatively high literacy rates among tribal women in urban areas. Kerala ranks the highest in the country in terms of women's literacy rates and gender development index. From a gender perspective, women in Kerala have made impressive gains in health and education, particularly when compared to other parts of the country. But from my interaction with Tribal Welfare officials and from the data and records maintained in the Tribal Welfare and Development office, it is clear that tribal education in Kerala has been a slow process of integration into formal mainstream education. It is replete with problems mainly due to lack of understanding of tribal culture; inaccessibility and the dispersed nature of tribal habitations; language barriers and thrusting of Malayalam, the official state language, as the medium of education in tribal schools; socio-cultural disparities between tribes as well as between tribals and outsiders; poverty; and, above all, neglect of development needs and basic amenities for either tribals or non-tribals posted as teachers in these areas and non-allocation of resources for tribal education. Even after 60 years of independence, education has not reached the tribal regions, largely owing to lack of political will in making the tribal communities a priority for development. This is further aggravated by the lack of infrastructure, the shortage of personnel like women wardens for girl's hostels, the lack of medical facilities, and sexual harassment with the culprits going scot-free while tribal girls get branded as 'immoral'. Such lack of sensitivity on the part of the government and cultural prejudices, especially with regard to tribal women and girls, are important factors that act against the education of the girl child in the tribal areas. The sudden 'affluence' of the government tribal teachers due to higher salaries and allowances than previously has created an elite segment among the tribals. Instead of being motivated to bring education opportunities to their communities, they have begun to exploit them. With market forces on the verge of invading these remote areas, cultural and social chaos is imminent with women as the worst victims.

Tribal Health

Health is a holistic issue and various micro and macro conditions affecting the people have both direct and indirect impacts on it. An analysis of a community's health status has to encompass its culture, its social and economic status and the larger external political influences and policies. In the existing situation, where government provides free healthcare in the primary health centres, the number of tribal women who have access to these facilities is minimal. The infant mortality rate is still high and 90 per cent of childbirths take place at home by traditional methods, without any access to professional medical services. Women have multiple pregnancies and miscarriages, and there is no tertiary care during or after pregnancy. Women and children are increasingly becoming vulnerable to new diseases hitherto unknown among tribals. In the tribal areas, family planning and population control seem to be the areas of concern for the government rather than immunization; safe deliveries and motherhood; and prevention of endemic diseases like malaria, gastroenteritis, communicable diseases, goitre, etc. In these areas neither the Tribal Welfare department nor the health departments provide for treatment of cases with serious endemic diseases such as goitre, sickle-cell anaemia, malaria, etc., although specific programmes exist in the policy. Owing to this neglect, the adivasis are largely dependent on health workers, quacks or traditional healers. From my visits to various tribal colonies I have come to understand that professional medical doctors show no motivation to work in these remote areas. After liberalization, there is a greater outflow of medical professionals for higher education or more lucrative job opportunities outside the country. There is a total absence of training or services in traditional systems or Ayurveda, which are most relevant to the tribal context and where the tribal women are themselves knowledgeable and have access to these sources of medicines. (But sadly many of the young tribal girls now living in urban areas especially those who have gained 'education' seem to have lost touch with their roots. Many confessed that they can hardly recall any of their traditional medicines nor can they even speak in their tribal dialects.) Research on traditional knowledge systems and herbal/natural forms of medicine by external research and donor agencies is on the rise but it in no way benefits the tribal people. Similarly, lack of provision for safe drinking water is another serious problem in the tribal areas. Every year there are widespread deaths during the monsoons as a result of diarrhoea and water-borne diseases.

Addiction is a common problem among both men and women. Illicit liquor brewing and *ganja* (cannabis) cultivation is rampant in many tribal areas, where large tracts of forests are destroyed to cultivate the killer plant. With so much illicit liquor flowing, the region is rift with signs of social cracks. Excessive drinking has left many young women as widows. On my visits to a few tribal colonies in my home district of Pathanamthitta, I have come across many tribal men, old as well as young, staggering on the road under the influence of alcohol. Ammani, the leader of the colony mainly inhabited by the Mala Vaden tribe and a close associate of C. K. Janu, the tribal leader from Kerala, narrated how the men in her village were exploited to carry out illegal activities for a few bottles of country toddy! Under the new economic policies of the state, revenues are to be earned from lucrative sectors like the sale of liquor. The ban that was imposed on sale and consumption of liquor after strong protests from women across the state was lifted by the present government. The heavy burden of debt accumulated by political decision-makers is inflicted on poor women whose hard-earned wages are utilized, not for better nutrition and quality of life, but to support their men folk's spending in the liquor dens. The state is responsible for such negative policies affecting women's health. There are reports of tribal women, who refused to allow the liquor mafia to set up its outlets in the tribal villages, being brutally 'punished' for daring to defy the local powers and excise authorities. Legal suits filed against the excise authorities have only led to constant harassment of the women.

The posting of police forces in interior tribal pockets has led to severe sexual abuse and exploitation of tribal women and girls. They have been exposed to new health hazards such as acquired immune deficiency syndrome (AIDS) and other sexually transmitted diseases. In a region where the government is unable to deliver basic healthcare, it has ignored the emergence of new health problems for tribal women. Gang rapes and sexual violence reported to the authorities were brutally hushed up and no punitive action was taken. Social evils and health problems like these were completely absent in their traditional way of life. In the present scenario, domestic violence, crimes by and against adivasis, and harassment of tribal women by outsiders are all alarmingly high. Psychic disorders and suicides, which were unheard of among the tribes until recently, are also on the increase. Whatever the men earn, they spend on liquor, and the women are forced to raise their families all alone. The excessive consumption of illicit liquor, that too on empty stomachs, has taken its toll of the health of the tribals. It has severely affected their fertility levels, and consequently the tribal birth rate is falling. Since almost all the tribal women are severely anaemic due to hard work and malnutrition and 80 per cent of newborns are underweight, their chances of survival are very low.

Tribal Economy

'Markets are vital mechanisms through which globalization extends its reach' (Singh 2000: 54). The tribals earn the greater part of their livelihood through collection of Non-timber Forest Products (NTFP), which they sell at weekly markets to private traders on highly exploitative terms. The monopoly law restricts them from selling for a better price in the open market. Tribal women, who are actively involved in the collection and sale of forest produce, bear the brunt of this exploitation and do not get a fair price. This market exploitation translates into poor nutrition for the women, for whom sale of NTFP is the only source of cash to purchase food or other domestic items. Hence the women are forced to sell their products 'illegally'. This is a clear indicator of how privatization is not for the benefit of the poor, especially the tribals. Women's knowledge in forestry is being undermined by the new tribe of external technical consultants forcing their expertise of forestry on them.

The externally-funded projects in the tribal areas, led by the World Bank, are mounting pressure for new forms of economy in these areas and are pushing for constitutional amendments to bring in corporatized agriculture, large farm holdings, hybridization, and extension of agricultural loans so that farmers can grow cash crops and high-capital intensive crops. In Kerala, the tribals have rich traditional systems of agriculture, horticulture and vegetable cultivation, which reflect the diversity of crops, the consumption-oriented nature of the economy and the optimal use of land and resources with minimum capital and external support. The government has, over a period, been trying to shift the economy of the tribals into new forms of monocultures without forethought to the risks they entail for the tribals, especially the women, who have an important role in the traditional form of agriculture. One of the most shocking aspects of this new shift is the general lack of any information transfer among tribals. Consequently they are mostly unaware of the influence of macro market forces on agriculture.

Tribals are highly dependent on land for their identity and livelihood (Patel 1974: 61). The nature of the economy that the new policies of the state government are ushering in through corporatization of forests, agriculture and other resources of the tribals are, in a sense, effectively driving them out of their lands. It is tribal women who are the worst affected as they can neither claim employment nor do they have the requisite skills to face the new economic situations. In fact, the present pathetic condition of tribal women in Kerala is a result of decades of displacement, industrialization and economic reforms. Forced into migration and facing harassment from revenue and forest officials over 'illegal encroachments', tribal women have been pushed into prostitution and other similar forms of livelihood. These are macro issues related to the entire tribal population, but they subtly yet very definitely intrude into tribal women's rights, status and health. In the traditional economy, a tribal woman had a vital role and control over the resources of the land, whether in agriculture or collection of forest produce. As a matter of fact the tribal economy cannot do without the contribution of women and in spite of the non-existence of written laws tribal women enjoy an economic status and decision-making power over the surrounding natural resources unlike women in most non-tribal societies. Custom ensures that resources are available, accessible and sustained for women's use — for food, medicinal purposes or domestic consumption. Their economy recognizes the needs of women from the land and the forests. But all these traditions are changing under the new threats of privatization and liberalization. 'Being in minority and economically vulnerable [the tribals] suffer the most in terms of loss of cultural identity in the process of globalisation' (Singh 2000: 55).

Conclusion

Our being human is no longer predicated on the fundamental human rights enshrined in all constitutions and in the UN Declaration of Human Rights. It is now conditional on our ability to 'buy' our needs in the global marketplace in which the conditions of life — food, water, health, and knowledge — have become the ultimate commodities controlled by a handful of corporations. In the market fundamentalism of globalization, everything is a commodity and for sale. Nothing is sacred; there are no fundamental rights of citizens and no fundamental duties of governments. The culture of commoditization has increased violence against women, whether in the form of rising domestic violence, increasing cases of rape, more instances of female foeticide, or higher incidence of trafficking in women.

Globalization as a patriarchal project has reinforced patriarchal exclusions. Globalization commoditizes. Tribal women are seen as erotic commodities because traditionally they are bare-shouldered, unlike other Indian women. And it is not taboo for them to drink alcohol — which makes them easier to seduce or assault. This perhaps is the single recurring reason why trafficking of tribal women has increased in recent years.

The mushrooming of tourist resorts in the hills of Kerala is a matter of concern. The tribal community's fear is that such tourist resorts would encourage sex tourism. Though adivasi women enjoy considerable freedom without the constraining moral rules of the 'civilized' world, they shoulder most of the work at home and in the fields while their men laze around in a drunken stupor. Ironically, it is the women who have to bear the brunt of exploitation. They are exploited alike by the *zamindars* (landlords), politicians and others. The number of unmarried mothers among the adivasi people is shocking. Social changes have also affected the traditional practices of tribals. Thus, immigration, population pressures, lack of facilities to maintain proper hygiene, dearth of educational services and awareness, and changes in cultivation patterns and environmental degradation have affected the *ooru* (land) system of the tribals. Marginalization, poor infrastructural facilities, neglect at the policy level, isolation, low acceptance of family planning and contraception, illiteracy, and traditional belief systems and practices have led to a number of health problems amongst the tribals.

The new generation of adivasis, evicted from the forest and settled in government-built colonies, which bear no resemblance to their settlements in the forests, find their old order of life evolved through centuries of close association with nature slowly slipping out of their hands. Those who found water by making pits in the ground now have to fight for water supply. The colonies and hostels built by the state, supposedly to bring tribals into the mainstream, have inculcated in them a whole new order of life. Though many of them accepted the new ways, the mainstream never accepted them. It is true that the Government of Kerala introduced free rations for adivasis who live below the poverty line (green card holders). These rations are their mainstay. It is true that the government has tried to induce the tribals to improve their living conditions by availing of welfare measures such as resettlement programmes and distribution of surplus land, hutment rights, free built houses, educational programmes. However the vast majority still have many unresolved problems, especially landlessness in their traditional homeland and no means to an assured livelihood. Conflicts involving tribal communities have their roots in both restrictive forest policies and misplaced development strategies, especially in the globalization context.

For the tribals, 'globalisation is associated with rising prices, loss of job security, lack of health care' and tribal development programmes (Mahbul ul Haq Human Development Centre 2001: 50). Markets are not very friendly to the poor, the weak or the vulnerable, either nationally or internationally. Nor are markets free. They are often the handmaidens of powerful interest groups, and are greatly influenced by the prevailing distribution of income. In a capitalist economy, all are not in a position to compete in the market. Some, like tribals and Dalits, who do not have enough education, health and nutrition to compete will fall outside the marketplace. The tribals are part of our society, and at the same time they are different. 'Special polic[ies] and programmes are required to address and redress these differences' especially in the context of globalization (Joshi 1998: 25). If globalization were superimposed on a poorly-educated and insufficiently-trained tribal people, it would not lead to growth nor reduce poverty. Therefore, it is shocking that, unmindful of the tragedy that confronts the tribals, the state government is going ahead with its liberalization policies in these remote tribal areas by inviting multinationals and non-resident Indians to take up tourism, and agri-based and other industries in the name of tribal 'development'. What happens to the tribal women and their health is of no consequence to the government as women's bodies are considered negotiable commodities in lieu of the economic prosperity of a few industries and political powers. This is the gender justice and gender equality situation of Kerala under the structural adjustment programme in the post-liberalized state.

References

Fuchs, Stephen. 1982. *The Aboriginal Tribes of India*. New Delhi: Macmillan India.

Hasan, Amir. 1988. *Tribal Administration in India*. New Delhi: B. R. Publishing Corporation.

Hopkins, Anthony G. (ed.). 2002. *Globalization in World History*. London: W. W. Norton & Company.

Joshi, Vidyut (ed.). 1998. *Tribal Situation in India*. New Delhi: Rawat Publications.

Kattakayam, Jacob John. 1983. *Social Structures and Change among the Tribals: A Study among the Uralies of Idukki District in Kerala*. Delhi: D. K. Publications.

Mahbub ul Haq Human Development Centre. 2001. *Human Development in South Asia 2001: Globalisation and Human Development*. Karachi: Oxford University Press.

Mathur, P. R. G. 1977. *Tribal Situation in Kerala*. Trivandrum: Kerala Historical Society.

Patel, Mahendra Lal. 1974. *Changing Land Problems of Tribal India*. Bhopal: Progress Publishers.

Samuelson, Robert J. 2000. 'Growing Market Offers Huge Potential — but also Peril: Globalization's Double Edge'. *International Herald Tribune*, 4 January.

Sikdar, Soumyen. 2002. *Contemporary Issues in Globalization*. New Delhi: Oxford University Press.

Singh, Yogendra. 2000. *Culture Change in India: Identity and Globalization*. Jaipur: Rawat Publications.

18 Eco-Fraternity of Kurum(b)a Tribes in Wayanad, Kerala

Nelson P. Abraham

Words like 'tribe' and 'tribals' have come to acquire a salience in any discourse on social science and social change. They denote both an anthropological entity and a metaphor for the most victimized of our society. The term covers a repertoire of social organizations at various levels of development. The origin of this concept dates back to the colonial period. Many present-day tribes were once nations with whom the colonists entered into treaties. Colonialism marked the beginning of radical change in the tribal situation in India, a land marked by an extraordinary range of ecological, cultural, religious, and linguistic heterogeneity. Tribal resources became a commodity. The tribal world was aggressively and brutally exploited. By the end of the British Raj, the Scheduled Tribes (STs) had emerged as a distinct constitutional category (Singh 2005: ii). Tribal situations are marked by diversity. The STs of Kerala form 35 to 38 distinct communities. *Adivasi*, the Malayalam term used in Kerala, is equivalent to the English word 'tribe'.

The tribes of Kerala have varied ethnic roots. Their cultures are autonomous, with their own sets of norms, values and beliefs that govern their struggle for existence. Wayanad and Idukki districts have the highest concentration of tribal communities in Kerala. The former, lying between 700 and 2,100 metres above sea level, is a picturesque mountainous plateau in the Western Ghats. This panoramic hilly region of Malabar, in north Kerala, is known as the 'Green Paradise' of God's own country. The etymology of the word 'Wayanad' is *vayal naadu*, which means 'village of paddy fields'. It is a serene place of scenic beauty with wildlife, indigenous culture and lush green vegetation, covering an area of 2,132 sq. km, extending between 70° to 76°25' E and 11°30' to 11°59' N. Its natural vegetation consists of evergreen, semi-evergreen, deciduous forest lands along with grassy and marshy lands. Now the land is famous for cultivation of black pepper, coffee, tea, cardamom, ginger and plantations of teak, albizzia, eucalyptus, etc.

Organized human life existed in these parts at least ten centuries before Christ. The Edakkal caves of Ampukuthimala located between Sulthan Bathery and Ambalavayal, with pictures and pictorial writing on their walls, speak volumes of the bygone era and civilization. This prehistoric rock shelter, formed naturally by a strange arrangement of three huge boulders, one resting on the other two, is a fascinating Neolithic cave. It is believed that Edakkal inscriptions were engraved in 4000 BCE in the Brahmi script by the ancestors of Mulla Kurumar.

The recorded history of this district is available from the 18th century CE onwards. In ancient times, this land was ruled by the Rajas of the Veda tribe and then came under the rule of the Pazhassi Rajas of the Kottayam royal dynasty. When the Raja was driven to the wilderness of Wayanad, he organized the Kurichiya tribals into a sort of people's militia and engaged the British in several guerrilla encounters. In the end, the British could get only the dead body of the Raja, who killed himself somewhere in the interior of the forest. Thus, Wayanad fell into the hands of the British and with it came a new turn in its history. The British authorities opened up the plateau for cultivation of tea and other cash crops. Roads were laid across the hazardous slopes of Wayanad, from Kozhikode and Thalassery. These brought in settlers from all over Kerala and the virgin forest lands were converted to a rich source of cash crops.

Wayanad is home to various tribal communities. P. R. G. Mathur (1977) classifies them into Kurichiyans, Paniyans, Adiyars, Tēn Kurumars, Bet Kurumars, and Mulla Kurumars, along with six other minor communities.

Kurichiyans

The Kurichiyans are an agricultural tribal community. Until recently they practised untouchability. Their social control mechanism was to excommunicate offenders. They have clean food habits and keep their houses, premises and dress always tidy. They are matrilineal and live in joint families, under the control of their chieftain called *Pittan*. The members of the extended family work together and put their earnings in the same purse. The Kurichiyans prefer cross-cousin marriage to any other marriage alliances. They do not practise polyandry. Many of the excommunicated Kurichiyans are now educationally and economically better off than the traditional Kurichiyans.

Paniyans

The vast majority of tribes in Kerala hail from the Paniyan clan. They inhabit Wayanad and the neighbouring parts of Kannur and Malappuram. The name 'Paniyan' means 'worker' as they are supposed to have been slaves of the non-tribals. Monogamy appears to be the norm among the Paniyans. Widow re-marriage is allowed. Their idea of religion is rather simple. Their major deity is Kali. They also worship the banyan tree, which they do not cut, and it is believed that if any of them attempts to cut such trees, he will fall sick. Owing to the various tribal welfare programmes of the government, their lifestyles are changing.

Adiyars

The Adiyars are traditionally known as 'Ravulayar'. Like the Paniyans, they are one of the slave tribes of Kerala. In the nuclear Adiyar tribal family the husband is the head of the house. Bride price is customary. They permit divorce and widow marriage. Polygamy is also practised. Unlike the Kurichiars, they have no punitive measures for sex offences (like ostracizing offenders). Even women committing such offences are allowed to undergo a purification ceremony known as 'Kalachu Veypu' and return to the community.

Kattunayakan (Tēn Kuruman)

The Kattunayakan (Tēn Kuruman) community is found in Wayanad, Kozhikode and Malappuram districts. They are also called Cholanaickan in the interior forests of the Nilambur area of Malappuram and Pathinaickans in the plains of Malappuram district. As their name denotes, they were the kings of the jungle engaged in the collection and gathering of forest produce. They are known as Tēn Kurumar since they collect honey from the forest. They have all the physical features of hill tribals, speak a mixture of all Dravidian languages, and are very familiar with the forest tracks. With an exceptional sense of sight and smell, their ability to identify the honeybee hives is well known. They move in the interior of forests in small groups to collect honey, staying there for weeks together and their familiarity with forest life forms enables them to live in the interior without disturbing them. They know how to interact with and escape from the larger animals in case of any intimidation. Though life in the forest interiors seems risky, they enjoy it owing to their love for nature and the spirit of earning livelihood from nature. They are engaged in agriculture, manual labour and collection of forest produce. They lead an accommodative, harmonious life little influenced by modernity. With their primitive worldview, they do not expect much of the modern world. They follow nature's laws, respecting everyone's rights without encroaching upon the territory of others.

They worship animals, birds, trees, rock hillocks, snakes, and stones placed under trees. They believe in black magic and sorcery, and worship their ancestors, besides Hindu deities. Local gods are also worshipped. At Begur in North Wayanad, Mariyamma is worshipped in the boulders under trees selected by the hamlet chief, called *Mooppan*. Annual festivals are held as part of their worship. Coconut, plantain, betel leaf, areca nut, sandalwood, and rice flakes are offered to the deities during worship. The Mooppan is the main priest as well as the chief administrator. Leadership among the Tēn Kurumars is hierarchically inherited within a family. Their annual feasts at Valliyurkavu and Thirunelli temples are famous. A Kuruma ritual — *daivam kaanal* (communicating with God) — is an important means of diagnosing disease and warding off evil spirits. The Mooppan performs this ritual. He makes prophecies by rolling the nuts of the forest rubber plant in a winnow and declares the need for *daivam kaanal*. In their rituals, the pollution codes are observed very strictly. They believe that diseases are due to the curse of gods and quarrels in the hamlet. After the conciliatory act, harmony between the members of the hamlets is restored in the Mooppan's presence. Slight shifts in these belief systems are now discernible. The educated younger generation prefers allopathic treatment. But the elders still rely on tribal medicines for most illnesses. They have concoctions for snake bites, indigestion, ulcers, fractures, eczema, stomach pains and disorders, cuts and bruises, headache, influenza as well as for inducing abortions. This practice is traditional and is never for sale. Scripts of the preparations are never made. The grace of God is believed to be the primary requirement for the cure of diseases.

Their life is in harmony with the forest. They believe that the forest fulfils all their needs from birth to death. Their lament — *Etu nangamadathu kuppu. Eegayavathu kani* ('we owned the forest, but now we have nothing') — echoes the paradigm shift in the life of the Tēn Kurumar to modernity, which spells the death of an ancient culture, a life concordant with nature.

The traditional rhymes of the Kattunaykka tribe reveal their history and tribal identity. Songs and sequentially added narratives of Tēn Kurumars reveal their sorrow:

Lallu purantathaa Kavery
Ullu puranthathoo poolooka
Kilakkelu oru swamiyeh kaavilammee
Eezhimala elli, gunam varuthamme (Puzha.com n.d.).

'The encoded ideas in these songs' reveal their 'eco-aesthetic view' of life, in which 'the flora and fauna ... are characters' like themselves. This is evident in the songs narrating 'the intricacies of hunting, gathering of honey, etc.' (ibid.).

A Sowing Song (Malavedar)

Thithannam teyyannam teyyannam taaree
Thithannam teyyannam teyyannam taaree (2)
Thrikkodi vazhayum vettichavitti
Thithannam teyyannam teyyannam taaree (2)
Thrikkodi vazhakku onnalloo kayyum vannee
Thrikkodi penninnu onnalloo masam
Thithannam teyyannam teyyannam taaree (2)
Thrikkodo vazhakku randalloo kayyum vannee
Thrikkodi penninnu randalloo masam
Thrikkodi vazhakku pathalloo kayyum vane
Thirikkodi penninnu pathalloo masam
Thithannam teyyannam teyyannam taaree (2) (ibid.).

The plantain developing its leaves one by one is compared with the 'growth and the stages of pregnancy of [a] tribal girl. This imagery is taken from their [*tinai*][1] concept, one of the sources from which [Tamil] Sangham literature also absorbed a lot of things. The five-fold categorisation of the biosphere — Aintinaii[2] — in Sangham literature is derived from this aboriginal aesthetic concept' (ibid.).

Urali Kurumas/Bet Kurumas

Urali Kurumas, the most versatile and colourful of the Kerala tribals, are one of the few artisan tribes in south India. They pursue a wide variety of occupations such as smithy, basketry, carpentry, and pottery. They supplied agricultural implements and earthenware to other communities. Their pottery, hand-made without a wheel, is famous.

---

[1] In the Sangam age, Tamil people had a common language and culture. They lived in five different landscapes and these geographical regions are called *tinais*.

[2] The five *tinais* are collectively called *aintinaii*.

Urali Kurumas claim to be followers of the ancient Kurumbas or Pallavas, who were once powerful in southern India. Urali Kurumas are also called Bet Kurumas. While the Bet Kurumas, found now in the Mysore district of Karnataka, speak Kannada, these tribals in Wayanad speak a mixture of Kannada and Malayalam. The Urali Kurumas choose their spouses from within their tribe. When a person dies they believe that the souls of the good become gods and those of the bad become devils. They worship deities such as Bettu Chikkamma and Bamadu, as well as demons and ancestral spirits.

They play the flute and drum on festive occasions. The *Uch-alkali* (dance festival to please the goddess) is played in the month of February. Some men dance while some beat the drums and play the flute. An old man in the group performs rites to their deity, Bettu Chikkamma. Women are not allowed to participate in these ceremonies.

Uralis were traditionally farmers and labourers, but many of them are now forced to quit these occupations owing to the forest policies. There used to be close harmony between the environment and their economic pursuits. Now aluminium vessels have rendered the product and the technology obsolete.

A people with little ambition in life, they live and die with modest hopes and desires, and are generally satisfied with two meals and *ganja*, or opium, to smoke. The so-called 'civilized' people consider them merely as people who fulfil the need for hard labour, meant to be exploited and not to be helped. They are the peasants 'blessed' to be brutally dominated over. There was a time when they were literally sold as slaves in Coorg — the cheapest commodity in the market. Quintessential children of nature, they are found in several places in Wayanad and in Attappadi in Palakkad District.

They have strong family bonding. Their liberal family mores allow remarriage on the death of the spouse as well as divorce. Inter-caste marriages were not allowed among Kurumars, but they are exploited by other people along with Adiyars and Paniars. Even if a woman is considered to have been morally lax, the act is condoned. There are no orphans in their society. Orphaned children are maintained by relatives or other people as their own family members. Elders are also similarly cared for. This fraternity is not seen prevailing to the same extent among them in contemporary times. Lacking self-esteem, they are trying to change their ways without realizing the cultural erosion affecting their society.

They live in harmony with the forest. Dwellings are built near rivers and forests for easy access to firewood, tubers and water. They live in groups. The very construction of their dwellings reveals their affinity for nature. They never use valuable tall trees for building their homes. Bamboo is the main construction material. Mud and husk mix are also used. Straw from local grass is used to thatch the houses, and these are decorated with pictures of animals and men using natural products like coal, red soil and lime. They usually cook in earthen vessels but aluminium and plastic have started replacing earthen vessels and bamboo baskets. Near their houses they maintain gardens where vegetables too are grown. They grow only elephant-resistant varieties as they live within forest boundaries. They are fond of pets like dogs and poultry, and also keep goats and cows.

The Uralis have in each hamlet a common east-facing place of worship called *Daivapura*, which also serves as a community meeting place. The *Gomalan*, or chief of the hamlet, chairs the discussions. Only men are allowed to sit inside the hall. He professes by rolling the nuts of forest rubber plant in a winnower and declares the need for *daivam kaanal*. The chief delivers the sermons of the *daivam kaanal*, generally at night. A fire is lit at two places. Near it, to its east, three mats are spread out. Two to five women sit near the fire and perform music. The men sit on the same side of the fire and listen. *Daivam kani* (chief priests) offer chants and prayers to the god by wriggling body movements wearing gingle bells (bracelet with brass balls) around their wrists. As the performance reaches its frenzy the *kani* perform a vigorous dance, pronounce the cause of the illness and prescribe the remedy. They pray for the diseased to be absolved of the sins committed, and he/she is given remedial medicines from the forest. The ritual is also believed to exorcize evil spirits. The wedding dress of the bride is also kept in the *daiva pura* (house of worship). Trials for sins are also conducted here by the chief. This belief system helps to preserve the group dynamics of the Uralis.

Their culture is agrarian. Grains of rice, ragi and *thina* (barley) are their major food. Ragi is also brewed, yielding the most sumptuous drink for them. They eat bamboo seeds, roasted fish and meat, use leaves to flavour their curries, and consume various kinds of leaves. This is considered to be the secret of their health, although they live in tough conditions. Tubers collected from the forests during the dry months are also part of their food. They are stored as such or in powdered form for use in the rainy season. Yams, colocassia, potato, etc. are cultivated. They eat plantains, gooseberries, mushrooms, and seasonal forest fruits. They also eat birds, which they catch using nets and other techniques. Fish is a delicacy. They use different techniques for catching it but all their activities are eco-friendly. Large fish catches are saved and used later. They eat crabs, tortoises as well as other flesh. They also poach small mammals using bows and snares. If somebody wants to eat the flesh of large mammals, the matter is reported to the chief, who prays, and the animal is caused to be killed by some other carnivore such as a wild dog, jackal or leopard. The kill is apportioned for dogs, the chief and helpers, and gods like Kuttichattan, Kali or Ayyappan. Sambar, spotted deer, toddy cat, pangolins, varanus (monitor lizard), hare, giant squirrel, etc. are favourite game animals. They never eat cow or gaur (Indian bison). Their food habits conform to nature and seasonal variations. But now they are tempted to change this habit due to the availability of other items provided by the food vendors in the village. The administration and other development projects aimed at their upliftment are actually alienating their soul and spirit from their traditional harmony with nature.

Mulla Kurumar

The Mulla Kurumars consider themselves superior to the other Kurumar tribals in Wayanad. They are found in southern Wayanad at Sulthan Bathery, Ambalavayal, Nulpuzha, Padri, Muttanga, and elsewhere. They are descended from the ancient Vishnuvarman dynasty, which reigned over Wayanad from 4000 to 3000 BCE. History claims that they even had scripts at that time — Brahmi. Pictures of the Neolithic age in the Edakkal caves are the remnants of the history of the ancestry of Mulla Kurumars. They are more hygienic than all other Kurumas and maintain a distinction from them in their customs and rituals. They believe in Hindu gods and offer worship in temples. While tribal medicine is their major mode of treatment, they also use allopathic medicines and go to hospitals for better medical care. They are considerably influenced by the local people and mingle with other communities and have more adaptive ability than other Kurumars. Their children are educated. They go for non-forest jobs and their elders are engaged in forestry operations. The women among them are generally housewives. The families follow matriarchy. They use forest produce for some of their food, particularly tubers and seeds of forest trees and shrubs. They eat meat and fish, and claim to be servants of the forest rather than its destroyers.

The Mulla Kurumars are agriculturists and possess land near the forest boundaries. Rice and ragi are the major crops. Plantains are also cultivated and sold in the market. They maintain close family relations. All members of the hamlets are considered equal and help each other in emergencies. They like pets and also keep hens and goats. Their premises are always clean unlike those of other Kurumars. They are dedicated to the forest and respect it and spend more time in it to seek relief during illness.

Narratives of Mulla Kurumars

A creation myth is fundamental to tribal spirituality. For tribals the land is home — the land is the 'land he lives on now, the trees and plants he relates himself with day and night, and even the whole earth' (Nalunakkal 1999: 198). Tribal life is based and built upon the vision of human existence in which they are aware that the land, forest and the country they occupy are gifts of God.

The aesthetic sense of the tribes is seen in their narratives too. They are mostly origin or creation myths. The origin of the universe, the earth, the tribe and the struggle against adversity are the main themes generally narrated. The creation myth of Mulla Kurumar goes like this:

> this universe was created splitting a huge egg from which Adimukhan Vellakkaliyappan and his vehicle the owl were born. The world above becomes the sky while the nether, the earth. As the sky was filled with stars and the earth with water, the owl finding no space requested Vellakkaliyappan for some place, and land emerged out from water. Plants and animals were born. After the creation of all these, the absence of one was felt and from the pangs of the primordial man was born a woman. Though he accepted her as his spouse they could be together only for one night, for soon Adimukhan left for the other end of the universe, the bereaved woman dreamt him out in a forest rivulet (Puzha.com n.d.).

The Kurumar tribe believe that their origin was from Vellakkaliyappan. This praises the glorious birth of the tribe and the narrative is related to their ecosystem and their nomadic life of the past. Earth, hill, tree, river, animals all become characters in such myths where ancestor worship is a main factor. The structural study of these myths shows each one's tribal fellowship in the vast composition of the universe and it becomes the tribal consciousness. 'I need some space', the pathetic request of the owl in the myth, is the desperate struggling voice of the reality of the tribes. The rivulet containing the soul of their father and the animals occupying the earth are looked upon with affection and reverence. This narrative is not anthropocentric; it shows the desire for sustaining diversity. Animals and plants are totems for the tribes who claim kinship with them, believing in the symbiotic relation between nature and themselves.

Conclusion

Natural forests have been converted to plantations, destroying the subsistence base of the tribal economy. The stringent enforcement of the Forest Conservation Act and expropriation of other resources have forced them to distant places. The symbiotic relationship between the tribal people and the forest has snapped. The rituals, language and customs of the Paniyans and Adiyars have been eroded a lot, but among the Tēn Kurumars and Urali Kurumars there is relatively little influence of modern life. Though they subscribe to traditional beliefs, there is a self-expressed beauty in their life. It is their lifestyle centred on the forest that enabled them to preserve their cultural individuality. Now the lost forest cover and government policies have caused the silent sighs of these people. Once the forest provided them with everything — food, shelter and refuge. The sky-high trees and honeycombs on the trees were always their personal possessions. The rice from fertile forest marshes nourished their life. Today they are alienated from all these by law. Under the pretext of the preservation of the forest they are denied their dreams, their life itself.

Until recently, adivasis had isolated themselves from modern man. They embraced and upheld their distinctive culture emanating from their generations-old lifestyle, beliefs and rituals. But of late, they have also been forced to merge with the mainstream. Despite such pressures, they preserve their lifestyle, customs and culture to a great extent. But no one can predict how long they will be able to withstand the challenges. They are now the victims of plunder by the so-called 'civilized'.

The Tēn Kurumars and Urali Kurumars, who once had agricultural land, are now driven into bonded labour in paddy fields and coffee plantations — a lifestyle they are not accustomed to. The national policy of cultural assimilation and attempts to shepherd tribal communities into the mainstream have impaired the development of their values, religions and lifestyles (Chacko 2005: 17–18). There are many aspects of tribal life that the mainstream can profitably assimilate. The growing awareness of ecological fragility demands a rethinking of our attitude to these children of the forest, and to nature and the significance of pre-modern realities.

References

Chacko, Pariyaram M. (ed.). 2005. *Tribal Communities and Social Change*. New Delhi: Sage.

Mathur, P. R. G. 1977. *Tribal Situation in Kerala*. Trivandrum: Kerala Historical Society.

Morgan, Lewis Henry. 1997 [1871]. *Systems of Consanguinity and Affinity of the Human Family*. Lincoln: University of Nebraska Press.

Nalunnakkal, George Mathew. 1999. *Green Liberation: Towards an Integral Eco-theology*. Delhi: Indian Society for Promoting Christian Knowledge.

Puzha.com. n.d. 'Original Aesthetics'. http://www.puzha.com/puzha/archive/aboriginal.html (accessed 12 April 2013).

Singh, K. S. 2005. 'Foreword', in Pariyaram M. Chacko (eds), *Tribal Communities and Social Change*, pp. i–ix. New Delhi: Sage.

About the Editors

Ganesh Devy is Founder, Adivasi Academy, Tejgadh, and Bhasha Research and Publication Centre, Baroda (Vadodara), Gujarat, India and is also a literary scholar and cultural activist who writes in three languages — Marathi, Gujarati and English — and has received prestigious literary awards for his works in all three languages. Between 1973 and 1996 he taught at the Maharaja Sayajirao University at Baroda, but gave up his academic position to take up conservation of threatened languages in India. Between 1978 and 1996, Devy held several fellowships such as the Rotary Foundation Fellowship, Commonwealth Academic Exchange Fellowship, Fulbright Fellowship, THB Symons Fellowship and Jawaharlal Nehru Fellowship. His major publications in English include *In Another Tongue: Essays On Indian English Literature* (1993), *Between Tradition and Modernity: India's Search for Identity* (1997), *Painted Words: An Anthology of Tribal Literature* (2002, edited), *Indian Literary Criticism: Theory and Interpretation* (2002, edited), *A Nomad Called Thief: Reflections on Adivasi Voice and Silence* (2006), *Indigeneity: Culture and Representation* (2008, co-edited), and *Voice and Memory: Indigenous Imagination and Expression* (2011, co-edited). *The G. N. Devy Reader* (Orient Blackswan) containing four of his book length essays was published in 2009.

Geoffrey Davis is Chairperson, European Association for Commonwealth Literature and Language Studies (EACLALS). He is the co-editor of the Rodopi Series on 'Readings in the Post/Colonial Literatures in English'. His published works include *Theatre and Change in South Africa* (1996, co-edited), *Beyond the Echoes of Soweto: Five Plays by Matsemela Manaka* (1997, edited), *Voices of Justice and Reason: Apartheid and Beyond in South African Literature* (2003), *Staging New Britain: Aspects of Black and South Asian Theatre Practice* (2006, co-edited), *Towards a Transcultural Future: Literature and Human Rights in a 'Post'-Colonial World* (2008, co-edited), *Indigeneity: Culture and Representation* (2008, co-edited), and *Voice and Memory: Indigenous Imagination and Expression* (2011, co-edited).

K. K. Chakravarty is Chairperson, Lalit Kala Akademi; Chancellor, National University of Education Planning and Administration (NUEPA); and Vice Chairman, Delhi Institute of Heritage Research and Management,

New Delhi, India. He has been an IAS officer and a distinguished scholar in the field of Culture Studies and Archeology. Previously he was Director, Museum of Man, Bhopal, and Member Secretary, Indira Gandhi National Centre for Arts, New Delhi. Apart from his numerous essays and journal articles, his recent works include *Restoring Human Culture and Biospheric Environment: A New Museum Movement* (2003, co-edited), *River Valley Cultures of India* (2005, co-edited), *Traditional Water Management Systems of India* (2006, co-edited), *Indigeneity: Culture and Representation* (2008, co-edited), and *Voice and Memory: Indigenous Imagination and Expression* (2011, co-edited).

Notes on Contributors

Nelson P. Abraham is Associate Professor, Department of Zoology, St Thomas College, Kozhencherry, Kerala, India. He obtained his doctoral degree with a thesis on wildlife biology, which concentrated on the habitat preference of larger mammals at Wynad, a hilly plateau in the Western Ghats of Kerala, and highlighted human pressures on the forest habitat which cause habitat deterioration and wildlife loss. Environmental education, fresh water habitats and tribal studies are topics he is especially interested in. He also works as a human resource consultant.

Zahid Akter is Assistant Professor and Chair, Department of English, East West University, Dhaka, Bangladesh. He has training in language and literature and is interested in documenting endangered languages. He has published books and articles in areas related to language endangerment, language teaching and post-colonialism.

A. O. Balcomb is Professor, School of Religion and Theology, University of KwaZulu-Natal, South Africa. He holds a PhD in Theology and has a particular research interest in the influence of Pentecostalism both in South Africa and further afield on the African continent. He has taught at the Akrofi-Christaller Institute for Mission and Culture in Akropong, Ghana, every year since 1995. His publications include *Third Way Theology — Reconciliation, Revolution, and Reform in the South African Church during the 1980s* (1993) and numerous articles in theological journals.

Vibha S. Chauhan is Associate Professor, Department of English, Zakir Husain Delhi College, University of Delhi, India. Her research interests lie in the area of local cultures and oral narratives of non-urbanized communities. She has surveyed, written and published several articles about social codes like caste and gender and their complex interaction with creative articulation. She is also deeply interested in Indian classical music and has co-authored the biography of Siddheshwari Devi, the legendary singer of the Benares *gharana*. Proficient in Hindi, English and Bhojpuri, Vibha Chauhan is a published novelist in Hindi. She also regularly publishes poetry in all three languages, besides being an active translator.

Bindi Cole is a Melbourne-based award-winning artist of Australian Aboriginal, English and Jewish heritage. Bindi's work exposes the latent and unspoken power dynamics of Australian culture in the here and now. She subtly but powerfully reveals some uncomfortable truths about the fundamental disconnection between who we are — the communities and identities by which we shape our sense of self — and how the prevailing culture attempts to place and define us. Cole won the Victorian Indigenous Art Award in 2009 and has been a finalist in numerous other art awards. Recent projects include 'Sistagirls', currently touring Australia; curating 'Nyah-bunyar (Temple)' for the Melbourne International Arts Festival at the Arts Centre Melbourne, Victoria, Australia; 'Not Really Aboriginal' at the Centre for Contemporary Photography, Fitzroy, Victoria, Australia; 'A Time Like This' at the Margaret Lawrence Gallery, Victorian College of the Arts, Melbourne, Victoria; and 'Post Us' at Boscia Galleries, Melbourne. Cole is currently represented by Nellie Castan Gallery, South Yarra, Victoria, Australia.

Ximena Córdova is a Bolivian national who has been living in Europe for the past 15 years and has a strong interest in the meanings and paradoxes of the concept of identity. She has a background in documentary filmmaking production and training, and completed a Masters in Documentary at Goldsmiths College, University of London, UK. She recently completed a PhD in Latin American Studies at Newcastle University, UK about the Oruro Carnival in Bolivia. Working at the crossroads of anthropology, history and identity studies, combined with a multi-media approach, her work focuses on the relationship between popular culture, performances of indigeneity and politics in Latin America, and particularly in the Andean region of Bolivia, Ecuador and Peru.

Emma Cox is Lecturer in Drama and Theatre, Royal Holloway, University of London, UK. Her research focuses on the representation and participation of refugees in the arts, indigenous performance and activism in Australia and Aotearoa–New Zealand and contemporary Shakespeare performance. She has published scholarly articles in these areas and is currently working on *Staging Asylum: Contemporary Australian Plays about Refugees* (forthcoming) and *Theatre & Migration* (forthcoming).

Leisangthem Gitarani Devi is Assistant Professor of English Literature, Shivaji College, University of Delhi, India. She is also working on doctoral studies on women's writing in Manipur. Her research interests include folk studies, women's writing and Manipuri culture studies.

Gail Fincham was Head, Department of English at the University of Cape Town, South Africa from 2006 to 2009. She is particularly interested in intersections between the metropolitan and the post-colonial. Her publications include *Under Postcolonial Eyes: Joseph Conrad after Empire* (co-edited, 1996); *Conrad at the Millennium: Modernism, Postmodernism, Postcolonialism* (co-edited, 2001); *Conrad in Africa* (co-edited, 2002); *Literary Landscapes from Modernism to Postcolonialism* (co-edited, 2009); and *Dance of Life: The Novels of Zakes Mda in Post-apartheid South Africa* (2011).

Vishvajit Pandya is Professor of Anthropology, Dhirubhai Ambani Institute of Information Communication Technology, Gandhinagar, India and has previously held teaching positions in the US and New Zealand. A social/cultural anthropologist, he has been engaged in ethnographic research primarily among the tribes of the Andaman and Nicobar Islands. He has published numerous papers in journals and edited volumes and his major publications include *Above the Forest* (1993) and *In the Forest* (2009).

P. K. Parihar is Vice-Principal, Dyal Singh College, University of Delhi, India and has 37 years of teaching experience. He obtained his PhD from the Delhi School of Economics, University of Delhi with a thesis on Ecological Aspects of Rural Housing in Punjab. Specializing in settlement geography, statistics and Geographic Information Systems, he is also an avid trekker.

Seema M. Parihar is Associate Professor of Geography, Kirori Mal College; Joint Director, Developing Countries Research Center; and Deputy Dean, Students Welfare, University of Delhi, India. She holds a PhD in 'Natural Resource Management of Bhagirathi Basin' from Delhi School of Economics, University of Delhi, India, was a Post-Doctoral Fellow at Faculty of Geo-Information Science and Earth Observation (ITC) in the Netherlands, and has more than 25 years of teaching experience. Her present projects include concerns related to climate variability, spatial topology, mapping glacial changes, and gender concerns. She was awarded the Bhoo Samman in 2005.

Dieter Riemenschneider wrote his PhD on *The Modern Indian Novel in English* (1971), taught Commonwealth/English-Language Literatures at University of Frankfurt, Germany (1971–99), and set up the 'New Literatures and Cultures in English' research and teaching centre there. He founded the newsletter *ACOLIT* and was Chair of the Association for the Study of the New Literatures in English (1989–93). His main research areas are: Indian, African, Australian Aboriginal, and New Zealand/Aotearoan Maori literature and culture. His recent publications include *Postcolonial Theory: The Emergence of a Critical Discourse: A Selected and Annotated Bibliography* (2004), *The Reception of the Indian Novel in English* (2005), and essays on Maori biculturalism/glocality, Maori poetry, theatre and film. He published a bilingual anthology of poems from Aotearoa/New Zealand, *Wildes Licht* [*Wild Light*] in 2010. His current research projects focus on the interdependence of aesthetic and evolutionary psychological theory building (eco-aesthetics) with reference to landscape poetry, writing and painting.

Soma Sarkar is a PhD Research Scholar working on *Fuzzy Logic in Wetlands of East Kolkata* at Kirori Mal College, University of Delhi, India.

Priscilla Settee is Associate Professor, Department of Native Studies, University of Saskatchewan, Canada, and a member of Cumberland House Cree First Nations from northern Saskatchewan. She is Chair of Saskatoon's only Aboriginal high school, *Oskayak*, and is a member of the *Iskwewak* group which focuses on disappeared indigenous women. She initiated a project with the University of San Marcos, Peru, which supported indigenous students making the transition from their home communities to university, and also developed youth leadership programmes locally (Saskatoon's annual indigenous music festival) and for internships in Fiji, the Philippines and Hawaii. She is currently working on a book presently titled *Akemeyimow, Indigenous Women's Stories*. Settee, who was honoured with a Global Citizen's award by the Saskatchewan Council for International Co-operation, is a board member for the Canadian Centre for Policy Alternatives and a Faculty Fellow at the Centre for Global Citizenship Education and Research, University of Alberta, Canada.

Shilpy Sharma is a Research Fellow working on a project on 'Integrated Environmental Resource Management of Bhilangana Basin using High

Resolution Remote Sensing Data and GIS' at Kirori Mal College, University of Delhi, India.

Alero Uwawah is Lecturer, Department of Theatre Arts and Mass Communication, University of Benin, Nigeria. She holds an MA in Theatre Arts. Recently, she has been involved in integrating theatre practice with learning and character formation at neighbourhood secondary schools in Benin City, Nigeria. Her interests also lie in theatre for integration and community development. She has attended and presented papers at conferences in Nigeria and elsewhere, and has published in local and international journals and book collections.

Lata Marina Varghese is Associate Professor, Department of English, Catholicate College, Trivandrum, India. She graduated from University of Mumbai, India and did her MA (English) and PhD (English) from Mahatma Gandhi University, Kerala; BEd from Kerala University; and MPhil from Madurai Kamaraj University, Tamil Nadu, India. She also did an MA in Women's Studies from Mother Teresa Women's University, Tamil Nadu, India, where she is currently pursuing her PhD in Women Studies. She has authored two books and published in both national and international journals, and has also been a resource person at the Academic Staff College, Trivandrum, India.

Chris J. C. Wasike is Lecturer in Literature and Cultural Studies, Masinde Muliro University of Science and Technology, Kenya. He recently completed his PhD in African Literature at the University of the Witwatersrand, South Africa. He has published various articles on Bukusu funeral folklore and masculinities in a number of journals. His other research interests include popular Kenyan music and East African drama and media. He is currently engaged in research on popular humour columns in Kenyan magazines and newspapers.

Perpetual Crentsil is Researcher, Social and Cultural Anthropology, Faculty of Social Sciences, University of Helsinki, Finland. Her areas of interest are HIV/Aids in Ghana (Africa), reproductive health, African medical systems, and kinship. Her other research area is migration and African Diaspora. She has conducted research on remittances, gambling, gender and identities among African migrants in Finland. Her current study focuses on mobile technology, gender and health development in Africa.

Israel Meriomame Wekpe is Lecturer, Department of Theatre Arts and Mass Communication, University of Benin, Benin City, Nigeria. He holds an MA in Theatre Studies from the University of Leeds and teaches and researches in the areas of contemporary Nigerian theatre, theatre for development, acting, and directing. His directing credits include Wole Soyinka's *The Beatification of Area Boys*; Ola Rotimi's *Ovonramwen Nogbaisi*, which was the command performance at the 2002 Festival of Nigerian Plays (FESTINA); Barrie Stavis's *The Man Who Never Died*; and Ngũgĩ wa Thiong'o and Micere Mugo Githae's *The Trial of Dedan Kimathi*. He is a member of the African Literature Association (ALA) and the Society of Nigerian Theatre Artists (SONTA), and has presented papers at conferences and festivals across the world and published in several academic journals.

Index

Aboriginal Australians 141; asylum seekers and refugees 143–49; child sexual abuse and neglect 143; current status of 144; Migration Amendment Act (1992) 143; migration zone 149; Northern Territory National Emergency Response 143; Racial Discrimination Act (1975) 143; self-identification 147
Aboriginal Protection Act (1956), India 25n6
Aboriginal Tent Embassy 144–45, 148
Achebe, Chinua 184
acquired immune deficiency syndrome (AIDS) 321
adimjanjati (primitive tribals) 17
Adivasi-Dalit Action Council 318
*adivasi*s 314, 317–18, 320–21, 324, 327, 336
Adiyars tribe 328–29, 332, 336
African–American cultural and political movements 170
African National Congress 58, 229
African Renaissance 60
African thanatology, analysis of 71
Agbonifo-Obaseki, Pedro 101–2
Ague-Osa ceremony 6
Aintinaii, concept of 7, 9, 331
alternative sovereignty 141–42
American Revolution 170
Anata festivity (Oruro) 245–47, 259
Andaman Adim Janjati Vikas Samiti (AAJVS) 24, 25n6, 27, 30
Anderson, Benedict 152
Aotearoa–New Zealand 150; asylum seekers 139; communication of citizenship 153; cultural heritage 140; cultural, social and diplomatic relations 152; indigenous activism 140; Maori juridico-political influence 142; Maori political representation in 142; *powhiri* (welcome ceremony) 140; reciprocal residency rights 152; relationship with Asia 152; Waitangi, Treaty of (1840) 140, 142, 151, 280–82; Welcome to Country rituals 142
apartheid system, South Africa 58
asylum seekers 139; Aboriginal supporters of 143–49; cross-cultural compassion and solidarity 147; detention of 147; migration zone 149; Pacific Island overstayers and refugees 149–55; refugee support movements 147
Australian Defence Force Border Protection 149
ayllu (cultural space network) 5, 249, 261–62
ayni, Andean concept of 5, 9, 263

Baan-*gosain* (community deity), myth of 3, 39–40, 47, 49
Babukusu Funeral Oratory 71; after-burial performance (*khuswala kumuse*) 72, 73–76; death and funeral practices 72, 73–76; *ekhorere* 75; morbid and sexual anxieties 72; mourning the dead man 81–85; phallic images and metaphors of fertility 81–85; religious reverence 76
Bacchae of Euripides, The (Soyinka) 185–86
Bali Jagar, ritual of 3, 35, 36
Bandopadhyay, Manik 37
Bandopadhyay, Tarashankar 3, 37
being in balance, notion of 54
Bewitched Crossroad, A (Head) 225
Black Skin, White Masks (Fanon) 178

blasphemy 136
britimoolak upanyas 37
British Raj 327
Bronner, Simon J. 128
Brueghel, Pieter 297
Bukusu community: 'anatomy of the phallus' and masculine anxieties 76–81; cessation of phallic desires 81; folklore 84, 85; hierarchy of masculinity and cultural identity 80; *kumunandere* tree 85; male circumcision 76, 78, 79; phallic images and metaphors of fertility 81–85; representation of women, in the public sphere 78; sexual licentiousness 85; *sioyaye* song 79; social significance of sexuality 80
Bulun Bulun case 11

Capitalism and Slavery (Williams) 168
Captain Singleton (Defoe) 180
carnival parade (Oruro) 247–49
Cary, Joyce 184
Castaway and Other Poems, The (Walcott) 179
castration anxiety, Freud's views on 72, 76–77
Catcher of the Sun 298
Cave of Barwa painting 290, 292–93, 295
Cell-Life project, South Africa 107
Chotro conference 1, 52
Christian myth, of state of original innocence 160
Church of the Mineshaft 5, 247, 251, 257
Cion (Mda) 289–91, 293, 302–7
circumcision: in Bukusu community 76, 78, 79; in European-Christian community 79; Freud, Sigmund, views on 76–77; in sub-Saharan African communities 79; symbolic and reproductive significance of 84
Civil Rights and Black Consciousness movements 183

Claerhout, Frans 7, 289, 291, 295–302
Clifton, Talbot 28
Coetzee, J. M. 180
Commission of Inquiry into Witchcraft Violence and Ritual Murder in the Northern Province, South Africa 229
communication of citizenship 153
community healing 53, 54; Oskayak High School 55–57
community knowledge 2, 11, 45
Confessiones (397–398 CE) 274
Congress of South African Trade Unions (COSATU) 58
Conrad, Joseph 180, 184
Convention on Biological Diversity (CBD) 63
Cosgrove, Denis 289
Cotton, Shane 277, 281–85
Country of My Skull (Krog) 58
Court Chronicle of the Kings of Manipur, The (Parratt) 126, 129
Coxon, Stanley William 28
cultural self-determination 10–11

daivam kaanal (communicating with God) 330, 333
Daivapura (place of worship) 333
Danse Africaine (Hughes) 175
Darcy, Nicholas 285
Deacon, Janette 293
Declaration on the Rights of Indigenous Peoples 144
Derrida, Jacques 160, 164, 293n4
Desiya Oriya (Indo-European language) 36
Devil Dance (*Diablada*) 247, 248
Diablada Auténtica 248, 251
dipheko (ritual murder), story of 6, 229, 231–34
Doodhatoli Lok Vikas Sansthan 212
Dow, Unity 226–39; AIDS pandemic 228; birth 226; *dipheko* (ritual murder) 231–34; education and career 226; on female empowerment 238; as

first female High Court judge 226–27; portrait of Botswana society 238; *Saturday is for Funerals* (Dow and Essex) 227; *Screaming of the Innocent, The* (Gagiano) 6, 229, 231, 234, 236; Women and Law in Southern Africa research project 227
Dream on Monkey Mountain (Walcott) 173, 174, 176, 178, 183–84, 197
Dream Play, A (Strindberg) 174
Drums and Colours (Walcott) 171
Dussel, Enrique 260

Eagleton, Terry 47
Earliece, Ossa 102
Eggleton, David 277
ekhorere 75
Emperor Jones, The (O'Neill) 174–78, 183–84, 196
ethnic identities 73, 251n6, 309
European enlightenment 9

Fanon, Frantz 178
Far and Beyon' (Dow) 228, 236
Farm Yard Manure (FYM) 209
Federación Sindical Única de Trabajadores Campesinos de Oruro (FSUTCO) 256, 262
festive practices, in the Highlands (Bolivia): on boundaries of national politics 256–60; carnival and the making of the national subject 250–55; Catholic Mestizo-white perspective 259; cultural heritage 242, 254; cultural manifestations 244; cultural space 243; Oruro Carnival 241–43; politics of recognition 260–64; religion and ethnicity 256–60; Revolution (1952) 252; selectiveness, principles of 244; significance for 252; Spanish colonialism 244, 253; *see also* Oruro's festive framework
For Whom the Bell Tolls (Hemingway) 193
Foster, Craig 293
Frankfurt School of philosophical thought 159
Freire, Paulo 52
French Revolution 170
Freud, Sigmund, views on: castration anxiety 76–77; penis envy 77
Further Selections from the Prison Notebooks (Gramsci) 65

gender development index 319
genocide 309
Geographical Indications (GIs) 200
Geographical Information System (GIS) 214, 215
Geographic Information Science 214
Geospatial Capacity Building Initiative 216
Geospatial Capacity Building Initiative Index (GCBII) 216
Ghana, healthcare communication in: benefits and constraints of using mobile phones 120–21; colonial media and social change 110–12; communication centres 113; doctor–patient communication 106; drama and films as channels for 112; face-to-face communication and 110, 112; health messages 109–10; HIV/AIDS and related health issues 118; indigenous communication systems 109–10; Information Services Department (ISD) 111; Internet and the mobile telephone 112–14; latest technologies in 112–14; mobile phone, use of 106–8, 118–20; modernization during British colonialism 110; National Communication Authority (NCA) 115; 'out of coverage area' 117; ownership, access, and affordability of mobile phone 114–15; Parliamentary Act (1996) 115; pattern of 108; patterns of mobile phone usage 116–18; penetration of mobile phones 115–16; potential for spreading health messages 111; social cleanliness and 109; tools of 112–14

Ghana Posts and Telecommunications Corporation (PTC) 112
Ghana Telecom (GT) 112, 113, 115
global capitalism 2, 159
Global Positioning System (GPS) 214, 215
Global System for Mobile Communications (GSM) 117
Grameen Bank project, Bangladesh 107
Gramsci, Antonio 65, 263
Gulf, The (Walcott) 173

Haitian Revolution 170–71
Hansuli Banker Upokatha (Bandopadhyay) 37–39, 43–45, 49
hapu (sub-tribal grouping) 140, 150–52, 282
Harlem Renaissance 170, 174, 175, 183
Head, Bessie 225
health issues, among adivasis of India 319
Heaphy, Charles 276, 283–84
Heart of Darkness (Conrad) 184
Heavens May Fall, The (Dow) 228
Heidegger, Martin 11, 158, 164, 203–4
Hemingway, Ernest 193
Henri Christophe (Walcott) 169–71
Hertz, Robert 71
heterosexual sexuality 77
Himalayan community 198; community-generated information 214; conceptualizing space 203–5; contextualizing relationships between 216–22; Doodhatoli Lok Vikas Sansthan 212; Farm Yard Manure (FYM) 209; Geospatial Capacity Building Initiative 216; geospatial tools, introduction of 214–16; Indian Forest Act (1927) 210; livestock, relevance of 211; man–nature inter-relationship 213; methodology for study of 202–3; *mole* 209; open-pit manure decomposition, practice of 209; spiritual values 213; study areas 200–202; traditional natural resource practices 206–13; water management-based model, creation of 212
Holstein, Jonathan 304, 306
'Hombre Solitario' (Morenada songs) 259
Homers Heimat (Schrott) 185
Hoppers, Catherine Odora 58, 60–66, 68
Hughes, Langston 175
Hussein, Ebrahim 89, 104

Idia, The Warrior Queen of Benin (Salami-Agunloye) 92
Imaguero (Ogieiriaixi) 102–3
Indian Forest Act (1927) 210
indigenous communication systems, in Ghana 109–10
Indigenous Knowledge Systems 51, 61; capacity-building for 68; community healing 54; creation of 53; healing aspects of 65; healing circles 54; implementation of 61; indigenous people and 205–6; integration of 63; learning from the Global South 57–66; medicine wheel teachings 54; modern scientific knowledge system, inclusion of 221; need for 63; at North-West University, North West Province 66–69; Oskayak High School 55–57; pedagogy of healing 53–55; protection of 63; struggle for re-establishing 65; web and space 222; WEB model 219
indigenous languages: condition of 309; current state of 310–11; English Language Teaching (ELT) industry 312; European colonization, impact of 310; in imperial context 311–12; inter-generational transmission of 313; in nation-states 312–14; third-world nationalist bourgeoisie 309
information and communication technologies (ICTs) 114

infra-nationalistic movements 10
Ingold, Tim 165–66
Intellectual Property Right (IPR) 10–11, 61–63
Inter-Apache Summit on Repatriation of Cultural Properties, USA 11
intergenerational 'grafting', O'Donoghue's idea of 148–49
Interim Constitutional Court of Kenya 227
International Commission of Jurists 227
international discourse of asylum 144
International English Language Testing System (IELTS) 312
international governance systems 64
International Refugee Convention 144
Ione (Walcott) 184
Isola, Akinwumi 93

Jarawa Reserve Territory 14, 17, 20, 22
Jarawa tribe 13; act of hostility with outsiders 15; Andaman Trunk Road (ATR) 14, 22–29; 'bizarre incident' 13–19; clothed civility 22; dressing and undressing, notion of 22; engagement with the Outsider 15, 30; friendly way of clothing of 19–21; human rights 24; identity of 18; Indian state's pacification of 19; as marginal community 18; naked primitiveness 22; protection of 17; relation with clothing 16–19, 27
Juggling Truths (Dow) 228

Ka Awatea (Karaka) 280–82
kahar community 38–39, 43; norm of sharing in 46
Kalahari Typing School for Men, The (McCall Smith) 226
Kant, Immanuel 9, 203
Karioca Declaration of Indigenous People's Earth Charter (1992), Brazil 11
Kattunayakan (Tēn Kuruman) community 329–31

khals 208
Khoi-San concept of *ubuntu* 4
Kinjeketile (Hussein) 89, 104
Kohanga Reo pre-school programme 142–43
Krog, Antjie 58
Kurichiyans community 328
Kurum(b)a tribes in Wayanad, Kerala 327

Lacan, Jacques 72, 76–77; concept of phallic symbolism 76
Lachmi Jagar, ritual of 34; emergence of rice, story of 45; narration of 35, 36, 45
La Philosophie Bantu-Rwandaise de l'Être (Kagame) 162
Leibniz, Gottfried Wilhelm 9, 203
lex mercatoria (law of the market) 11
literacy rates, among adivasis of India 17n3, 318–19
Lord Krishna, story of 47–48

MacKinnon, Catherine 77
Macmillan, Harold 170
Madam Tinubu: The Terror in Lagos (Isola) 93
Madonna of Excelsior, The (Mda) 289–93, 295–301
Mahabharata 47
Mamdani, Mahmood 68
Mangere Refugee Resettlement Centre, Aukland 153–55
Manguliechi, John Wanyonyi 72–74, 76, 81–85
Maori paintings, pictorial representation of: concept of 273; landscape and land 270–77; Maori land paintings 277–85; *Sketches of a Maori muru at Parawera* 272; technique of 273; Western landscape painting 275
Maori tribes 140–41; activism 149–55; juridico-political influence 142; Kohanga Reo pre-school programme

143; *manaakitanga*, value of 154; paintings of, see Maori paintings, pictorial representation of; political representation 142; Waitangi, Treaty of (1840) 140, 142, 151, 280–82
'Maps with Belongingness' 214–15
Maru (Head) 225
Mataatua Declaration of Cultural and Intellectual Property Rights of Indigenous People (1993) 11
Mataora: The Living Face — Contemporary Maori Art: Te Waka Toi (Adsett et al.) 271
Mda, Zakes 7, 289–93, 295–99, 301–4
Meaning of Folklore: The Analytical Essays of Alan Dundes, The (Bronner) 128
Meitei folklore: arrival of *Konok*s 129–30; discrimination against the tribes 133; forms of 125; game-rhyme 130–32; Hindu festivals 137; and Hinduization of Meitei society 126–28, 132–33; Hindu rites and ceremonies 136; ideological territorialization 133; Kabui Keioiba 133–34; myths associated with 127; *Puyas*, burning of 136; religious and political space 130; revivalist movement 135; Sanamahi Movement (Naoria Phullo) 135–37; socio-religious life 127; values and Brahmanical Hindu ideology 126
Merak asylum seekers 139
Mestizo identity 255, 257
mestizos 5, 249, 255, 257, 262, 264
metropolitan hybridity 257
Middle Passage, The (Naipaul) 168–69, 175
Migration Amendment Act (1992), Australia 143
Ministry of Arts, Culture, Science and Technology, South Africa 63
Mister Johnson (Cary) 184
mole 209
Morales, Evo 254, 264–66
Morality for Beautiful Girls (McCall Smith) 226

Moreno Dance (*Morenada*) 248
Mugo, Micere Githae 89, 104
Mulla Kurumar tribe: Brahmi script 334; creation myth of 335; Edakkal caves 334; narratives of 335; tribal medicine 334; Vishnuvarman dynasty 334
Muthanga agitation (2003) 318
My Heart Stands in the Hill (Deacon) 293–94
myths, narration of 34, 36–39, 43–44, 47–49, 78, 127, 129, 179, 277, 279, 335

nagini kanya (snake girl), myth of 40
Nagini Kanyar Kahini (Bandopadhyay) 37–38, 40–44
National Press Club of Australia 146
National Steering Committee, South Africa 62–63
Native Survival School 57
Nekighidi (Earliece) 102
No. 1 Ladies' Detective Agency, The (McCall Smith) 226
Non-timber Forest Products (NTFP) 322
Nupi Lan (Second Women's War in Manipur, 1939) 3, 130

Oba of Benin, in Nigerian literature: Benin people's perception of 90; British Punitive Expedition 88, 90, 96; divine kingship 91; folktale associated with 90–92; personification as demi-god 88; playwrights 93; Rotimi's portrayal of 89, 93–98; spiritual duties and functions 96; stature of 103; Yerima's portrayal of 98–101
Obaseki: A Historical Play (Agbonifo-Obaseki) 101
O'Donoghue, Lowitja 148
Odyssey, The (Walcott) 173, 185–89
Ogieiriaixi, Evinma 102–3
Omeros (Walcott) 173, 185
O'Neill, Eugene 174–78, 183, 184, 196
Ongee community 3, 13, 19n4, 29

ooru (land) system of the tribals 324
Organization of African Unity 61, 63
Oruro's festive framework 5; Anata 245–47; Association of Folkloric Troupes 245; carnival parade 247–49; festive actors 249–50
Orwell, George 10
Oskayak community, Canada: quality of life for 51; storytelling among 51
Oskayak High School: *Big Bear Walk* 55; community healing, model for 55–57
Ovonramwen Nogbaisi (Rotimi) 89, 92, 93–98

Pachamama deity 5, 257, 262
Padmanadir Manjhi (1939) 37
Painting the Frontier — The Art of New Zealand's Pioneers (Filer) 270
Paniyan clan 328, 329, 336
Pantomime (Walcott) 180–81, 184
Parratt, Saroj Nalini Arambam 126, 128n5
patriarchal white sovereignty 142
Pengo (Dravidian language) 3, 36
'penis envy', Freud's concepts of 77
Perception of the Environment: Essays in Livelihood, Dwelling, and Skill (Ingold) 166
performativity, ideas of 242
Personal Digital Assistants (PDAs) 214, 215
Pfaffenberger, Bryan 108, 120
phallic symbolism, Lacan's concept of 72, 76
Phenomenology of Perception (Merleau-Ponty) 163
Pieced Quilt: An American Design Tradition, The (Holstein) 304–5
pimatisiwin, concept of 4, 9, 60, 69
Primal Vision, The (Taylor) 162–63
Primitive Tribal Groups (PTGs) 13, 16–17, 30; definition of 18

Prior Informed Consent (PIC) 63
Prometheus in Greek legend 158; *versus* Hermes the trickster 161; Western civilization, crisis of 159
Putul Nacher Itikatha (1936) 37

racial casting, issue of 184
Racial Discrimination Act (1975), Australia 143
Ramcharitmanas (Tulsidas) 39
Red Cross 111
refugee support movements 147
representation of women, in the public sphere 78
Ringatu movement 280
Rose, Jacqueline 80
Rotimi, Ola 89–94, 96–97, 100–101, 103–4

Saint-Réquier, Diane 234, 238
Salami-Agunloye, Irene Isoken 92
Samuelson, Robert J. 317
Sanamahi Movement (Naoria Phullo), Meitei community 135–37
Saturday is for Funerals (Dow) 227
Sbisà, Marina 153
Scheduled Tribe (ST) 16n3, 17n3, 200, 205, 318, 327
Schrott, Raoul 185
Screaming of the Innocent, The (Dow) 6, 228, 229, 231, 234, 236
Serowe: Village of the Rain Wind (Head) 225 sexual dominance 77–78
Shakespeare, William 169, 171, 173, 180
She Plays with the Darkness (Mda) 289, 290, 291–95
Smith, Alexander McCall 225
social construction of technology (SCOT) 108
social identity 242
Socialist Alliance Indigenous Rights 145
Soja, Edward W. 204
space and indigenous knowledge, concept of 198, 203–5; evolved relationship of 217–18

Space and Place: The Perspective of Experience (Tuan) 204
Srimad Bhagwat 47
srishtitatva (cosmogony) 37–39
Stevenson, Robert Louis 192
Strindberg, August 174
sui generis, principle of 11
sustainable development 10, 63, 67–68

taonga, concept of 7, 9, 142, 280–81
Taylor, John V. 162–63
Te Kotuku's Bush (Nicholas) 277–78, 285
Tempest, The (Shakespeare) 180
Things Fall Apart (Achebe) 184
Tija Jagar, ritual of 35
Ti-Jean and his Brothers (Walcott) 171–72
Tiwi Land Council 149
tiyospaya 54
Tohunga Suppression Act (1907) 284
Trade-Related Intellectual Property Rights (TRIPS) 200n1
Treasure Island (1883) 192
Trial of Dedan Kimathi, The (Ngugi) 1976) 89
Trials of Oba Ovonramwen, The (Yerima) 89, 92, 99
tribal community, in Andaman island *see* Jarawa tribe
tribal women in Kerala: addiction issues 320–21; agitation to regain the forests and lands 318; culture of commoditization 323; economy issues 322–23; education of 318–19; family planning and contraception 324; female foeticide, instances of 323; health of 319–21; illegal encroachments 323; knowledge in forestry 322; literacy rates and gender development index 319; living below poverty line 318; Muthanga agitation (2003) 318; natural wealth of the tribal areas 317; pathetic condition of 322–23; sex tourism, issue of 324; special policies and programmes 325; struggle against multinational companies 317; trafficking in women, incidence of 323
Trinidad Theatre Workshop 171
Truth and Reconciliation Commission, South Africa 4, 58
Tulsidas 39
Turner, Harold 160

ubuntu, Khoi-San concept of 4, 9, 58; African philosophy of 60; contributions of other cultures 60; life-giving knowledge force of 60
UN Charter for Human Rights 144
UN Declaration of Human Rights 323
United Nations Development Programme 59
United Nations Educational, Scientific and Cultural Organization (UNESCO) 5, 242, 244, 254
United Nations Interagency Steering Committee on Education for All 61
United States Agency for International Development (USAID) 256n8
upobhasha (dialect) 37, 38
Urali Kurumas/Bet Kurumas community 331–34

varna, hierarchy of 46
View (Cotton) 283
Visible and the Invisible, The (Merleau-Ponty) 163
visual arts 280, 289

Wahine Toa: Women of Maori Myth (Kahukiwa) 278
Waitangi, Treaty of (1840) 140, 142, 151, 280–82
Waitangi Tribunal 281–82
wakotawin, concept of 4, 9, 58
Walcott, Derek 168–69; and African Caribbean oral tradition 171–73; and

American tradition 173–78; Blind Billie Blue, figure of 191; 'A Caribbean Tragedy' 170; *Castaway and Other Poems, The* (Walcott) 179; *Dream on Monkey Mountain* (Walcott) 173, 174, 176, 183–84, 197; *Drums and Colours* (Walcott) 171; and Great Tradition 179–84; and Greek Classics 184–93; *Gulf, The* (1969) 173; *Henri Christophe* (Walcott) 169, 171; *Ione* (Walcott) 184; *Odyssey, The* (Walcott) 173, 185–89; *Omeros* (Walcott) 173; *Pantomime* (Walcott) 180–81, 184; *Ti-Jean and his Brothers* (play) 171–72; Trinidad Theatre Workshop 171

Wayanad tribal communities, Kerala: Adiyars tribe 329; Kattunayakan (Tēn Kuruman) community 329–31; Kurichiyans community 328; Mulla Kurumars 334–35; Paniyan clan 329; Urali Kurumas/Bet Kurumas 331–34

Ways of Dying (Mda) 290–91, 293, 295, 302

Western civilization, crisis of 159

'Western Gaze' 295–98, 300

Whale Caller, The (Mda) 295

When Rain Clouds Gather (Head) 225

whenua, concept of 9, 271, 273, 277, 279, 281

'Wind of Change' (1960) 170

World Economic Forum 61

World Intangible Heritage 5, 242, 254, 260

World Intellectual Property Organization (WIPO) 61

Yerima, Ahmed 89, 92–93, 98–104

*zamindar*s 324

Zuna, Irineo 256, 260–62, 266

'Sistagirl'

Bindi Cole

The term 'Sistagirl' is used to describe a transgender person in Tiwi Island culture. Traditionally, the term was 'Yimpininni'. The very existence of the word provides some indication of the inclusive attitudes historically extended towards Aboriginal sexual minorities. Colonization not only wiped out many indigenous people, it also had an impact on Aboriginal culture and understanding of sexual and gender expression. As Catholicism took hold and many traditions were lost, this term became a thing of the past. Yimpininni were once held in high regard as the nurturers within the family unit and tribe much like the Faafafine from Samoa. As the usage of the term vanished, tribes' attitudes toward queer indigenous people began to resemble that of the western world and religious right. Even today many Sistergirls are excluded from their own tribes and suffer at the hands of others.

Within a population of around 2,500, there are approximately 50 'Sistagirls' living on the Tiwi Islands. This community contains a complex range of dynamics including a hierarchy (a queen Sistergirl), politics and a significant history of pride and shame. The 'Sistagirls' are isolated yet thriving, unexplored territory with a beauty, strength and diversity to inspire and challenge.

During August and September of 2009, I was fortunate enough to have the opportunity to spend a month living with the 'Sistagirls' on the Tiwi Islands creating a series of highly stylized portraits of them. I loaded a barge with a four-wheel drive, lights, a generator, cameras, and enough film to fill a suitcase. Each day brought an emotional rollercoaster — from moments of elation around what was being achieved with the images to complete anxiety from the many dramas that occurred. This time has affected me in a profound way. The 'Sistagirls' have touched my heart. I only hope that in some way I have captured the essence of who they are and the spirit of their community. I know that they will always be a part of me and that I will be a regular visitor to Tiwi to visit the 'Sistagirl' community for the rest of my life.